Inuit Stories
of Being and Rebirth

CONTEMPORARY STUDIES ON THE NORTH

ISSN 1928-1722

CHRIS TROTT, SERIES EDITOR

6 *Inuit Stories of Being and Rebirth: Gender, Shamanism, and the Third Sex*, by Bernard Saladin d'Anglure, translated by Peter Frost

5 *Report of an Inquiry into an Injustice: Begade Shutagot'ine and the Sahtu Treaty*, by Peter Kulchyski

4 *Sanaaq: An Inuit Novel*, by Mitiarjuk Nappaaluk

3 *Stories in a New Skin: Approaches to Inuit Literature*, by Keavy Martin

2 *Settlement, Subsistence, and Change among the Labrador Inuit: The Nunatsiavummiut Experience*, edited by David C. Natcher, Lawrence Felt, and Andrea Procter

1 *Like the Sound of a Drum: Aboriginal Cultural Politics in Denendeh and Nunavut*, by Peter Kulchyski

Inuit Stories of Being and Rebirth

Gender, Shamanism, and the Third Sex

Bernard Saladin d'Anglure

Translated by Peter Frost
Preface by Claude Lévi-Strauss

UNIVERSITY OF MANITOBA PRESS

Inuit Stories of Being and Rebirth: Gender, Shamanism, and the Third Sex
© University of Manitoba Press 2018

Originally published as *Être et renaître inuit, homme,*
femme ou chamane © Éditions GALLIMARD, Paris, 2006

22   21   20   19   18   1   2   3   4   5

University of Manitoba Press
Winnipeg, Manitoba, Canada
Treaty 1 Territory
uofmpress.ca

Cataloguing data available from Library and Archives Canada
Contemporary Studies on the North, ISSN 1928-1722; 6
ISBN 978-0-88755-830-6 (PAPER)
ISBN 978-0-88755-559-6 (PDF)
ISBN 978-0-88755-557-2 (EPUB)

Cover design by Marvin Harder
Interior design by Jess Koroscil
Cover art: Pitaloosie Saila, *Arctic Madonna*. Collection of the Winnipeg
Art Gallery. Reproduced with the permission of Dorset Fine Arts.

Printed in Canada

The University of Manitoba Press acknowledges the financial support for
its publication program provided by the Government of Canada through
the Canada Book Fund, the Canada Council for the Arts, the Manitoba
Department of Sport, Culture, and Heritage, the Manitoba Arts Council,
and the Manitoba Book Publishing Tax Credit.

We acknowledge the financial support of the Government of Canada
through the National Translation Program for Book Publishing,
an initiative of the *Roadmap for Canada's Official Languages 2013–2018:*
Education, Immigration, Communities, for our translation activities.

Funded by the Government of Canada | Canadä

Contents

xi   **PREFACE TO THE 2006 EDITION**
BY CLAUDE LÉVI-STRAUSS

xiii   **FOREWORD**
IGLOOLIK ISLAND, A MYTHICAL PLACE

xxi   **THE STORYTELLERS**

1   **INTRODUCTION**
IQALLIJUQ, UJARAK, KUPAAQ, AND THE OTHERS

9   **INTERLUDE 1:** SONG OF *SAITTUQ*

11   **CHAPTER 1**
SAVVIURTALIK IS REINCARNATED

28   **INTERLUDE 2:** *IQALLIJUQ* REMEMBERING

39   **CHAPTER 2**
INUIT GENESIS AND THE DESIRE FOR CHILDREN

57   **CHAPTER 3**
NAARJUK: THE GIANT BABY WITH PROMINENT
GENITALS AND THE MASTER OF *SILA*

74   **CHAPTER 4**
INCESTUOUS MOON BROTHER CHASES SUN SISTER

101 **CHAPTER 5**
A HEADSTRONG DAUGHTER: THE MOTHER OF ALL
HUMAN RACES AND ALL MARINE MAMMALS

121 **CHAPTER 6**
A CHEATED HUSBAND AND THWARTED
LOVE IN THE ANIMAL WORLD

141 **CHAPTER 7**
GIRLS SHOULD NOT PLAY AT MARRIAGE

152 **CHAPTER 8**
A BATTERED WIFE CHOOSES TO BE REBORN IN
ANIMAL FORMS, THEN AS A MAN

177 **CHAPTER 9**
KAUJJAJJUK, A MISTREATED ORPHAN
RESCUED BY THE MOON MAN

197 **CHAPTER 10**
THE DANGER OF BEING IMPREGNATED BY A
SPIRIT WHEN YOU HAVE A JEALOUS HUSBAND

210 **CHAPTER 11**
ITIRJUAQ, THE FIRST WOMAN HEALER

220 **CHAPTER 12**
THE STRANGE MAN AND HIS WHALE

232 **CHAPTER 13**
ATANAARJUAT, THE FAST RUNNER: A MYTHICAL HERO

247 **CHAPTER 14**
ATAGUTTAALUK, THE CANNIBAL FOREBEAR
(OR THE BIRTH OF A MYTH)

274 **CHAPTER 15**
QISARUATSIAQ: BACK TO HER MOTHER'S WOMB

283 **CONCLUSION**

291 AFTERWORD
305 GLOSSARY OF INUKTITUT TERMS
319 NOTES
337 BIBLIOGRAPHY
349 PHOTO CREDITS
351 INDEX

To my Inuit teachers, now departed:

Iqallijuq (d. 2002), who introduced me to the enchanted world of life in the womb and to many other aspects of Inuit symbolism;

Ujarak (d. 1985), who through a shamanic song made me realize that the dome of an igloo could represent the vault of the heavens, and who patiently showed me the social rules of his group;

Kupaaq (d. 1997), a tireless storyteller, who greatly contributed to this book. Facing south, with his arms stretched out wide, he taught me how to identify the time of the spring equinox, for making safely long dog-team journeys on the sea ice.

To all of my other Nunavik and Nunavut friends who agreed to share their knowledge with me.

To Françoise, who braved with me at Igloolik the Arctic cold and night with me during our honeymoon, in order to observe a circumpolar full moon in late December 1990. With affection and intelligence she accompanied the slow progress of this book while bringing me into the movement to defend the rights of Indigenous peoples.

To Guillaume-*Iktuksarjuat*, my son, who introduced me into the world of Igloolik's young Inuit and who shared my enthusiasm, in January 2006, when we saw four sun dogs in the sky surrounded by a rainbow, at –50°C near Igloolik. Through Artcirq he has given new generations of Inuit a renewed confidence in life. May this book have the same effect!

SNOW VILLAGE OF THE ESKIMAUX.

Winter Island.

FIGURE 1. Inuit village on Winter Island, part of the Iglulik
extended group, winter 1821–1822. Engraving after a drawing by
Captain Lyons, 1824 (Lyon 1824, 110–111).

FIGURE 2. The two British Admiralty ships, *Fury* and *Hecla*, wintering in the ice near Igloolik Island, 1822–1823. Engraving after a drawing by Captain Lyons, 1824 (Parry 1824, frontispiece).

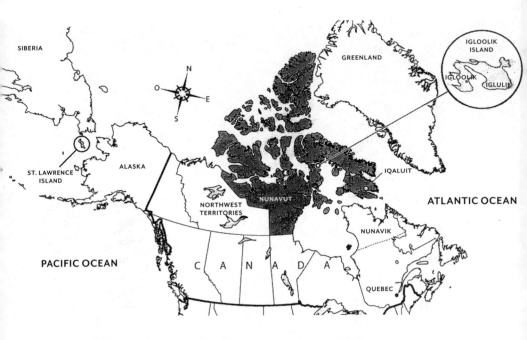

FIGURE 3. Map of Igloolik, Nunavut, and Nunavik in the Canadian
Arctic, and St. Lawrence Island in the Bering Strait. Drawn by
B. Saladin d'Anglure and made by Félix Pharand-Deschênes, 2005.

Preface to the 2006 Edition

BY CLAUDE LÉVI-STRAUSS
TRANSLATED BY PETER FROST

In Chapter 9 of *The Fourth Book of Pantagruel* (1684 [1552]), Rabelais recounts Pantagruel's visit to the island of Ennasin, whose people addressed each other strangely. For instance, an old man would call a girl "father," and she would call him "daughter."

A comical invention, undoubtedly. But anyone reading Saladin d'Anglure can have fun imagining that Rabelais was simply echoing an account by one of Jacques Cartier's shipmates who had journeyed as far afield as Arctic Quebec. This way of addressing kin has been observed by d'Anglure among the Inuit, and his book shows how it functions. It rests on the belief that one can choose, while alive, to reincarnate in a descendant, even someone of the opposite sex, and that the fetus is free to decide its sex at the time of birth, regardless of the sex of the ancestor the fetus is reincarnating. Indeed, and this is what Saladin d'Anglure discovered, among the Inuit are people who, without ever having had contact with each other, claim almost in the same terms to remember their life in the womb and describe it in great detail, from conception to birth.

Depending on how one stands in relation to surrounding family members, such an individual lives a life where forms of social conduct and kinship ties are alternately male and female. This gender instability calls for mediation. Inuit society performs this mediation through the shaman, who is seen as the representative of a third sex, which is intermediate between man and woman and which, by transcending how society defines the sexual division of labour, also transcends the other dualities: the human world versus the animal world, and the human world versus the spirit world. This ternary vision of the individual—man, woman, or transgender—extends to society and the cosmos. One response to this vision is the title of d'Anglure's book.

This book presents a selection of myths that the author collected in Inuktitut, a language he understands and speaks fluently. He takes care to compare them with the versions published by his predecessors, first of all those by Franz Boas and Knud Rasmussen. These Inuit myths are often similar to myths from other Amerindian peoples, a proof of contacts and exchanges down through the centuries. They differ from these other myths in their intensely poetic expression and a tendency to push the treatment of some themes to an extreme and give the narrative a tragic tone.

These characteristics are highlighted by Saladin d'Anglure's way of presenting his texts. He separates his informants' mythical narrative from his own commentary and divides both of them into short sequences that are more or less juxtaposed, giving the reader the impression of seeing the story on screen and arranged in longer sequences while hearing the commentator's voice in the background.

Speaking about the comments, is it necessary to emphasize how interesting and rich in meaning they are? When this book is published, more than fifty years will have elapsed since Saladin d'Anglure chose to devote himself to studying the Inuit and their lives up close. And more than thirty of those years have focused on the community of Igloolik. This long intimacy with the Inuit has given him an incomparable understanding of their family and social life, their culture, their beliefs, their worldview, and their philosophy. Such devotion lends distinction to an exceptional case in the history of anthropology. This lovely book bears witness to his work. It will become a classic.

Igloolik Island, a Mythical Place

Between the Melville Peninsula and Baffin Island at the northern end of Hudson Bay and north of the Arctic Circle (69° 23′ N), lies a small island. It has fascinated many in the Western world since 1824, when a London publisher made available the narratives by Captain Parry (1824) and his second-in-command, Captain Lyon (1824), describing the two long years they spent looking for the mythical Northwest Passage to the Indies. The island is named Igloolik, literally, "the place where there are igloos." Off its shores the two ships of the expedition, HMS *Fury* and HMS *Hecla*, cast anchor for the winter. Their names were given to the newly discovered strait northwest of the island.[1]

Both ships spent the winter of 1822–23 trapped in pack ice. At nearby Iglulik camp,[2] officers and sailors alike got to know the local Inuit, then called Eskimos (Figures 4 and 5). Lyon even managed to learn enough of their language to talk with them, notably with their shamans. Thanks to this uncommon experience, Inuit customs were written up in two accounts that showed much empathy for this people, something very new at the time. Parry's and Lyon's narratives were a great success and were republished many times. It was the first time that this endearing people

FIGURE 4. Inside of a multi-family igloo in the Igloolik region during the winter of 1821–22. On the left, a mother and her baby near an oil lamp; above, a stone pot and a leather bucket. Engraving after a drawing by Captain Lyons, 1824

had been described with more emphasis on their humanity than on their strange customs.

One hundred and eighty years later, in May 2001, the Cannes Film Festival jury honoured the Iglulik Inuit by awarding one of them, Zacharias *Kunuk*, the Caméra d'or for his film *Atanarjuat: The Fast Runner*. In fact, the film had been conceived, written, produced, and performed collectively by the people of Igloolik through the efforts of three Inuit: scriptwriter Paul *Apaaq*, elder Paul *Qulittalik*, and director Zac *Kunuk*.[3] Also helping was their friend and videomaker Norman Cohn. Together, they had formed a small production company, significantly named Isuma (reason), and created their first full-length film from one of the region's great myths: the story of *Atanaarjuat* and his brother *Aamarjuaq* (Chapter 13). The film was a hit on all continents, and Igloolik could now show millions of viewers its wondrous legends. Everyone acclaimed the profound humanity and courage of the Inuit (Saladin d'Anglure and Igloolik Isuma Productions 2002).

Meanwhile, in the wake of Parry and Lyon's expedition, these distant islanders had also piqued the interest of science—in the person of the German Franz Boas, the founding father of American anthropology. He left Germany for Baffin Island in 1883 to study how Inuit relate to their environment. His first destination: a scientific station in Cumberland Sound that German researchers had used the previous year for the International Polar Year.

Boas took Parry's and Lyon's narratives along with him in his luggage with the intention of going to Iglulik by dogsled. He also had travel accounts by the explorer Charles Francis Hall, who had gone to the same region between 1864 and 1869 to inquire about the 1847 disappearance of Rear Admiral Sir John Franklin's naval expedition. Hall had inaugurated a new approach to travel, unusual for his time, of learning to live like Inuit and getting about by dogsled. This was the model that Franz Boas wanted to follow. Unfortunately, a severe outbreak of canine disease kept him from putting together a dog team for such a trip, and he had to make do with studying the Inuit of Cumberland Sound and neighbouring groups (Boas 1888).

Iglulik remained inaccessible to Boas. Eventually, through Captain George Comer, a famous American whaler, he managed to contact several of its inhabitants, who supplied him with ethnographic collections that are now kept at the American Museum of Natural History, in New York.[4] Comer was based in New England and regularly went whaling in northwestern

FIGURE 5. The return of an Inuk hunter after a seal hunt at the open water along the floe edge near Iglulik, winter 1822–23. With his kayak on his head and shoulders, he is wearing a coat made of eider duck feathers. His wife holds his harpoon, and their pack dog is following them (Parry 1824, 274–275). Archival fonds of B. Saladin d'Anglure.

Hudson Bay. He also gathered myths and accounts for Boas about the region's recent history and its inhabitants' oral traditions. This material was published by Boas (1901, 1907), together with Baffin Island material that had been gathered for him by another whaler, Captain J. Mutch, and by Reverend Peck, an Anglican missionary stationed at Blacklead Island on Cumberland Sound (Boas 1888).

The project was taken up forty years later by Knud Rasmussen and the members of his Fifth Thule Expedition (1921–24). One hundred years after Parry and Lyon, Rasmussen, who could draw on all of his predecessors' publications, chose the Iglulik Inuit to be the first destination of his expedition. Though not visiting Igloolik Island, he did meet many of its families and sent several of his assistants there. He had actually established his base camp on an island several hundred kilometres south of Iglulik, but not far from the winter dogsled trail running from that community southwest to the Repulse Bay trading post. Rasmussen complicated matters a bit by applying the term Iglulik to all Inuit in the huge territory from North Baffin (Pond Inlet and Arctic Bay) to the south of Repulse Bay. Later research by Dorais (2010 [1996]) has shown that linguistic and cultural differences justify classifying the inhabitants of the Repulse Bay region with another group: the Aivilik ("The walrus people"). Rasmussen eventually took his scientific expedition as far as the Bering Strait.

Rasmussen was the son of a Danish Lutheran pastor but spoke the Inuit language fluently, having learned it as a child in Greenland from his Inuit maternal grandmother. He thus had an edge over all of his predecessors and even most of his successors. Rasmussen's major monograph, *Intellectual Culture of the Iglulik Eskimos* (1929), became a must-read for anyone interested in the cosmology, shamanism, and oral traditions of Canadian Inuit.

Thus for the century stretching from Parry and Lyon to Rasmussen the Iglulik Inuit were seen as the quintessential Inuit group. Unknown to Westerners until 1821, they lived away from the sea lanes of Euro-Americans for several centuries in the marine cul-de-sac of Foxe Basin, which is often clogged by drifting pack ice in summer. There they remained beyond the reach of whalers, traders, and missionaries, unlike many other groups.

In 1931 the first white man, Father Étienne Bazin OMI, a French missionary, came to live among them in their winter camp at Avvajjaq, several kilometres from Igloolik Island, in a semi-subterranean Inuit house. Then in 1937, a Catholic mission was built on the island itself, on Ikpiarjuk Bay

("The little bag"), which offered better moorings than either Avvajjaq or the old Iglulik winter camp. Two years later it was the turn of the Hudson's Bay Company to build a store, not far from the mission (Laugrand 2002). In 1959 an Anglican mission was erected a bit farther away and an Inuit minister placed in charge. That same year saw the arrival of the Canadian government's first administrator, and with him several civil servants who set out to develop the infrastructure of an organized village.

The people were still living in traditional seasonal camps, while regularly coming to Ikpiarjuk for trade and religious services. Then the first pupils were sent to the Catholic boarding school in Chesterfield Inlet, and several families came to live in the village and do the first service jobs. Others left to live near the U.S. Army radar station at Hall Beach, around fifty kilometres south of Igloolik Island, where many job opportunities were available.

From then on, the Inuit became more and more sedentary. A school was built in the village, then a nursing station and a police station, and finally a co-op store. The site previously known as Ikpiarjuk was officially renamed Igloolik and given an elected municipal council. In 1966 there were already fifty or so little prefab houses, followed later by the same number of new multi-room family homes. By the late 1960s only a few families were still spending winter in camps, living either in semi-subterranean homes of sod, stones, and hides or in igloos of snow. Most igloos were now temporary shelters for hunting or for visits to other villages.

I witnessed similar changes in Arctic Quebec between 1955 and 1970. In 1956 most families were still living in snow igloos; five years later they had to move to Euro-Canadian settlements for compulsory schooling of their children. This settlement policy entailed the rapid abandonment of snow igloos, kayaks, dogsleds, and a diet based mainly on local resources.

In 1971, when I first came to the village of Igloolik, I intended to complete the study I had been conducting for nearly six months in Arctic Quebec (present-day Nunavik) on the way Inuit imagine the reproduction of life, on the customs surrounding the socialization of their children, and on the beliefs, rules, and myths that explain, uphold, or justify those customs. My plan was to spend December in Igloolik gathering comparable data on these themes. I already knew the Tarramiut Inuit dialect, which the people of Igloolik easily understood although it differed slightly from their own.[5] An Inuit assistant, Jimmy *Innaarulik* Mark from Ivujivik, Nunavik, accompanied me. He had worked with me for two years and had assisted me in developing my research project, using previously gathered data, and in transcribing recorded interviews into standard written form.

Two researchers had come to the area several years before. The first, David Damas, an anthropologist, spent a year (1959–60) examining the kinship and residential patterns of Inuit camps (Damas 1971). The second, Jean Malaurie, a geographer, spent several months in the region in 1960 and 1961 studying the ecology of hunting among local families and their micro-economic structures (Malaurie 2001). Both had learned some rudiments of the Inuit language but could not speak it well enough to conduct interviews without an interpreter.

Upon my arrival in Igloolik, I visited the local Anglican minister, Reverend Noah *Nasuk*, an Inuk native to the region. He received me very simply, and to my question about which elders could best help me in my research he unhesitatingly referred me to his uncle *Ujarak* and his female cousin *Iqallijuq*. The first elder, an Anglican convert, was around seventy years old, and the second, a baptized Catholic, several years younger. I went to visit each of them, and they agreed to come and work with me the next day. To avoid any misunderstanding due to differences in dialect I hired another assistant: a young local Catholic girl, Bernadette *Imaruittuq*, who had gone to the boarding school in Igluligaarjuk (Chesterfield Inlet).

The two elders' names were not unknown to me, but I could not remember where I had seen them. I looked up the population list that Rasmussen's team had made in 1922 and found the names there: *Ujarak*, the son of the great shaman *Ava*; and *Iqallijuq*, his girlfriend. They had been living together in the shaman's igloo where Rasmussen had spent several days. Surely they had been the namesakes of my two future assistants, who now lived in separate homes at one end of the village. At the appointed time the next morning, I greeted them and offered tea. To lighten the mood I smiled and mentioned that fifty years earlier a man called *Ujarak* had lived in Iglulik with his girlfriend *Iqallijuq*. Were they named after those two? They looked at me with surprise and, laughing, told me: "That was us. We were young back then!" Before me were two witnesses to Knud Rasmussen's visit. And what witnesses! They had lived in the same igloo as the Danish explorer and had attended his discussions with *Ujarak*'s father—the shaman *Ava*—and his mother, *Urulu*, herself a shaman.

This unforeseen meeting turned all of my plans upside down. Both elders would be remarkable informants. They had spent most of their lives in the camps and fully remembered the pre-Christian period. They soon became my friends and my teachers of Inuit culture and history. Until *Ujarak*'s death in 1985 and *Iqallijuq*'s in 2000, I would work with them and their families to gather the oral traditions of their people—a period totalling thirty years. The quality of their accounts, which differed from and complemented each other, especially on the subject of shamanism, justified suspending all of my other research projects in Nunavik, where I returned only after their deaths. Even then, I still kept in touch with my many Igloolik friends, who since 1998 have taken an active part in producing films about their history and culture. It is at their request that I have dusted off the abundant material I accumulated over the past thirty years about their oral tradition, in order to make it available to them and to a broader audience. One outcome is this book.

The Storytellers

Saladin d'Anglure's Main Informants

(MICHEL) *KUPAAQ* (c. mid-1920s–1997) was married to *Iqallijuq*'s oldest daughter, *Arnainnuk*, and together they had eight children, two of them adopted. He himself had been adopted at a very early age by his paternal grandparents, had lived in their home with his father and his mother *Alariaq*, and had learned their knowledge and stories. He was a good hunter and probably the best local storyteller. He was the oldest grandchild of *Ataguttaaluk*, who had died in 1948 and been dubbed by white people the "Queen of Igloolik." A former shaman, she was forced to eat the corpses of her first husband and their children in 1905 to survive a terrible famine (Chapter 14). *Ataguttaaluk* remarried *Iktuksarjuat*, who died in 1944. He was nicknamed the "King of Igloolik" because he was the best hunter of the region and was a trained shaman. The couple converted to Catholicism in 1931. *Kupaaq*'s older children went to a Catholic residential school in Chesterfield Inlet and spoke English. They helped Saladin d'Anglure (with the collaboration of some of their cousins) transcribe and translate interviews and visited various families in the village with him. In 1972 Saladin d'Anglure joined *Kupaaq*'s family on a hunting expedition and listened to him sharing his stories in the evenings

with his children. After their return to Igloolik, Saladin d'Anglure spent another month recording *Kupaaq*'s stories and myths. Saladin d'Anglure asked
Kupaaq's daughter Élise *Ataguttaaluk* to help him keep track of the interviews and monitor the recording equipment. The recordings, which date
from 1972 and were completed in 1973, provide most of the myths and
stories in this book.

(ROSE) *IQALLIJUQ* (1905–2000), daughter of the shaman *Ittuliaq* and his
wife *Nuvvijaq*, granddaughter of *Savviurtalik*, a great bowhead whale hunter
and shaman, and a daughter-in-law of *Ataguttaaluk* by her marriage with
Ukumaaluk. *Iqallijuq*'s oldest daughter, *Arnainnuk*, had married a cousin,
Kupaaq. She was the girlfriend of *Ujarak* when Rasmussen met her in 1922.
Ujarak's father *Ava* was the younger brother of *Iqallijuq*'s maternal grandmother and both *Ujarak* and *Iqallijug* were fifth cousins and descended
from *Qingailisaq*, the shaman from whom Captain Comer had bought a
shaman's coat for Franz Boas and the American Museum of Natural History in the late nineteenth century. But she subsequently married shaman
Amarualik, who had lost his wife. She had several spouses and many children
before Bernard interviewed her in 1971, when she was probably in her late
sixties and a baptized Catholic. She is also a cousin of Reverend Noah *Nasuk*.
Iqallijuq was in a class of her own when talking about rules, ritual injunctions, and prohibitions. In Chapter 1, she shares with Saladin d'Anglure and
Alexina *Kublu*—her granddaughter—a story about her life in the womb as
well as about changing her sex while she was born and about being cross-
dressed until puberty.

(JUANASI) *UJARAK* (c. 1900–1985), son of the great shaman and storyteller
Ava and his wife shaman and storyteller *Urulu* and younger brother of *Atuat* and *Nataaq*. When Rasmussen met him in 1922, *Ujarak* lived with his
girlfriend *Iqallijuq* in his father's igloo. After *Iqallijuq* married another man,
Ujarak had several spouses and children. He was interviewed by Bernard
Saladin d'Anglure in 1971 when he was around seventy and had become
an Anglican convert (baptized by the Rev. Turner in 1943). His parents,
two sisters, and two uncles had been shamans, and *Ujarak* spoke about them
in spite of his nephew Noah *Nasuk* being the Anglican minister for Igloolik. In his stories *Ujarak* was able to illustrate Inuit rules and prohibitions
with precise and detailed examples. He told Saladin d'Anglure that he was

cross-dressed as a child. *Ujarak* had worn braids and girl's clothing until the age of eight because of the female names given him at birth. He might have become a shaman had he not been Christianized as a child or teenager.

Other Storytellers

AGIAQ was *Ijituuq*'s younger brother and one of the elders interviewed by Saladin d'Anglure. He recounted the beginning of time starting with two male beings and placed the event on Igloolik Island. He was told the story by *Ulluriaq*, a very old shaman woman from Iglulik who died in the 1930s.

ATUAT (1894–1976), also called *Ittukusuk*, was adopted by *Tagurnaaq* but was the biological daughter of shamans *Ava* and *Urulu* and *Ujarak* and *Nataaq*'s sister. She was a witness to *Ataguttaaluk*'s story, being eleven years old in 1905 when her party discovered *Ataguttaaluk* on the brink of death after she consumed some of her dead companions' flesh to survive. Father Guy Mary-Rousselière recorded *Atuat*'s version of *Ataguttaaluk*'s story in 1968 and Saladin d'Anglure took down another version when he met her in 1974.

AVA (c. 1870–after 1922) was a great shaman and storyteller, husband of the shaman *Urulu*, father to *Ujarak*, *Nataaq*, and *Atuat*, son of shaman *Qingailisaq*, and younger brother of *Natsiq* and *Ivaluarjuk*. He met Rasmussen in 1922 and they hunted walrus together. He and his wife hosted Rasmussen in their igloo compound among their kinfolk. He told Rasmussen many stories and Rasmussen considered him an authority not only on folklore and customs but also on supernatural matters and rites and observances related to taboo subjects. As with many other people born in winter, *Ava* had been rubbed at birth with a skin of the raven and wore the same skin as his first clothing. Afterwards, he treated the raven as a powerful sign and amulet.

IGJUGAARJUK was a Caribou Inuit shaman, chief of the Paallirmiut—people of the willow, encountered by Rasmussen near Lake Hikoligjuaq. His two wives were *Kivkarjuk*, also a storyteller, and *Atqaralaq*. As a young man he was visited by strange unknown beings in his dreams and was trained to become a shaman by fasting and by being exposed to the cold.

INUKPASUJJUK was a great storyteller and a native of the neighbouring Natsilik region. In 1922, Rasmussen met him and his party at Pikiuleq (Depot Island) near Chesterfield. Rasmussen stayed with *Inukpasujjuk* and wrote down many of his stories. The storyteller also was able to repeat to Rasmussen some of the knowledge of a well-known Natsilik shaman *Anaituarjuk* about life after death and among other stories discussed with him observances and rules regarding death.

IVALUARJUK was *Ava's* older brother, shaman, storyteller, and singer. Rasmussen met him in 1922 at Repulse Bay and then again at Lyon Inlet hunting camp and recorded over fifty of *Ivaluarjuk's* stories. He credited *Ivaluarjuk* with the greatest contribution of legends, myths, and folk tales of all of his informants during the Fifth Thule Expedition. *Ivaluarjuk* also drew the map of the coastline from Repulse Bay right up to Baffin Island, familiarizing Rasmussen with all the Inuit place names and thus assisting his work.

IJITUUQ (born c. 1912 at Wager Bay), baptized Catholic in 1935, was an Inuk from Igloolik, *Agiaq's* older brother and one of the elders Saladin d'Anglure interviewed in 1971, along with *Ujarak* and *Iqallijuq*. He shared a story about an amulet his shaman grandfather had given him.

NAUKAJJIK was one of Rasmussen's storytellers and informants. Among the stories he tells is one about *Kaujjajjuk* (Walrus-Skin). Rasmussen does not introduce him as he does his other informants.

(HERVÉ) *PANNIAQ* (born 1933) was *Kupaaq's* younger brother. Baptized Catholic at birth in Avvajjaq (near Igloolik), he contributed a variant of the *Taqqiq* (the Moon Man) myth. Because he was adopted by another family at a very early age, he had access to other sources than those of *Kupaaq* and his original family. Along with his own interviews, Saladin d'Anglure referenced some of *Panniaq's* stories collected and published (1998) by John MacDonald, the former Director of the Igloolik Research Centre (Nunavut).

(NOAH) *PIUGAATTUQ* (born c. 1908), baptized Anglican, was an elder interviewed by Saladin d'Anglure in 1990 who contributed to the discussion of *Sila* in this book.

TAGURNAAQ was an older woman from Iglulik who had shamanic powers. She had a troubled married life with several ex-husbands before she married *Padluq*, a shaman, and adopted *Atuat*. She met Rasmussen in 1922 and was the first of the Hudson Bay Inuit to befriend him. She shared with him the story of her life as well as the story of *Ataguttaaluk*, as she was one of the sled passengers who discovered *Ataguttaaluk* near death after she consumed some of her dead companions' flesh. She and *Padluq* joined Rasmussen and his group on Danish Island and stayed with them one winter.

UNALIQ was an old shaman who was a Netsilik immigrant. With his wife *Tuulliq*, he had come from the Pelly Bay region some twenty years earlier. Rasmussen met him in 1922 near *Tagurnaaq*'s village and at Lyon Inlet hunting camp. *Unaliq* discussed his ten helping spirits with Rasmussen, and he and his wife shared stories about the earliest history of mankind and creation. Rasmussen had doubts about *Unaliq* skills as a hunter and a shaman, and more faith in the accounts told by his wife *Tuulliq*.

URULU was a female shaman and storyteller, the wife of shaman *Ava,* and the mother of *Ujarak*, *Nataaq*, and *Atuat*. She spent time with Rasmussen in 1922 and, along with her husband, she hosted him in their igloo compound among their kinfolk. Among other stories, she told Rasmussen the story of her life: being born on Baffin Island, experiencing the deaths of her father and brothers, living through her mother's several marriages, and finally marrying *Ava*. Rasmussen considered her highly knowledgeable about old traditions and a faithful storyteller.

Other Informants

(GEORGE) *ANNANAK* (1904–1968) was an Inuk from Kangirsualujjuaq (George River or Nouveau-Québec) on Ungava Bay. In 1967, he was the first to tell Saladin d'Anglure his own birth memories but died the following year before Saladin d'Anglure could question him further.

DAIVIDIALUK AMITTUQ ALASUAQ (1910–1976) was an artist and an informant from Puvirnituq. He told and illustrated several myths for Saladin d'Anglure in 1971.

(JIMMY) ETTUK (1908–1975), also known as *Ittuq*, was an Arctic Bay artist who made drawings of various episodes of the story of *Atanaarjuat*. Saladin d'Anglure used what Ettuk (1964) wrote about the drawings to supplement *Kupaaq*'s *Atanaarjuat* account.

GEORGE KAPPIANAQ (1917–unknown) was an Inuk man who grew up in the Salliq area. His father was *Kappianaq*, his mother *Uviluq*. When his family moved from the Salliq area (Southhampton Island) to the coast of Keewatin (Nunavut), he became a Christian. There were several shamans in his family. Saladin d'Anglure uses his variant of the Moon Brother and Sun Sister story, published by MacDonald (1998).

ALEXINA *KUBLU* (born 1954) is a daughter of *Kupaaq* and a granddaughter of *Iqallijuq*. She earned a university degree and taught at various educational institutions in Nunavut, including Nunavut Arctic College in Iqaluit, where she was a professor for over ten years in the Inuit Studies Program. She was appointed the first justice of the peace in Nunavut. Saladin d'Anglure uses her published story (Kublu 2000) of Brother Moon and Sister Sun, which is based on what she heard from her father, to supplement *Kupaaq*'s story. *Kublu* assisted Saladin d'Anglure in interviewing and filming her maternal grandmother, *Iqalijuq*, in Igloolik, and also in Sanirajaq (Hall Beach), the former *angakkuq Sapangaarjuk* (born c. 1889)—son of *Mirqutui*, the most powerful shaman of the country at the time of Knud Rasmussen's Fifth Thule Expedition.

MOSES NUVALINGAQ was a young man from Sanikiluaq (Belcher Islands, Nunavut) who shared with Saladin d'Anglure in the spring of 2004 a custom that was observed whenever one entered a new territory for the first time.

(PIITA) *PITSIULAAQ* (c. 1902–1973) was a man of around sixty from Kinngait (Cape Dorset) on Baffin Island. He shared with Saladin d'Anglure his recollections of prenatal life and birth in 1971. Several years later,

Dorothy Eber (Eber and Pitseolak 1975) helped him write his life's story, in which he shared some of these prenatal memories.

QISARUATSIAQ (born 1956) was a female informant Saladin d'Anglure met when he returned to the Belcher Islands in 2003. She worked for the local high school and arranged to share with Saladin d'Anglure her own womb memories.

AANI QITUSUK (c. 1930–unknown) was a female informant Saladin d'Anglure met in Sanikiluaq on the Belcher Islands. She was the first in 1971 to recount to him memories of her birth.

FRANÇOIS QUASSA (1927–unknown) was the father of Paul *Quassa* (the fourth premier of Nunavut); he provided a version of the *Atanaarjuat* story that Saladin d'Anglure uses to supplement the story told by *Kupaaq*. *Quassa's* variant (1998) describes how *Aamarjuaq*, *Atanaarjuat's* brother, murders one of his wives.

PAULUSI SIVUAK (1930–1986) was an Inuit artist from Puvirnituq. Some of the illustrations in the text, such as those accompanying the story of Walrus-Skin, are based on his drawings and text.

GRACE SLWOOKO (1921–2013) was a Yupik woman from Sivuqaq (Gambell) on St. Lawrence Island, Alaska, who took down the Alaskan myth of a strange man and his whale in the Yupik language and translated it into English in 1979. Saladin d'Anglure met her nephew Chris Petuwak Koonooka, a schoolteacher, in 2004 and he was also familiar with this myth.

SAKARIASI ARNATUQ TARQIAPIK (1911–1977) was an elder from Kangirsuk Saladin d'Anglure interviewed in Kuujjuaq, where he was living during the 1960s. Tarqiapiq told him that the *Itiqanngittut*, the anus-less people of Chapter 4, were actually *ukpiit* (snowy owls) in human form.

DALASI KIMMIITUQ TARQIAPIK (1904–1997) was the wife of Sakariasi. She described the custom of how, when the wind blew in the same direction for a long time, breech-born individuals were made to go outside to reverse the wind direction.

Note: In Franz Boas's publications, stories are not accredited to single story-tellers but are more generally described as stories from a certain geographical region. In many cases, they were compiled from the notes of several sources, for example, in the publication *The Eskimo of Baffin Island and Hudson Bay* (Boas 1901).

Inuit Stories
of Being and Rebirth

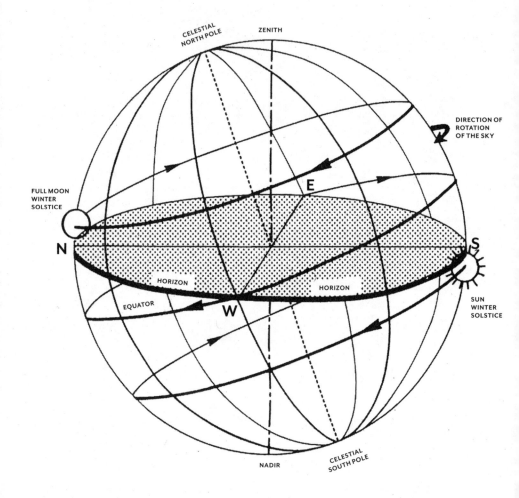

FIGURE 6. The celestial sphere showing the apparent trajectories of the full moon and the sun at the winter solstice at 70° latitude North, Igloolik. It helps explain the phenomenon of the circumpolar moon. Drawn by B. Saladin d'Anglure and made by Johanne Lévesque, 2005.

Iqallijuq, Ujarak, Kupaaq, and the Others

The sun had disappeared for nearly a week when I came to Igloolik Island on 1 December 1971. It reappeared only in mid-January, and very gradually at that. The small village of Igloolik, with its 500 inhabitants, was bathed in a semi-darkness in which the only sources of light were the moon and a few streetlights along the village's icy streets. I arrived on the day of the full moon, and its size, brightness, and omnipresence as it rose and fell in the sky were striking wherever one stood. At midday it was due north, as if placed on the horizon. Due south, a small reddish glow bore witness to the sun's furtive presence a few degrees below the horizon. At midnight the moon was at its apogee, very high to the south, its pale light illuminating the snow-covered ice and land. In early morning it still appeared in the sky, but now to the west on its downward course to the horizon. Never did I suspect it had been circling around the winter sky and not setting for at least three days. Nineteen years later, thanks to an astronomy software package, I discovered that at Igloolik's latitude (69° N) the full moon rotates around the sky without ever setting between November and February (Saladin d'Anglure 1992),[1] its path inversely symmetrical to the sun's path in summer, that is, to the north at midday and to the south at midnight. So the moon is full at midday during the Arctic's long winter

1

night. I later established a relationship between this astronomical peculiarity and the moon's prevalence in Inuit shamanism (Saladin d'Anglure 1993a [1990]).

Two weeks after my arrival, a new lunar month began under a sunless and moonless sky. *Tauvijjuaq*, "the great darkness," is the Inuit name for this time on the lunar calendar, which coincides with the winter solstice and the longest night (Saladin d'Anglure 1992; MacDonald 1993). This was the time of the *Tivajuut* festival, which featured many contests of strength and singing, games, and exchanges of spouses. The festival was motivated by a fear of the end of the world and by a corresponding need to restart the cycles of life and the cosmos.

The thermometer ranged between −30° and −50° Celsius, temperatures one could endure with appropriate clothing as long as the north wind was not blowing. The local administrator had given me a house in the centre of the village, of the same type as the neighbouring Inuit family dwellings. There were around sixty such dwellings. Mine was for visiting researchers and had been home that year to biologists working for the International Biological Program. This was where I would live and conduct my interviews, while my assistant Jimmy *Innaarulik* stayed in an Inuit family of his choice.

Iqallijuq and Ujarak

I regularly met with *Iqallijuq* and *Ujarak* every morning because they preferred to start work early.[2] They seemed to enjoy discussing this past I wished to learn more about. After Rasmussen had left for the Western Arctic, they did not stay betrothed to each other for long. *Ujarak*'s father, the shaman *Ava,* died the following year, and *Iqallijuq*'s parents decided to marry their daughter to *Amarualik*, a shaman who had lost his wife the year before. *Iqallijuq* and *Ujarak* each subsequently had several successive spouses and many children, yet they still called each other *aippaksaq* (fiancé), a term of address I found touching.

After several interviews about the beliefs and rituals surrounding conception and pregnancy, I came to the theme of birth and asked *Iqallijuq* whether she had known anyone who remembered being born. She looked at me, amused, and answered, "If you're interested, I can tell you about my birth and even my life from before!" I could not hide my satisfaction and urged her to tell me her memories. She began a fabulous story about her life in the womb and earlier still, when she was her maternal grandfather (see Chapter 1). She then told me how she had changed sex while being born and been cross-dressed until puberty.

Not to be outdone, and while *Iqallijuq* was having tea, *Ujarak* told me he too used to be cross-dressed. He had worn braids and girl's clothing until the age of eight because of the female names given him at birth. An uncle then decided to help him make his first kill. The man cut his braids, dressed him as a boy, took him to the hunting ground, and guided his hand as he shot an arrow at a young caribou fawn. This feat was celebrated, and the young hunter learned how to do a man's job under the authority of his older brothers and uncles (Saladin d'Anglure 1980a).

My two new friends provided me with a month of fascinating discoveries in Igloolik. *Ujarak*'s father was the younger brother of *Iqallijuq*'s maternal grandmother. Both of them were therefore descended from *Qingailisaq*, the shaman from whom Captain Comer had bought a shaman's coat for Franz Boas and the American Museum of Natural History in the late nineteenth century. So they were fifth cousins and thus close to each other, while differing considerably in their ways of discussing Inuit culture and the history of their group. *Iqallijuq* was in a class of her own when talking about rules, ritual injunctions, and prohibitions, while *Ujarak* could endlessly illustrate these rules with precise and detailed examples. Until the age of twenty he had been raised by shamans: his father, his mother, two of his sisters, and two uncles. He spoke about them without the least reserve or fear of being disowned by his nephew *Nasuk*, the Anglican minister for Igloolik.

One morning I got the two elders talking about the womb-igloo symbolic equivalence, which had come up the day before. They had spoken about a rule requiring a future father to place the igloo keystone perpendicular to the entrance to ensure a fast, trouble-free childbirth. *Ujarak* stared at me, concentrated for a moment, and began to sing the words of an old infirm shaman, *Saittuq*, who had once stayed for a while with his family. Because the old man could no longer get around, he shrank the outside world to the different parts of his igloo: the sleeping platform became the land, the floor the sea ice, the ice window the sun, the opening for the entrance the moon, and the dome the vault of the heavens. He thus had a means to find game animals and help hunters capture them. *Ujarak*'s song showed me that an igloo is not only a large womb but also a microcosm of the universe (see Figure 34).

Time went by very fast. Christmas was coming, and the Catholic mission busied itself with preparations. The whole community would come and dance to the drum and join in a traditional feast of frozen raw caribou and gamey walrus meat, both steeped in rancid oil. The Catholic missionary, a French man from Corrèze, with whom I had talked about my research, warned me against putting much faith in the stories of *Iqallijuq*, one of his worshippers. She was known, he said, for her tall tales. Unlike other missionaries I had met, he seemed to be more of a church builder and a mystic than an anthropologist.

Clearly, I viewed this woman differently, being struck by her depth and genuineness when interviewed. I nonetheless realized that much work remained to complete, transcribe, translate, and analyze the recorded texts. I took stock of the time I would need to get to know this group, its oral traditions, its social life, and its recent history. Never in my ten years of fieldwork among the Inuit had I encountered such a wonderful opportunity to study their system of thoughts and beliefs—too wonderful for me to let it slip through my fingers. I was caught up in something that would bring me back to this region every year, for over thirty years. My research focused on its inhabitants.

Kupaaq and the Others

Iqallijuq's oldest daughter, *Arnainnuk*, had married a cousin, *Kupaaq*, the oldest grandchild of *Ataguttaaluk*, who had died in 1948 and been dubbed by white people the "Queen of Igloolik."[3] A former shaman, she was forced to eat the corpses of her first husband and their children in the early twentieth century to survive a terrible famine (Chapter 14). *Ataguttaaluk* remarried with *Iktuksarjuat*, who died in 1944. He was nicknamed the "King of Igloolik" because he was the best hunter of the region, and he himself had trained to be a shaman. The couple converted to Catholicism in 1931 while on a trip to Pond Inlet,[4] and they asked Father Bazin to come to Igloolik, to their camp at Avvajjaq. The descendants of this blended family now form the largest subgroup in the community of Igloolik. In May 2004, around 100 of them gathered in the interior of Baffin Island at the site of Inukturvik, "The place where someone ate human flesh," to commemorate their ancestor's heroic adventure.

I was greatly helped by *Kupaaq*, *Arnainnuk*, and their eight children, two of whom were adopted. In this family the parents spoke only Inuktitut[5] and knew the traditional way of life, which they had practised until the early 1960s. The mother was skilled at working hides and sewing. The father was a good hunter and probably the best local storyteller. He had been adopted at a very early age by his paternal grandparents,[6] had lived in their home with his parents, and had learned their knowledge and stories (see Figure 33). As for *Kupaaq* and *Arnainnuk*'s children, the older ones had been educated from 1962 to 1967 at a Catholic boarding school in Chesterfield Inlet, 400 kilometres to the south, and got along well in English. They were able to help me transcribe and translate the recordings of my Inuit-language interviews and guide me through the meanders of the village on my visits to various families. In short, this family offered me a mixture of tradition and modernity that reflected the situation of this changing community.

In August 1972, during my second Igloolik stay, I travelled with them and a related family on a whaling boat powered by a small gas engine. We were going to hunt caribou along the coasts of Baffin Island, three days by boat from the village, caribou fur being ideal at that time of year for making winter clothes. There was no night yet. Each evening, from my small back-packing tent pitched next to their large family tent, I heard *Kupaaq*'s expressive voice slowly telling his fascinated children the myths of long-ago times.

The expedition lasted a month. We then left for home, but our boat was soon trapped by large slabs of ice. To keep it from getting smashed up, we used a makeshift hoist to pull it up onto a small ice floe. There we stayed for twelve hours, bivouacking inside the boat under a tent canvas. Our group was made up of fifteen people, plus the same number of dogs and about twenty caribou carcasses, as well as bundles of hides. There we waited for a passage of open water to form. Lookouts were continually watching the condition of the sea, while *Kupaaq* remained imperturbable and told one myth after another.

When a narrow channel opened up we emptied the whaling boat, put it back in the water, reloaded it, and scrambled aboard. We had to advance slowly while pushing the ice aside with our oars until we finally reached open water. Other hunters had come in canoes and remained stuck for several days. On the way home *Kupaaq* commented on the various place names and the memories, history, and legends they brought to mind. We soon reached the Qikirtaarjuk headland, where he used to spend winter in the 1950s. Here, too, lived at the dawn of time *Uinigumasuittuq*, the mother of the different human races and marine mammals (Chapter 5). We then rounded the little cape that once sheltered the old Iglulik camp. A fine layer of ice, a few millimetres thick, covered the sea surface. The boat broke through the ice as it moved forward. The time of year was late August—we had to get home now to avoid being trapped by the freezing sea.

After our return to Igloolik I spent another month recording myths told by *Kupaaq*. I had asked one of his daughters (Élise *Ataguttaaluk*) to help me keep track of the interviews and monitor the recording equipment. The recordings, which date from 1972 and were completed in 1973, provide most of the myths and stories in this book.

During the summer of 1973, my ties with *Kupaaq*'s family and with my two old friends *Iqallijuq* and *Ujarak* grew stronger. I brought a cameraman from Université Laval in Quebec City to film in Inuktitut several stories and myths I had recorded during my two previous stays.[7] I also brought my young six-month-old son, Guillaume, whom *Arnainnuk* immediately offered to babysit at her home during the day. *Iqallijuq* saw in him a reincarnation of her father-in-law, the old chief *Iktuksarjuat* and the grandfather of both *Arnainnuk* and *Kupaaq*. Because the child's right eye was slightly lazy at the time, a condition called strabismus, everyone thought he was the deceased chief, who had lost his right eye in a hunting accident. And so, as *Iktuksarjuat*'s father, I entered the group's complex and tightly woven web of kinship.

Although *Arnainnuk* and *Ujarak* died in the mid-1980s, followed by *Kupaaq* in 1997 and *Iqallijuq* in 2000, their descendants have maintained these ties of kinship. Guillaume, alias *Iktuksarjuat* and now an adult, has fully accepted this kinship and has since 1998 organized youth activities with the community of Igloolik and Igloolik Isuma Productions to help give meaning to the lives of young people. Together with the introduction of compulsory schooling and its very colonial mindset, the intrusion of television into the community, which came later than elsewhere, has pushed young Inuit toward a new world and away from the world of previous generations. To them, the village seems like a prison they dream of getting away from—hence a teen suicide rate eleven times higher than among

Canadians in general. To fight the suicidal tendencies of these teens, whose Westernized schooling encourages individualism and discourages traditional collective values of "living well" and sharing, Guillaume-*Iktuksarjuat* created Artcirq with other young Inuit friends. The first Inuit circus troupe, Artcirq is inspired by the genre of contemporary circus that developed in Quebec during the late twentieth century. Cirque du Soleil, Cirque Éloise, and Cirque Les sept doigts de la main have assisted Artcirq by sending equipment and circus performers from southern Quebec. They have successfully trained young people in the circus arts and helped them express their emotions with their bodies.[8]

Memory, Culture, and History

Many anthropologists and archaeologists have viewed Igloolik as a centre of religious activity. The site was a crossroads for all of the great migrations that spread out of northern Alaska, through Arctic North America, and into Greenland. The first migration brought the people of the Pre-Dorset culture, who came 4,000 years ago, just after the melting of the great ice sheets that had until then covered the land. They were replaced 2,000 years later by the Dorset people, who are called *Tuniit* in Inuit myths. Then, around 1,000 years ago came the Thule people, who were bowhead whale hunters and the direct ancestors of today's Inuit. Local oral tradition has it that it was on Igloolik Island that the first two humans emerged from the earth (Chapter 2).

Over the past half century, and spurred on by the elders, a keen interest in culture, collective memory, and history has developed among the Iglulik Inuit. The Inummariit ("Real Inuit") Cultural Association was founded with the help of the Catholic missionary,[9] then the Inullariit ("Authentic Inuit") Society with the help of a federal civil servant,[10] and finally Igloolik Isuma Productions. This company has organized cultural and social activities while producing world-renowned films.[11] I worked with all three organizations for a period of thirty-five years. More recently it was in this village that the Nunavut territorial government decided to locate its Department of Culture, Language, Elders and Youth, with a view to decentralization. In April 1999, Nunavut gained official status as a self-governing territory, and the Inuit were recognized as having collective ownership over much of the land and its resources. The territorial capital is Iqaluit (formerly Frobisher Bay; see map), but several departments have been relocated to the major subregions. The population of Igloolik has tripled over the past thirty years and today exceeds 1,500 people—1 percent of the world's total Inuit population.[12]

In such a society, which did not know writing until the early twentieth century,[13] you learned by imitating, by experiencing with your senses, and by receiving what had been passed down orally. You also learned by dreaming or by contacting spirits. Memory was the tool for retaining knowledge. Memory aids were taught from early childhood so that children could orient themselves in their kin group (through kinship terms), in space (through place names), and in time (through your family tree and life stories). According to Inuit, you could also learn from a spirit encountered in a dream or in a seldom-visited place, and it would then make you forget the encounter. Nonetheless, such erased memories could be remembered in special circumstances, like during the approach of death or a serious illness. Spirits were also said to have the gift of making themselves invisible at will; they would show themselves to ordinary humans to seduce them or to take revenge. Shamans, however, were chosen by spirits and would form close relationships with them.

Individuals differed considerably in their knowledge. If raised and brought up by their grandparents, they would know more of the traditional knowledge. They would know less if raised by their parents, who were much less available. Moreover, at birth some children received a gender identity that differed from their biological one because their name came from a deceased person of the opposite sex. They were then brought up according to their assigned gender. Such children developed talents as mediators that predisposed them to shamanism. This was the case with *Iqallijuq* and *Ujarak*, who might have become shamans, like *Kupaaq*, had they not been Christianized as children or teenagers.

Song of *Saittuq*

This is the song of the invalid shaman *Saittuq* who lived in the home of the shaman *Ava*; *Ujarak*, *Ava*'s son, had long known this song.[1]

Ajaa uvanga ajaja ajaja,
iglirli[2] majja ijigivara aa
nunarjuarli Sunauvva mannaa
ajaja ajaja ajaja ajaja ajaja ajaa
ajaa I'm the one ajaja ajaja who's looking at this platform
and to my great surprise there's now the vast land
ajaja ajaja ajaja ajaja ajaja ajaa

natirli[3] majjaa ijigivaraa,
sikuliajuarli[4] sunauvva mannaa
ajaja ajaja ajaja ajaja ajaja ajaa
this ground I'm looking at here,
now to my great surprise there's the big ice floe,
ajaja ajaja ajaja ajaja ajaja ajaja ajaa

**kataglii[5] kannaa ijigivaraa
taqqirjuarli sunauvva kannaa,
ajaja ajaja ajaa ajaja ajaja ajaa**
and this entrance way I'm looking at below,
now to my great surprise there's the huge moon down there,
ajaja ajaja ajaja ajaja ajaja ajaa

**Igalaarli[6] pikka ijigivaraa
siqinirjuarli sunauvvali unaa
ajaja ajaja ajaja ajaja ajaja ajaa**
and this windowpane I'm looking at up there,
now to my great surprise there's the huge sun,
ajaja ajaja ajaa ajaja ajaja ajaa

**Akili[7] majja ijigivaraa
imarjuarli[8] sunauvva mannaa
ajaja ajaja ajaja ajaja ajaja ajaa**
and this meat larder I'm looking at here, now to my great surprise
there's the big sea here very close,
ajaja ajaja ajaja ajaja ajaja ajaa

**igluli[9] majja ijigivaraa
silarjuarmi[10] sunauvva mannaa
ajaja ajaja ajaja ajaja ajaja ajaa**
and this dome of the igloo I'm looking at up there,
now to my great surprise there's the vast universe,
ajaja ajaja ajaja ajaja ajaja ajaa

**kangirli[11] pikka ijigivaraa
ullurialli sunauvva makua
ajaja ajaja ajaja ajaja ajaa**
and this air shaft I'm looking at up there,
now to my great surprise there are stars,
ajaja ajaja ajaja ajaja ajaja ajaa

CHAPTER 1

Savviurtalik Is Reincarnated

Memories from the Womb: A "Narrative Genre"?

Six years before my arrival in Igloolik, when I was doing my first fieldwork on Inuit oral tradition in Nunavik (Arctic Quebec), elderly informants had told me about a long-dead woman called *Irqaviaq* who would talk about her own birth. Intrigued, I investigated such memories systematically in the various Inuit locales where my research took me. It was a good line of inquiry. On my next mission I had the luck to meet someone who remembered being born.

He was George Annanack, an old man from Kangiqsualujjuaq (George River) who could trace his family tree back to the mid-eighteenth century. He had travelled a lot and knew a lot. In 1967, he told me his memories of being born and promised to write them down for me in syllabics, which he had learned by reading prayer books. Unfortunately, he died the next year before I could see him again. Then in the early summer of 1971, at Sanikiluaq (Belcher Islands), I met a woman who was around forty years old, Aani Qitusuk, who likewise told me she could remember her birth. A more detailed recollection of prenatal life and birth was shared with me a little later the same year by Piita Pitsiulaaq, a man of around sixty from Kinngait (Cape Dorset) on Baffin Island. Several years later, Dorothy Eber helped him write his life story and provided the following account, which largely matches the one I had gathered:

> It will be hard to believe what I am about to write: I can remember before I was born. It seems like a dream. I remember I had to go through a very narrow channel. The passage was so narrow I thought it would be impossible. I didn't realize the passage was my mother—I thought it was a crevasse in the ice. That ice crevasse must have been my mother's bones. I remember it took a long time to go through. Once I turned back—it was too hard. But finally I was outside; I was born. I think I opened my eyes inside my mother but after I was born I opened my eyes again and all I could see were two little cliffs on either side of me. I often remember this: I saw something blue and those cliffs which were exactly the same . . . which were probably my mother's thighs (Eber and Pitseolak 1975, 49).

In telling me this story he also mentioned his surprise at finding lush vegetation on the ground. This was, he told me, the hairs of the caribou hide on which his mother was squatting.

Not only did the people who shared these stories not know each other, they also lived hundreds of kilometres apart. This type of reminiscence seemed more widespread than I had initially thought, being perhaps a latent "narrative genre" of Inuit culture that some individuals would use in certain settings.

Memories from beyond the Grave[1]

Several months later in Igloolik, I was fortunate to collect *Iqallijuq*'s account of her earliest memories, as described above in the Introduction, when she had been the soul of her maternal grandfather, *Savviurtalik* (who died c. 1904). She bore his name and assumed his identity to some degree.[2]

> I knew I was going to become a fetus while still in the grave. It was very cold there.

Souls of the dead, fetuses, and spirits can know the future and have a sensory acuity beyond that of humans.

The blocks of snow [forming the grave] had been solidly put together, so I pushed out the end one and made an opening. I slid out and began looking around for my "favourite sister," my daughter [*Nuvvijaq*].

In life, *Savviurtalik* had addressed his daughter *Nuvvijaq* (the mother of the narrator *Iqallijuq*) by the term "favourite sister." She indeed had his dead sister's name. Now, on leaving his grave, he begins to look around for her because he wishes to reincarnate through her.

I hoped to myself she would want to urinate and go outside. And I saw her leaving her igloo, going down below, to urinate in the small igloo made for that purpose.

To reincarnate, the dead person's soul leaves its former body and the grave where the body lies. The woman it wishes to penetrate has to leave her home to urinate and thereby open a passage for it to enter. Its wish immediately makes the woman feel a corresponding desire. Such power of thinking is common to all fetuses, spirits, and shamans. It need not be expressed in words—a simple wish is enough.

In the Land of the Dead, souls live in completely enclosed homes with no doors, because souls can pass through walls. In the Land of the Living, a home must have an opening for going in or out. Such an opening is needed for a dead person to reincarnate and rejoin the Land of the Living. A female cousin of *Iqallijuq* dreamed one night that a deceased relative came by dogsled and stopped in front of her igloo. He was thirsty and was looking for the entrance to pay her a visit, but not finding it, he went far away. On awakening, she realized that the dead man had wished to reincarnate and that she had become sterile. So she adopted a child and gave it the man's name.

As I was very thirsty, I went down to her.

Note the inverse symmetry. The woman desires to urinate as a prelude to opening up to the dead person's soul. Conversely, the soul is thirsty, a sign of its desire to reincarnate. When a game animal is killed, its soul is likewise thirsty, and the hunter has to quench the thirst by dripping several

13

FIGURE 7. Memories from beyond the grave by *Iqallijuq*. The soul of her namesake grandfather, *Savviurtalik*, comes out of his grave of snow to reincarnate in his daughter's womb. Black and white copy of a colour drawing by Leah Idlout from the comments by *Iqallijuq*, 1974.

drops of fresh water onto the animal's lips. It can now reincarnate as another animal of the same species.

I was a man wearing a *qiqpaujaq* [a man's parka], *silapaak* [a man's outer pants], and *miqquliik* [a man's boots with fur outside]. I had a beautiful appearance. While going down to her, I truly had the impression of being alive.

This is *Savviurtalik*'s double-soul. It was a miniaturized double of the old man when he was alive. At his death it changed scale, taking on his size and appearance and becoming an ethereal image, a reflection of himself before dying.

I was cold and thirsty. I approached her and asked her for something to drink, but she didn't hear me. She didn't even realize I was there, for I was a dead man.

The souls of the newly dead are cold and thirsty, like travellers who have arrived after a long trip. To express their need to reincarnate and live again, they ask for food and shelter from people they like. Usually, this desire is expressed in a dream where they visit their future parents and ask for something to drink. Outside this dreamlike setting the souls of the dead are invisible to ordinary humans. Only spirits, animals, and shamans may see them or detect their presence. *Nuvvijaq*'s misunderstanding in this story shows the gap between the two levels of reality: the reality of the double-soul, which conscious humans cannot perceive, and the reality of *Nuvvijaq* in her day-to-day space-time.

I knew she and her husband couldn't have children and I felt sorry for them.

Savviurtalik's daughter *Nuvvijaq* had initially married the son of a great female shaman. She had been his second wife, his first wife being unable to bear him children. Whenever their shared husband was away, the first wife would abuse her so often and humiliate her so much that *Nuvvijaq* decided to run away to her father's place. This displeased her shaman ex-mother-in-law, who cast a spell on her future pregnancies to make them miscarry. No punishment could be worse. A young woman was destined to perpetuate her family's work force and reincarnate the deceased members of her lineage.

She entered the *quijaturvik* [a small igloo where she would go to urinate] and began to urinate in a squatting position. I approached the rear panel of her parka and told myself that if I were to touch the end of her *unngiqsaq* [the sinew belt holding up her pants] I could probably enter her.

The rear panel of a woman's parka is the last barrier protecting the crotch of a woman crouched down and urinating. The belt, the upper bootlaces, or any other cord-like objects are often mentioned metaphorically when people talk about the reproduction of life, be it conception, as here, or birth. In the latter case, people are afraid of the umbilical cord getting wrapped around the neck of the child being born. To make movement easier in both directions, one has to loosen the mother-to-be's belt and any other cords binding her body. The crotch is a way in for the soul and a way out for the fetus.

I touched the loosened belt of my "favourite sister" and all of a sudden found myself before an igloo. I entered without knowing how I made my way in.

This touching of the loosened belt is a key moment in the story. It immediately fulfils three wishes: *Savviurtalik*'s wish to reincarnate in his daughter's family; *Nuvvijaq*'s wish to have a child; and her wish to see her father again. The soul fulfills all three by touching her belt. It can enter her womb, which now becomes an igloo by analogy and by change of scale.

Memories from the Womb

I was inside her *igliaq* [womb]. While before I was warmly clothed, I was now stark naked, with no memory of ever taking my clothes off.

This remark about old *Savviurtalik*'s sudden nudity, as told by *Iqalli-juq*, his reincarnation, is all the more intriguing because the narrator has no memory of getting undressed. She was a warmly dressed old man and is now a male fetus—as we will learn a little farther on in her story. What happened?

The explanation lies in the Inuit theory of the soul and reincarnation, which may be summarized as follows: when alive, everyone has a double-soul (*tarniq*), a miniature image of oneself, which is encapsulated in an air bubble (*pudlaq*) and lodged somewhere in the groin. Everyone also has a name-soul (*atiq*), a psychic principle inherited from a dead person or a spirit, which encompasses all of the experiences and abilities accumulated by everyone who previously held that name. At death, the double-soul escapes from the bubble and expands to the dead person's size, becoming his or her ethereal replica. It will then roam around the grave until the name-soul manages to reincarnate. The two souls then part company: the double-soul goes to live eternally in the hereafter, looking like the person did just before death, whereas the name-soul lives again in a fetus and enters a new cycle of human life. *Savviurtalik*'s double-soul, looking like an old man dressed in winter clothing, goes to live in the hereafter when his name-soul reincarnates. But let us listen to *Iqallijuq*:

> Then she [*Nuvvijaq*] came home and, after a certain number of nights, she realized she was pregnant while feeling her belly. Lying alongside her husband, she said, "*Uik!* [Husband!] I'm again pregnant, and again it [the child] won't live!" and she began to cry. She cried because I was going to die. My five older siblings were stillborn, and I was going to follow them by dying like them. She cried because she wanted at any price to have a child. I knew if she didn't stop crying I would be stillborn, and if she stopped I would be born alive. I was full of compassion for my "favourite sister" and decided to do my utmost to live. She then stopped crying.

A fetus, like a spirit, has clairvoyance. It immediately understands what is happening outside, and by listening to its parents it learns about its situation and the threats to its fate. Here it keenly feels what its mother, *Nuvvijaq*, feels. It becomes sad when she feels sad, and reciprocally she calms down when it decides to live.

> My father [*Ittuliaq*, the narrator's real father] then told her, "We're going to try hard to keep it alive."

17

To neutralize the shaman's curse from *Nuvvijaq*'s ex-mother-in-law, her second husband *Ittuliaq* decides to use his own shamanic powers. He calls upon his helping spirit *Iqallijuq*, whose name he will give the child.[3]

I was conscious that a very old woman, *Arnartaaq*, came to visit *Nuvvijaq*'s igloo, and I heard her say, "I want to have the child as my namesake. Give it my name and it will live, for I will thereby bind its life to mine." I then understood that her vitality was going to strengthen my own.

Not only does the fetus hear what is said outside the womb but it also understands the full meaning.

I had indeed become a fetus. I was inside her womb. I realized she went out every morning as soon as she woke up. I knew when she slept and when she was awake, when she went out and when she was home.

A sensory symbiosis exists between the fetus and the expectant mother, but only the fetus is aware of the relationship. The fetus is still half in the spirit world, and the expectant mother simply experiences the effects of what it wants. Inuit custom has it that every woman of childbearing age should rush out each morning after waking up, to help her deliver her present or future fetus quickly. The aim is to have sons, who are believed to come out faster than daughters, or to have daughters who will become skilled garment makers and give birth to many boys. This custom may also be practised by little girls, men, and boys so that their sons will be agile runners and able hunters. In the eighteenth and nineteenth centuries, Greenland's first explorers and Moravian missionaries were intrigued by the custom (Cranz 1767, quoted by Oswalt 1979), thinking the Inuit were performing a solar ritual and offering a salutation to the sun (Saladin d'Anglure 1993a [1990b]).

I made out the shape of an igloo and mistook her womb for an igloo. I thought I was in a very small igloo where I was cramped for space.

The womb-igloo metaphor appears elsewhere in Inuit oral literature. One example is the myth about the origin of the first humans, among the Inuit of South Baffin (Chapter 2). There is also the myth of *Arnakpaktuq*

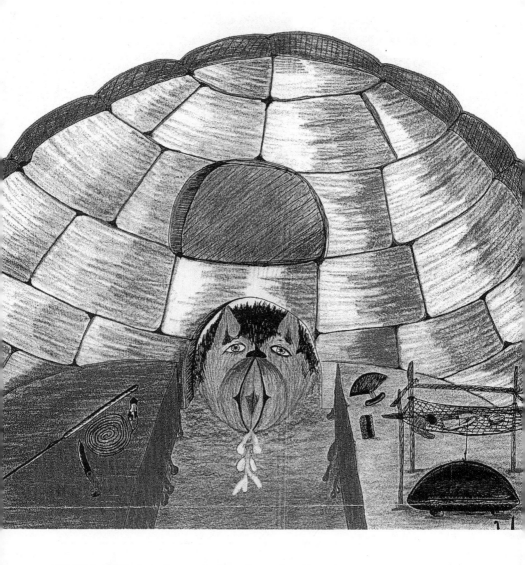

FIGURE 8. *Iqallijuq*'s womb memories. From time to time a dog
with a vertically slit mouth would appear at the entrance of the
small igloo/womb and vomit white food. Black and white copy of a
colour drawing by Leah Idlout from comments by *Iqallijuq*, 1974.

(Chapter 8), about a soul migrating to one animal species after another before becoming a human fetus.

> Now a dog appeared from time to time in the entrance opening. Its mouth was slit vertically. In fact, each time it appeared in the entrance, it was my father having sex with my mother. It was his penis, which I mistook for a dog. Whenever it got ready to leave, it vomited, and I really wanted to eat its vomit. I undoubtedly ate some, and I grew bigger.

The dog-penis metaphor (see Figure 8) also appears in a myth reported by Boas (1907) about the first humans. As in the previous metaphor, there is a change of scale from human to fetal size: the womb becomes an igloo in the eyes of the fetus, and the intruder (the father's penis) becomes a dog. When Inuit travel in winter they feed their dogs in the evening and let one dog after another poke its head through the igloo entrance. Here, however, we see two differences: the intruder's mouth (urinary meatus) is slit vertically instead of horizontally; and it vomits food instead of ingesting food. According to the Inuit theory of the reproduction of life, sperm serves two purposes: first, to plug the womb to keep the woman's blood from flowing out; and, second, to form the fetus and consolidate its structure.[4] According to the same theory, if men other than the husband have sex with a pregnant woman, the fetus will dislocate and the pregnancy will not come to term.

> I was now in a cramped space. My igloo had become very small and tiny. My mother's womb was dripping with liquid. While looking at the door, I began to think I would like to get out. I couldn't stay put anymore. I had previously been on the platform, but now there no longer was any platform, and the little igloo was no bigger than me. Drops were falling from the dome, which wasn't lined with hides. I wanted to get out because the entrance was no longer clean.

At the end of its life cycle in the womb, a fetus is like an Inuk in an igloo near the end of winter, when the snow walls begin to drip water and the sleeping platform shrinks and begins to melt. Sewn hides usually line the inside of the snow dome of large family igloos, but there are none here. The womb-igloo is more like a traveller's temporary shelter. The darkness of winter corresponds to the early months of pregnancy, and the end of pregnancy to the warm onset of spring.

Neonatal Transsexualism

I was having trouble, however, getting through the entrance. To the left were tools for a man. I stretched out my hand and grasped them, but I had a premonition that my father [*Ittuliaq*] would die by drowning while hunting on the ice. My namesake *Savviurtalik* had also expressed a wish before dying to live again as a woman because he was weary of the cold, the fatigue, and the risks of hunting. Thinking I could get cold and die like my father if I used those tools, I put them back and instead took the tools for a woman: an oil lamp and an *ulu* [a woman's knife shaped like a half moon].

Before going out, *Savviurtalik*, now reincarnated as a fetus, has to choose a sexual identity. He does so metonymically by choosing either a man's tools (a harpoon shaft with its thong and detachable head, as well as a cutlass) or a woman's tools (a half-moon knife, a small cooking pot, and a soapstone oil lamp). The two sets of tools symbolize the sexual division of labour among the Inuit (see Figure 8). At this point in time, the fetus is anatomically male, like the dead man who has reincarnated in it. This anatomy also matches the wishes of the mother, who every morning after waking would rush out to help the fetus come out fast and therefore as a boy. Her wishes are shared by all of the deceased man's kin, since the child will be his reincarnation.

A little drama is now playing out, however, because these wishes clash with those of the fetus, which fears accidental death if it becomes a hunter, and with those of the dead man, who wishes to live again as a woman.

I then closed my eyes and with much effort got out of the igloo. On my way out, however, my penis retracted, my perineum split open into a vulva, and I went from male to female, becoming a *sipiniq* [a transsexual].

Inuit still believe that a newborn can change sex during delivery, usually from male to female, but also from female to male. For this reason, the midwife keeps her eyes on the baby's genitals, touches them with her hand,

INUIT STORIES OF BEING AND REBIRTH

or grabs them between two fingers to keep them from being reabsorbed. This custom varies from one region to the next.

On my way out, I saw my mother shrouded by a sort of cloud. The cloud was denser than [tobacco] smoke. It was caused by my birth, by my coming out. I opened my eyes. I was in the *irnivik* [a small tent for childbirth]. I had been delivered and wanted to say *Ujuu!* ["Whew!"], but only the sound *Ungaa!* ["Wah! Wah!"] came out of my mouth. I was chilled to the bone. I was thirsty and wanted to say "I'm thirsty!" but again only the sound "wah!" came out of my mouth.

This cloud is invisible to ordinary humans but perceptible to spirits, animals, shamans, and newborn babies, who retain for some time the properties of fetal life. Blamed on the blood of childbirth, the cloud is dangerous and makes game animals run away. Hunters and women of childbearing age must take care to stay away from such blood. This is why a new mother and her newborn child are confined to a small personal hut throughout her time of postpartum bleeding. Similarly, women have to let everyone know when they are menstruating. At that time they must eat by themselves and refrain from any contact with hunters and hunting tools.

With its life in the womb now over, the newborn child begins a new life cycle without its fetal abilities for thought transmission and clairvoyance. It can no longer communicate with humans, just as *Savviurtalik* could not when his double-soul left his grave and he tried in vain to make himself heard by his daughter *Nuvvijaq*. A newborn will fit poorly into its human environment for a year after birth. It will be in transition between the name-soul identity of its previous life and the new identity that develops with its social and physical environment through its new sensory experiences and interactions with people:

When the cloud dissipated, I found myself in an old woman's arms and I looked at her while smiling. She then turned toward my mother and I saw her lips move. I could very clearly make out [what surrounded me] and I smiled at my mother while seeing the movements of her mouth. Outside, two people were practising divination. I turned toward them and smiled at one of them whose mouth was moving and who undoubtedly was speaking. Whereas I could hear very well when inside [the womb], now that I had come out and was born I could no longer hear anything. The two people were practising divination for me to come out faster because my birth had taken a long time, due to my having initially chosen a man's knife, harpoon, and harpoon head. That was why I took time [to be born].

These memories are from the newborn's first few seconds of life and its very first visual discoveries. The child sees the midwife who helped it come into the world but does not hear her words. It also sees two women practising divination. According to comments later made by *Iqallijuq*, one woman is lying on the ground while the other is trying to raise the reclining woman's head by fits and starts, using a band of cloth, while putting questions to the spirit in that woman's head. The two of them want to know why the child is taking so long. When asked whether the delay is due to the fetus changing sex, the spirit answers in the affirmative.

Uviluq cleaned me and, after cutting my umbilical cord, gave me back to my mother, who placed me in the back pouch of her parka.

The midwife cleans the newborn. If the child is born in winter or spring, she uses the skin of an *aqiggiarjuk* (willow ptarmigan, *Lagopus lagopus*) with its feathers still attached, or the skin of a winter land bird, like a *tulugaq* (common raven, *Corvus corax*) or an *ukpik* (snowy owl, Nyctea nyctea). If the birth is in summer, the skin comes from an *aggiarjuk* (long-tailed duck, *Clangula hyemalis*) or any other migrating sea bird. The skin will later be used as an amulet, and people believe that the bird's species will protect the child all life long (Saladin d'Anglure 1989).[5] The bird may even become one of the child's helping animals if the child wishes to become a shaman.

The midwife's key task is to tie the umbilical cord with caribou sinew. Once the cord has been cut with a stone blade—never with one of imported metal—the knot becomes the child's first social marking. These two acts of tying and cutting separate the child from its biological mother and bind it to the group and the group's rules. The child can then be given back to its mother for her to nurse and put in the back pouch of her parka, where it will be warmed by the skin of her back.

After spending some time in the *irnivik* [birth hut], we went to stay in the *kinirvik* [postpartum confinement tent]. This tent was more spacious and had an oil lamp over which seal stew would be prepared. It was nonetheless small and would be thrown out afterwards and buried under stones with my *arraaq*[6]—this was what the afterbirth was called—and also with the skins [used to deliver the child].

The time of confinement follows the actual delivery and may last four to six weeks. The new mother now moves to a more spacious place where meals can be prepared. Because of her postpartum bleeding, she is forbidden to have any contact with raw food and has to cook the meat and boil the water she consumes. The midwife, or another postmenopausal woman, may help her cook. By custom, the special tents, the skins used as childbirth mats, and the skin huts must be buried beyond the reach of dogs. This has to be done quickly so that the child will grow up to be an able hunter, if a boy, or an able garment maker, if a girl.

Uviluq, my midwife, boiled the [seal] meat in a small cooking pot. Then, when my mother began eating the stew, I felt very hungry [for meat], even though I was being breastfed. My mother then took a few morsels of chewed meat from her mouth and pretended to put them into my mouth while only touching my lips. Nonetheless, I had the impression of chewing and eating. She did the same with some of the stew, by letting a drop of stew fall onto my mouth, and I had right away a feeling of having eaten my fill. She next retrieved the morsels of meat she had made me touch and placed them in a *minguliqtiqutiqarvik* [a small funnel-shaped leather pouch].

The small leather pouch is cone-shaped and represents the dead namesake's stomach. Metaphorically, the namesake is fed when morsels that have touched the newborn's lips are placed in the pouch. The little symbolic stomach gradually fills up and when full is emptied into a crevasse on the sea ice. It is thought that the morsels will come back to life as a seal. Later, when the child can hunt, he will catch many seals, and they will recognize him.

When my mother finished eating, I was full and fell into a deep sleep. In fact I died.

The dead man's name-soul is not yet firmly set in the newborn, who is furthermore exposed to many death-seeking forces. There is the shaman's curse on *Nuvvijaq* from her ex-mother-in-law. There is also the beckoning from the newborn's five older brothers and sisters—all of them stillborn— who shared the same umbilical cord and who want the baby to join them. In the Inuit language, this sibling solidarity is called *miksliaqatigiit*. The term *tuqujuq* is used here, meaning "he's dead" or "she's dead," while also meaning "he's inanimate, he's unconscious," or "it's numb" when said about a limb. The sleep metaphor here expresses the child's near-death.

She cried out to my father to come, but he answered that he was performing *sakaniq* [a shamanic seance] to ask me to live, me being *Savviurtalik*. And I, *Savviurtalik*, realized that I was at the home of my *najannaaq* ["favourite sister"] and that I would live again.

To fight these death-seeking forces, the child's father *Ittuliaq* uses shamanic powers to call out to the name-soul of his father-in-law *Savviurtalik*, who is regaining consciousness through the child.

But now, a little later, without knowing how, I fell back into a deep sleep. I fell asleep, being very tired, and awoke only when I heard the words of an old woman, *Arnartaaq*, "May this one be me! May I have her as *kiiguti* [support]! May she have me as *kiiguti*! Through her may I bear the name of *Iqallijuq*, for I am tired of hearing the name of *Arnartaaq*!" She wanted me to live and, as our two lives would now be bound to each other and strengthened by each other through this relationship, I would probably live to be old because she was very old. I emerged from my torpor. I was now fully alive.

This is the same *Arnartaaq* who during *Nuvvijaq*'s pregnancy wished to strengthen the child's life force by binding its life to her own. She wants to provide the child with a relationship of *kiigutigiik* (mutual support), a dual term that in the language of shamans means a relationship between namesakes. She wishes to give the baby her second name *Iqallijuq*, thus guaranteeing it a very long life. Reciprocally, the old *Arnartaaq*, who no longer has any descendants, will be able to have an abundant posterity through the newborn.

I saw people entering. I could make out my father and *Uviluq*. We then moved to my father's tent, and my parents slept once more together. I was a *sipiniq* [transsexual] because *Savviurtalik* had wanted to live again as a woman and not as a man. He no longer wanted to hunt because hunting took too much effort and for him meant a high risk of getting cold. So I had become a girl after changing sex at birth. I previously had a penis but then got a vulva; this is how it is with *sipiniit* [transsexuals].

Here, *Iqallijuq* talks again about her change of sex. We have seen previously that this transformation was ascribed to the slowness of childbirth, but the narrator now puts forward the ultimate cause: the wish of her namesake, the old *Savviurtalik*, expressed before his death, not to reincarnate as a boy.

Transgendering of Children

And until my first period I wore male clothes and very often accompanied [for hunting] my *ataatakuluk* ["sweet father," stepfather] because my real father died of drowning the autumn after my birth. I wore boy clothes for a long time and even thought I was a boy rather than a girl.

Contrary to the wish of the grandfather, who wanted to reincarnate as a girl and no longer have to hunt, we now see *Iqallijuq* dressed as a boy and learning all the secrets of hunting. Her mother *Nuvvijaq* still sees the child as her beloved father *Savviurtalik*, and calls the child "sweet brother" (*aniannuk*). In return, the child calls her by the term "sweet sister" (*najaannuk*).

Iqallijuq's father *Ittuliaq* dies soon after her birth, as she foresaw while still a fetus. Her mother remarries, and her second husband *Kublu* shows the little girl much affection. She calls him "sweet father" (*ataatakuluk*), and he calls her "sweet daughter" (*panikuluk*). With no son of his own, he initiates *Iqallijuq* into male activities and takes her with him on his hunting expeditions. She learns so much about how to drive a sled, how to care for dogs, how to build an igloo, and how to hunt all kinds of animals that she admits to thinking she is a boy.

When I became an adolescent and had my first period, my mother began to make me a *minguttinaaqtuq* [parka for a young teen girl], as well as a woman's pair of trousers. While making them, she started to cry because of the name I had; she thought I was her father and refused to make women's clothing for her father. This was how I realized I was a woman, during my first period.

We have here a real *mise en scène* and dramatization of *Iqallijuq*'s debut on the stage of life. It began with her first menstrual bleeding. That blood struck deep at her identity, as did the tears of her mother while making a young teen girl's clothes: a pair of trousers with female decorations and, above all, a parka with a very long rear panel unsuited for male hunting and travelling. Her mother, too, was emotionally caught up in the gender roles she had assigned her daughter, who had been born a girl and yet was the reincarnation of *Savviurtalik*—and therefore a man. Mother and daughter spoke to each other in ways that implied a brother-sister relationship, as had existed two generations ago when the young *Savviurtalik* had a sister named *Nuvvijaq*. That sister died prematurely, and he later named his daughter *Nuvvijaq* after her. Such ambiguity would always persist to some degree in their use of the terms "favourite brother" and "favourite sister." At some point, however, a change took place. The girl became a woman and a potential mother, as shown by her periods. She now had to wear the clothing required by tradition and get ready to start a family with the man chosen for her. *Iqallijuq* later told me the following incident. After her mother made her a pair of woman's trousers, she pulled them on and, furious to see her gender identity so pointedly challenged by this piece of woman's clothing, she tore them apart. It took her time to accept wearing woman's clothing and to learn the tasks that a woman should know to keep house. Her mother refused to teach her. Her aunts and female cousins helped her learn, and later her first mother-in-law. But she never forgot her male upbringing. And the different men she married greatly valued her double ability to be both a good housewife and a prized hunting and travelling companion.

Iqallijuq
Remembering

IQALLIJUQ [SAVVIURTALIK]: Taima singainguniaq&unga qaujilauqsimavunga iluvirmii&&unga niglasuktualungmi.
At the time that I was going to be conceived, I recall
being in the grave, which was very cold.
Tavva ukua auviit ilisimangmata uvuuna isuk&iqpaaq una makpiq&ugu anigama qinilirama takanna najannaara.
These *auviit* were in place, so I opened the end one and went
out. When I started looking around, I saw my *najannaaq*.

KUBLU: Kisu auviit makpiq&ugu?
You opened what? *Auviit?*

IQALLIJUQ: Imaak uvuuna ajak&ugu auviit makua iliuqaqsimasuut, auvirnik qaujimaviit?
I pushed it out, *auviit* are placed together, do you know what *auviit* are?

KUBLU: Aputiniik?
Out of snow?

**IQALLIJUQ: Ii! Aput ajak&ugu paali paangulirmat
tavvuuna anigama takanna takugakkit
najannaakukka anaanakkukka anaanaga.**

Yes! I pushed the snow out, making a door which I went out through,
and I saw my *najaannaaq*'s dwelling, my parents, my mother.

**Imiruktualuugama takanunngauliq&unga imaak angutaullunga
qiqpaujaqaq&unga silapaaqaq&unga miqquliqaq&unga.**

As I was very thirsty, I went down there. I was a man wearing a
qiqpaujaq parka, *silapaak* outer pants, and *miqquliik kamiik* with hair.

**Inuuqquujittiaq&unga takanunngaullunga
tavva sanittianganuarama.**

I seemed to be alive going down there, and when
I got to her, I stopped beside her.

Imirumallunga uqaraluarama tusanngimmat imiriaqturniraq&unga.

I said that I wanted a drink, but when she didn't
hear me I said, I came for a drink.

KUBLU: Nanii&&uni?

Where was she?

**IQALLIJUQ: Quijaqturvingminii&&uni igluungmat
quijaqturvigingmagu tavvunga quijaqturvingminut quiliqtuq.**

She was where she would go to urinate. An igloo was set
for her to go and urinate. She was there urinating.

Upaktaraluara qaujinngi&&uninga suuqaima tuqungagaluaramali.

I went to her but she was not aware of me, which
was no wonder because I was dead.

Unngiqsangaqai akturukku itirunnaqpunga.

I thought maybe if I were to touch her *unngiqsaq*,
the sinew tie for her pants, I would enter.

**Asuilaak akturakku itiq&unga qamunga iglianganut
naukkut itiriaksak qaujinngilanga tamauna kisiani
unngiqsanga atuq&ugu iglianganuaqtunga**

So, when I touched it, I entered her womb. I was not aware of how I
entered but when I touched her *unngiqsaq*, I entered her womb.

**Tavva itiq&uni, qaulaasillugu siniqattalauq&utik qaujilirami
imaak tassikkaminga uini uqautivaa innangagaluaq&tik:**

She entered her igloo. They slept for several nights and when she
became aware of me, by touching her belly, she said to her husband:

**"Uing'aasin tavva singaili&&araluaqpunga
inuujjarminanilu" uq&unilu qialiq&unilu.**

"Husband, I am pregnant once again, and yet again
this one will not live," and she started to cry.

KUBLU: Qanui&&uni qialiqpa?

Why was she crying?

**IQALLIJUQ: Tuquniarasugilluninga ukua angajukka
tallimat taimanna inuusaaq&utik tuquinnarmata
tuquqattarmata amma maliksar&unga tuquniarasugilluninga
nutaraqtaarumaluamut qialiq&uni.**

She thought I was going to die, as five children before me had died
while they were infants. She thought I was going to likewise die, and
because she so very much wanted a child, she started crying.

Uqautilluniuk ataatama: "Inuutitaujunnarniaqtuksauvuq."

My father said to her, "This one could probably be made to live."

**Asuilaak singainguvakkama manna igliap
iluanii iglianganii&&unga.**

So, I was a fetus inside her womb.

**Anisaaliqattarlunilu isumagigakku anisaalivak&uni
ullaakkut tupakkaangami.**

It was my thought that she should go out early. She would
go out early in the morning when she woke up.

**Iglulu tautuk&ugu igliangalu igluunasugillugu
iglumii&&ungaugaluaq.**

I could see the igloo. I considered her womb to
be an igloo, that is I was in an igloo.

KUBLU: Igluuquujittiaq&unii?

It seemed to be an igloo?

IQALLIJUQ: Igluuqqujittiaq&uni nirukittukuluugami.

It seemed to be an igloo that was very snug.

Tavva asuilaak pangmiuliqtualuuliq&unga qimmiq una atausiq katangmuaqattaqtuq qaninga tukingalluni katangmuaraangat sunauvva kujaliraangagu nuliani una usua qimmiunasugijara.

I was now feeling very crowded, and there would be this dog, with its mouth slit upright, that would come to the entrance. It turns out that it came to the entrance when he (my father) was having sex with his wife (my mother). I thought that his penis was a dog.

Anigiaraangami miriaqpak&uni miriaqtanganik nirijumallungaugaluaq nirivaqquulauqtunga angiliqpallialauqtunga.

The dog would vomit, just as it was about to exit, and I would eat what it vomited and therefore I grew.

KUBLU: Taanna miriaqtanga angillivalliajjutigilluguu?

Was the vomit making you grow?

IQALLIJUQ: Iinguqquujijuuq.

It seemed that way.

Taimanna usunga sunauvva qimmiunasugillugu katangmuarasugiqattaqtara.

I thought that what turned out to be his penis was a dog that would come to the entrance.

Asuilaak pangmiuliqtualuugama taanna iglukuluga nirukittummarikuluulirmat mannalu kuuktualuuliq&uni iglianga kuuktualuuliq&uni.

So, I became very crowded in my little igloo, and the sides started dripping. Fluid started pouring from her uterus.

Takanna katak tatukkakku anijumallunga isumalirama.

I could see the entrance while I was thinking about getting out.

Asuilak nuqqanganngiliq&unga iglirmiittialauraluaq&unga igliqtaqarunniirmat tavvunga naammagituinnalirakku iglukuluk.

At this point, I no longer was just lying there, because though at first I had been on the bed, there was no longer a bed and I could barely fit in the little igloo by then.

Katak takanna tikiqqangiarjukkakku.

I couldn't quite reach the entrance.

Angutisiutin' ukua kataup tassuma saumittianganiittut isak&ugu tavva tigullugu tavva ikkiiqattalaami

ikkiinguqattarniarilluni taakkua aturlugit ilillugit arnaq taakkua qullikulullu ulukulullu tigugakkit anigiaqtualuugama.
I reached for the male implements that were on the left-hand side of the entrance and I grabbed them. Then I thought if I was going to use them, I would experience being cold. So I put them down and grabbing a woman's little *qulliq* and a little *ulu*, I attempted to get out.

KUBLU: Arnaujumangaaliravit taakkua arnaqsiutit tigullugiit?
Because you wanted to be female instead? This is why you took these implements?

IQALLIJUQ: Ii suuqaimma Savviuqtalik atira arnaujumalaurnirmat.
Because my *atiq* Savviurtalik had wanted to be female.
Anillunga anillunga ilaa anigama ui&&araluarama pujuuqtualuk supuuqtuutit makua supuuqtuutit pujuqaqpangmata taimanna anginiqsaalungmik pujuuqtualuk . . .
I went out. I was born. When I came out, I opened my eyes but all I saw was smoke like what comes out of a pipe but much larger.

KUBLU: Qanuinnami pujuuqtualuk?
Why was it all blurry?

IQALLIJUQ: Anisaarama uvanga pujualunganik uuminga irniangunirmik asuilaak , . .
It was the smoke resulting from my birth, after the delivery.

KUBLU: Tamanna tautuktatuarilluguu?
Was this all that you could see?

IQALLIJUQ: Ii asuilaak takuttiarama pujuurunniiq&uni ilaak qungannama aulalluni anaanagalu qungannakku qaninga aulagilluni.
When the blurriness ended, I could see well. I saw my mother and her mouth was moving. When I smiled at her, her mouth moved once again.
Amma takkikkuak paamiittuuk qilajuuk sunauvva qilajuuk qiviarakkik qungakaluarakkik amma uqaIlaktuksaugaluaq&uni qaninga aulalluni.

There were those two people at the door who were *qilajuuk* [trying to know from a spirit what was happening with the fetus]. I looked at them and smiled at them. One of them was probably talking because his/her mouth was also moving.

Iluanii&&ungali tusaattialauq&unga anigamali tusaajunniiq&unga irniangugama . . .

While I was still inside (the womb), I could hear very well. When I was born, I couldn't hear anymore . . .

KUBLU: Qannuinnamik taikkua qilavat?

Why was it that those people were *qilajut*?

IQALLIJUQ: Irniangusaaliqunikumut uvanga—hiii . . .

Because they wanted me to be born sooner—hiii . . .

Akuni irniangunngilirnirama sakkuniglu savingmiglu unaarmik tigusinasuqattarnira taanna akuniujjutiginnirakku.

It was taking a long time for me to be born because my trying to take the knife and the harpoon had prolonged my birth.

Tavva irnivingmi irnivinganuaq&ungaa irnivinga taanna takuttiaq&ugu tavva ikkiiqtualugama imirlangaaraluaq&unga ungaa ungaa ungaa ungaalasijualuugama.

So, I then ended up in the birthing tent, which I could then see very well. As I was cold (and thirsty), I tried to say "let me drink" but ended up only saying "*ungaa, ungaa, ungaa.*"

Qummiutilluninga anaanama tassumali Uviluup salummaqsalauq&uninga tavvunngaqtaanga anaanannuaqtaanga mannalu mik&iaruluga kipilluniuk Uviluup anaanannuaqtaanga tavva tavvaniilaupilak&unuk.

My mother put me in the front of her *amauti*, where *Uviluq* placed me after cleaning me up. *Uviluq* cut my umbilical cord and gave it to my mother. We were here for a short while . . .

Kinirviginiaqtangaguuq takkikaungmat takkiunga imannali tupillattaakulungmut nirutuniqsaujumut qulliqattiaq&unilu asuilaak tavvunngarami uujuliuliq&uni.

The place where she was going to stay during the time of post-natal bleeding was right next door. It was a small tent larger than the one I was born in and had a *qulliq,* so when my mother entered it, she started cooking some meat.

KUBLU: Tainnali irnivik tupituinnakuluullunii?
The place where you were born was just a little tent?

IQALLIJUQ: Iksinnaqtaullunilii taannalu arraaara arraaruluqaqpangmata nutaralaat unalu allirarijanga taannalu tupikuluk anitaullutigli.
It was discarded. My placenta, the skin that I was born on, and the little tent were thrown away.
Tavva ujuliurmat taassuma pimajigijama Uviluup pimajigijannuk uuk&ingmagu ujuliuq&uni ujuqtusigiarmat.
My caregiver, our caregiver *Uviluq* cooked meat. When she started to eat . . .
Tavva kaaktualuullunga imiraluaq&unga imiqattaliraluaq&unga anaanannit, niqikulungmik piiqsigami.
I was very hungry although I would drink, I was drinking from my mother.
Mikittummarikulungmik amaaraminga tamuali&&uninga.
I was in her *amauti* when she took off a very small piece of meat and put it in my mouth.
Ammailaak nirilauq&uni nirianikkami qajurmik qalusigami niuqsi qajuqtuq&unga.
After I had eaten, she scooped up some broth and gave me some.
Sunauvva imanna qanira aktutuinnaq&uniuk tamualitaunasugijunga nirinasugijunga.
It turns out that she had only touched the meat to my mouth but I thought that I had been given a bite of meat.
Ammaluuna qajurmik qanira kusirvigiarjungmagu aqiatturasugijunga tavva.
Also, when she poured a tiny amount of broth into my mouth, I thought I became full.

KUBLU: Taakkuali niqikuluit tamuatianikkamigit illingnut qanui&&unigit?

What did she do with the small piece of meat after she gave you a bite?

IQALLIJUQ: Puuq&unigit kisumugguurngaa taimannaittukulungmut inikuluanut.

She placed it in a . . . what was it called, [*mingulirtiqutiqarvik*] anyway into a special place for it.

KUBLU: Inikuluqaqpak&utiik?

There was a special place for it?

IQALLIJUQ: Ii inikuluqarmata ilaa inikulua tainna atinga puigurakku qujana puigurlugu.

Yes, there was a special place for it but [a little cone made of leather] I've forgotten what it was called, it's alright that I've forgotten it [*mingulirtiqutiqarvik*].

Tainna tautuqquuttiaraluaq&ugu tavvali nirianiktillugu aqiatturama siniliqtualuullunga sunauvva tuquliqtunga.

I can clearly picture it. After I ate the piece of meat, I became full then I fell asleep. It turns out that I was dying.

KUBLU: Siniqquujivit tuqullutiit?

Did you seem to be asleep when you (actually) died?

IQALLIJUQ: Ii ataataga tavva tuq&ulalluniu'qai sakangmagguuq Savviuqtalik uumaqulluningailaak Savviuqtaliglu qaujittialirillugu.

Yes, my father yelled. They said that he was *sakajuq*, he wanted *Savviuqtalik* to live, and I was very aware of *Savviuqtalik*.

Tavva najannaanniinnama inuunialiq&unga.

I was with my *najannaaq* and I was going to live.

Asuilaa amma tavva kingurngagut qanuiliramakiaq amma siniliqtualuungmigama sinililiq&unga uirngaqtualuulirama.

And once again, later on, although I don't know what was wrong with me, I fell asleep again. I fell asleep for I was very sleepy . . .

ammailak tupattialarivunga Arnaqtaat uqallaktuq.

. . . and I then became wide awake again and heard *Arnaqtaat* talking:

**"Uvanga 'una Arnaqtaat tusannguqtaalugigakku
Iqallijuuqtauqattarluni attirlaurlagu attiqtaulaurlanga
kiigutiginiarakku kiigutiginiarmanga."**

"I am tired of hearing *Arnaqtaat*, I will name her *Iqallijuq*. Let me be
her namesake, let me lock her in so that she can lock me in."

KUBLU: Suurlu kiiglunitiit?

As though she were locking you in?

**IQALLIJUQ: Imaak kiigluninga qanukiaq inna
kiigutiqarumava imaak inuusiqaqaulluninga.**

She would lock me in. I don't know what she wanted to use to
lock me in, but that she wanted me to have a life to live.

**Imaak ningiuraaluugami inuusiqpuk suurlu attattaq&uni
kiik&uni taikunga inuutuqaujarnialirama.**

As she was a very old woman, it was as though she was splicing our lives
together, so that my life was locked to hers, so that I could live longer.

**Tavva kinirunniiq&uni ilaa inuuttialiq&unga ukua takuvak&ugit
isiqtut ataatakkukka qaujimattialiq&ugit taannaluunniit Uviluq.**

I was now well and alive. I would see them enter and knew them well,
my father and even *Uviluq*.

**Ilitariumattianginnaq&ugu qaujimattianginnaq&ugu
tupirmuaq&unuk ataatama tupinganut
tutiqattaliq&utik ataatakkukkak.**

I recognized him and continued to know my father. We went to the tent where
my father was and my parents were once more sharing the same bed.

Tavva minguttinnaaliurnialiq&uninga sunauvva arnatut . . .

She was now going to make a *minguttinnaaq* for me, as for a girl . . .

**KUBLU: Nutarakuluullutiit? [eighteen-year-old *Kublu*
interrupts and sixty-year-old *Kublu* feels bad]**

When you were a young child?

**IQALLIJUQ: Aakka innaarauliq&ungali
aunaariurnialiq&unga ilaa sipinikuunnirama
Savviuqtalik angutaujumalaurningimmat arnaujumalilaurnirmat.**

No, when I was a young adult and started my periods, because *Savviuqtalik* had not wanted to be male but wanted to be female instead.

Angunasuqattanngurnirami ilaa angunasuk&uni aksuruluarnirami ikkiiqattanngurnirami arnaulilaurama sipillunga usuqalauraluaq&unga uttuktaarniq&unga taimanna sipisuungunnirmata . . .

He no longer wanted to go hunting because he had got tired of hunting, as it was exhausting, and he got tired of being cold. So my body went through the *sipiniq* process. I had a penis but then I ended up with a vagina. That is how they would *spipijuq.*

KUBLU: Angutaulauraluaq&utit arnannguq&utit?
You had started out as a boy but you became a girl?

IQALLIJUQ: Ii usuqalauraluaq&utik uttuktaaraangamik sipisuungungmata taimanna angutaulauraluaq&unga arnanngurnirama . . .
Yes. When children start out with a penis and end up with a vagina, the term is *sipijuq.* So, in that manner I was a boy and then became a girl . . .

KUBLU: Angutisiutinik annuraaqaq&utiit?
You were dressed as a boy?

IQALLIJUQ: Ii angutisiutinik annuraaqainnattiaq&unga aunaariurniluktaannut ilauqattalaurama ataatakulunni, ataatagali ukiatuinnaqtillugu upirngaakkut juunmi inuulauq&unga ukiatuinnaqtillugu tuqulaurmat ataatallattaara imaaq&uni.
Yes, I was always dressed in boys' clothing up to the time I started menstruating. I used to accompany my *ataatakuluk.* My *ataata,* my biological father, died by drowning in the fall after I was born. I was born in June.

Tavva taimanngat angutisiutinik annuraaqainnaq&unga aglaat angutaunasugiinnaq&unga arnaunasuginngit&unga.
So, I was always dressed as a boy and therefore I never considered myself to be a girl.

Asuila innaulilirama aunaariurama anaanama minguttinnaaqtumik atigiliuliq&uninga qarliliurniaq&uningalu atigiliurliraminga asuila qialiq&uni ataatani ataataginasugilluninga ilaa attiarimut taimanna annurajjiurumanngikkaluaq&uniuk ataatani ataatagigaminga qialiq&uni.

So, when I grew up and started menstruating, my *anaana* made me a *minguttinnaaqtuq atigi* and made *qarliik* for me as well. When she made the *atigi* for me, she started crying because she considered me to be her father, since I was named for him. She did not want to clothe her father as such, and I was her father, which is why she was crying.

Tavva arnannguq&unga kisiani aunaariurama arnaunasuginngiinnaq&unga.

Then I became female, though I never thought of myself as female until I started my periods.

Suli taima naluliqpara nalulinngikkaluaq&ugu taanna.

There is still more but I've forgotten it, though I know this part.

KUBLU: Maannamut tiki&&uguu?

Even up to now?

IQALLIJUQ: Ii maannamut.

Yes, up to now.

CHAPTER 2

Inuit Genesis and the Desire for Children

In Canada's Central and Eastern Arctic, there are no great myths about the origin of the world and humans. There are only short stories collected by the first anthropologists who travelled through that part of the world, Franz Boas and Knud Rasmussen in particular. Boas, a German Jew, and Rasmussen, a son of a Danish Lutheran pastor, both brought up in a religion of the book, hoped to find more than terse accounts of this major theme of Judeo-Christianity. They were deeply disappointed. After compiling the data then available from other Arctic regions of the Inuit, Boas summed up their cosmology: "The world has always been as it is now; and in the few stories in which the origin of some animals and of natural phenomena is related, it is rarely clearly implied that these did not exist before" (1904, 504). Elsewhere, Boas (1910) wrote that Inuit folklore also contains some heroic epics and stories about accidental events of limited scope. As for Rasmussen, who fluently spoke the Inuit language, he wrote that we should not look for logic in their origin myths (Rasmussen 1929). Such assertions presume that this people, obsessed with survival, devoted their energy wholly to that goal and had no time to philosophize or think up coherent myths. Such stereotypes still prevailed in the first half of the twentieth century and reflected a Western mindset dominated by written tradition, rationalism, and a linear conception of history.

Rasmussen had long been interested in Inuit oral literature and became known to the public through several collections of Eskimo tales that showed his knack for writing up and popularizing the many stories he had found in various Greenland villages (Rasmussen 1998). His writings about the Iglulingmiut and their close neighbours provide the first pieces of a puzzle I hope to solve—the puzzle of origins.

Inuit Prehistory

According to the oral tradition of the Inuit, other humans preceded them on earth. This is what the people of Igloolik say:

> There was once a world before this, and in it lived people who were not of our tribe. But the pillars of the earth collapsed, and all was destroyed (Rasmussen 1929, 252).[1]

The Inuit of the neighbouring Netsilik region add:

> Then forests grew on the bottom of the sea, and it is the remains of those forests that to this day tear themselves loose when the storms blow, so that we find driftwood on our shores. . . . Great showers of rain flooded the land. All the animals died" (Rasmussen 1931, 208–9).

The homeland of the Inuit has many signs of a past that is not theirs, beginning with the presence of marine fossils on the hills of Igloolik Island. For this people, the fossils come from the habitat of early humans, a place where islands floated on the sea and could tip over (Boas 1901, 173). Numerous prehistoric remains are scattered over the whole region and attest to earlier cultures that are close to but different from the culture of the Inuit of historical times, whose ancestors arrived as bowhead whale hunters 1,000 years ago—the Thule people, as archaeologists call them. Those earlier peoples eventually became the source of various human-like spirits, dwarfs, giants, and different monsters that are today visible only to shamans.

The 1930s saw the beginning of active Christianization among the Iglulik Inuit, but they still saw the earth as a flat disc surrounded by the sea, with everything tenuously balanced on four pillars standing over a lower world. Upon the earth stood four other pillars that supported the firmament and the upper world. The shamans interviewed by Rasmussen (1929) said they would sometimes go to adjust a shaky pillar. In short, Inuit believed that human life, before being what it is now, had gone through various avatars and that the world was still in a precarious balance.

The Earth Brings Forth Two Adult Males

In those times, when no one dwelt on it, the earth brought forth human life in the form of two Inuit, *Uumarnituq* and *Aakulujjuusi*:[2]

It is said that two males, two men, were born; that two *niaquqtaak* [hummocks of earth] turned into two human beings.[3]

Rasmussen adds the following key detail:

They were already fully grown when they emerged from the ground (1929, 252).

In Igloolik, a very firm belief still survived in the first half of the twentieth century that living things could emerge from hummocks of earth.[4] People believed themselves to be autochthonous—sprung from the soil itself—although they actually descended from the last migratory wave to enter North America from across the Bering Strait and were, furthermore, semi-nomadic in this Arctic region.

For the first humans, *Nuna* (the earth) was female. She was not only the original womb but also a supplementary source of nourishment—one could say a placenta. This is seen in an answer by *Inukpasujjuk*, a native of the neighbouring Natsilik region, to questions from Rasmussen:

I heard old people say that once, long long ago, men ate of the earth. Our forefathers ate of the earth (1929, 253).

The earth's female identity in the Inuit symbolic system is demonstrated in several ways. To have daughters, pregnant women in Nunavik (Arctic Quebec) would go away from the seashore and squat facing inland to urinate. To have sons, they would instead go near the sea and squat seaward. Some men, it was said, would make love to the earth and ejaculate into the ground—a serious transgression in people's eyes (Rasmussen 1929, 98). Finally, eggs would sometimes come up through the ground surface and produce fantastic beings: *Silaat*, children of *Sila* (the atmosphere, the air) and *Nuna* (the earth). We will come back to this point in Chapter 3.

Day did not exist, neither did death or war; nor were there any seasons; no light, no sea ice, no gales, no storms, no lightning, no winds. The ground was covered with snow (see also Rasmussen 1929, 252–53; Rasmussen 1931, 208).

The Creation of Woman and the Gendering of the World

According to Rasmussen's handwritten notes in Inuktitut (see Chapter 2, note 1) and *Agiaq*'s comments, the first two men wanted to multiply after living together awhile:

One of them [*Uumarnituq*] was taken by the other [*Aakulujjuusi*] as a wife and became pregnant;[5] his belly became prominent. When he was about to deliver, seeing he [the fetus] had no way out, his companion composed an *irinaliuti* [magic song]:
"A human being here, a penis here. May its opening be wide and roomy. Opening, opening, opening!"
When these words were sung, the man's penis split and a male baby came out, and saw the light of day.

Humans discovered they needed a female sex to reproduce. They also discovered the magic power of singing and speaking.

These [first three Inuit] were our earliest forefathers, and from them all the lands were peopled (Rasmussen 1929, 253).

Gathering Babies from the Earth, or the Origin of Adoption

I questioned *Iqallijuq* about these mythical times. She answered:

I heard that in olden times women who couldn't have children could get them by going to look for and gather babies from the earth, and they found them. They raised them and thereby had many descendants. In this way, you could get babies.

Ivaluarjuk, for his part, provided interesting comments:

And when people were out on a journey and settled at a place, one might see them going round about the camping ground, bending down and searching about in the earth. It is said that in that way they sought for children from the earth, the children of earth. And with the children they found on the ground it was in this wise: a long search was needed to find boys, but one had not to go far to find girls. Not all, however, were equally lucky. Some found only girls, perhaps because they would not take the trouble to go far, being lazy, but those who were not afraid of walking, those who were not lazy, they had sons. As soon as a child was found on the ground, it was picked up at once and put in the *amaut* (back pouch of a woman's parka), and carried off home. The women who came home with children they had found observed precisely the same taboo and the same rules as those who had themselves given birth to a child, and were similarly regarded as unclean. They were given a birth hut of snow, or if it happened in summer, a small tent, and there they stayed for the time prescribed after childbirth, during which the woman must live apart from her husband (Rasmussen 1929, 254).

This belief provides a kind of mythical basis and justification for adoption, a common Inuit practice. Even today, around 40 percent of all newborns go to parents other than their own. In reality, as in the myth, it is harder to get boys than girls because boys are given up less easily. Boas published another variant of this myth, collected by Captain J. Mutch in Cumberland Sound, on Baffin Island. It describes how babies were gathered:

Akkalookjo [*Aakulujjuk*] and his wife, Owmirneto [*Uumarnituq*][6] were living at Kinerto. They had no children. One day *Uumarnituq* went out early. She found a baby girl, which she took home and brought up as her own. When the child was almost grown up, *Uumarnituq* found another baby girl, which she took and brought up as her own. When this child was almost grown up, she found a third one; and after a number of years, when the third also was almost grown up, she found a fourth one. All these she brought up. When the first girl was grown up and able to look after a child herself, she went out early one morning, before her mother. She found a baby boy, whom she took home and brought up as her own child. When this boy was almost grown up, *Uumarnituq* and the first and second girl whom she had found went about looking for children, and *Uumarnituq* found another baby child. When this one was almost grown up, *Uumarnituq* and the two girls whom she had found first were again looking for children. Her first daughter found another girl. About this time her third daughter began to look for children too, while *Uumarnituq* had grown so old that she did not look for any more to bring up. About this time the third girl found a child; and when this one had grown up, the first girl found another one.

So far, the second girl had been unsuccessful, although she was very anxious to find a child. When the last one had grown up, the third daughter found a child, and so they lived on for many years. Finally, they decided that the second girl should marry the boy which the first girl had found. Although she now had a husband, she still continued to look for children (Boas 1901, 178–79).

After reading this long description about how the first humans got babies, we can make several remarks. First, boys were hard to find and girls plentiful. Only one of the ten children from the earth was a boy, the nine others being girls. Second, the mother waited until the first child had sufficiently grown up before looking for another to raise. So there was considerable spacing between births at a time when death did not exist, as we will see further on. Finally, the myth states that some women could not get babies this way from the earth. Such women included one of *Uumarnituq*'s adopted daughters, who for this reason married the son that her older sister had found. This mythical reality is the reverse of human reality, where procreation is the rule and adoption an expedient.

In 1907, Boas published another variant, likewise from Cumberland Sound and from Captain J. Mutch. It nonetheless differs on several key points from the previous ones:

> Omerneeto [*Uumarnituq*] used to wear her husband's boots. She did not fasten the upper strings properly, but allowed the boot-leg to sag down and the boot-strings to drag over the ground. One day the soul of an infant that was on the ground crept up the boot-string and up into her womb. Up to that time, children had been found in the snow. The child grew in the womb, and finally was born. It began to cry, and gradually became old enough to speak. One day it told its parents how it had crawled into *Uumarnituq*'s womb. It continued, "There I was as in a small house. Every night when you cohabited, a dog would come in and vomit food for me to make me grow. Finally I longed to get outside; and when I got out, I wanted to speak, but all I could do was to cry. When I wanted other food than milk, I could only say '*apaapa*';[7] and when I wanted to say 'I am thirsty,' I could only say '*uu, uu!*'" (Boas 1907, 483).

This variant is consistent with *Iqallijuq*'s pre-birth memories recounted in the previous chapter, and it shows that reversibility of perspective is important in the Inuit way of thinking.[8] Again, the reversed perspective is a fetal one. Also important is the fact that the child's soul chooses to incarnate. During gestation, the mother is its home and the father its food provider. As in *Iqallijuq*'s story, a fetus is distinct from a baby. A fetus is fully aware, while a baby cannot express its thoughts and desires other than by crying or by imitating sounds.

In the Iglulik Inuit variants, however, the first two humans invent procreation and gather babies from the earth to make up for sterility. Here, baby gathering precedes the discovery of gestation and leads to it.

Adopting Animals: A Palliative for Childlessness

Let us come back to the first variant published by Boas. *Uumarnituq*'s second daughter failed to find any babies from the earth and has married a husband who is too young to procreate. She again starts looking for a baby.

Finally she found a *miqqulingiaq* [a fuzzy caterpillar].[9] She allowed it to suck the blood from her own body. Therefore she needed a vast amount of food, and she had to go to the houses of her neighbors to ask for it. Her husband was so young that he did not go sealing yet. When she had eaten enough, she went home, and let the caterpillar suck her blood. While she was outside, she left the caterpillar in her stocking and in one of the legs of her trousers; and when she came back, it would suck the blood from various parts of her body. The caterpillar was growing all the time, and now entirely filled the stockings and the trousers. The larger it grew, the oftener she had to go and ask for food. Her husband stayed in the house all the time. He sat on the bed and trimmed the lamps.[10] It was very warm inside, and he sat without a shirt on. One day the caterpillar became hungry while the woman was away. It left its bed, and began to suck blood out of the man's side. It hurt him, and he threw it into the porch, where the dogs were. He heard them howling when they were bitten by the caterpillar. Very soon they stopped. They had killed it and devoured it. Its blood was spattered all over the porch and over their pelts. When the woman came back, she saw the blood, and asked her husband, "Is that the blood of the caterpillar?" She looked at her trousers, and found that the caterpillar had disappeared. Then her husband told her what had happened. He said, "That was not a human being. Why did you want to raise it?" She cried, went to bed, and soon she died (Boas 1901, 178–79).

In the variant told by *Ivaluarjuk* to Rasmussen, from the Iglulik Inuit, the woman bursts into tears but does not die (1929, 268–69). In a myth told by *Inukpasujjuk* to Rasmussen, an Inuit woman adopts another animal, a bear cub:

There was once an old woman who took in a bear's cub to live with her. She brought it up and taught it, and soon it was big enough to go out and play with the children in the village, and the bear and the children fought and wrestled and played together. The bear grew up and was soon so big that some of the people in the village wanted to kill and eat it. But the old woman wept, and prayed for her bear and did so wish that it might live. When at last she dared not keep it any longer, she urged it to run away. But before the bear left its foster-mother, it spoke to her thus: "You shall never suffer want. If you should be in want, go down to the edge of the ice, and there you will see some bears. Call them, and they will come." The woman did as the bear had said. When she began to be in want, she went out on to the sea ice and began looking about for bears. She saw a bear on a drifting icefloe, and called to it, but when the bear saw and heard her it fled away. The old woman went on until she saw another bear, and called to this one also. The bear heard her, and as soon as it had seen her, it ran over to the other bear, that was close by, and began fighting with it. It soon killed the bear it was fighting, and hauled it in to land, and left it there even before the foster-mother had reached the spot. After that the old woman lived in abundance on the meat of the bear that had been given her, and even gave her neighbours some for themselves. Thus it came about that greedy people in the village themselves caused a bear, that might have procured meat for them all, to go away and leave them (Rasmussen 1929, 267–68).[11]

By describing attempts to adopt animal offspring to make up for a woman's sterility or the solitude of old age, these mythical stories show how hard it is for a hunting society to have real social relationships with animals, particularly the ones they hunt. Here, we see filiation by adoption. In other myths, we see marriage or procreation. Although these experiences seem positive at first, they always end badly because of lack of understanding by other Inuit, be they neighbours from the same camp or people from other camps (Chapter 12). The same goes for real life. It is not unusual for a hunter to bring home a wild baby bird or more rarely a young bear cub, which he entrusts to his family. The whole family raises, feeds, and plays with the animal until it has grown up and is now, in everyone's eyes, a game animal. It becomes a target and ends up getting killed, sometimes by the very people who cared for it.[12] Yet in mythical times humans and animals lived together in harmony and could go from being animal to being human, or vice versa. This former time was also, however, one of darkness, lack of differentiation, cold, hunger, and obscurity.

FIGURE 9. In mythical times, humans and animals were very close, and they could marry, adopt each other, or exchange identities. From a drawing by Daividialuk Amittuq Alasuaq, Puvirnituq, 1971. Made by Johanne Lévesque. Archival fonds of B. Saladin d'Anglure.

Ukpikarniq: Somersaulting to Renewed Youth

In the beginning, Inuit did not die and knew how to rejuvenate when they reached an advanced age:

> It is said that very long ago, when men and women reached an advanced age, or even when they only began to get old, they would somersault head first from the edge of the sleeping platform in their home and get up standing on the floor, having been made young again. That was how they regenerated (Iqallijuq 1971).

This mythical life cycle sees an individual enter a new age group at regular intervals and form new relationships with people younger or older. Assuming a difference of around twenty years between generations, the system works as follows.

PHASE 1: Ego is born. The parents are around twenty and the grand-parents around forty.

PHASE 2: Ego is twenty. The first child is just born, the parents are around forty, and the grandparents, having reached their sixties, re-juvenate and become once more young adults in their twenties—the same age as Ego.

PHASE 3: The grandchildren are born. The children are entering their twenties, Ego and the grandparents are forty, and the parents, having reached their sixties, in turn rejuvenate and become young twenty-year-olds—the age of Ego's children.

PHASE 4: The cycle begins anew with the birth of Ego's great-grand-children and his grandchildren entering their twenties. Ego enters his sixties, rejuvenates, and becomes a young twenty-year-old like his grandparents—and like his grandchildren.

The system is thus circular, with three age classes: children under twenty; parents aged twenty to thirty-nine; and grandparents aged forty to fifty-nine. If we exclude children, every other generation belongs to the same age class.[13] This mythical renewal of youth brings to mind two rituals that were practised until recently and still are to some degree. In 1971 *Ujarak*, from Igloolik, recalled the following:

> When, in my youth, I first went from Igloolik to Arctic Bay by dogsled, we came to the border of the two territories, and we stopped. I was made to get off the dogsled, take off my parka, and remove my outer caribou trousers, and I was asked to fall head over heels and stand up. I was told this was so the spirit of the place, who didn't know me, would accept me as a newcomer and protect me.

This custom was observed whenever you entered a territory for the first time. The somersault corresponds here to a rebirth. The outsider becomes a native of the region, and a link is made with the spirit of the place. In the spring of 2004 I heard an account with many analogies to the last one. This was at Sanikiluaq (Belcher Islands, Nunavut), several hundred kilometres south of Igloolik, and I heard it from a young adult, Moses Nuvalingaq:

> When you come to a place for the first time ever and set foot on the shore, you must right away get down on all fours, like a baby, and go forward while saying, *"Ungaa! Ungaa! Ungaa!"* to imitate a newborn's wailing.

This ritual injunction also appears in an account gathered by Comer from the west coast of Hudson Bay and published by Boas. In the sea is a low rock called Marble Island:

> When the people go to this island in winter, they step from their sledges a short distance from the shore, and crawl up on their elbows and knees. When they visit the island in the summer, they do the same, after landing (1901, 151).

Rasmussen himself heard about the Marble Island ritual from *Tagurnaaq*, an old woman from the Igloolik region. The island was named Ursuriaq (from *ursuq*, "fat") because its rocky, quartzite structure looked like blubber:

Before that time, it was nothing but a heap of pressure ridges in the ice. It was not until later that the ice turned to the white stone we call *ursuriaq*. I remember the first time we came to that island, we had to crawl up onto the land, and were not allowed to stand upright until we reached the top. That was done then, and it is done to this day, for the Island is a sacred place; magic words made it, and if we do not show respect for it by crawling it will change to ice again, and all the people on it will fall through and drown (1929, 26–27).

Neither Comer nor Boas nor Rasmussen seems to have suspected the symbolism behind this commandment to crawl. In light of *Ujarak*'s and Nuvalingaq's explanations, the aim clearly was to win over the benevolence of the spirit of the place by making it think the visitor had been born there and therefore had roots there (Saladin d'Anglure 2004). Each visit was a symbolic rebirth. In mythical times, when death did not exist, one would be reborn as a young adult. In the present time, when life is short, one is re-born as a baby. Remember, too, just as Ursuriaq Island is made of crushed ice that turned to stone, a human being is made of liquid elements (blood and sperm) that take shape, like the ice, and become a fetus.

The Origin of Daylight

According to Rasmussen, in ancient times night reigned permanently over the world, and there were no stars in the sky. This darkness made survival difficult for humans and animals alike:

It is said that in the days when the earth was dark, the only creatures men had to hunt were ptarmigan and hare, and these were hunted by wetting the forefinger and holding it out in the air; the finger then became luminous and it was possible to see the animal hunted. . . . In those days, men were not clad as now, in warm caribou skins, but had to use skins of birds and foxes (1929, 253).

In the beginning, small animals were the only source of food or clothing. This point requires two comments. First, in times of scarcity, such animals were the only ones easily available. The willow ptarmigan and the Arctic hare were not very hard to kill with bows and arrows, while the Arctic fox could be captured in stone traps, whose vestiges are often seen almost everywhere in the Inuit homeland. Mythical times are described in a way that implies food scarcity, as seen in people's clothing. Winter clothes were once made from bird skins with the feathers still attached. This very special technique, which requires forty or so bird skins to make one parka, was still in use on the Belcher Islands in the mid-1960s after caribou went extinct on the islands. Parry and Lyon's 1821–23 Arctic expedition encountered several hunters, including some Iglulik Inuit, who wore eider-skin parkas. In the legend of *Atanaarjuat* (Chapter 13), one of the protagonists wears an eider-skin parka. This custom may go back to the early days of humankind or to times of scarcity in historic times. It may also echo the custom of using such a skin to wipe a newborn child, who would later often be dressed in a bird skin (Chapter 1).

Let us continue with *Ivaluarjuk's* story on the origin of daylight:

Among the earliest living beings on earth were the raven and the Arctic fox. One day they met, and fell into talk. "Let there be no daylight, let there be no daylight," said the fox, who likes to hunt in the darkness. But the raven, who moves by flying and not by walking, and who constantly strikes its head—no wonder!—got angry and said, "*Qau! Qau!* May the light come, may the day come!" "*Taaq! Taaq!* May it be night, may it be night!" replied the Arctic fox. It is said that day has alternated with night ever since (Rasmussen 1929, 253; Rasmussen 1930b, 26).

In those days, words had magic power. Being a scavenger that fed on animal remains and human refuse, the raven wished for daylight to find its food more easily. Inuit believe animals once had the gift of speech and could easily take human form. The raven's cry *Qau!*, which means "day, daylight" in the Inuit language also means "forehead" and is the root of *qaumaniq*, "light" or "aura" (the one that surrounds a shaman) and *qaujimaniq*, "knowledge." Paradoxically, the black raven preferred the lightness of day, and the white fox the darkness of night.[14] Originally, according to another variant told by *Ivaluarjuk* to Rasmussen (1929, 277–78), the raven did not have that colour. To summarize this variant: the raven and the loon decided one day to tattoo each other, this being in the time when both could take human form. The raven tattooed the loon's body wondrously. It was then his turn to be tattooed, but he felt uncomfortable and became so restless that the loon lost patience and poured the bucket of soot all over his body. All ravens have since been black.

Because the Arctic fox finds its food during nighttime plundering, it prefers the darkness of night. Its cry *Taaq! Taaq!* means "darkness." In a Greenlandic variant of the same myth, a man takes the raven's place and a woman the fox's place. Now although the Inuit language does not have gender, the universe and its components are noticeably gendered, as much in cosmology as in technology, rites, and myths. The raven usually takes a man's role, and the fox a woman's role.[15] Among the Alaskan Inuit, the raven plays the role of a demiurge. Thus, from the clash between heavenly male forces and underworld female forces came the first differentiation of the heavens: the alternation of day and night.[16] In Inuit symbolism, the eastern sky (*Ulluqarvik*, "The place where daylight appears") became the birthplace of life and hope, often associated in rites with the flight of a raven. This is seen in a magic formula that the shaman *Ava* recited when his little baby namesake left on his first journey (Rasmussen 1929, 47; Saladin d'Anglure 1980a):

I arise from rest with movements swift as the beat of a raven's wings. I arise to meet the day, *wa wa!* My face is turned from the dark of night to gaze at the dawn of day, now whitening in the sky.

As with many other people born in winter, *Ava* had been wiped at birth with a raven skin, which was also his first clothing. Thereafter, he treated it as a powerful amulet. As an adult, according to his son *Ujarak* (1971), *Ava* fell one day into the water while hunting on the sea ice and clung to a floating slab of ice, but the wind and currents took him farther out to sea. He summoned his guardian raven. Soon he heard a flapping of wings and saw a raven appear:[17]

The raven flew in the night, coming from where the light appears, from where the break of day is seen. . . . Then the raven drew nearer, circling [in the direction of *Sila*], and now it was bringing the drifting slab of ice back toward the land-fast ice; [the slab] came alongside the land-fast ice, and my father clambered onto it.

The bird saved *Ava*'s life and at the same time gave him great power through this ordeal. By the same token, night and symbolic death were key to a shaman's initiation, and thus to gaining clairvoyance and access to the invisible world.

Woman Brings Death and War

With the two-fold procreative power of the earth and of women, the population soon grew so much that the island home of the first Inuit began to sink into the sea and tip over. This is reported by Boas in one story:

There were a great many Eskimo [Inuit] on [the island of] Midliqjuaq. There were also a great many people in all the other places. At that time there had never been a death. There were but few islands, which were floating about. They did not touch the bottom of the sea. The people on Midliqjuaq came to be so numerous that the island became top-heavy, and turned over. Thus a great many of the people were killed. A long time after this event had happened the waters began to recede, and the islands went aground. These were the first deaths; and ever since that time, man has continued to die (Boas 1901, 173).

Rasmussen reports another variant:

In the very earliest times, there was no death among human beings. Men took women to wife, and women bore children, and mankind grew so numerous that at last there was not room for all. The first human beings lived on an island, and there are those who maintain that it was the island of Mitligjuaq, in Hudson Strait. But the people there propagated their kind, and as none ever left the land where they were born, there were at last so many that the island could not support them. Very slowly, then, one side of the island began to slope down towards the sea. The people grew frightened, for it seemed as if they might slip off and be drowned. But then an old woman began to shout; she had power in her words, and she called out loudly, "Let [it] be so ordered that human beings can die, for there will no longer be room for us on earth." And the woman's words had such power that her wish was fulfilled. Thus death came among mankind (Rasmussen 1929, 92).

In 1974, *Iqallijuq* provided me with further details on the origin of death:

It is told that the Inuit, who lived on the island, didn't know death. . . . Because their numbers had grown considerably, their land, which was floating, began to sink. An old woman then took fright and cried out, "May they die! May they wage war on each other! Death! Death! War! War!" It is said that they began to wage war on each other and that they began to die. But an old man, a very old man, who was lying down, cried out on his own behalf, "May they not die! May they not wage war on each other!" The people who were gathered . . . built small boats and left for uninhabited places. Although each group now had its territory, death continued to do its work, even though the people no longer waged war on each other as much.

According to *Agiaq*, this happened on Igloolik Island, and the two old people were the man *Aakulujjuusi* and the woman *Uumarnituq*. All of the accounts agree on one point: the land of the first humans was unstable and floated on the sea (Chapter 2). This island was an ideal location for Inuit, who lived essentially from hunting of marine mammals. Archaeology has long shown that islands located along migration routes of large marine mammals were occupied by humans in very ancient times.

With war the Inuit dispersed to other lands, and with death their numbers fell. The earth regained its stability. They were saved from being swallowed up by the sea, but at the price of losing immortality and the ability to regenerate. They could no longer pick up babies from the earth; nor could they eat the earth anymore. This shorter lifespan increased the value of women, who played a major role in striking a new balance and who assumed the task of perpetuating human life with no help from the earth and no regeneration. Men could now hunt more easily, thanks to daylight, and became providers for their families. Life was brought into balance—at the price of war, dispersal, and death.

Death also ushered in a new cosmic age, with the population of human souls expanding into other worlds. These souls, after separating from the body, now migrate either to the upper world or to the lower one. For all those who have died prematurely through violence, war, or difficult childbirth, their souls are promised an eternal life of bliss, joy, and games in a heavenly hereafter among the Ullurmiut ("The people of the Land of Day"). On beautiful winter nights, you may see them in the sky playing ball with a walrus skull. They form the *aqsarniit* (aurora borealis). For those who have died in other circumstances, their souls live on in the lower world of the *Qimiujarmiut* ("The dwellers in the narrow strip of land").[18]

By bursting the *pudlaq* (the bubble containing the soul), death frees the life-giving air inside and sends it into the atmosphere and thence into *Sila*, thus enabling the *tarniq* (double-soul) to live in the hereafter. Instead of endlessly increasing human life and disturbing the balance of the universe, *Sila* now presides over a much more limited capacity for increase. Souls, however, are non-material and can populate the uninhabited realms of the hereafter without limit. Paradoxically, death and war ensure the continuity of life,[19] which is no longer about the perpetual existence of individuals but rather about the perpetual existence of the group, its society, and its culture.

CHAPTER 3

Naarjuk: The Giant Baby with Prominent Genitals and the Master of *Sila*

When the Inuit were still new on the earth, they lived alongside other humans who looked strikingly different in shape and size. These were dwarfs and giants. Did they come from an earlier peopling of the world, before the Inuit? The myths do not say so explicitly, but this is implied. Stories abound of encounters and interactions between the Inuit and these other humans.

The most imposing of them is beyond doubt *Naarjuk* ("Big Belly"),[1] also known as *Silaap Inua*—the master spirit of *Sila*, the atmosphere, and the universe. *Naarjuk* may move in regular, orderly, and foreseeable cycles, or he may exhibit turbulences and antagonistic tensions that are paradoxical, ambiguous, and unforeseeable. His many avatars transcend boundaries and scales of existence, and command the motions of heavenly bodies and the dynamics of life. I will review his main characteristics here, as revealed in myths, rites, and beliefs. First, however, let me describe some of the problems encountered by those who have tried to grasp the meaning and importance of *Sila* and its master spirit.

The Crux of Inuit Cosmology: *Sila*

Sila is a puzzling concept that has discouraged most people who have made it their object of study. It means several things at once: the universe; that which envelops; that which is most external to humans; and also that which is most internal to humans—reason and intelligence. According to Rasmussen (1929, 73), "*Sila* is doubtless the original world power, which at one time, when the Eskimos had not yet become a coastal people dependent on the sea, was the principal spirit, on which all religious ideas were based."

Rasmussen believed that the Inuit came from the North American interior and that the Caribou Inuit are therefore the last living representatives of this original stage (Rasmussen 1930a, 5–8). The Caribou Inuit, together with the Copper Inuit, whose ancestors split off from them according to recent research, consider *Sila* to be the main cosmic force, from which all others emanate. Unfortunately, archaeology has refuted Rasmussen's theory. Savard wrote in 1970: "Of all the Eskimo divinities, this one remains by far the hardest to grasp. Although at first sight it seems known throughout the territory, one ends up wondering whether it always is the same religious concept. Because little material about it appears in myths, it will probably long remain one of the main puzzles for religious ethnology in this region of the world."

In an essay that describes the religion of the Iglulik and Netsilik Inuit and which draws on Rasmussen's monographs (1929, 1931), Oosten wrote (1976, 23): "The *inua* (master) of the air was a vague and abstract figure among most *inuit* groups. . . . Such an abstract religious force, however, did not play any part in inuit religion. *Sila* clearly was an individual spirit and not an abstract spiritual force among the *netsilik* and the *iglulik*."

On this subject, and in this culture area, Oosten relied mainly on Rasmussen's meagre collected data. Later, he recognized the importance of the *Sila* concept and its associated heavenly entity (Oosten 1989). In all fairness, when he first wrote about it there was little new research on the master of *Sila*.

Sila thus seems to have two contradictory meanings: intelligence and atmosphere. The contradiction is only an apparent one, in my opinion (Saladin d'Anglure 1980a, 1986). The concept has to be understood on three scales of existence: the infra-human scale of dwarfs and fetuses; the human scale; and the supra-human scale of giants. Changes of scale are made possible by the master spirit of the cosmos *Silaap Inua*, or *Naarjuk* in the language of shamans, who enables people and things to go from the microcosm to the macrocosm. His place is well-known in the macrocosm, where he animates the surrounding universe and is everything that is most external: the air, the atmosphere, and the cosmos. The microcosm is a lower level of ontogenesis. It is a living individual's soul.

The soul looks like a miniature of the individual (a tiny model a few centimetres tall) and is enclosed in a sort of compressed air bubble (*pudlaq*) the size of a small egg (Chapter 1). This bubble contains the air of a baby's first cries. The air is borrowed from the great *Sila* (the atmosphere) and will return to *Sila* at death, when the bubble bursts. The air surrounds the soul in the microcosmic bubble, being external to the miniature individual and internal to the human body. This air is what gives its possessor strength and intelligence.

So there is no contradiction between the two meanings of *Sila*. The concept is the same but applied differently in two different settings, from two different perspectives, and on three different scales of existence.

The Revenge of *Naarjuk*

I have collected many stories about dwarfs and giants in the Igloolik region and in Nunavik, but Rasmussen (1931: 229–231) has the myth that best explains *Naarjuk*'s origin. It comes from the Netsilik Inuit, who live next to the Iglulik Inuit:

> The giant Inugpasugssuk [*Inukpasujjuk*][2] and his adoptive son, who was an ordinary human, were once out walking. They came to a lake covered with ice, where they fell in with another giant, the enormous Inuaruvligasugssuk [*Inugagulligaarjuk*], who was even bigger than Inugpasugssuk [*Inukpasujjuk*]. He was standing there fishing for Arctic char,[3] horrible to look at, and then he had only two teeth in his mouth.

This scene brings human life into play on three scales of existence: the *Inugagulligaarjuk* (a special kind of dwarf); the *Inukpasujjuk* (a giant); and the Inuk (an ordinary human). The giant has adopted the Inuk, who is nearly ten times smaller than himself. They encounter a special dwarf, who is normally three or four times smaller than the Inuk, but unlike the other two he can become as big or small as the people or animals he has to contend with.[4] Because he is fishing for giant trout, he had taken on the size of a giant. This is a mythical time when the boundaries between the various types of humans are still blurred, as well as the boundaries between humans and animals. We will come back later to this point.

Inukpasujjuk and his foster son went up to him and saw that he had caught two salmon, giant salmon. They asked to be allowed to eat with him, but as *Inugagulligaarjuk* would give them none of his catch, they went back to the shore again and there *Inukpasujjuk* said to his foster son: "Shout as loud as you can: *aybay*, he has only two teeth in his mouth!" At first the foster son was afraid, but when *Inukpasujjuk* urged him, he shouted at the top of his voice "*Aybay*, he has only two teeth in his mouth!" This he kept on shouting. At last *Inugagulligaarjuk* became angry and shouted: "One gets tired of hearing him shouting about the two teeth, he who is no bigger than that one could have him between one's teeth like a shred of meat!"

According to Rasmussen's unpublished Inuktitut manuscripts and my senior Inuit informants, the son is comparing the special dwarf's two remaining teeth to those of a *siksik*. This is the Arctic ground squirrel (*Citellus parryi*), a small tundra rodent between a groundhog and a squirrel in size. Like many rodents, it has two big incisors in its upper jaw.

The two parties have broken two key rules. The special dwarf has refused to share his catch with the giant, after being asked to share, and the Inuk has mocked the special dwarf's physical disability—his toothlessness, aside from two remaining teeth. The allusion to a *siksik* is all the more insulting because it reduces the supersized dwarf to the scale of a small animal, and thus back to his normal size. It is an especially nasty insult because it comes from an Inuk who is much smaller, although the reverse is normally true. With a fight brewing, we can see the giant's stratagem. He is facing a creature bigger and stronger than himself, and he is using his adopted son to set up a fight that the special dwarf thinks will be easy to win as the stronger opponent.

Furious, he waded to the shore, threw the two giant trout down on a rock, and they fell with such force that they made quite a hollow in it:

and then *Inukpasujjuk* said to his foster son: "Now when we start to wrestle, hamstring him!"

For though *Inukpasujjuk* was tall, he was no match for *Inugagulligaarjuk*, neither in size nor in strength.

Then the two giants ran at each other and began to wrestle. It was easy to see that *Inugagulligaarjuk* was the stronger. It was only when the boy had cut one of his hamstrings that the two contestants became equal. But then when the other had been cut, *Inukpasujjuk* threw him and killed him. But before he died *Inugagulligaarjuk* howled loudly: "*Uhuu, uhuu, uhuu.*"

In most Inuit stories with differently sized protagonists, the smaller, more cunning one usually wins, especially when the larger or stronger one abuses his power. Thus, one myth tells how a dwarf almost smothers an Inuk by sucking his breath away after the latter challenges him for his catch of meat. Here, the Inuk and the giant are the ones in a position of weakness. Their cunning brings down the oversized dwarf.[5]

A moment afterwards an enormous topknot came in sight over the summit of the hills; it was his [*Inugagulligaarjuk's*] wife coming at his call, and she was so big that her breasts lay like two large bearded seals over her body. She seized *Inukpasujjuk*, and as she did so her breasts swung against him with such force that he almost fell. But his foster-son hamstrung her too and, as she sank down, *Inukpasujjuk* killed her.

A favourite form of Inuit humour is one where beings of different size confront each other. Dwarfs from the infra-human world are projected into the supra-human world of giants, while being observed by the master of the game—an Inuk from the intermediate world of humans. When the storyteller gets to the part where the special dwarf's wife almost knocks out the giant with her breasts as big as bearded seals (*Erignathus barbatus*), the Inuit audience always responds with howls of laughter (a bearded seal weighs 250 kilograms on average.)

Then they followed the giant-woman's footprints back and found her child, an infant who had fallen out of her *amaut* (back pouch of a woman's parka) as she ran, and there it lay on the ground squalling "*Ungaa, ungaa, ungaa.*" Its mother had been so excited and so eager to come to her husband's aid that she did not even notice that her child had slipped out of her coat.

The baby is clothed in laced skin underwear called *ungirlaq*, with an open crotch to urinate freely while squatting. This is how his penis can stick up in the air. There were some people close at hand, and when they came up to look at the baby, *Inukpasujjuk* amused himself by setting the women up on the child's penis; and so enormous was this infant that four women could sit on it side by side; and when the infant trembled a little they could not hold themselves on and all fell off. So immense was his strength.

Inuit humour also targets the sexual characteristics of the human body, and these characteristics are laughed at when different sizes are compared. Sex between giants and humans, and the resulting problems, is a theme of several stories, such as the one about the Inuk who marries a giant woman and gets lost in her vagina, and the one about the Inuit woman who marries a giant and is run through by his penis.

The most popular stories are about huge male erections. One is about a giant who walks in the sea looking for *kanajuq*, a sculpin of the *Cottidae* family, which he bludgeons with his club. On a human scale, the fish are in fact *arviit* (bowhead whales, *Balaena mysticetus*), which the Inuit are simultaneously pursuing in their kayak. The giant is up to his belt in water and, suddenly, a form with a round end emerges some distance ahead. Thinking he sees a *kanajuq* (sculpin), he clubs it, only to topple over lifeless as the surprised Inuit hunters look on. In the excitement of the hunt, he had an erection and mistook the head of his penis for a sculpin. On top of the humour of this incongruous situation, one might add that Inuit hunters call the bow of a kayak *usuujaq* ("that which looks like a penis").

Later on that infant [the special dwarf's child] went up to the sky and became the Spirit of the Air to avenge mistreated orphaned children.

Brutally deprived of both parents and made fun of by everyone present, the child flees up into the sky and becomes *Silaap Inua*. This is the master of the cosmos who commands the cold northwesterlies, the storms, the snow, and the rain.

When questioned about the meaning of this myth and the special dwarf's child—a symbol of weather and atmospheric disturbances, *Iqallijuq* (1974) likened the unpredictability of a child's mood to that of the weather, and the impulsiveness of male sexual arousal to that of storms. When next questioned about the meaning of the name *Naarjuk* ("Big Belly"), as shamans called the child, she mentioned that atmospheric turbulences and intestinal disorders bring to mind the fickleness of children.[6] Rasmussen (1931, 230) provided a few details on *Naarjuk's* behaviour:

When women are secretive about their uncleanliness, that is to say when they tell nobody that they have their menses, or that they have had a miscarriage, *Naarjuk* punishes their village with storms; he loosens the thongs of his skin napkin and lets it blow, rain, snow or drift. If bad weather continues, great seances are held and the boldest and cleverest shamans then have to go up to that place in the air where *Naarjuk* is hovering. There they have to fight with him, and not until they succeed in tying his skin napkin tight about his body will the weather settle again.

Kupaaq (1974) gave me a few complementary details. He had heard the following:

The shaman sometimes had to whip *Naarjuk* until he bled, or cut one of his tendons, and in any event lace up his wide-open clothing again to calm the storm.

The atmospheric rages of *Silaap Inua*, the master of the cosmos, are feared and his cosmic farts dreaded. *Iqallijuq* (1971) also provided some comments:

I heard that in winter when *Uannaq* (the northwesterly wind) blew for a long time, the stores of food would soon run out. When a snowstorm from the northwest lasted too long, the shaman would consult his helping spirit; he would try, through shamanism, to fasten the wind's clothing. Whenever an opening appeared in its clothes, the wind could be felt blowing through.

FIGURE 10. A giant walking on the bottom of the sea, hunting for sculpins with a club. To the Inuit, these are bowhead whales, which they are hunting from kayaks. Excited by the hunt, the giant has an erection, and when his penis appears on the surface, he mistakes it for a sculpin and gives it a blow with his club. From a text and drawing by Daividialuk Amittuq Alasuaq. Puvirnituq, 1971. Made by Johanne Lévesque. Archival Fonds of B. Saladin d'Anglure.

Born under a Sign of *Sila*

In Inuktitut, *silaittuq* ("devoid of *Sila*," foolish) describes a young child who disobeys the rules of adults and will not listen to anyone else. Conversely, *silatujuq* ("endowed with *Sila*," wise) describes a child who has reached the age of reason and follows the advice of elders. Applied to an adult, *silaittuq* means to lack prudence, judgment, discretion, self-control, or intelligence, and can even mean madness, whereas *silatujuq* signifies someone who is shrewd, cunning, responsible, reserved, and commonsensical. It is the quality of a good leader (*isumataq*).

I mentioned above that each living thing has a certain amount of *Sila* encapsulated inside a bubble (*pudlaq*) with the soul. When a child is born, its soul—a miniaturized image of itself—is set in the bubble with the ambient air of that day, including the climatic conditions. If the weather is bad, people will say the child is *silaluttuq* ("a bearer of bad weather"). If it is good, people will say the child is *silattiavak* ("a bearer of good weather"). This encapsulated air brings the same climatic conditions at death as at birth. At death, the bubble bursts, the soul escapes into the hereafter, and the air of the bubble returns to the ambient air, influencing it near and far. This influence can also occur in the course of one's life during a seasonal move, such as from an igloo to a tent in the spring or from a tent to an igloo in the autumn. During a lengthy spell of bad weather, a *silattiavak* ("a person born on a day of good weather") might be asked to go outside and undress with arms raised above his/her head to be recognized by *Sila*. The individual then cries out, "*Silaga nauk? Ungaa!*" ("Where is my *Sila*? *Ungaa!*"), while rolling on the ground. This was supposed to bring back good weather, as shown by the example of *Iqallijuq* (1971):

> I was born in the spring in warm, sunny weather, in very good weather. . . . One day, my stepfather—my mother's second husband [*Kublu*]—and his hunting companions didn't come back when the weather was very bad and the wind very strong. I didn't know the gale was keeping them from coming back because they had left by boat. It was autumn and because my grandmother was worried, she told me to undress and go outside to face north, and then, with my arms raised above my head, roll several times on the ground while saying, "But where is my *Sila* [the good weather of my birth]? *Ungaa!* [sound of a baby crying]." Because it was very cold, I went back in right away and we went to bed. When we awoke, the weather was once more fine and the boat in sight.

This evocation of the weather of one's birth is addressed to the great cosmic guardians, *Sila* and *Nuna*, and its metonymic action appeals to the main human senses: hearing, when a baby first cries *Ungaa!*; sight and smell, when one exposes one's bare body to *Sila* with arms upraised; and touch, when one rolls on the ground, on *Nuna* (the earth).[7]

A *silaluttuq* ("a person born on a stormy day") could bring the other kind of birth weather, but that option was seldom exercised. It is exercised, however, in the epic of *Kiviuq* (the diver),[8] whose adventures are summarized in Chapter 6. The version told by *Kupaaq* (1972) is much more explicit on this point than those of Boas (1888, 1901) or Rasmussen (1929, 1930a, 1931). Here are some excerpts:

> *Kiviuq* and his younger brother had many camp playmates they often played ball with. These boys included a small orphan who lived alone with his very poor grandmother. The orphan's clothes were continually being torn by the others, but he had no spare clothing. Only *Kiviuq* would give him some to replace them, but these in turn got torn. The grandmother then asked her grandson to get the skin of a baby seal's head. When he brought her a skin, she chewed it, moistened it with saliva, and stretched it out so she could adjust it to the orphan's face. She then placed it on his face, saying, "You'll go to sea and act like a baby seal. You'll surface near kayaks, taking care not to get caught, then you'll swim out to open sea. When you're very far from the coast, you'll cry out, 'But where is my [birth] weather?' while shaking your left arm and hand in the air and crying '*Ungaa! Ungaa!*'" . . . The young boy followed his grandmother's instructions and was pursued by hunters in kayaks. When he made it to open sea, he shook his left arm and hand while crying out, "*Silaga nauk?* [Where is the bad weather of my birth?] *Ungaa!*" Then a very strong wind began to blow from the mainland. The men in kayaks could no longer advance, and everyone capsized and drowned except for *Kiviuq* who, unable to go home, went far away.

The left arm was used in rituals to summon supra-human power. It was the arm with which a shaman would operate. With this gesture, the orphan brings the bad weather of his birth by means of the *Uannaq* (the northwesterly wind). This avatar of *Sila* raises a storm and drowns the pursuers, sparing only *Kiviuq* because he showed the orphan compassion.[9]

For a human being, birth was the first exposure to *Sila* and one's master, an exposure that marked one until death. The rituals of initiation into sha-manism provided a second exposure, at least among the Caribou Inuit, as re-ported by Rasmussen (1930a, 51) in an account by the shaman *Igjugaarjuk*:

> The novice exposes himself to cold and hunger, to drowning and to death by shooting. The manner selected by *Igjugârjuk* for 'exhibiting' him-self was to starve and expose himself to cold.
>
> For the novice receives his special powers by "exhibiting" himself to Hila [*Sila*]—by letting Hila [*Sila*] see him and take notice of him. One says: . . . Hila [*Sila*] must see you and take notice of you. Hila [*Sila*] must keep her eye on you.

For Inuit everywhere, to gain a shaman's clairvoyance was to be reborn. *Iqallijuq* (1971) told me about a rule that a woman in her first pregnancy should also be exposed to *Sila*:

> When a young woman was pregnant for the first time, when she had missed her period, her mother or grandmother would try to find out if she were pregnant by palpating her belly. . . . Next, she was told to go outside for *Sila* to see her, to ensure that her future child would be a boy. For that, she had to go to a place where the snow had no footprints and, with her foot, remove a little snow, which she would put in her cooking pot. That would help her give birth to sons.

When a very young infant receives its soul from a dead person and the soul is positioned in the air bubble inside its body, this positioning is fragile and remains so for the first year after birth. The soul is not yet accustomed to its new body and may escape via the anus or the mouth—openings through which air passes as breath or body exhalations. When a child farts or sneezes, this is a sign of the soul escaping from its *pudlaq* (bubble). You must whistle softly, as when calling for a dog, to bring it back to its place. Such was the custom, which applied to women too, as *Ujarak* (1971) explained:

> A woman thus has to say "*Qaaq!*" (a bursting noise) when, not thinking of anything, a tickling sensation invades her nostrils and makes her sneeze.

She must say that, even if completely alone with no witnesses. Also, when a woman is working on the sleeping platform of her home, when she is sewing, even if her children have gone out and no one is beside her, when she has a sudden urge to fart and farts, she must say "*Qaaq!*" This was really what women would do, to keep their *inuusiq* [life] from escaping out of the *pudlaq* [bubble containing the soul]; this was what they had to say, to ensure that their life wouldn't escape from them, in order that their soul not be diminished, and their life not shortened. This rule didn't apply to men. It was as if your soul and your life were full of air and as if some of it would come out when you sneezed or broke wind. . . . By saying "*Qaaq!*" a woman would keep her life from bursting.

Inuit ethnography is very patchy in describing the movements of body fluids and gases, whose religious value is nonetheless attested by myths, rituals, and beliefs.[10]

Sila's Children

In Igloolik, *Silaat* (*Sila's* children) are certain fantastic animals, often white-coloured and unusual in size, which may not be killed or else one's life will be shortened. Some *Silaat* are said to be bearded seals, polar bears, or caribou. The most often-mentioned ones are caribou. They are said to hatch from *silaaksait* (*Silaat*, embryos), which look like large eggs believed to emerge from the ground (Ujarak 1971). *Silaat*, according to *Ujarak*, are male animals. Their female counterparts are *Pukiit*:

A *silaaksaq* [egg from which the *silaaq* hatches] was seen here on the ground. . . . The *silaaksaq* seen on the ground had the size of a very large egg, but it wasn't a bird's egg. There has also been found a *pukiksaq* [egg from which a *pukiq* is born] . . . A *pukiksaq* is a white-coloured egg, larger than a bird's egg, but smaller than a *silaaksaq*. *Silaaksait* eggs are blue-green in colour. Birds don't hatch from these ground eggs [but rather *Silaat* and *Pukiit*. In this case, strange caribou hatch from them].

They must above all else not be broken when found, or else the consequences will be disastrous for hunting. *Ujarak* (1971) said:

When an egg from the ground is broken, be it a *silaaksaq* or a *pukiksaq*, there will be thick fog and heavy rain.

In Igloolik in 1978, fog covered the village for much of the summer after a dog had broken a *silaaksaq* in a neighbouring camp. From these eggs are hatched *Silaat*—grey-brown, lemming-coloured male caribou almost as big as horses. *Ujarak* (1971) added:

My father tried to catch a *Silaaq*, but he didn't succeed. The *Silaaq* fled, making splashes as it took flight. He continued to pursue it, and the splashing got stronger and stronger. There was fog and rain, and he had to give up the pursuit, for [the animal] had vanished from sight.

Pukiksait are smaller eggs, which hatch into *Pukiit*—white female caribou. *Pukiit* and *Silaat* are very close to *Ijiqqat* ("The invisible ones"). These beings live inland in the mountains and, like white people, are descended from "the girl and the dog" (Chapter 5). *Ijiqqat* live very near caribou and can even turn into caribou (Boas 1907; Rasmussen 1929, 204–8; Saladin d'Anglure 1983). Like *Silaat* and *Pukiit*, they have the power to cause fog and become invisible to their pursuers. In human form, they are invisible to ordinary mortals but visible to shamans. *Sila*'s children include all humans. According to *Iqallijuq* (1971), because humans are children of *Sila* and therefore brothers and sisters of *Silaat* and *Pukiit*, it is forbidden to kill these extraordinary animals and especially to eat them.

Sila's Atmospheric Turbulences

Although the bad weather of *silaluttuq* generally refers to overcast sky with rain and wind, bad weather means any meteorological turbulence of some importance, with or without precipitation. Weather is named after the current wind direction. Its positive or negative value depends obviously on its intensity, on the season, and on special contexts in various places and at various times of the year. Turner (1894) wrote that the Ungava Inuit divide the wind into two systems. The first one encompasses winds from the west, the northwest, the north, and the northeast and is controlled by male spirits. The second system encompasses winds from the east, the southeast, the south, and the southwest and is controlled by female spirits.

This is what Igloolik elders would say (Ujarak, Iqallijuq, and Ijituuq 1971):

> I heard that in the winter, when *Uannaq* [the northwesterly wind] often blew, the stores of food would run out . . . It truly seems that *Uannaq* is a man . . . In the winter it's very cold when he blows . . . The female wind isn't cold enough to make your skin freeze . . . *Nigiiq* [the southeasterly wind] is a woman . . . When *Nigiiq* blew, soft snow would fall, forming a spongy layer . . . The temperature would be warmer . . . Although *Kananniq* [the northeasterly wind] sometimes blows in winter, he especially shows himself in the spring . . . *Kananniq* isn't at all feared because he usually blows in the spring.

Uannaq is the great male northwesterly, bringing cold violent blizzards. *Nigiiq* is his female southeasterly opposite, a gentle wind accompanied by soft, slushy snowfalls. The two are antagonists: when one blows, the other stays calm, and vice versa. They were the winds that Inuit feared the most. The first wind prevented winter hunting at the breathing holes of marine mammals, and the second one melted igloos and made travel by dogsled very hard. When either blew for a long while, a shaman had to be called in to try to calm the wind. Both master spirits, like those of the other great atmospheric entities, are, as I see it, avatars of *Naarjuk*, the master of *Sila*. The closest avatar is *Uannaq*. It is said of him, as of *Naarjuk*, that he is dressed in a laced hide and that the wind comes from the air that escapes through gaps when his laces are distended.

As for *Nigiiq*, she lives in an igloo with her oil lamp. When it becomes too hot inside, the igloo's walls begin to melt and holes form. Through them escapes the warm southeasterly wind, and a shaman would have to go and plug the holes. Such operations took place during public seances, with a stretched hide as a screen between the shaman and the audience. If the wind was *Uannaq*, the hide represented his laced garment, and the shaman had to tighten the lacing. If the wind was *Nigiiq*, the hide represented the walls of her igloo, and the holes had to be fixed.

These characteristics and practices show us the same symbolic system we have already found in Inuit cosmogony. The forces of nature are conceptualized against a background of sexual differentiation, in a relationship of opposition/complementarity. Man possesses the north, the cold, the winter, the qualities of strength and violence, and the activities performed outdoors, with Moon Brother as his symbol. Conversely, woman possesses the south, the warmth, the thaw, the lamp, and the home, with Sun Sister as her symbol. This is according to *Ujarak*'s account, for whom the moon controls one wind and the sun the other (Thérien 1978).

In addition to these forces of nature, we should add the master of the fog (*Taktuup Inua*), another avatar of *Sila*. We know little about him other than a curious ritual. Whenever a dense, persistent fog covered the area and prevented all hunting, the Iglulik Inuit would ask a teenager to attach an artificial penis to his pants. He had to hold it erect and make suggestive gestures, as if making love, while saying:

"Taktuup nuliirpara! taktuup nuliirpara!" ("I've taken the fog's wife! I've taken the fog's wife!").

He would say this while walking in a big circle in the direction of *Sila*—the sun's circular path around the sky. The aim was to shame the fog into going away (Piugaattuq 1990; Iqallijuq 1990; Aipili Inuksuk 1991).

Sila and the Direction of the World

The direction of the world, the direction of the universe, the direction of *Sila*—this is the apparent motion of the entire sky along the trajectories of the sun and the moon, as we will see in the next chapter. It is one of the keys to Inuit cosmology and ritual practices. It is the symbol of the great cycles of reproduction of life and the cosmos: the nycthemeral cycle (twenty-four-hour cycle); the lunar cycle; the cycle of the seasons; and the cycle of human life. Many rituals refer to it. According to *Iqallijuq* (1971):

In the autumn . . . when a family had built their first igloo of snow, . . . they would go out and walk around the new igloo, the man in front, followed by his wife and their children. Then, when they went inside for the first time, they would chew a small piece of meat . . . in honour of their birthplace, whose name they would say. . . . For myself I would say, "I swallow this in honour of my birthplace Qatiktalik." They would also pay homage to the deceased person whose name they were given. People think your birthplace becomes your distinguishing feature. It's the place where you got your name. It's the place where the deceased person's soul changed body.

Thus the whole family, before spending their first night in the igloo, had to walk around their future home by following the sun's path around the sky. The next morning, before sunrise, the children again had to perform this type of ritual (Iqallijuq 1971):

We had to wake them early in the morning, since it was the first night in the igloo. They had to get out right away. . . . the little girls had to go and see *Sila* in order to have fast childbirths later. . . . For the boys, it was to help them catch game animals. For the girls, it was for their future children. . . . It was also to have a long life. . . . They would walk in a circle, following the sun's path.

Festivities were held at the winter solstice, during the darkest days without sun. The Iglulingmiut had the *Tivajuut* festival, when widespread spouse exchange was organized. Each of the festival's newly formed couples had to walk several times along the path of the sun around an oil lamp in the middle of the ceremonial igloo, without making the slightest smile (Rasmussen 1929; Saladin d'Anglure 1993b). In Cumberland Sound, Boas (1964 [1888], 196) recounted that early in the morning men would assemble in the middle of the settlement. As soon as they had all gathered together, they would run screaming and jumping around the igloos, following the path of the sun. A few, dressed in women's jackets, would run in the opposite direction, these being the ones who had abnormally presented at birth. In Igloolik, children born on their belly (*pammangajut*) would walk in that direction (Iqallijuq 1977):

Those ones, the children who were born on their back [would walk in a circle] following the path of the sun. . . . Those who were born on their belly [would walk in a circle] following the sun's path in the opposite direction.

A *nirralajuq* (a baby born on its back), that is, with its face turned up, was believed to have had a normal birth (Saladin d'Anglure 2001b

[2000]).[11] According to elderly Igloolik women, this type of birth was the most common one in olden times. A much less common and particularly abnormal presentation was breech birth—being born feet first. It was also hazardous. Children born that way would have the direction of the fur reversed on their first hat and on their first caribou-skin clothing. Later, they were always supposed to shake a visitor's hand with their left hand. In Kangirsuk (Nunavik), Dalasi Taqqiapik described this custom: when the wind blew in the same direction for a long time, breech-born individuals were made to go outside to reverse the wind direction.

Finally, we should mention a ritual of circumambulation during funeral ceremonies, likewise in the direction of *Sila*. When a corpse had been laid on the ground and covered with stone blocks or snow, the next of kin would slowly walk three times around the grave along the circular path of *Sila* and the sun (Chapter 14, the case of *Ataguttaaluk*).

The relationship between the life cycle and the path of the sun or *Sila* was expressed more explicitly by the direction in which the corpse and the grave were oriented. The orientation varied with age of death. Lieutenant Hooper (1823, 797), who wintered in Igloolik with Parry and Lyon's expedition in 1822–23, gives us a valuable description: "The body was placed, by the husband's direction, on its back with the feet to the Southward, as it is custom for full grown persons. Infants are placed with the feet eastward, half-grown persons South-east, those in the decline of life South-west, and very old people have their feet laid to the westward."[12]

Thus are laid out, from the direction of sunrise to that of sunset, those whom death strikes down between childhood and old age. Thus is kept a harmonious balance between the microcosm of a body that *Sila* shapes and dwells within—for the time of a life—and the macrocosm that animates this body through orderly cycles and unforeseen happenstance.

CHAPTER 4

Incestuous Moon Brother Chases Sun Sister

I recorded this myth with *Kupaaq* in Igloolik, in 1972. One of the best-known myths of the Inuit homeland, *Kupaaq*'s variant has five episodes. It features a brother and a sister who became the moon and the sun after many adventures. Elsewhere in the Inuit Arctic, some of the episodes have other characters: *Kiviuq*, the epic hero of the Copper Inuit; and *Atungaq*,[1] the shaman who in stories of the Nunavik Inuit travelled around the world. Elsewhere, too, some episodes stand alone as independent myths.[2]

Kublu's Story

Thirty years after I recorded this story and its narrator now dead, his daughter *Kublu* (2000) published a much more detailed variant, which she had heard from her father.[3] It differs in many ways from the first one, and I am inclined to think that it either includes details from the tradition of southeast Baffin Island, where *Kublu* had long been living, or combines several versions heard during her childhood. This is the beginning of the second variant, which nicely introduces the one *Kupaaq* told me:

In the spring, when the Inuit had gone to their summer camp, a brother and sister were left behind with their cruel mother; they no longer had any provider because of their father's death during the winter. The brother was left behind because he was blind although he was of hunting age. Before being abandoned, they had nonetheless been given a small piece of meat, a dog, a bow and arrows, and a harpoon, although they were thought incapable of using the weapons. The boy's name was *Taqqiq* [Moon] and his sister's *Siqiniq* [Sun], but between the two of them they would use the terms *aningaq* ["favourite brother"] and *najangaq* ["favourite sister"].[4] *Siqiniq* tried to take care of her *aningaq* because their cruel mother mistreated him. It was the season when people lived in tents, but as they had no tent they stayed in their *qarmaq* [semi-subterranean house].

We learn that the young orphans live with their cruel mother,[5] and that the brother is blind (*tautunngittuq*, "he cannot see").[6] This is one reason why their campmates went off and left him with his family. He cannot join them anymore on the great summer hunts.

Abused by His Mother, the Blind Son Eats Forbidden Meat

The first episode begins in the spring. The sun is at its highest in the sky, and its unbearable brightness reflects off the carpet of snow, forcing the men to wear goggles of wood, antler, or ivory with narrow eye slits to reduce the intensity of the light as much as possible—otherwise they risk getting conjunctivitis or snow blindness.[7] Blindness may last a few days to several weeks, as with *Aningaq*, the young hero of the myth. This is what *Kupaaq* told me:

Three Inuit and their dog found themselves alone when their campmates left them behind. Only one of the three was male, and he was blind. With him were the only two kin he had: his mother and his sister. The brother was blind and couldn't hunt, while being the only one who knew how. Their provisions were quickly running out, and no one else could help. While they were there, a polar bear appeared suddenly and headed for the [skin] window. Since it was in direct view from the window, the mother adjusted the bow and arrow in her son's hands and guided him so that he could aim and shoot at the animal. He shot the bear with his arrow, and a loud noise was heard.

In late winter, starving polar bears often wander close to camps in search of food, in particular the blubber of marine mammals. To kill a polar bear for the first time is indispensable to gaining the status of an adult and provider. The young man's blindness keeps him from seeing his prey, making him depend on his mother. The situation is paradoxical. Normally, to get close to a polar bear unseen and to attack it fearlessly with a spear or a knife, a boy would have been prepared by making him sleep against the back of his father, who would provide him with symbolic protection. This was part of a culturally encouraged process of detachment from the mother, once a boy had been weaned after extended breastfeeding often lasting three years. In the story, however, the young man is not only fatherless but also blind, and far from him being invisible to his prey, it is the prey that cannot be seen by him.

The old woman said, "You've shot the *iqqut* [window frame]! You've shot the *iqqut!*"

A semi-subterranean house usually had a large window above the stone casing of its entrance. The window was a frame of assembled pieces of driftwood and bone, over which was stretched a pane of translucent walrus-penis skin. Using a Greenlandic variant of the myth, Savard (1966) showed the equivalence between the power of sight and sexual potency. This point is borne out later on in the story. In the variants from Nunavik (Arctic Quebec), *Iqqut* is the name of a dog that the mother claims has been hit by the arrow. In either case, she clearly wants to mislead her blind son.

The mother secretly asked her daughter to go and see if the bear was dead. She told her to throw a stone at it for this purpose. When she did so, the bear didn't move. She then asked her to kick it, and she did so, but the bear still didn't move. When they were sure it was dead, the mother began to skin the animal, and then she killed their dog and skinned it too. When she began to cook pieces of bear meat, she also cooked pieces of dog meat. She gave her son dog meat because he was blind. She gave her daughter bear meat because she wasn't blind.

The mother makes her son think she has killed their dog for want of food. The replacement of bear meat with dog meat is doubly interesting.

ᑕᑐᑕᓄ ᐋᓇᒪᓗ ᐱᐱᒐᐃᑕᑕᑯᐸ ᐊᑕᐊᒪ ᐱᐱᓪᐸᑉ ᑕᑐᑕᓄ

FIGURE 11. Moon Brother myth. The blind son shoots a bow and arrow at a
bear as it enters the dwelling. The Inuktitut text says: *Taannataga tautunngituq
anaanaminut pitigiartitausijuq Asuilaa pitigiarsijuq tautunngituq*—This is the
blind boy whose bow and arrow was shot by his mother. Surely the blind boy shot
the bow and arrow. From a drawing by Daividialuk Amittuq Alasuaq, Povungnituk,
1971. Made by Johanne Lévesque. Arichival Fonds of B. Saladin d'Anglure.

First, Inuit have a very special relationship with dogs. These are their only domestic animals and the only animal species to receive personal names. They are thus not seen as potential food.[8] Only when driven to an extreme, during famines, do Inuit decide to kill one of their dogs for food. Second, and more symbolically, dogs and bears are considered to be cross-cousins and opponents in tournaments of strength. On a bear hunt, dogs are used to pursue and corner the prey. Though not the same size, bears are seen as counterparts to dogs, and great spirits harness bears to their dogsleds (Chapter 10); conversely, for newborn children, a dog represents a bear. According to *Iqallijuq* (1971), when a mother finished her postpartum seclusion and returned with her baby to the family home, she would pretend to cook a dog's head and then grab a meat spike, place it in the baby's hand, and make the baby prick its head. The child would thus become a great bear hunter (see also Rasmussen 1929, 176).

His sister put bear meat in her sleeve while she and their mother ate. She would then bring it to her brother for him to eat, unbeknownst to their mother.

The mother cannot mislead her daughter, who saw what happened, but she pressures her to say nothing to her brother about him killing the polar bear. *Najangaq* wishes to help her brother and supplies him secretly with bear meat. In so doing, however, she becomes an accomplice to a serious offence. A hunter is forbidden to consume the meat of his first kill (Rasmussen 1929, 179).[9]

With spring well under way, the mother said to her daughter, "Why did you finish your share of the meat so fast?" She answered that she was very hungry. Actually, she had consumed it so fast because she had been regularly taking some to her brother. Spring was in full swing, and the brother asked his sister, "Is there still ice on the lake surfaces?" She replied, "No, there's no more ice!" "Are there qaqsaut [red-throated loons] on the lake waters?" "Yes, there are qaqsaut on the lake!"

Lake ice lasts long after the snow has melted from the ground and even after the sea ice has broken away from the shore. Loons, like other migratory water birds, wait for the ice to go away before they come to lay their eggs and sit on them by the lake shore. They have very keen eyes. It is claimed they can spot caribou from very far off and will show a hunter the direction in which the caribou may be found by a special motion of their wings and feet. Several species nest in the Arctic, in the spring. The largest loon is the *tuulliq* or common loon (*Gavia immer*), but the most abundant one is the *qaqsauq* or red-throated loon (*Gavia stellata*).

He then wanted to go to the shore of a lake where there were red-throated loons. She led him there, and he told her to return to their tent and erect several cairns on the way back. So she left her blind brother alone by the lake shore [Figure 12].

He must be alone for the success of the healing experience he desires. He must also find his way back after getting healed, using the small piles of stones along the way home.

A Red-Throated Loon Gives Moon Brother His Sight

When no one else could be seen, a red-throated loon came in a kayak to the lake shore and said to him, "Get in behind me, on the stern!"

It is a loon that has metamorphosed into a man. Part of its bird body has become a kayak, with its tail forming the stern.[10] For short kayak journeys, a man customarily made his passenger lie face down on the stern. As Inuit see it, animals conceal human attributes—language, social life, and practices—beneath the attributes of their own species.

He got in, and they went farther and farther away from shore. Suddenly, he was dragged under water while clinging to the bird's back. They didn't stay under for long, for the blind boy was soon out of breath, and they resurfaced.

The man in the kayak once more becomes a bird to dive under water. A loon can move in the air, under the water, on the water's surface, and on the land, although in the last case it does so very awkwardly because of its short feet. Inuit thus consider it a go-between, a mediator. They are awed by its ability to fish under water during lengthy dives while holding its breath for a long time. Because breath (*anirniq*) matters so much to the

FIGURE 12. Continuing the Moon Brother myth. The blind man hears a
red-throated loon and calls out to it for help. The Inuktitut text says: *Taanna
angut sinittasuni ullaakut tuullimut pavviujuviniq qaujigiurtuviniq tikulatsuni
najjitusunilu aulijuq mitsaanut najjituriik taajausuut*—In the morning the man
who was sleeping becomes aware of the annoying loon. From a text and drawing by
Daividialuk Amittuq Alasuaq, engraving on stone. Federeation of Cooperatives of
New Quebec. Made by Johanne Lévesque.

Inuit way of thinking and is associated with *Sila,* they understandably ascribe shamanic powers to this bird. It will give the blind boy clairvoyance
by dragging him down until he is about to suffocate and die.

The red-throated loon asked him, "Do you see something now?" He
answered that what he had seen resembled light. But that was all. They
dove again, and stayed under water longer. He was almost suffocating
when they resurfaced. The red-throated loon asked him again, "Do you
see something now?" He answered that what he had seen looked tall. They
dove again, and when they resurfaced, it was high time for him to breathe
because they had stayed under water much longer. The red-throated loon
asked him again, "So you see something now?" What he had seen hazily
the last time, he now saw very distinctly. He answered he had seen the
shore of the lake. They dove again, and they stayed even longer under
water. When they resurfaced, the red-throated loon asked him, "Don't
you see the lyme grass?"[11] "No," he answered. He hadn't seen any, but he
could see far away. They dove again, and when they resurfaced long after,
the red-throated loon asked him, "You still don't see the lyme grass?" "Yes I
do," he answered. He had seen the lyme grass and the mist rising from the
ground. The red-throated loon then took him back to dry land.

This episode, where *Aningaq* gains superior visual acuity, brings to
mind an initiation ritual where a master shaman makes a novice dive under
water to make him clairvoyant (Rasmussen 1930a). The light (*qaumaniq*)
enables shamans to see spirits, which are invisible to other humans. It also
enables them to read people's thoughts and gain access to knowledge of
the future and the past. Among the Copper Inuit, some shamans would
attach a loon's bill to the front of their headdress.

The red-throated loon went back onto the water, and the man set off
on his way home. He made himself a sling with the top of one of his boots
and, using stones, he tried to hit the cairns his sister had made along the
way. He finally caught sight of the place where he lived. As he came closer,
he saw a polar bear's hide drying on the ground. When he got home he
asked his mother, "Where does that polar bear hide come from?" She
replied, "Some people who came here by boat left it with me when they

went away." It was the hide of the polar bear he had killed, but she claimed that a passing boat had left it with her.

The unworthy mother piles one lie on top of another, thus signing her death warrant. Inuit thought highly of confessing to misdeeds, considering it to be restorative, and it was sought at public confessions—this is why the mother's attitude to her son is so serious. *Kublu*'s variant, by depicting her as a cruel mother to the boy, has a moral message that makes the story more uplifting. The mother violates the family duty to share food and, even worse, denies the boy's achievement—his first kill. The relationship is more ambiguous between the boy and his sister. Out of compassion, she feeds him forbidden meat from his first polar bear, but, fearing their mother, she makes him think it comes from the dog. Her complicity in this transgression paves the way for other transgressions, as we will see further on.

Moon Brother's Revenge and the Origin of the Narwhal

The myth continues with a second episode. Summer has come, the sea ice has gone, and the family still lives isolated in abject poverty.

Since *qilalugait* [beluga whales] were passing by not far from shore, Moon Brother made himself a harpoon. He then kept a lookout on the shore, after tying the end of the harpoon line to his sister's waist, so she could help him hold onto his prey once he had harpooned it.

Beluga whales (*Delphinapterus leucas*) are the size of large dolphins. They are migratory marine mammals that abound in the Arctic in June and July and have a habit of coming very close to shore once the ice has gone. This was where hunters would wait for them, on small rocky headlands. When an adult beluga was harpooned from shore, one man was not enough to hold on to it. He needed a helper whose belt would anchor the harpoon line.[12] Hunting from a kayak was different. At the end of the harpoon line, a float would slow down the fleeing wounded animal so that the hunter could follow it by sight and spear it to death when it resurfaced.

He soon harpooned one. When the time came to eat it, they gave their mother only a small morsel because she hadn't let her son eat any of the bear meat. He told her that if she wanted to get more food, she should help him by tying the end of the harpoon line to her waist.

Aningaq is invoking here an old rule of sharing. To be entitled to a share, one has to take part in the hunt. If one receives a share, other rules allow one to decide how to divide it up with members of one's family, with neighbours, and with any needy person. His words to his mother are all the more persuasive because Inuit love to eat beluga skin (*maktaaq*), which they consider a delicacy, especially after not eating any for a long while. He convinces her by dangling the prospect of her getting a share if she helps, thus exploiting her craving for *maktaaq*.[13]

When some belugas again passed close by shore, his mother said, "That one, that one, the one that is dark grey-blue!"

The mother asks her son to harpoon a very young calf, grey-blue in colour, which is swimming among the pod of whales. That one is easier to catch because it stands out from the white-coloured adults.

He pretended to want to harpoon the one she wished for, but he actually harpooned a big male, which dragged the old woman along and into the water. She began to run on the water surface, while singing, "My son, my son, why do you want me to die? I was the one who cleaned up your pee and poop long ago! I want to go up there to the top of the hill where everything is dry!"

The trap has sprung on the unworthy mother, who has too late understood that her son wants her to die. She wishes to be on dry land atop a hill because women have to make something solid (babies) out of something liquid (their own blood), and because women are secluded during wet menstrual or postpartum periods. After menopause they can finally hope to live as dry people with no restrictions. Hilltops are certainly the driest places you can find in the Arctic, in early summer. Most of the old Inuit myths have a part that is sung.

FIGURE 13. Moon Brother's unworthy mother is pulled into the sea by the beluga her son has just harpooned. The Inuktitut text says: *Tavva nukilauraluarsutik qilalugaq piinngimat sakkusijuq taima anaananga luumartusivuq taannataga qilalugaq*—Here because he harpoons the strongest beluga whale, his mother cries out "lumaaq" from this beluga. From an original drawing by Daividialuk Amittuq, Povungnituk, 1971. Arichival Fonds of B. Saladin d'Anglure.

While she sang, her hair wound itself around the line to which she was tied. She was dragged under water and when the whale resurfaced, she appeared in its wake. After a while she behaved exactly like a whale. She had turned into a narwhal. Her hair, wound up into a coil, had become its ivory tusk. This is why a narwhal's tusk is twisted.

The Iglulik Inuit call the narwhal and the beluga by the same name, *qilalugaq*. To avoid ambiguity, people simply add the qualifier *tuugalik* ("which has a tusk"). The narwhal's tusk looks like a long twisted length of hair. In the Nunavik region, where the myth is very well-known but where narwhals are rare, the mother becomes a beluga tied to another animal of the same species but bigger. In that region she is called *Lumaajuq* ("She who says *lumaaq*"). This is the cry she purportedly makes when surfacing.[14]

Misadventures among the People with Long Claws, the *Qittuarjuit*[15]

The brother and sister were alone now, and they got on their way after abandoning their camp. They walked until winter came, when they reached a camp composed of a single igloo. *Aningaq* began to build one by himself. No one left the other igloo, and he asked his sister to go there and ask for water. He was very thirsty.

When travellers arrive, custom has it that the camp dwellers will go out to greet the newcomers. They must be offered food and drink and helped to put up their tent or build their igloo. This is not the case here, however. *Aningaq* should have been wary.

She went to the door and said, "My *aningaq* ['favourite brother'] is very thirsty, and I've come to get some water!" She was told this answer, "Come in! The top of our door is leaking, so come in backwards!" She lifted the *akuq* [rear panel] of her parka and entered backwards, as she had been asked.

A woman's parka had two panels: a shorter one in front and a longer one behind. For a young single pubescent girl, the rear panel went down to the ground.[16] To have sons, she even had to let it trail on the ground because men must get dirty to find and kill their game animals. It was, however, unseemly for a woman to crawl backwards into or out of a home. She might have complications during future childbirths because her fetuses would likewise want to come out backwards.

But the denizens of the place were in fact *Qittuarjuit* ["Those who have a habit of clawing"]. As soon as they saw her skin appear [because her parka was lifted up], they began to claw at it. And try as she might to call her brother, he didn't hear her right away because he was inside the igloo he was building. He eventually heard her, however, and when he came over he saw that his sister's back was now a big wound, with her flesh scraped raw from the clawing she had received. Once inside, he grabbed a tent pole and used it to spear the igloo's denizens [Figure 14]. They included an old fellow who said to them, "I really tried to warn you about her brother!" He tried to clean his claws, which were still all bloody, and, when he was struck down in turn, he cried out before dying, "*Uggussuk!* [I'm sorry!]."

The old man is the head of the household, and his warning went unheeded by the other family members. His bloody claws nonetheless show he took an active part in assaulting the young girl.

His sister had been so badly clawed that she was very weak. He had to carry her off on his back. He decided to go far away, and for a long while he had to carry her on his back until her wounds eventually healed.

Living among the People without Anuses, the *Itiqanngittut*

The brother and sister continue their quest for social life and campmates, with winter coming to an end.

Then, in early spring, they came one evening to a village. He saw there many chunks of *tunnu* [caribou suet] scattered all around the igloos—morsels of caribou fat that had long been chewed by the camp dwellers. The sister picked up one of the morsels, put it in her mouth, and began to chew, while trying to avoid being seen by people.

FIGURE 14. Moon Brother gets ready to kill a *Qittuarjuk* that has tortured his sister (Sun Sister). From a drawing by Daividialuk *Amittuq* Alasuaq. Engraving on stone, Federation of Cooperatives of New Quebec.

Caribou fat is especially thick in late summer in large males that have spent several months in lush lichen pastures. This fat is much prized by Inuit, who eat it raw along with slices of fillet. With the brother and sister having lived on so little food over the past year, *Najangaq* cannot easily resist the urge to eat a morsel of *tunnu*.

When she put the morsel in her mouth, someone exclaimed, "Those are turds! Those are turds!" These people were *Itiqanngittut* ["People without anuses"]. They had no anuses and consequently put morsels of caribou fat in their mouths and kept them there until a taste/smell of excrement was given off. Only then would they spit them out. It was their way of defecating.

The *Itiqanngittut* are another group of human-looking non-humans. How can we interpret their anatomical uniqueness?[17] In one variant, found in Nunavik during the 1960s, my informant Sakariasi Tarqiapik offered me an interesting interpretation. According to him, these anus-less people were *ukpiit* (snowy owls) in human form. A snowy owl (*Nyctea scandiaca*) mostly feeds on lemmings, swallowing them whole. It keeps them for a long time in its stomach and then throws them up whole. This is why the dried remains of regurgitated lemmings are sometimes found on the tundra, as pellets of compacted skin and bone.

The brother and sister lived among the people without anuses. The sister married one of them. They had sex by using their armpits. She was soon pregnant.

Besides lacking anuses, these beings have no male or female sexual organs. When they make love, the man sticks his elbow under the woman's armpit. In this way, *Najangaq* is impregnated by her *Itiqanngittuq* husband and becomes pregnant.

Her brother likewise married one of them, but since she had no vagina he left her because he was an Inuk [human] who was normally formed. His sister's pregnancy soon came to term, and, when it was time to deliver, her mother-in-law began to make braids from sinew fibres of different sizes. She also made sure her *ulu* [woman's knife] was still well-sharpened. She got herself ready to make an incision in her daughter-in-law's belly for the delivery. She planned to re-stitch the uterus with a finer braid of sinews and then the skin of the belly with a thicker braid.

This is a description of a Caesarean section (incision and then suture of the abdominal and uterine walls). Apart from this mythical reference, no one has ever reported to me any cases of such operations in Inuit oral tradition of the Central Arctic. Nor have I found any mention in the available literature. If, however, prehistoric humans knew how to perform trepanations, why should ancestral Inuit have been unable to do Caesarean sections in desperate circumstances? The question remains open. Braids were woven with caribou sinews and used specially to make watertight flat seams (for boots, kayaks, and tents).

When his sister was about to deliver, *Aningaq* [Moon Brother], who didn't want her to be cut and re-stitched, said to her mother-in-law, "Give her a chance to deliver on her own! If she can't, only then will you cut her!" She gave birth in fact before her mother-in-law had to cut her. She delivered like the real Inuit woman she was. Her mother-in-law then began to shout, "Our daughter-in-law has given birth to a child with an orifice, with an anus, with a vagina! Make yourselves an anus! Make yourselves a penis!" She wanted to give the baby a name, and she said to the mother, "Who will she be? Let's call her *Pualuuk* ['Pair of mittens']!" The mother put a pair of mittens on her baby's hands because she hadn't understood she was supposed to give it a name. Her mother-in-law repeated, "Make yourselves an anus! Make yourselves a penis!" So the people tried to make themselves penises out of oil lamp pokers.

An Inuk would use a homemade poker to adjust the wick and flame of an oil lamp. The poker (*taqqut*) was usually cut out of soft stone. Its long shape and curved end made it an explicitly male symbol, with the oil lamp as a female counterpart. A myth tells how an old woman, who lived alone with her daughter, turned herself into a man by making a penis out of her poker.[18] She then cut off her large lips to make a sled and used her turds to make dogs.

Her mother-in-law was cut so she could have a vagina. But the incision was made too far to the side. She cried out, "My husband has stabbed me, he has stabbed me with a knife! I now have no more hope that my wound will heal!" And she died.

In *Ivaluarjuk*'s variant, *Aningaq* is the one who decides to cut his anus-less wife (*Itiqanngittuq*), so he can procreate with her. And she is the one who cries out her despair before dying (Rasmussen 1929, 80).

Some women survived the incisions but the ones cut at the wrong place died.

The story does not say what happened to the men who made penises for themselves out of pokers.

Moon Brother's Incest with Sun Sister

The last episode likewise takes place among the people without anuses, after Sun Sister (*Najangaq*) gives birth to a daughter. She is then confined to a small personal igloo until her postpartum seclusion is over. Meanwhile, Moon Brother (*Aningaq*) feels sexually frustrated because he cannot find a woman who can meet his needs.

The local people then began to celebrate and dance in a *qaggiq* [a large ceremonial igloo]. While everyone was gathered together in the *qaggiq*, someone sneaked into the little igloo where Sun Sister, who had just given birth, was confined. He blew out the flame of her oil lamp, raped her, and fled.

Confinement to the igloo of reclusion [*kinirvik*] could last a month, until postpartum bleeding had stopped. Only postmenopausal women could visit such recluses. This is the first transgression, with serious consequences for the man and for his community. The second transgression is incest. Although cases of brother-sister incest have been widely reported among the Inuit in settings where young unmarried people live together in close proximity, this practice is just as widely condemned. The third transgression is the deceit of Moon Brother, who has sexually assaulted his sister in the dark while hiding his identity. One may object that Inuit men before the coming of Christianity did not always see rape as a wrong-doing—other than to the victim's husband, who would obtain redress from the assailant. Spouse exchange was relatively common at that time, to the point of making sex more of a community activity than is the case in other cultures.

Unable to discover who had committed the wrongdoing, she relit her lamp and placed her cooking pot above, to blacken it with soot. Several days later the people of the camp were again dancing in the qaggiq when the unknown man came back to blow out the flame of [Sun Sister's] lamp. He fought with her and, finally, raped her again. She rubbed her hand on the bottom of the cooking pot and smirched her assailant's face with the lampblack to reveal his identity. After he left, she put on her boots and went out. She saw that the unknown man was heading for the qaggiq, and she followed. As she got closer, she heard someone say, "Taqqiq [Moon] got his face blackened with soot while trying to have sex with a single woman."

In *Ivaluarjuk*'s variant (Rasmussen 1929, 81), she runs to get her half-moon knife (*ulu*) from her little igloo and hurries back to the *qaggiq* to confront her brother:

There she hacked off one of her breasts, threw it down in front of her brother, and cried: "You are so fond of my body; eat that too!"

The semantics of food and sex overlap in the Inuit language. When in Inuktitut the suffix -*turniq* is added to the name of a food item or a person, the word now means "to eat food" or "to have sex with someone." In the same way, the expression *mamaqpuq* means "that's good" when referring to a food item or a smell, and "good" when referring to a sexual partner. Beyond this semantic overlap, Sun Sister is likening her brother's incest to cannibalism, another practice deemed contrary to nature by Inuit. She offers him her breast to eat, thus merging dietary and sexual codes of con-duct, as Lévi-Strauss (1966 [1962]) would say (see also Savard 1966).

She tried in vain to give it to him, so she set it alight and went out, using it as a torch. He grabbed a portion of a lighted wick from an oil lamp and ran after her.

It may seem surprising to see a breast cut off, streaming with blood—and turned into a torch. The surprise is short-lived if one knows the rich diversity of the Inuit language, which from the root *auk* (blood) has constructed a whole series of terms, like *aumak* (ember) and *aupartuq* (red colour).[19]

They were running away from the *qaggiq*, and the flame of *Aningaq's* torch went out because it no longer had any blubber to burn. The wick merely glowed like an ember, whereas the one held by his sister kept on shining. They rose up in the air, she becoming the sun, and he the moon. The moon is dimmer because his torch has burned out. The sun is bright and warm because hers has not.

In the variant told by *Ivaluarjuk* to Rasmussen (1929, 81), the brother chases his sister around the ceremonial igloo and falls over a block of snow, causing his torch to go out. Their race becomes one of the expressions of *Sila*—a circular motion that expresses the direction of the world. From an Inuit standpoint, the motion is clockwise, from left to right.[20]

The oil lamp symbolically represents the sun. It lights up the microcosm of the home, the family, and the exogamic social order. It also makes cooking possible and definitely separates the bleeding, menstruating woman from the bleeding, raw meat, and by metonymic extension from the meat-providing male hunter. This separation now marks women's faces in the form of a radiant facial tattoo, which symbolically cooks their faces and is made by inserting soot under their skin when they are young girls who have menstruated for the first time.[21]

Sun's brother *Taqqiq* (Moon), with his powerful eyesight and overpowering sex drive, leaves his adventurous earthly existence frustrated and darkened. Yet in the sky he is no less crucial to maintaining and reproducing this order. The moon's cycle is the basis for the Inuit calendar. He also has the tasks of impregnating barren women, bringing game animals to unlucky hunters, and defending mistreated orphans and the disadvantaged of the earth, as we will see further on.

With this myth about the origins of the sun and the moon, we come to a new stage of Inuit cosmogenesis and see a strengthening of the major rules of human society: prohibition of incest, to promote exogamy and exchange of women between groups; solidarity with kin and care for widows and orphans; and sharing of game meat. The two heavenly bodies follow paths across the sky that run parallel to those of the stars. For the Inuit, these paths symbolize the cosmic order and are the major frame of reference for cosmology and for the great rituals, especially rites of passage.

The second and fifth episodes show the two heavenly bodies ending up in symmetrically opposite positions. In one episode, the unworthy mother spirals down into the submarine animal world, her hair becoming the narwhal's spiral tusk. In the other episode, brother and sister spiral up into the sky, after chasing each other around an igloo whose blocks are laid in an ascending spiral.[22]

Disorders on Earth and Voyages to the Stars

Several myths recount the human or animal origins of the constellations.[23] One of the most exemplary ones is the myth of *Ullaktut* ("The Bear Hunters"). On a night of the full moon, a bear is sighted very near a camp, and some hunters immediately go after it on dogsled. Four brothers are on the sled (or three brothers and their brother-in-law, according to another variant; Iqallijuq 1990). One brother's wife has just miscarried and looks at the bear—a forbidden act in her condition (a Natsilik variant states that the brothers' sister is the one who has miscarried and who looks at the bear from the threshold of her *kinirvik*, the igloo where a woman is confined after giving birth). Just then, the youngest brother loses one of his mittens, and the oldest brother tells him to follow the sled tracks back to them. He alone returns to the camp.

Meanwhile the bear, the dog team, and the sled's passengers begin to rise higher and higher into the sky, in the direction of *Sila*. The hunters have unharnessed their dog team so that the dogs can stop the bear (see Figure 15). The dogs become the Pleiades (*Sakiattiat*; or Atlas, Maia, Taygeta, Pleione, Electra, Merope) and surround the bear, which assumes gigantic proportions (*Nanurjuk*; Alcyone). The three hunters form Orion's Belt (*Ullaktut*, "Those who run" [Alnitak, the older brother; Alnilam, the younger; and Mintaka, the brother-in-law]). The old red sled dog is slower

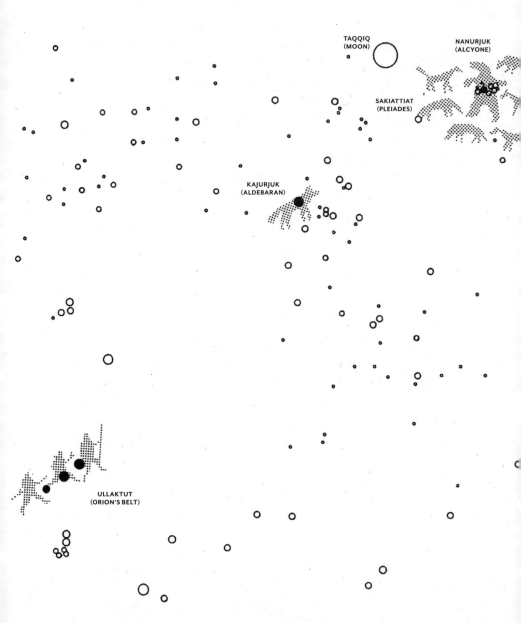

FIGURE 15. Myth of the bear hunters and their dogs becoming
Orion's Belt, Aldebaran, and the Pleiades. Sky over Igloolik (69°
latitude North), 20 December 1988, at 11:00 pm. Designed by B.
Saladin d'Anglure and drawn by Johanne Lévesque.

than the others and remains halfway between the hunters and the bear. It becomes Aldebaran (*Kajurjuk*, Big Red). Part of Orion is thus joined to the Pleiades and Aldebaran in a single Indigenous constellation that seems very frequent among Amerindian peoples, especially those of South America, as Lévi-Strauss eloquently showed in his extensive writings on them (*Mythologiques* 1–4; see Lévi-Strauss 1969b, 1983, 1978, 1981, [1964, 1966, 1968, 1971]).

In Igloolik, after a woman had given birth or miscarried, or during her periods, she was forbidden to look at live game animals, especially big game like bears or walruses. If she did, it was said that the animal would shrink from a large scale to a small one (grow smaller), or the woman would lose her sight. This was how an *aiviq* (walrus, *Odobenus rosmarus*) could shrink to the size of a *kanajuq* (sculpin, *Oncocottus hexacornis*), or a *nanuq* (polar bear, *Ursus maritimus*) to the size of a *tiriganniaq* (Arctic fox, *Alopex lagopus*). In the present story, the scale grows larger and the characters become heavenly bodies. This larger scale creates a gap with the human scale of existence, as does a smaller scale. We will later see the importance of the full moon in this story and the importance of the bear, a mediating animal closely associated with the moon.

Another star-related myth told by *Kupaaq* (1972) is the story of a young orphaned boy who lives with his grandmother. Both of them have been left behind by their campmates, and the young boy is poorly received whenever he tries to get food from their neighbours. One day, while visiting the home of *Utuqqalualuk*, an old man, he helps himself to food, and the old man begins to sing maliciously:

"You orphan, go and gnaw on your mother's tailbone!"

On hearing this curse, with its implied cannibalism, the child runs away and tells his grandmother everything. She replies that if the same thing happens again, he should respond by singing:

"You the wicked *Utuqqaluk*, what have you done with your brother-in-law? Didn't you drown him in the crevasse down there, unbeknownst to everyone?"

So that is what he does on his next visit. The old man responds by going after him with a knife. The child tries to return to his grandmother's igloo, but seeing himself about to get caught near the entrance, he begins to run around the igloo with the old man in pursuit.

On hearing them, the grandmother goes out and in turn begins to run around and around behind them.

They now rise higher and higher into the sky, with the child becoming Muphrid (Mu Boötis) or *Iliarjugaarjuk* ("The little orphan"), the old man becoming *Arcturus* (Alpha Boötis) or *Utuqqalualuk* ("The great wicked *Utuqqaluk*"), and the grandmother becoming Vega (Alpha Lyrae) or *Ningiuraaluk* ("The very old woman"). The first two are commonly called the *sivulliit* ("Those who are ahead") and the grandmother, *kingulliq* ("She who is behind").

This myth is about two transgressions. The first one is the curse on a young, defenceless orphan. Respect for young children and sharing of food with needy visitors are among the most sacred of all Inuit rules. The second transgression is the concealed crime against an in-law, which has been neither confessed nor redressed.

The characters rise up into the sky after chasing each other around the igloo, thus evoking the rising moon and sun, as described earlier. This aerial chase follows *Sila's* general movement along a path from left to right.

The Antagonism of Sun versus Moon and the Dynamic Unity of Opposites

Throughout the last two chapters, I have tried to show that the storyline of the myth may be seen as a long process in which a primordial, undifferentiated state has differentiated into opposing antagonistic and complementary forces. The process began with the differentiation of the sexes. It was followed by other differentiations: day and night, the dead and the living, and war and peace. *Sila* has thus given us good weather versus bad weather, *Uannaq* (the northwesterly wind) versus *Nigiiq* (the southeasterly wind), and Moon Brother versus Sun Sister.

I would like to say more about the last pair and their key role in the Inuit theory of climate variation. Each year Inuit closely monitor the motions of Moon Brother and Sun Sister. They think that each of them wants to triumph over the other by being the first to reappear in the dark January sky. Because of refraction, the sun first becomes visible due south on the horizon for a few minutes on 13 January—instead of 18 January—if the sky over Igloolik is clear. Moon Brother triumphs if he is in his waxing phase when the sun returns. If he is in his waning phase or is absent, Sun Sister triumphs. A victory for Moon Brother, especially a clear-cut one, heralds a cold spring and summer and a long sea freeze-up. Conversely, a victory for Sun Sister heralds a warm spring, an early breakup, and a very warm summer. This antagonism is seen in the term for the January lunar month, *Ingiaqqaqattauk* ("They are competing against each other").

When the full moon shines brighter at night than usual, people in Igloolik see it as a sign that hunting will be poor during that lunar month. Conversely, if it shines less brightly, and if the blue-tinted blackness of the sky stretches to the horizon, game animals will be easier to catch (Kupaaq 1990).

Solar eclipses (*Siqiniq pulamajuq*) are feared. They used to trigger an obsessive panic, as described by Lyon (1824): "An eclipse of the sun took place in the afternoon, while a number of Eskimaux (Inuit) were on board. They appeared much alarmed, and with one accord hurried out of the ship. Before they were all on the ice a brisk squall came on, and added not a little to their terrors. Okotook [*Uquutak*?] ran wildly about under the stern, gesticulating and screaming to the sun, while the others gazed on it in silence and dread. The corporal of marines found two of the natives lying prostrate with their faces to the ice quite panic-struck." The elderly Inuit of Igloolik still remembered the fright of the old female shaman *Ulluriaq* during the total solar eclipse on 31 August 1932 (Kupaaq 1990): The air became very cold all of a sudden, breath turned to mist, and darkness came over the sky. Everybody feared that these conditions would worsen. *Ulluriaq* repeated over and over:

"Sun has gone to earth to give birth! Sun has gone to earth to give birth!"

At that time, when shamanism was still very present, people feared that the pillars holding up the earth and the sky would tremble and collapse, thus destroying the world. I obtained no other comments, but *Ulluriaq* likely feared what seemed to be a sign of Moon Brother's incestuous passion for Sun Sister. This passion would cause an eclipse: the exceptional occultation of one heavenly body by another, but not in the sense of a conjunction. The terms for both kinds of eclipses refer etymologically to the absence of one of the two heavenly bodies. During a solar eclipse, the most spectacular kind, Sun Sister goes down to earth to give birth, according to *Ulluriaq*. This means that Moon Brother has again come to her and

FIGURE 16. *Tivajuut* festival on the Igloolik Island around 1910.
People born during the winter compete against those born during
the summer in contests of strength, skill, and song. After a drawing
by *Atuat* (Blodgett 1986). Made by Johanne Lévesque. Collection of
Terry Ryan.

made her pregnant. The shamans tell us that Moon Brother and Sun Sister share the same double igloo in the sky (Chapter 10). But we also know that no one gives birth in the heavens. Even when Inuit women are taken up above by Moon Brother and made pregnant by him, they still come back to earth to deliver afterwards. The entire order of *Sila* is threatened whenever the act of incest is repeated, the sign being a solar eclipse. As Inuit see it, this order is fragile because Moon Brother's behaviour is unpredictable.

Lunar eclipses are more frequent but less visible and do not arouse the same fear. When one happens, people believe that the lunar month will be shorter, the weather more favourable, and game animals more available. Inuit social and religious life is dominated by an antagonism between the seasons due to an antagonism between the two heavenly bodies, one associated with warmth and summer and the other with cold and winter (Mauss 1979 [1906]). This duality plays out against a background of confrontation and complementarity between male and female (Saladin d'Anglure 2005 [2004b]).

The Cycle of the Seasons

In Igloolik, this antagonism was expressed in an original way. People born in an igloo or a semi-subterranean winter house were called *aqiggiarjuit* (willow ptarmigans, *Lagopus lagopus*), and people born in a tent were called *aggiarjuit* (long-tailed ducks, *Clangula hyemalis*).[24] They played against each other in community games and tournaments of strength or singing ability. The tournaments took place in large ceremonial igloos (*qaggiq*) at the winter solstice. Opponents faced each other, singing songs of derision or playing games of strength or skill (see Figure 16; Saladin d'Anglure 1994b [1986]). Spring contests were outdoors. Adults of both sexes were split into two camps by season of birth and played a sort of football. To win, the *aqiggiarjuit* had to push the ball as far inland as possible, while the *aggiarjuit* had to push it in the opposite direction, as far onto the sea ice as possible. If the first group won, spring and summer would be cooler. If the second group won, spring and summer would be warmer.

Other games corresponded to the winter sun's departure or return. Cat's cradle (*ajaraq*) was mainly for women and not to be played in Sun Sister's presence because it might injure her and make her bleed. It was played especially during the mid-winter time of *Tauvijjuaq* ("The great darkness"), when the sun is totally absent (Boas 1901, 1907; Rasmussen

1929, 183; Saladin d'Anglure 2003a). *Iqallijuq* (1971) confirmed to me the existence of this rule:

> People were not supposed to play cat's cradle in the sun's presence because they might make cuts to her knees . . . , cuts due to playing cat's cradle. Indeed, when the sun had suffered such cuts, it would hide behind the clouds and the weather would get colder for a long while.

Cat's cradle was played during the time of darkness, according to *Iqallijuq* (1971), in order to hold on to the sun and keep it from vanishing for good (Chapter 10). When the sun returned, the game was put aside and replaced by another one, for men: the game of cup-and-ball described by *Iqallijuq* (1971):

> When the sun had come back, people played *ajagaq* [cup-and-ball] a lot. They tried to make the sun climb higher. When they tossed [the ball on the string] into the air, it was as if they were trying to push the sun [to climb] by playing.

We should also mention a solar ritual that was practised at the same time of the year and which, in my opinion, nicely illustrates the dynamic of opposites that characterizes *Sila* and its avatars. This is the ritual of the "twisted smile" or "paradoxical smile" (*illuinanganik qungaujaqpuq*). People pretended to smile with half of their face when the sun made its first appearance of the year. This is what *Iqallijuq* (1971) said:

> When the sun reappeared for the first time, the one who saw it come up was supposed to smile at it with half of his face only, to make the sun shine brighter . . . in fact, it was being made to think, "Since he's making fun of me, I'm going to shine my burning rays on him."

A fact worth mentioning is that in traditional Yupik pictographic art from the Lower Kuskokwim, Alaska, a sad face was usually female, and a happy face male (cf. Saladin d'Anglure 1993b, 84, Figure 13a and b [1989, 155, Figure 13a and b], after Fitzhugh and Kaplan 1982).

Thus once again the antagonistic and complementary duality of male versus female and moon versus sun, already so often evoked, leads us to a dynamic unity of opposites, to *Sila*—source of renewal of the cosmic and life cycles.

CHAPTER 5

A Headstrong Daughter: The Mother of All Human Races and All Marine Mammals

Along with the myth of Moon Brother and Sun Sister (Chapter 4), this myth is the one most often cited from the Inuit mythology of the Central Arctic (Figure 17).[1] *Kupaaq*'s variant, presented here, has two major episodes: the origin of human races, and the origin of marine mammals. These episodes are considered to be two distinct myths outside the land of the Iglulingmiut.[2] The main character is *Uinigumasuittuq* ("She who refused to marry"), who becomes *Kannaaluk* ("The great one down below"). Better known in the literature by the name of *Sedna* ever since Boas popularized that name in his writings, she is also called *Nuliajuk* ("The great wife") by the Aivilik Inuit. Rasmussen (1929, 63–68) published an English translation from a variant he heard in 1922 from the mouth of *Urulu*, the mother of *Ujarak*.

Most of the Inuit from the territories around Iglulik locate the myth there and say they descend from its heroine. The first written reference to this myth, from the Central Arctic, comes from Captain G. Lyon (1824): "The above important personages [shaman's helping spirits] are thus named: Ay-williay-oo [*Aiviliajuk*], or Nooli-ay-oo [*Nuliajuk*], the female spirit . . .; her father Nappa-yook [*Nappajuk*] . . . Out of this host of superior spirits the two first are pre-eminent, although the female is decidedly

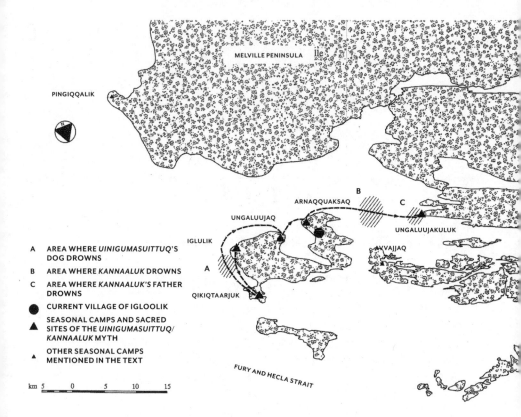

A AREA WHERE *UINIGUMASUITTUQ*'S DOG DROWNS

B AREA WHERE *KANNAALUK* DROWNS

C AREA WHERE *KANNAALUK*'S FATHER DROWNS

● CURRENT VILLAGE OF IGLOOLIK

▲ SEASONAL CAMPS AND SACRED SITES OF THE *UINIGUMASUITTUQ/ KANNAALUK* MYTH

▴ OTHER SEASONAL CAMPS MENTIONED IN THE TEXT

km 5   0   5   10   15

FIGURE 17. Map of the Igloolik region illustrating the movements of the main characters of the myth of *Uinigumasuittuq/Kannaaluk*. After a story by *Kupaaq*. Designed by B. Saladin d'Anglure and made by Johanne Lévesque.

the most important in the eyes of the Eskimaux generally . . . In addition to her power over animals, Aywilliayoo [*Aiviliajuk*] has a boundless command over the lives and destinies of mankind. . . . Immediately within the door of her dwelling, which has a long passage of entrance, is stationed a very large and fierce dog, which has no tail, and whose hinder quarters are black. This animal is by some called the husband, and by others merely the dog of Aywilliayoo [*Aiviliajuk*]; but he is generally considered as the father of Indians and Kabloona [*Qallunaat*, whites] by the conjurers."

She Who Refused to Marry (*Uinigumasuittuq*)

According to *Kupaaq* (1972), the story happened long ago on Igloolik Island:

This is the story of *Uinigumasuittuq* ["She who refused to marry"]. It happened in winter at Iglulik camp. Several suitors wished to marry her and came to propose to her, but she absolutely didn't want to have a husband, and that's why she was called *Uinigumasuittuq*.

Inuit parents customarily decided a child's marriage at birth or during early childhood. The story of this headstrong daughter is surprisingly important in Inuit cosmology and the Inuit belief system. Traditionally, when a male baby reached two years of age, a little newborn girl was betrothed to him. Both would be raised with the idea of later becoming husband and wife. As soon as they could speak, they learned to address each other by the terms of husband-to-be (*uiksaq*) and wife-to-be (*nuliaksaq*), or by the reciprocal term of "future spouse" (*aippaksaq*). In everyday life, it was not unusual for one of the two children to die before reaching adulthood. Other arrangements would then have to be made for the surviving party. The betrothal could likewise be cancelled if one of the families left the territory, or if one of the couples died before their children were old enough to marry.

The myth of *Uinigumasuittuq* is about an isolated family, a fairly rare circumstance, whose daughter has no husband-to-be and no evident wish to leave her family. The rule was that, once married, a woman should go and live with her husband's family, unless she had no siblings. In that case, the parents, rather than resigning themselves to seeing their only child leave, would try to find a son-in-law who would agree to come and live with them.

Her father was angry and, in a rage, told her to marry their dog. . . . She lived in that camp alone with her mother and father, but they had a male dog, *Siarnaq* ["Grey"], a grey-haired dog, which was very often outside.

Family life is not meant to be lived in a vacuum. You need neighbours, hunting partners, and allies. To build such a network, the best way was to start with a double arrangement: a simple exchange between two families where the son and daughter of one would be betrothed to the daughter and son of the other. Boas (1901, 165–67) published two variants of this episode. In the first one, a stone with white and red speckles turns into a dog and marries the girl. In the second one, the father, angry with his daughter's attitude, says to her:

"You don't want to take a husband. Why not marry my dog?"

The next night a man wearing trousers of red dogskin comes to visit and lies down with her. This reference to the dog's colour may be explained by Inuit colour symbolism. White is male, being the colour of the moon, ice, and bone. Reddish brown (and its derivatives of yellow, red, and brown) is female. The dog is associated with both red and white and is thus androgynous, in keeping with its place in Inuit social organization. It is a means of production that a man uses to hunt and transport, and also a domestic animal that is subject to a man and fed by him—the opposite of an ideal son-in-law. But back to *Kupaaq*'s story:

Uinigumasuittuq didn't want a husband, but she nonetheless wanted sex. One night, a visitor, a very handsome man, showed up at the entrance to the family igloo. He wore a necklace with a dog tooth. He was invited to come in, eat, and spend the night with them. He stretched out on the couch and made love to *Uinigumasuittuq*, and then he left before the night was over. He was in fact *Siarnaq*, the father's dog, now metamorphosed into a man. People say he often came back at night in his human guise, and for a long while no one knew he was *Siarnaq*. And so he came back each night that whole spring. When summer came, they realized their dog had been coming regularly in this guise.

Yet he wears a distinctive sign of his metamorphosis, a necklace from which hangs a dog tooth. No one seems to have caught on.

Uinigumasuittuq became pregnant, and her father got angry. He didn't accept his daughter having a dog for a husband, and he decided to take his pregnant daughter and her dog lover to the neighbouring island of Qikirtaarjuk.

Today, Qikirtaarjuk ("The little island") is a headland linked by a narrow strip of land to the much larger Igloolik Island, even at high tide (see Figure 17). But it used to be an island, linked to Igloolik Island only at low tide. Oral tradition has kept the memory of that time when Qikirtaarjuk was an island.[3] It served until recently as a winter camp and, as such, was greatly prized, especially by *Kupaaq*'s family (see Introduction).

Banishment was a traditional Inuit way of punishing blood relatives or in-laws who disobeyed the group's rules. Their lives were spared, but they had to go and live elsewhere. Until the 1970s there was also a custom of leaving sled dogs alone on certain islands in summer and letting them find food on their own, while their masters went inland to hunt caribou with only one or two pack dogs specially trained for stealth hunting.

She and her dog husband now lived on the island. When they no longer had any food, Siarnaq would swim across to get food from her father's camp and then return with the food carried on its back, in a knapsack.

Unlike its cousin the *amaruq* (wolf, *Canis lupus arctos*), a *qimmiq* (sled dog, *Canis familiaris borealis*) is not a predator and cannot, except during the short summer, meet its food needs for long other than by plundering and by eating carrion or its own excrement. In contrast, a son-in-law is sought not only for his ability to reproduce and continue human life, thus ensuring that the names of the dead are reincarnated, but also for his ability to produce and feed his family while also, in due course, providing for his children's grandparents. Here, however, the onus has shifted to *Uinigumasuittuq*'s father to feed his daughter, his dog son-in-law, and their future offspring.

Murder of the Dog Son-in-Law by Drowning

But the father grew irritated at the frequency of these trips. He thought the dog was wearing out its welcome by coming so often for food. So the next time he filled the dog's knapsack with stones, and when the dog went into the water with the sack on its back, it sank straight to the bottom while howling very loudly. The knapsack, overloaded with stones, filled up with water right away. And so the former family dog drowned, going down to the bottom of the sea without ever reaching the island's shore.

Facing a situation with no way out and contrary to the social life and reproduction of the community, *Uinigumasuittuq*'s father has no choice but to get rid of his high-maintenance son-in-law. He cannot kill it, however, as one does a game animal or any other animal. It is the family dog and has a name. So the father uses trickery. Has not the dog deceived him by assuming a human guise and thereby abusing his hospitality and his daughter? In the variant collected by Rasmussen (1929, 63), the father deceives the dog by laying stones in the bottom of a container and covering them with meat. This act calls to mind the dog's origin in Boas's variant (1901), in which the dog is initially a white and red stone. Here, it is drowned by a load of stones and red meat.

For a man to kill one of his sled dogs was serious and exceptional. We will see further on how a man kills his lead dog because it has cried out like a human (Chapter 8). A dog would also be killed if guilty of killing a human, for fear it would kill others. Sometimes, a dog might be killed to save the life of its seriously ill master, in the belief that the dog's life force would strengthen his. The killing was thus a ritual canicide.[4]

In the above episode, the drowning of the dog is accompanied by desperate howling. Inuit sled dogs do not bark. They howl like wolves when something odd happens, such as when they nowadays hear the sound of a bell or a high-flying airplane. When mourning, Inuit express their grief without words, through a sort of collective sobbing that resembles the howling of a dog or wolf.

Once it [the dog] had sunk to the bottom, the father began taking food to his daughter by kayak. But when he got to Qikirtaarjuk he saw the many offspring of his daughter and the dog. They too were very hungry, and the father often had to bring food by kayak. Even after eating, they weren't full and would lick the blood that stained the kayak. One day when he came by kayak with a load of food, they ate all of the provisions without leaving a thing, and then licked all of the blood on the kayak.

In *Kupaaq*'s variant, the children of *Uinigumasuittuq* and her dog husband are born after their father drowns, unbeknownst to the grandfather until he finds out he has half-human, half-canine grandchildren. Having caused the death of his troublesome son-in-law, he must now be the male provider for his daughter in almost incestuous circumstances (Savard 1970).[5]

After her father left, *Uinigumasuittuq* said to her offspring, "When your *ittuq* [grandfather, literally 'your old one'] comes back, pretend to lick his kayak but devour the skin that covers it." And so it was done. When he came back by kayak with food, they greeted him on the shore and, pretending to lick his kayak, they ate its skin covering after ripping it apart with their teeth.

Uinigumasuittuq decides to get back at her father. By attacking his kayak, she in fact attacks his male identity as family provider and head of the household. The kayak was a key social symbol for Inuit. Just as the igloo represented a woman's body, the kayak represented the body of a producing and reproducing man. It had a backbone, ribs, and a phallic bow, which in Inuktitut was called *usuujaq* ("that which looks like a penis").[6] To get married, a young man needed a kayak, his main tool for being productive in summer, just as he needed a dogsled in winter. The sled's slightly erect front likewise had a phallic connotation (it was called *uirniq*, "that which lifts itself onto," a term related to *uik*, "husband"). In the Kangiqsujuaq region, where kayaking persisted until the mid-1960s, only the kayak owner's wife was allowed to sew the rawhide covering the bow.

The father is thus castrated when the skin on his kayak's frame is eaten. In a variant published by Boas (1901), *Uinigumasuittuq* tells her pups to attack and devour her father, and this they do. There are parallels here with Moon Brother's murder of his mother. *Uinigumasuittuq* tries to cut her ties to her father, who fed her with his sperm when she was a fetus. Similarly, Moon Brother figuratively cuts the umbilical cord that has tied him to his mother since his life in the womb. He then ties himself to another line, a harpoon line, and sends her to the world of marine mammals for the rest of her life (see Figure 13).

The father could no longer go home. He waited for low tide and managed to cross when a strip of land linked Qikirtaarjuk to Igloolik Island. He got home and made a small open boat with a walrus skin over a frame of assembled bones.

This is an *umiaq*, a multi-passenger boat that is open on the top and used to transport family members in summer. Such boats came in several sizes. In the Eastern Arctic, *umiat* (plural of *umiaq*) could each carry thirty or so people with their luggage and were still being used in the early twentieth century. A single boat was covered with around seven bearded seal skins. In the Igloolik region, the *umiaq* fell out of use earlier, undoubtedly under the influence of American whalers who were sailing the waters of Hudson Bay as early as the mid-nineteenth century. They provided whaleboats to Inuit who helped them hunt bowhead whales. This myth describes a small *umiaq* whose frame of assembled bone and driftwood pieces is covered with a single large walrus skin.

The Mother of the Different Human Races

Because their grandfather had left Qikirtaarjuk Island and would undoubtedly not come back anymore, *Uinigumasuittuq*'s children were hungry and whimpered for more food. Their mother tore off an old sole from a boot and, hoping her children would find a safe haven, put some of them on the sole, which she placed on the water of the sea and sent away from shore, southeastward, while there was heavy fog.

Through this founding act, born out of desperation, *Uinigumasuittuq* begins to populate the world by sending her offspring away in different directions, first southeastward. The presence of fog alludes to an act of magical transformation and change of scale. The spirits are thus shielding themselves from human eyes.

Because of the fog, they soon could no longer be seen, but metallic noises were heard. The sole had turned into a large ship of the whites, which left for the country of the white people, where they found a home.

Although she gradually loses sight of the frail boat as it goes off into the mist, *Uinigumasuittuq* can hear the signals of its transformation—metallic noises, which at that time are still unknown to the Inuit but will soon mark their first encounters with white people. A shamanic seance would likewise take place out of sight of its attendees once the oil lamps had been extinguished. People had to use their sense of hearing.

When the Inologenous people of the Caribbean met Christopher Columbus and first heard the sound of a bell, they too were surprised. For the Inuit, the coming of the Europeans was associated with the discovery of new sounds. Many ships of exploration left Europe for Arctic shores with musicians aboard who, as the ship came close, would play to the Inuit on shore to gain their curiosity and friendship (Saladin d'Anglure 1981).

The first whites came to Igloolik Island from the southeast in 1822 with the British expedition commanded by Parry and Lyon (see Foreword). This first stage in the dispersal of *Uinigumasuittuq's* children extends the myth into the historical era in a very shamanic, circular fashion, as will the succeeding stages with her other children. As *Uinigumasuittuq's* descendants, the *Qallunaat* ("Those with long eyebrows," the white people) are cousins of the Inuit, and their return was, in a way, determined in advance.

The mother sent others [of her children] to the mainland, southwestward, and they became the *Iqqiliit* ["Those who have nits," the Indians].

The Chipewyan inhabit the woodlands just below the Inuit-occupied tundra. They therefore live to the southwest and inland, whereas the Inuit are more coastal. Relations were historically hostile between the two groups, and Inuit have memories of many bloody clashes with the Chipewyan in the second half of the nineteenth century. These memories still feed into a negative image that Inuit have of the Chipewyan being cruel and bloodthirsty like wolves and covered with nits.

With European trading posts being first established in woodland areas, the First Nations clearly had greater access than the Inuit to firearms and metal. These trading contacts aggravated the hostility that already existed between the two peoples. At the limits of James Bay and Hudson Bay, traders from the Hudson's Bay Company encouraged the Cree to launch punitive raids on the Inuit whenever the latter murdered any of their agents. This led to a traffic in Inuit scalps that, according to archival records, extended even to First Nations in the Montreal area. Thus, First Nations were traditionally both neighbours and enemies.[7]

[She sent] others [of her children] northwestward, and they became the *Tuniit*. The *Tuniit* differed from the Inuit in that they were much stronger.

Tuniit is the name Inuit give their predecessors on the land—its first inhabitants.[8] In this, the *Tuniit* differed from the whites, who have since established themselves amid the Inuit and the First Nations, who still live to the south. By making the *Tuniit* descendants of *Uinigumasuittuq* and her dog husband, the myth reverses archaeological findings, which show that they actually preceded her and other Inuit in the Arctic. The myth reverses historical reality a second time by having the *Tuniit* go off in the direction from which they actually came: in the direction of Alaska and Asia.

The Boas (1901) variants do not mention the *Tuniit* among *Uinigumasuittuq*'s descendants but instead speak of the *Inugagulligait* (or *Inugagulligarjuit* in the Iglulik dialect), a dwarfish, human-looking people discussed in Chapter 3.

Finally, she sent the last ones [of her children], northeastward, where they became the *Ijirait* (Figure 18), whom she made very powerful. Their power is unknowable to Inuit, but they know Inuit very well and know what caribou hunters do, wherever these may be. They know all about humans, even when very far away and themselves invisible to humans.

The *Ijirait* or *Ijiqqat* (plural of *Ijiraq*), whose name means "the invisibles," are a human-looking people who lead lives parallel to those of the Inuit, but inland. They live mainly on the mountainous plains of Baffin Island, northeast of Iglulik. Their name comes from their ability to make themselves invisible. They are great caribou hunters, and it is said that they can run and catch up to a caribou and, using a stone, knock it out with a blow to the skull. It is also said that they can turn into caribou and have exceptional vision. They feel much compassion for unfortunate humans and seek to establish emotional relationships with them. Inuit shamans were happy to have them as helping spirits, and more than one ancestor of Igloolik's current inhabitants is supposed to have gone to live with them.

So this is how Inuit describe the descendants of *Uinigumasuittuq* and her dog husband—the *Ijirait*, the First Nations, the white people, and the *Tuniit*—and these attributes help define Inuit identity by showing the various forms of otherness. The First Nations coexist belligerently and are cruel, being often compared to wolves; they live to the southwest. The *Tuniit* lived in the Inuit homeland at an earlier time and were strong, but their strength was indiscriminate and fragile; they fled to the northwest. White people are skilled in navigation and technology, making episodic voyages from the southeast. Finally, the *Ijirait* are gifted with clairvoyance, Herculean strength, and great speed for travel; they occupy the northeastern mainland of Baffin Island, a country of caribou and a paradise-like refuge in the Inuit imagination. In the variants published by Boas and Rasmussen, the Inuit consider themselves also to be *Uinigumasuittuq's* descendants. When I questioned my Igloolik informants on this point some thirty years ago, none doubted that white people were their distant cousins.

Two Suitors Are Turned Away

Now that he had a new boat, made from a large walrus skin, the father joined his daughter *Uinigumasuittuq*. She had been alone since the dog's death and her children's dispersal. Her father, who was getting ready to move away, came to get her with his skin boat and take her to his place [to Iglulik camp]. When she arrived [at the camp], it was now summer. They packed their possessions and moved a little farther away on the island, following the shoreline to a place called *Ungaluujaq*.[9] As they pitched tent at *Ungaluujaq*, a man arrived by kayak, a handsome, long-haired man. His hair was done up in a topknot above his forehead [*suluvvaut*], and he wore a splendid caribou-fur ceremonial coat [*qaliruaq*], wondrously decorated with white fur and with slits on both sides and also in front and behind. He was in fact a *pangniq* [adult male caribou] that had metamorphosed into a man. He had arrived in front of the tent, at low tide, and now cried out, "May *Uinigumasuittuq* come down to the shore!"

ᑕᐃᒪᓓ — ᐃᐱᒪᓓᒋᑕᐅ� ᐅ

ᐃᑉ ᕋᐅᓂ ᕋᑕᐅᔪᕐ ᓇ

ᑐ ᑐ ᒥ — ᐊᑎ ᒋ ᖃ ᕐ ᓓ ᑎ

FIGURE 18. Representation of an *Ijiraq*, dressed in a caribou skin coat, who is invisible to common people. These beings, whom the shamans can see, live in the interior caribou-hunting country, and their faces possess some caribou features. They can also become caribou. The Inuktitut text says: *Taimanna – isumannartuksauvuq Ijiraunirartaujuq, tuktumik – atigiqarlutik*—Thus one would think when speaking of *Ijirait* that they are wearing caribou skin coats. Drawing by *Agiaq*, Igloolik.

The topknot above the forehead is one of the distinctive signs of a *tuktu* (caribou, *Rangifer tarandus*) that has turned into a human. Its front antlers have become a forehead topknot, such as men sometimes wore. Another sign is the splendid coat, wondrously decorated with trimmings of white fur (*pukiq*) and made with four slits, these being characteristic of a ceremonial garment (*qaliruaq*). In Chapter 8, we will see a caribou metamorphose and turn its chest into a kayak to cross lakes and rivers. The tip of the caribou breastbone is called *uirniq*, the same name as the raised tip of a sled, and is a phallic symbol like the bow of a kayak (see above). A little girl would wear an amulet made from the tip of a caribou breastbone, and she would hang it from her neck to give birth to sons later.

But *Uinigumasuittuq* didn't even answer. And the man who came for her left as he had come. Another man in a kayak showed up, and his hair was cut short [*kijjaq*] above his forehead. He was a metamorphosed wolf.[10] He in turn began to cry out, "May *Uinigumasuittuq* come down to the shore!" Again she didn't answer, although she was there, and he went away.

The Fulmar Husband

After he left, there arrived a third kayak whose occupant wore snow goggles and a *natsiruti* [sealskin garment]. He looked tall, but in fact he sat on his tail to make himself seem taller. When he landed in front of the tent, he cried out, "May *Uinigumasuittuq* come down to the shore!" *Uinigumasuittuq*'s mother then said to her daughter, "It's for you. Only you are called 'She who refused to marry!'" The daughter acquiesced, saying, "Here I am!" She took a small sewing bag, made from a walrus kidney membrane, and went down to the shore, thus accepting his marriage proposal. She crouched down in the back of his kayak, and the man with eyes covered by snow goggles went out to sea, toward the drifting ice floes.

In Nunavik in the mid-1960s, one could still see passengers travelling this way, crouched down or lying face down in the back of a kayak.[11] When the kayak was large enough, more than one passenger could be carried inside. Of course, the sea had to be very calm. A woman usually had little luggage, her sewing equipment being most important. Her husband could make everything else for home life on site (oil lamp, stone pots, various scrapers, and so forth).

When they drew up alongside an ice floe, he got out to urinate. Only then did the girl notice with astonishment his very small legs, for he used his tail to sit on. He then turned to his new wife and burst out laughing, "Do you see my stool? *la-a-a-a!*" He then took off his snow goggles and said, "Do you see my eyes? *la-a-a-a!*" His lidless eyes were completely red. He looked handsome with his goggles on, but in reality he was hideous. He was a hideous *qaqulluk* [northern fulmar]. She wanted to leave him but no longer could, and once again she had to get into his kayak and squat in the back.

Her disappointment is great. The tall, young, and handsome man she thought she had married is in fact a northern fulmar (*Fulmarus glacialis*, also known as stormy petrel).[12] In the variant reported by Rasmussen (1929, 64), the daughter begins to cry, and her bird husband bursts into laughter again. When travelling in a kayak or an *umiaq*, it was not unusual for the travellers to stop off on a drifting ice floe to urinate or to get fresh water.

He thus brought her to his camp, at Arnaqquaksaq.[13] This was where he lived. This was where his tent was pitched. He told her to go in and take her place on the left. It was a tent made from *nattiaviniit* skins [young ringed seals].[14] He often left to go hunting, leaving her alone in the tent. One day *Uinigumasuittuq*'s parents decided to relocate in their walrus-skin boat to Ungaluujakuluk [little Ungaluujaq],[15] on the mainland. On the way, they came within sight of Arnaqquaksaq and stopped to visit their daughter. On reaching her place they saw she was alone and unhappy and decided to take her with them.

This second experience with marriage takes *Uinigumasuittuq* from one extreme to another. Whereas her first husband, a domestic dog, did not know how to hunt, her second husband, a wild bird, spends his time looking for food far away. She who had refused so long to leave her father's home is now reduced to solitude and remoteness from her family.

The Origin of Marine Mammals

Because her husband had gone hunting far away in his kayak, she had no way to tell him about her departure. Her father nonetheless decided to take his daughter away without delay, and everyone embarked to cross the arm of the sea that separated them from the mainland.

Parents had a responsibility to ensure that their daughter was well treated by her husband and, if need be, to take her back home if they felt she was unhappy. Here there is no mistreatment but rather deceit, disillusion, and solitude. The father may also be acting out of excessive attachment to his daughter. After killing his first son-in-law, is he seeking to get rid of the second one? I earlier mentioned the problem experienced by couples without sons, who would try to find a son-in-law willing to come and live with them.

After travelling some distance from their starting point, they noticed a kayak following them. It was the *qaqulluk* [fulmar] husband pursuing them to take his wife back. This was out of the question for her father. The *qaqulluk* man then stopped paddling, leaned toward the front of his kayak, and vanished from the view of those he was pursuing. Then suddenly a large fulmar appeared in the air, flew up into the sky, and then, nosediving on the fugitives, flew down to the surface of the sea, which it beat with its broad wings. The water darkened and a strong wind was created by the wings of the fulmar, which kept on nosediving until it stirred up a violent storm.

A fulmar is a seabird with very long wings that enable it to fly very great distances. Although it can nosedive to the sea surface to snatch a fish it sees from the air, its thick plumage makes underwater diving impossible (Randa 1994). Like the loon, the raven, the peregrine falcon, and the eagle, the fulmar has, according to Inuit, magic powers, which it uses when mistreated, deprived of its eggs, or robbed of its nestlings. It notably has the power to stir up bad weather and storms.

Despite being a bird, it asked to see its wife when it flew very close to the boat. In his skin boat, the father took fright and began to throw his daughter's boots into the sea, and then one by one all of her clothes.[16] For a few moments the pursuing bird stopped, but on discovering this trickery it began nosediving again and making the storm even worse.

The variant of this myth reported by Rasmussen (1929, 65) provides fewer details about the preceding episodes but much more about the fulmar's confrontation with the fugitives. The fulmar first calls out to its father-in-law:

"Let me but look at those dear hands that belong to me." This he said because the girl lay covered up with skins in the middle of the boat, and no part of her could be seen. But the girl's father answered scornfully, "How can one who is only tall with a stool to sit on, one whose face is covered by spectacles, how can such a one ever have sweet little hands belonging to him?" At this the stormy petrel [fulmar] grew angry and flew over the boat; it made first some powerful movements with its wings, and then sailed in over the boat, so that a storm arose from the beating of its wings: the waves rose, and the water began to come in over one side. Then again the stormy petrel [fulmar] cried: "Only her hands, the dear little hands that belong to me: you must let me see them."

But the father will have none of it. The bird then flaps its wings all the more, and the storm becomes so strong that the boat almost capsizes. It may seem surprising to hear the fulmar refer to its wife as "those dear little hands," but in Inuit culture a wife's ability to sew was highly valued. Now back to *Kupaaq*'s story:

There were no longer any clothes to toss into the water, and his daughter was naked. Panic-stricken, the father threw his daughter overboard into the sea.[17] But she clung with her hands to the gunwale. He chopped off the fingers of one hand with his axe, and the severed fingers turned into ringed seals. She was still hanging on with her other hand, so he chopped it off as well and then punctured her eyes. Completely blind and no longer able to hang on, she sank to the bottom of the sea while her severed members turned into ringed seals and bearded seals.

No longer will the "dear little hands" ever be used for sewing, and an interesting reversal now takes them from the female world of sewing to the male world of hunting. Versions of this scene differ from one region to the next.[18] *Kupaaq*'s story has the father puncturing both of his daughter's eyes. Other versions have him puncturing only one. In any case, he harms her ability to see. We have already seen the key role of vision in the myth of Moon Brother and Sun Sister (see Chapter 4). *Uinigumasuittuq*'s punctured eyes—her second disability—exclude her for good from all housework and all body care, such as combing her hair. From now on she will be called *Kannaaluk*. In the oldest recorded reference to *Nuliajuk* (*Kannaaluk*), by Captain G. Lyon (1824), she was the helping spirit of the shaman *Tulimaq*, who freed the various animals by amputating the young woman's hands. This may have been a shamanic ritual related to the one reported by Boas (1888) from Cumberland Sound, where the shaman harpooned *Sedna* (another name for the same character) through the ice to make her free the marine mammals. This ritual seems to re-enact the myth. Here is what Lyon (1824) wrote: "But as the spell by which the animals are held lies in the hand of the enchantress, the conjuror makes some bold attempts to cut it off. . . . If deprived of her nails, the [polar] bears obtain their freedom; amputation of the first joint liberates the netyek [*nattiq*], or small seal [ringed seal]; while that of the second loosens the ooghiook [*ujjuk*], or larger kind [bearded seal]. Should the knuckles be detached, whole herds of walrus rise to the surface; and should the adventurous annatko [*angakkuq*] succeed in cutting through the lower part of the metacarpal bones, the monstrous [bowhead] whales are disenthralled."

Among the Iglulik and Aivilik Inuit (Rasmussen 1929, 127), shamans would instead try to win over *Kannaaluk* by gentle and seductive means—by combing her hair and by speaking to her softly—to make her free the animals she held prisoner as head lice for human wrongdoings. Whereas human finger bones become marine mammals in the myth, in daily Inuit life the little bones of marine mammals (ringed seals) were specially set aside for complex games.[19] These games, like cat's cradle, had countless versions and variants. Each finger bone might be a human or animal figure, a part of the home, a litter of pups, or something else. Be it a game of chance or skill, the fun of play showed how unequal everyone was in reproduction, hunting success, manual dexterity, and longevity. For the time of a game, the players had a chance to replay their destinies on a small scale, in a circular and ever-renewable space-time.[20] But back to *Kupaaq*'s story:

The despairing father rushed back to dry land at Ungaluujakuluk, where he landed at low tide. While his wife pitched their skin tent, he took the bearskin they used for a mattress, spread it out not far from the water, rolled himself up in it, and let himself be covered by the rising tide. He thus joined his daughter at the bottom of the sea, where together they would be called *Kannaaluuk* ["The two great ones down below"].[21] They have with them their big dog *Siarnaq*, which likewise drowned and has become the guardian of their underwater home.

In his story, *Kupaaq* (1972) added:

It is known through the shamans that those who have committed wrongdoings, especially sexual offences, are sent after death to the home of *Kannaaluk* and her father. When the deceased is a woman, the father tortures her by clawing her vulva with his nails. When the deceased is a man, the daughter tortures him by clubbing his penis with a snow stick.

When humans disobey the rules of social life and the rules governing animals or the environment, *Kannaaluk* keeps the marine mammals in her tangled hair, in the form of head lice. Because she no longer has hands or the use of her eyes, she can no longer untangle her hair. To plead on behalf of humans and to release the marine mammals, as we have seen above, a shaman has to visit and seduce her by combing her hair. The shaman promises that the rules will be scrupulously obeyed and then goes back to tell his group about the success of his effort.

This great myth, which dominates the mythology and ritual system of the Inuit of the Central and Eastern Arctic, reaches its most elaborate form at Iglulik. It categorically condemns any inclination to female sexual autonomy and any rejection of the parents' authority to arrange their children's marriages. In the myth of Moon Brother and Sun Sister, we see condemnation of marriage between partners too closely related, that is, incestuous marriage. This is why the lunar and solar cycles were created and why the right distance must be kept between siblings of the opposite sex and between the sun and the moon. In the myth of *Uinigumasuittuq/Kannaaluk*, we see stigmatization of marriage between partners too distantly related, such as a human marrying an animal, here a domestic animal like a dog. Although the heroine manages to have offspring with her dog husband, she does so at the price of losing him and being separated from her children, who become those human groups that are farthest from the Inuit in time and space. Therefore, animals should be respected, but they should also serve humans. Dogs serve humans as a means of transport or as help for hunting. In return, they are fed. Wild animals offer humans their bodies as food or as raw material for making clothes, homes, boats, or tools. In return, humans must show them esteem and respect.

When questioned in the early 1970s about the seriousness of disobeying parents when the time comes to choose a spouse, the elders answered that such a wrongdoing was much more serious than Moon Brother's incestuous rape of Sun Sister.

Kannaaluk dislikes light, which takes away her power. This was why a shaman would extinguish the oil lamps when going to visit her during a community seance. This was also why her dictates and prohibitions were stricter during the long winter nights from the autumn equinox to the spring equinox. After being deprived of her offspring and her two successive husbands, *Uinigumasuittuq* alias *Kannaaluk* became the mistress of marine mammals and the guarantor of rules governing marriage and sex. She is excluded from women's housework and family life, and she ensures obedience of the rules governing reproduction of human life and production of game animals.[22]

Kannaaluk and Shamanic Space-Time

A single group of siblings—*Uinigumasuittuq*'s offspring—thus includes several peoples: the Chipewyan, a people next to the Inuit; the *Tuniit*, a people before the Inuit; the *Qallunaat*, the white people, who have recently come by sea; and the *Ijirait*, an invisible inland people. This inclusiveness expresses a circular view of space-time where the before time and the after time, the visible and the invisible, the episodic and the permanent share the same plane of reality. This view of space-time is also expressed in the greater whole that encompasses all marine mammals: polar bears, ringed seals, bearded seals, walruses, and bowhead whales, which all come from *Kannaaluk*'s hands and are held in her home when humans commit serious wrongdoings.

Finally, this view of space-time is expressed in the shaman's belt, which brings together the wearer's manifold experiences and powers. Let me quote Rasmussen (1930a, 56–57) and his example of a belt belonging to the shaman *Kinaalik* of the Caribou Inuit:

> She . . . had a special shaman belt, to which were fastened the following:
>
> —a piece of a gun butt, which she had to carry because she had become a shaman through "death visions," i.e., death by shooting;
> —a piece of sinew thread which had held two tent poles fast and had been used for *qilaneq* (divination);
> —a ribbon that had once been tied round a piece of tobacco she had been presented with . . . the ribbon that had been round the gift acquired miraculous powers, when placed on the shaman belt;
> —a piece of the cap of . . . her dead brother [who had become her helping spirit];
> —feet [of] a polar bear that was her helping spirit;
> —an ordinary piece of white caribou skin, which had received magical powers because it was a gift;
> —a piece of knitted vest that had belonged to a white man;
> —a caribou tooth;
> —mittens of caribou skin;
> —a piece of skin from a seal flipper.

Thus, gifts from her various Inuit or white patients were next to objects and relics that evoked her shamanic training, her dead or living helping spirits, and various land or sea animals. All of these elements from different worlds, times, and places joined forces when fastened to her belt. In her work as a shaman she recreated the unity of the cosmos, making herself stronger, more powerful, and more effective.

CHAPTER 6

A Cheated Husband and Thwarted Love in the Animal World

This chapter has three stories that in the Igloolik region are told as a single myth featuring an unhappily married man in a loveless marriage.[1] *Kupaaq* told me the stories in 1973, in Igloolik. He in turn had heard them from his mother *Alariaq*, who had died in 1972. The first story is about a childless couple. While her husband spends his days away from home hunting *tuktu* (caribou, *Rangifer tarandus*), a woman lets herself be seduced by a lake spirit, in fact a lake penis. The second story tells us the man's misadventures with a new wife, a fox woman. The third story is about the same man, unhappily married this time to a goose woman.

An Unfaithful Wife Devoured by Maggots (*Qupiqruqtaujuviniq*)

A man and a woman had no children. They lived alone and inland, where they hunted caribou. They lived there completely alone. The man hunted caribou with his bow and arrows (Kupaaq 1973).

Childlessness, which the narrator highlights as the story begins, was considered a calamity. A couple should ideally have at least one daughter, to help the mother, and one son, to help the father. When a couple could not have any children, they would try to adopt or temporarily exchange spouses with another sterile couple to increase their chances of procreating.

When he came home, his wife would make a fire with the brushwood she had gone to gather to cook the meat he had brought.

In the variant published by Rasmussen (1929, 221), the hunter leaves home for very long periods. Such absences, though frequent, are considered risky. To venture alone into remote areas far from dwellings and far from footprints means risking encounters with spirits. This is as true for a man hunting by himself as for a woman getting brushwood for her cooking fire or gathering wild berries.

She would go off for a long time looking for brushwood to feed the fire.[2] One day she went out looking again, and he followed her unseen.

The husband is suspicious. According to other variants, the home is disorderly when he comes back from hunting, and the housework neglected. What has she been doing with her time? The food has not been cooked yet, and he has to wait longer than usual for his caribou stew—his homecoming meal.

She began to gather brushwood, while he watched closely. After picking up the kindling, she went to the shore of a lake and cried out while throwing a pebble into the water, *"Usuk! Mauna nuili!"* ["Penis, emerge here!"]

In the variant published by Rasmussen (1929, 222), she cries out:

"Oh penis of the Lake Spirit, come up to the surface and show yourself!"

Lakes, rivers, mountains, rocks, or islands are possessed by spirits (*inuat*) that respond to the presence of humans, especially humans who are lonely or in distress. Spirits try to come to them, either to seduce and drag them into their world or to partner with them, as they do with shamans. It is implied here that the woman is suffering from her childlessness and solitude. *Kupaaq*'s story continues:

Then, so it is said, after she threw the pebble, a penis appeared at the water surface. She right away took off her *qarliik* [trousers][3] and waded out to the penis.[4] Seeing this, the husband seethed with anger against his wife who was behaving so wrongly.

He is angry at her not only for having sex with a man other than her husband but also for doing it in hiding and neglecting her housework. Inuit, as we will see later, did not mind exchanging spouses, but such exchange was prearranged. Moreover, except for shamans, anyone who had such relations with a spirit risked dying or being taken away into another world (Morin and Saladin d'Anglure 2006).

When he went caribou hunting again, he began looking for *qupiqruit* [maggots] on the ground and filled up his quiver with them. When it was full, he left it there and filled his mittens with maggots, which he likewise left there.

The narrator uses the term *qupiqruit*, which may mean all sorts of insects, larvae, worms, maggots, sand hoppers, and so on (Randa 1994). But we are inland, and he adds that the man is looking for them on the ground. So I have translated the term as "maggots." During the warm season, many insect larvae can be found on decaying scraps of flesh, particularly blowfly maggots of the genus *Calliphora* (Randa 1994).

When he got home, he told his wife he had lost his mittens. She made him another pair, which, afterwards, he again claimed to have lost. He filled them with maggots and left them there on the ground after gathering a large amount. He then went home.

We see here a murder being premeditated, in keeping with Inuit tradition. If you intend to do a lot of harm, such as shedding blood, you should wait for the right moment to punish the culprit.

The next morning, while his wife was still asleep, he went to the shore of the lake and began to throw stones into the water while crying out, "Penis, emerge here!"

The variant told by *Ivaluarjuk* has him mimicking his wife's voice to deceive the lake spirit (Rasmussen 1929, 222). This detail is plausible. In general, beings from a larger scale of existence were easily deceived by those from a smaller one (Chapter 3).

When it appeared, the man waded out to it. He cut it off and carried it home, his wife still asleep. Back home, the man made a fire and got to work boiling caribou meat, to which he added the big penis. When his stew was cooked, he awakened his wife and fed her the big penis while he contented himself with having caribou stew.

Remember, the Inuit language uses the same terms for sexual and dietary codes of conduct (Chapter 4). The wife has shirked her wifely duties, namely the duty of making meals for her husband. She has instead gone off to consume a non-food item, a sexual and illicit one. The sex roles are then reversed again—the husband makes his wife a meal. And what a meal it is! The penis of his wife's non-human lover!

His wife began to eat the big penis and asked, "What is this? It's so nice and crunchy!"

There is a touch of humour in this question from his wife, who still does not know what she is eating. Her remark makes sense. Inuit love crunchy food, like muscles or cartilage. It also makes sense when someone is having sex—a hard penis is a source of great pleasure.

He answered, "It's your lover's penis!" She then said, "It's no surprise that it's so good and hard!" His anger mounted against his wife and he asked her, "What do you fear more, a hunting knife or maggots?" She replied she feared a hunting knife more because maggots can be crushed. He unrolled the hide of a *pangniq* [big male caribou], which had been laid on the ground to dry, and poured onto it all of the maggots he had gathered. He then told his wife to take off her *qarliik* [trousers] and sit on the hide. She removed her trousers and began to sit with the *akuq* [rear panel] of her parka pulled down under her. He then cut off the rear panel of her parka, and she sat with the *kiniq* [front panel] pulled down under her.

That, too, he cut off with his knife, and she had no choice but to sit down with her bare buttocks on the large maggot-covered hide.

Whether squatting like a woman or sitting with legs stretched out like a man, she is still exposing her genitals to the maggots, and on this point her husband remains inflexible.

As soon as she sat down, the maggots began to slither into her and devour her guts. She died.

This is the tragic and horrible ending of almost all variants of the myth. Perhaps it explains why most women are terrified by the sight of some insects, like larvae, maggots, sand hoppers, and even bumblebees.

Avingait [lemmings] began to crawl out of her nostrils. The maggots, which had slithered into her, had turned into lemmings. A *tiriaq* [ermine] also crawled out of her mouth.[5] The man found himself all alone, alone in his camp, the maggots having killed his wife.

Lemmings and ermines are small burrowing animals, like Arctic foxes, which we will meet in the next episode. They belong to a scale of existence smaller than that of humans but larger than that of maggots. It is as if the maggots, after devouring the woman, have risen to the larger scale of lemmings and ermines. Alternatively, the wife, after cheating on her husband with a non-human entity, has fallen to a smaller scale and reincarnated in smaller forms. As noted above, if a woman broke the menstrual taboo by looking at a game animal, it would turn into a small game animal.

While he slept, a lemming tried to slide under him. He grabbed it and threw it into what remained of the fire he had lit. The animal was severely burned, and its belly cracked open on one side, its skin having shrunk so much.

The lemming here is the wife, now reduced in size, trying to snuggle up to her husband. The burned lemming will reappear in the next episode, with its skin shrunken and split open by the fire.[6] Children use a lemming skin in games where they pretend it is the hide of a caribou, another land animal. Here, the scale is smaller. A lemming is to a child or to a dwarf as a caribou is to an adult human. We will now return to the caribou hunter and the rest of his adventures.

The Fox Woman

The man left again to go caribou hunting. When he came back, he thought he would find his meat stew cold, only to discover that someone had reheated it.

The dietary code of conduct again alerts us that an effort to seduce is now under way. Someone, undoubtedly a woman, has come to reheat his food, as any good wife should.

The next day when he again came home from hunting, he saw a *tiriganniaq* [Arctic fox][7] leave his tent. The day after, pretending to go caribou hunting, he erected two large stone cairns some distance from his tent, one nearby and the other farther off. He hid behind the far one and waited. He saw the Arctic fox come near his tent, take off its skin and hang it on the leather guy rope of his tent. Then she [the fox had metamorphosed into a woman] began to make a fire to cook the meat. She went to and from the tent to stoke the fire with *qijuttaq* [kindling].

In a landscape without a single tree, like the Arctic tundra of this story, the only way to watch unseen is to hide behind a pile of stones (*inuksugaq*). Caribou hunters use this technique when lying in wait. When an animal metamorphoses into a human, it has to take off its skin from its head down and gradually reveal its human form.

It was a fox woman. When she went into the tent, the man drew near and hid behind the second cairn. There he waited some time and, when the fox woman went back in again, he ran to the tent and grabbed the animal's skin. The fox woman came out when she heard the man's footsteps and asked him to give her back her skin. He refused, saying he wished to marry her. The fox woman refused and said, "Give me my skin!"

We have here the story of a man in love with an animal that has metamorphosed into a pretty woman. This theme recurs in the mythology of many peoples, as does the theme of a man blackmailing such a woman into marrying him after seizing her animal skin.

"Do you want to become my wife?" "No!" she said. "Give me back my skin!" "Become my wife!" he now demanded. They continued this exchange until, weary of resisting, she finally agreed. He handed over her skin, and this is how he got a new wife. When he had taken the fox woman to be his wife, he was visited by a *qavvik* [wolverine],[8] which stayed to live with them. The wolverine, which had no wife, said it wished to have one and would make a turd that would be a beautiful woman, a tall brown woman with a big topknot and a long nose . . . it defecated a woman, but she didn't have a long enough nose. So it defecated a second woman just as it wanted her to be, a tall brown woman with long hair, a big topknot tied up above the back of her neck, and a long nose. And she became its wife.

The characteristics the wolverine has chosen for its turd wife include some that identify a wolverine, such as brown fur, and others that do not, like a long nose. A wolverine's snout is short, and the fox woman's husband (the Inuit man) sees this as a defect. Because the wolverine wishes to sleep with the fox woman, it has tried to make the turd woman attractive to the Inuit man. In *Ivaluarjuk*'s variant, the visitor is not a wolverine but rather a raven whose wife is a dog turd in human form (Rasmussen 1929, 224). The two species share a common trait. Both are scavengers and both eat excrement.

It may be surprising to see a human made from a turd, but Inuit view excrement as a link in the chain of life. This chain begins when meat (an animal) is eaten and gradually turned into excrement. This excrement can be eaten again by a coprophagous animal and recycled once more. This episode may be so scatological because Inuit ascribe a very unpleasant smell to wolverines, and also to ermines (Chapter 9).

The wolverine then wanted to swap spouses with the man and his fox-woman wife. But she wouldn't go along because she had a very special smell in a class of its own. She eventually gave in, while requesting that nothing be said about her *tiriganniasunniq* [fox smell].

The suffix *-sunniq* most often means "which has a smell of," while also referring to taste on some occasions. It is alternately used with two other suffixes, *-arniq* and *-nippuq*. In Inuit language and culture, these two meanings of taste and smell overlap considerably; to convey this overlap, the term "flavour" would be more appropriate.

For the 1910–45 period, when conversion to Christianity became complete, I found evidence of regular spouse exchange among twenty or so couples from the Igloolik region (Saladin d'Anglure 1993b, 85–89 [1989, 156–61]). As for the peculiar smell of the Arctic fox, Inuit say it is like urine. We again see this "defect" being internalized by the woman and former animal, although the smell is specific to foxes and not to her or to women. The fox woman is very touchy on this point, all the more so because the man blackmailed her into marriage as the price for returning her animal skin.

Despite being forewarned, the wolverine very much wanted to talk about the smell and cried out, *"Nakininna salunippa nurannippa?"* ["But where does this nice little smell come from?"].[9] The fox woman burst into tears. She took her desiccated skin and began to chew on it, to soften it up for her to wear. She slipped it on and fled out the door opening after regaining her appearance as an Arctic fox.

Inuit did not know how to tan leather. Hides were first dampened, dried, and hardened. Later they were chewed, moistened with saliva, and smoothed with a scraper to make them soft and supple. When the frail fox woman is faced with a devious partner like the wolverine, she cannot stand her ground. She instead chooses to return to her animal world, but her transformation will take place step by step.

The wolverine cried out, "I made my partner's wife run away!"

Its bad reputation is not exaggerated. Not content with breaking up the couple who welcomed it into their home, it goes on to brag about its misdeed.

The man who had just lost his wife said, "But where does this turd stink come from?"

Because his fox woman has run away, the man gives the wolverine a taste of its own medicine with a disparaging remark about the smell of its turd wife.

Then the wolverine's wife turned into excrement. She who had been brown and long-haired again became just a turd.

She returns to her original condition—excrement—simply because the man has mentioned her smell, thus revealing her origins. So metamorphosis into a human does not fully erase all traces of one's origins, which may show up in linguistic, cultural, morphological, dietary, or olfactory characteristics (see Descola 2013 [2005] for a general discussion of this point).

Neither of them had a wife now.

They differ, though, in that the man once had a fox companion, before the wolverine's visit, whereas the wolverine lived alone before making itself a turd wife. A wolverine is a solitary animal that does not willingly stand the presence of another male on its territory. It can push away any animal, even one stronger than itself, that encroaches on its turf. We can imagine the wolverine of our story going away alone.

The man began to follow the Arctic fox tracks to a few small mounds of peat. On one side, the tracks were those of a fox. On the other, they were human footprints.

The Inuk wants to find his beautiful, fragile, and tender-hearted little fox. She has fled but is only gradually reverting to her animal form. This is customary when one goes from the human world to the animal world or vice versa while travelling. She transforms first in one way and then in another, as seen in her half-human, half-animal tracks (Figure 19). As she gets nearer to her burrow, the fox woman completes her reversion to her original animal form.

The footprints stopped at a fox burrow. When the man reached it, he cried out, "Is my wife here?"

FIGURE 19. The woman gradually loses her human appearance and regains an animal appearance. From a drawing by Paulusi Sivuak, 1973. Made by Johanne Lévesque. Archival fonds of B. Saladin d'Anglure.

He tries to start a dialogue with her, but she is not alone. Several intermediaries will stand in the way between her and him.

When someone answered that she was there, he asked her to come out. A mosquito came out and said, "They want you to take me!"

Animals of different species exit the burrow in human form, each one retaining some distinctive traits from its origins. They present themselves in order of increasing size: a mosquito, a spider, a wolverine, and a wolf.[10]

"I don't want you! Your tuft of hair looks like smoke!" he said, and he again asked, "Is my wife here?" When someone answered that she was there, he asked her to come out. A spider came out and said, "They want you to take me!" He replied, "Your mouth is vertical! I don't want you!" The spider went back, saying, "He says that my mouth is vertical and that he doesn't want me." A wolverine then came out and said, "They want you to take me!" He replied, "Your nose is too short. I don't want you!" It went back, saying, "He says that my nose is too short and that he doesn't want me." The man cried out again, "Is my wife here?" Someone answered that she was. He asked her to come out. A wolf came out and said, "They want you to take me!" He replied, "Your nose is too long! I don't want you!" It went back, saying, "He says that my nose is too long and that he doesn't want me!" The man followed the wolf into the burrow, where he saw his wife combing her hair in a room. Just then, a horrid lemming appeared and, seeing the man, said, "This is the man who burned me, who caused my skin to be stretched!"

Until now, the man has remained at the burrow entrance, away from the animal world. He now decides to cross the threshold of this world that is taunting him. The burrow becomes a semi-subterranean home scaled up to his size, and the Arctic fox is now a woman combing her hair. In a Netsilik variant, where the main hero is *Kiviuq*, a lemming asks him to crawl into the burrow backwards with his eyes closed, thus reversing the normal order of things. Inside, he finds a large home with several rooms where many animals live in human form, including his fox wife (Rasmussen 1931, 371).

In the present variant, the lemming with burned, stretched skin comes from the first episode of the story, where we saw it appear after maggots had killed the caribou hunter's human wife. The lemming is also a prey of the Arctic fox. Here, it is alive but half-cooked, and living with its predator.

The man noticed that the lemming's skin was very taut on one side.

The man in turn recognizes the lemming he tried to kill by throwing it into the fire.

The lemming spoke again: "This is the man who made my skin shrink on one side!" Then it cried out, "Ow-ow-ow!" and in pain went back into its hole. Another lemming was above the entrance. It was big and brown and was scratching itself.

There are two types of lemmings. The first one is the northern collared lemming (*Dicrostonyx groenlandicus*), or *amiqslaq*, which turns white in winter and varies from beige to brown in summer. This is the type discussed so far. The second is the North American brown lemming (*Lemmus trimucronatus*), or *kajuji*. Both are found in the Igloolik region. The brown lemming's presence above the entrance requires comment. "Above" (*qulissiaq*) refers here to the entranceway of the burrow, but it also means the meat boiling in a stone pot above an oil lamp. The lemming, too, is meat, but very much alive. It is scratching itself like a live animal and is a preferred prey for the fox woman who is combing her hair like a human.

The man wanted to sit next to his wife but was unable and found a seat elsewhere. He then pointed his index finger at his wife and made a big fart. All of the animals scampered off into their holes. The lemming jumped and fell onto the ground, and the woman too ran off, going out the way she had come in. The man never retrieved her.

Unable to control the situation and discouraged by his failure, he shows his dissatisfaction and decides to break off the dialogue he has been trying to have with his ex-partner. For this, he uses a magical tactic, a bit unusual, which we will return to in Chapter 13 when discussing the magical value of farting. This unseemly finish brings to mind how an Inuit song contest comes to an end in the ceremonial igloo (*qaggiq*): the winner humiliates the loser with a fart accompanied by the same gesture.[11]

With this end to the fox woman story, things return to the way they were initially and the characters regain their original forms and roles. The story ends here, at least according to the narrator; however, he immediately launched into the next story, another episode of the same myth that exists in several variants.

The Goose Woman

This Inuk, though an adult, still had no wife. He customarily went for long walks by himself. On one of his long walks, he saw *nirliit* [Canada geese] that had taken human form and were swimming in the waters of a lake. They had taken off their clothes and were human-looking. He stole up to their clothes unobtrusively and unseen. When he got to the clothes, he picked them up. There were two sets of plumage for *mitiik* [eider ducks] and two for *nirliik* [Canada geese], which belonged to the women swimming in the lake.[12] When they saw the man with their clothes, they went up to him and demanded he give them back. The man gave the clothes back to the two eider ducks and to one of the two Canada geese. They put them on right away and flew off. But he liked the remaining goose and didn't wish to give her clothes back. She kept asking him for her clothes, but he didn't want to give them to her. She then began to cry. The man told her he would give them back if she agreed to become his wife. She eventually agreed, and he gave her back her clothes. She kept her human likeness, and the man married her. They went to his camp and stayed married for a long time. They had a child, exactly like the children of other humans, for its father was an Inuk. But the woman refused to touch seal blubber. She loathed it because she was a Canada goose. She would do no work that had anything to do with the blubber of marine mammals.

As in the last episode, the couple begins to enjoy a time of happiness. The goose wife unquestioningly adopts the Inuit rule that a woman should live with her husband's family. Differences in way of life soon appear, however, again leading to separation. When the man made his first try at marriage, in the autumn and farther inland, he and his spouse had no child, and he killed her because she was cheating on him with a spirit. When he tried a second time, the new human-animal couple likewise had no child, and the marriage broke up when he exchanged his wife in the winter with a dubious pair of partners. Now he is trying a third time. The human-animal couple have a child and seem to enjoy some stability when problems in their social environment arise. The goose wife belongs, however, to the migratory world of water birds that graze in summer on low ground plants. Unlike sea birds, she will have no contact with marine products, especially not with the blubber of marine mammals. This is a source of conflict with her husband, whose fellow Inuit are preparing for the summer whale hunt.

One day, the men caught an *arviq* [bowhead whale].[13] When the meat was cut up, the men began to carry the chunks away to their tents, with the help of their wives.

Catching a bowhead whale was a major event in the life of a community. Everyone had to work together to carry away the heavy quarters of meat, blubber, or *maktak* [the edible skin of a bowhead whal].[14]

The man wanted his wife to help, but she refused and her refusal angered him. He took a small chunk of whale blubber and threw it at her. She was hit in the leg, her trousers were dirtied, and she began to cry.

The husband no longer understands his wife. There is plenty of food for everyone and for a long time. In return, everyone has to work together to cut it up and carry it away. The goose woman's public refusal hurts his status as a hunter in his group. He becomes enraged and assaults her by forcing her into contact with whale blubber. This is going too far. Inuit social and ritual life rests on a separation between the land world and the sea world. The goose woman belongs to the former, and the Inuk to the latter. This division is compounded by another: she comes from the south, where she usually spends winter, whereas he lives in the north, where migratory animal species like Canada geese and whales go to breed. Finally, these two divisions are compounded by a third: the man/woman duality already encountered in preceding chapters. Women are associated with the land, the south, the sun, and the summer. Men are associated with the sea, the north, the moon, and the winter.

The goose woman went to the shore of the river with her child, and they began to gather goose feathers that had washed up along the shoreline. They put some feathers between their fingers, turned into geese, and flew off while honking like geese.

There is a total lack of understanding. His wife has been publicly assaulted in her own person and in her identity. She decides to go back to her kith and kin, taking with her the son she had with the hunter. Whenever an Inuit couple breaks up, the woman usually takes her young children along.

The man saw his wife and his child fly away, and he began to follow them on foot. He continued to walk in the direction of their flight and, while doing so, composed a song.

She has left for the south by air, which is inaccessible to humans.

He sang, "Over yonder, ya, yaa, I walk in vain, beyond the mountains, to the Land of the Birds, ukiujuittuq ['where there is no winter'], where there is no ice, over yonder, ya, yaa."

By singing, he tries to exorcize the terrible fate that has befallen him. He walks south for a very long time to the Land of the Sun from which migratory birds come every year, to where the sun seems to seek refuge in early winter, and from where it comes back a few moons later. *Ukiujuittuq* is the Land without Winter. It is the opposite here of *Aujuittuq*, the Land without Summer, the Land of Glaciers and Eternal Snow.

He kept walking in the same direction as his wife and child, and he kept singing. Then he came to a very big oil lamp burning with great flames, alone in the middle of the *nunainnaq* [tundra]. He tried to walk past the lamp, but it barred his way each time, so he composed a song about the lamp. He sang, "This big lamp on the ground, which tries to scare me away; it's impossible to walk past it; it's impossible to walk around it. If I jump on it and walk on the blubber residues, stepping from one to the next, then I'll be able to continue."

However stubborn the man may be in pursuing the two escapees, he is now confronted with obstacles of a scale larger than his own. At the outset of his adventure with the goose woman, he was in charge of the situation. Now his way is barred by a giant lamp and a giant flame, two female symbols, which he can overcome only by using his magic song and the large bits of blubber floating like slabs of ice on the sea. These bits are remnants of the pieces of blubber that have been chewed or crushed to get their oil.

So he jumped onto the lamp, walked on the *uqummiagait* [blubber residues], hopping from one to the next. He arrived at the other side and composed a song. He sang, "Over yonder, *ya, yaa*, I walk in vain beyond the mountains, to the Land of the Birds, where there is no winter, where there is no ice, yes, over yonder, *ya, yaa*." He sang as he walked. He then met a large pot, a very hot vessel containing meat stew. The stew inside the pot had been cooking over the big lamp he had walked past, but the pot was far from the lamp. He tried to walk past the pot, but it kept barring his way, so he began to sing again. He sang, "This big pot on the ground is trying to scare me away. It's impossible to walk around it. If I jump from one piece of meat to the next, I'll be able to get past."

The new obstacle likewise belongs to a larger scale of existence. This female symbol is a stone container, an *ukkusiq* (a woman is metaphorically referred to as a *puuq*, "container," in the language of shamans). It is used for cooking and sets the raw, bloody meat of a game animal apart from the body of a woman, who bleeds periodically and must shun all contact at such times with hunters. The largest stone pots of the Inuit could contain between five and ten litres of stew. This pot, however, is huge. The man manages to step across it using the pieces of boiled meat, which float on the surface like large ice cubes, thus getting past the obstacle.

He set his foot on the meat that simmered in the big pot and made his way to the other side. He began walking to the Land of the Birds, singing, "Over yonder, *ya, yaa*, I walk in vain beyond the mountains, to the Land of the Birds, where there is no winter, where there is no ice, over yonder, *ya, yaa*." He then met two big *akslaak* [black bears], which were fiercely fighting and trying to bite each other. He tried to pass by on one side, but they kept moving forward and backward, and he couldn't walk past them, so he began to sing. He sang, "These big black bears fighting each other are trying to scare me away. I can't go around them, and they won't stand aside for me. I'll have to charge right through between them."

Black bears (*Ursus americanis*) or *akslat* are associated with the boreal forest and its borderlands—the zone south of the tundra where the Inuit live. The bears feed mainly on plants (fruits, berries, leaves, nuts, roots). They are land animals and close to the world of women. It seems as if the flyaway wife has been slowing down her unwelcome pursuer by creating scaled-up obstacles from her world.

So he headed for the two black bears, and when they moved apart from each other a bit, he passed between them. He kept walking and sang, "Over yonder, *ya, yaa,* I'm trying to walk beyond the mountains to the Land of the Birds, where there is no winter, where there is no ice, over yonder, *ya, yaa.*"

He then met a large pair of women's thighs on the ground. He tried to walk around or past them, but they still barred his way, so he began to sing. He sang, "These two big thighs right on the ground, which are trying to scare me away, they're barring my way. They'll not let me go around. I'll get through only if I make love to them."

The obstacles seem meant to slow down his progress rather than to keep him from getting through. When he first encountered the goose, he was seduced by her appearance as a nude woman. Now she has created an obstacle in the form of a woman's nude body, reduced to its lower portion.

He made love to the big thighs and went on his way. After walking past them, he kept walking and said, "Over yonder, *ya, yaa,* I walk in vain beyond the mountains, to the Land of the Birds, where there is no winter, where there is no ice, over yonder, *ya, yaa,* over yonder, *ya.*" He sang as he walked. He then met two big *ujarasujjuuk* [stone blocks][15] battering each other. He couldn't pass between the two. So he sang once more, "These two big *ujarasujjuuk* on the ground are trying to scare me away. It's impossible for me to go around them. I'll get through only if I slip between." And while the two stone blocks were apart from each other, he ran through, but he had scarcely made it to the other side when the blocks collided again, and the *akuq* [rear panel] of his parka stayed stuck between them, for he had a caribou-skin *akutuinnaq* [man's parka with a rear panel]. He had to tear off the panel and leave it behind. He began walking again in the direction of his fleeing wife and son, while continuing to sing. He sang, "Over yonder, *ya, yaa,* I'm trying to walk beyond the mountains to the Land of the Birds, where there is no winter, where there is no ice, over yonder, far away, *ya.*"

Throughout this obstacle course, the man's song has shown its magic power. It has given him the strength to take on entities that belong to a larger scale of existence than his own by bringing him up to that scale. This trip has initiated him into shamanism.

An Encounter with *Iqallijuq,* the Creator of Atlantic Salmon and Arctic Char

He kept walking, and then up ahead he saw a stark naked man working with an axe. He approached the man from behind and, through the man's anus, glimpsed the glottis at the far end of his throat. His digestive tract was indeed very wide and cylindrical. The Inuk came near to him on one side. The hollow man slowly turned to him and asked, "From what direction did you approach me?" The Inuk answered, "I came to you from the left, a bit in front." The hollow man said, "If you had come from behind, I'd have split you in two with that," and he showed the big axe he was working with. The Inuk told the hollow man he had come from the side, although he had in fact come from behind. The hollow man believed him. He was cutting wood chips beside a river and making something. The Inuk asked him what he was making. He answered he was making *iqaluit* [fish in general, and especially salmonids like Arctic char and Atlantic salmon]. After cutting many wood chips, he stopped and went to the pile of chips he had cut. Using his penis, he smeared them with sperm and carried them to the river. When he dropped them into the water, they became Atlantic salmon and Arctic char, and the current right away carried them off. This was how he made the fish.

When pieces of driftwood wash ashore, some have a colour and texture that makes them look like Atlantic salmon (*Salmo salar*) or Arctic char (*Salvelinus alpinus*). Some Inuit, such as the Belcher Islanders, can identify whether the wood is male or female. They can tell by its "flavour" by sniffing and licking.

Inuit call the creator of Atlantic salmon and Arctic char *Iqallijuq*. The term is apt, being constructed from the root *iqaluk*, which means fish of the Salmonidae family and may be extended to fish in general. *Iqallijuq* was a helping spirit valued by shamans, his name being given for instance to the heroine of Chapter 1 to help her live. In some regions, people called this fish creator *Putulik* ("The one with a hole" or "The hollow man"). He was also said to be the patron spirit of successful childbirths.[16]

The Inuk watched him for a moment and then asked, "Do you know if people are around?" The hollow man answered, "Put your ear to the ground and listen." The Inuk stretched out on the ground and began to listen. He heard geese playing on the other river bank. He wanted to be taken to the other bank, so the fish-making hollow man cut down a tree trunk and told him to sit on it. The Inuk took his place on the log, and the hollow man pushed it out into the water. It floated to the other bank. Once there he began walking again.

A Hopeless Love Comes to a Dead End

He soon reached a lake and saw a village on the opposite shore, on a point of land. He sneaked unseen into the village and stayed hidden for a long while. The village dwellers finally stopped playing and went into their tent. A little boy stayed outside, and the man recognized his son. He began to walk toward the child. When the boy saw his father, he came to him, and they walked together to the tent. The child went in and said to his mother, "My father's here!" His mother said, "Your father can't be here because we left him near a whale." "My father's really here!" "Your father can't be here because we left him near a whale." "My father's really here!" The boy was close to tears, and she thought about the man whose arrival he announced. She said, "Tell him to come in!" The little boy went to tell his father to come in, and his father came in. The woman who had once been his goose wife was very far into her pregnancy. Next to her was an old goose man, her husband.

When this episode began, the bird woman was not alone while bathing in the lake. Another Canada goose accompanied her, and a pair of eider ducks. The second goose was undoubtedly her husband, since these birds migrate north as breeding pairs. Later, after leaving her Inuit spouse, she found her original husband and fled south to the Land of the Birds.

The old man said, "Give me that little bag, there, on the ground!" She gave it to him and opened it. It contained bird feathers. The old man, the woman, and the child put on their plumages and flew away. The woman was very fat and the last to fly off. When she was in the air, the man took an arrow and shot at her, aiming for her big belly. The egg inside fell to earth and bounced. The woman died, and the Inuk was once more a widower. He no longer had the strength of heart to go home. Although he had found his wife, the man began to sing again: "I forgot about the little goose and her little bag. She's gone. She tried to get away. *Qarii, qarii,* when the ice and the ice floes are breaking up." He had come all this way to find his wife and did find her, but he was unsuccessful in taking her back and killed her. He could no longer return to where he came from. It was too far away.

This is the tragic end to an impossible love story. One half of the couple is a migratory bird that spends winter in the south and summer in the north while feeding on the produce of the land and the lakes. The other is an Inuk who alternates between hunting caribou on the tundra and hunting marine mammals in Arctic waters. These two ways of life are so different. How could they ever be reconciled?

CHAPTER 7

Girls Should Not Play at Marriage

This marriage story is the reverse of the one told earlier about *Uiniguma-suittuq*, "She who refused to marry" (see Chapter 5). Here, four single girls play at having a husband. Both this story and that of *Uinigumasuittuq* are a stern warning to girls who wish to choose their mates freely. There is also perhaps a warning against misusing words or games and thereby sending a challenge to animal spirits or the stone spirit. Finally, the myth shows a cyclical view of life: a bone is both what is left of a dead animal and what may become a live one. The variant I present below was given by *Kupaaq* in 1972, in Igloolik. Though more succinct than some variants published earlier, only it and the one published by Rasmussen (1929, 281–84) have a storyline that includes all four girls and all four episodes.

Four girls were playing by the shore at having a husband. For this role, one girl had chosen a bone from an *arviq* [bowhead whale], the second had chosen a bone from a *nakturalik* [eagle], the third a *kanajuq* [sculpin], and the fourth an *ujarak* [stone block]. The girls were only playing at having a husband, but the four husbands they playfully chose soon became their real husbands.

The variant published by Boas (1901) has only three girls, who make their wishes after seeing live animals rather than bones (a bowhead whale, an eagle, and a stone block). This is also the case with the more detailed story by *Ivaluarjuk* and published by Rasmussen (1929, 281–84). It has four girls of marriageable age playing together at choosing a husband. One sees a bowhead whale spouting at sea and says, "That shall be my husband!" and so it comes about. Another catches sight of a sculpin[1] lying in shallow water and utters the same words, followed by the same effects. The third finds a stone she thinks very handsome and says the same thing. The fourth sees an eagle and says, "That eagle shall be my husband!" and the eagle takes her away. But back to *Kupaaq*'s story:

> The girl with a sculpin husband was kept on the shore. The one with a stone block husband stayed stuck to it. The one with a whale-bone husband was taken away to an island by the whale. The one with an eagle-bone husband was taken away by the eagle to the top of a cliff. The bone had turned into an eagle.

Kupaaq does not say how the transformation takes place, but it seems that as soon as the words are uttered the bones and stone, formerly inert in appearance, become alive with intentions, awareness, and feelings. In the Inuit way of thinking, there is a visible world of animals, plants, and elements of nature—water, fire, air, earth and minerals, and remains of living things—and there is an invisible spirit world in the background. The invisible world may at any time interfere with the visible one and bring an inanimate object to life, endowing it with very human-like appearances and behaviours (Descola 2013 [2005]). These are the consequences when the girls' ill-timed words cross the boundary between the two worlds.

> The sculpin's wife was building a fire at low tide. People saw her and went to watch her at work. As for the girl who had stayed stuck to her stone husband, no one could see her from the shore.

While none of the myth's variants say much about the relationship with the sculpin, all of them dwell on the strange fate of the girl with the stone husband.

The Stone Husband

The stone husband's girl stayed stuck to him, and whenever she saw a kayak pass by she would cry out, "Come to my rescue! This stone has stuck to me!"

Ivaluarjuk is more specific about the cry for help, which takes the form of a song that begins as follows (Rasmussen 1929, 283):

"Men in kayaks, come hither to me and be my husbands: this stone here has clung fast to me, and lo, my feet are now turning to stone!"

So begins a long repetitive lamentation as she gradually turns to stone while still offering herself in marriage. *Kupaaq*, too, has her making cries for help:

When her feet began to turn to stone, she cried out:
"Come to my rescue, this stone has stuck to me, my feet are turning to stone now."
"Come to my rescue, this stone has stuck to me, my shinbones are turning to stone now."
"Come to my rescue, this stone has stuck to me, my behind is turning to stone."
"Come to my rescue, this stone has stuck to me, my guts are turning to stone."
"Come to my rescue, this stone has stuck to me, my heart is becoming stone." Then she died.
Even after death, her metamorphosis continued, until she was only stone.

A sad outcome of what was supposed to be just a game. The variant provided by Comer (Boas 1901, 319) has a detail that the others lack:

But the people used to bring her food as long as there was any life left in her. This stone is also pointed out to children.

The myth's moral dimension, mentioned at the beginning of this chapter, is confirmed by a short Cumberland Sound variant published by Boas (1901, 172–73):

A young girl refused to take a husband. Finally the people grew angry, broke up their tents, and deserted her. The day after they had left she saw the men sealing in their kayaks. She had climbed a steep cliff, where they saw her standing. Then she shouted to one of the men, "Come and fetch me! I will marry you." But they did not believe her. Then they heard her saying, "I wish my feet would be turned into stone!" and they were turned into stone; "I wish my hips would be turned into stone!" And they also were turned into stone; "I wish my arms would be turned into stone!" And they too were turned to stone; "I wish my chest would be turned into stone!" and then it became stone; "I wish my head were turned into stone!" and it too became stone. Now she was entirely transformed into stone. And there she is still. The people hear her when they pass by in their boats.

This is no longer a cry for help, but rather a gesture of despair after being ostracized. As a side note, while I was investigating place names in the Igloolik region and Nunavik, several were identified to me as sites where one could see the girl who had changed to stone. We see this with many myths. The action is said to have happened at different sites of the Inuit homeland, as if a single myth has been appropriated by the inhabitants of one territory after another. Today, many place names, sometimes very far apart, refer to the same myth.[2]

The Whale Husband

The whale husband takes its young wife to an island. *Ivaluarjuk* added that it builds her a home using the bones of its body and feeds her pieces of its flesh and *maktak* (edible skin) (Rasmussen 1929, 282).[3] Just as a mammal closer to human size can take off its skin and assume a human appearance, a whale can turn its body into a home or a boat once it assumes human form. To make a home, it uses its ribs for the frame—a method introduced by the Thule ancestors of the Inuit to build their semi-subterranean dwellings (*qarmait*).

According to *Ivaluarjuk*, the whale husband is madly in love with its wife and fears she will escape. It never lets her go out alone without tethering her, even when she has to relieve herself. It kisses her so passionately and makes love to her so often that *maktak* begins to form about her nose and genitals. They kiss as Inuit do by sniffing each other, nose against nose. The girl is turning into a whale through repeated intimate contact with her insatiable lover. *Kupaaq's* story continues:

> The girl with a whale husband began to live on the island. Their home was the whale's body, and its bones served as a frame. When she wanted to go out to urinate, her whale husband would tie a line around her waist. They used the whale's carcass as a home, and the husband would stay inside on the sleeping platform. "Haven't you finished urinating?" the whale husband would ask, and when she finished, it would pull her into the home.

Ivaluarjuk added a few spicy details to the delight of young and old listeners alike (Rasmussen 1929, 282): when the girl wants to urinate, her husband tells her to do it in its huge mouth, and if there is any more, she can relieve herself in one of its fore flippers.

> A kayak had come, and she left with the line tied around her. The whale husband asked, "Are you still relieving yourself?" "Yes I am!" she answered. She then tied a post to the end of the line and went to the kayak, which took her to the mainland. The whale husband asked, "Are you still relieving your bowels?" The post answered for her, "Yes I am!" Each time the whale husband asked the question, the post answered, "Yes I am!" Then the whale husband tugged at the line. Instead of the girl, it discovered a bone post. The whale husband began to take down the home and put its bones back on. It acted so hastily that it forgot to put one of its ribs back and left without that bone. It gave chase in a kayak and finally caught sight of her, only to be forced back to look for the bone it had forgotten. It then got on its way again and caught up to the runaways (Kupaaq 1972).

This part of the story greatly resembles the description of *Uinigumasuittuq* fleeing in her father's *umiaq* to escape from her fulmar husband (Chapter 5); only the ending differs.

One of the girl's boots was thrown into the water, and the whale husband began to beat it with its flippers and tear it apart. The whale was meanwhile outdistanced and, after tearing the boot apart, gave chase again. The other boot was thrown into the water, and the whale, catching it, began to tear it apart as well. When it had been ripped to pieces, the whale gave chase again. They then threw the girl's trousers into the water, and the whale tore those apart as well when it reached them. This time it took longer and then gave chase again (Kupaaq 1972).

The variant published by Rasmussen (1929, 283) makes several references to the sense of smell, which are implicit in *Kupaaq*'s story. They show the whale husband's insatiable desire:

The breeches, which smelt of her body, kept the whale back so long that the boat got far ahead, and reached the shore, running in with such force that it dashed up on land, over two high terraces on the beach.

The terraces here, also known as raised beaches, correspond to earlier sea levels that existed after the melting of the ice sheets that had covered the Arctic during the last ice age. With the weight of the ice removed, the land gradually rebounded, the result being a succession of beaches in line with this isostatic uplift. *Kupaaq* adds:

They reached the coast, and when the whale made land, it turned to bone because that is what it had been before.

The girl is saved but only narrowly, and her visit to the enchanted spirit world, where bones come back to life, has ended. She is once more in the reality of the human world.

The Eagle Husband

The third girl, who chose an eagle bone to be her husband, has an experience comparable to the last one. Unlike whales, eagles are not often seen in the Igloolik region.[4] They are found more easily on the mountains and cliffs of North Baffin. They are nonetheless popular figures in Inuit oral tradition, undoubtedly because of their predatory qualities, their strength, their speed, and their visual acuity.

This episode, as told by *Kupaaq*, is known in many Inuit Arctic regions, especially in Nunavik. It has been used to illustrate many prints by contemporary Inuit artists.[5] The eagle is thus shown carrying its wife through the air in its talons to a clifftop. In fact, an eagle can capture live Arctic hares (*Lepus arcticus*) and caribou calves (*Rangifer tarandus groenlandicus*). Here, the eagle husband is a very good hunter, and its wife has plenty of meat and hides, as *Ivaluarjuk* says in his variant (Rasmussen 1929, 284). Eagles have a habit of making their nests in places inaccessible to humans.

The girl with a *nakturalik* [eagle] husband had been taken to a clifftop, at the bottom of which was a camp. The eagle hunted for food and caught several hares to feed its wife. It also caught some caribou. It would take the animal in its talons, fly away with it, and then let it fall, thus killing it instantly. The eagle brought the animals back to its wife, who, while her husband was away, weaved a braided line of caribou sinews (Kupaaq 1972).

Again, the girl has been caught in a trap of her own making and is now devising a way to get out. Sinew weaving is very widespread among the Inuit. It is essentially women's work and indispensable to making flat waterproof seams, which are needed to make skin tents, kayak skirts, and backings and strings for bows.

When she judged that the braided line was long enough to reach the cliff bottom, she made herself a pair of mittens out of a hare's skin. Whenever the bird came back to its home, she hid the sinew braid and the mittens. When the bird left one more time, she unwound the sinew braid and slid down (Figure 20).

She will use the braided sinew rope to escape, and the mittens are meant to protect her hands on the way down. In *Ivaluarjuk's* variant, the girl catches sight of an *umiaq* from the clifftop. Aboard are her kinfolk, looking for her. She then tells her eagle husband that caribou are plentiful at some faraway places, and the unsuspecting husband leaves on a long hunting trip. Because the steep cliff falls straight down to the sea, the girl has to coordinate her descent with the boat's occupants. And that is what

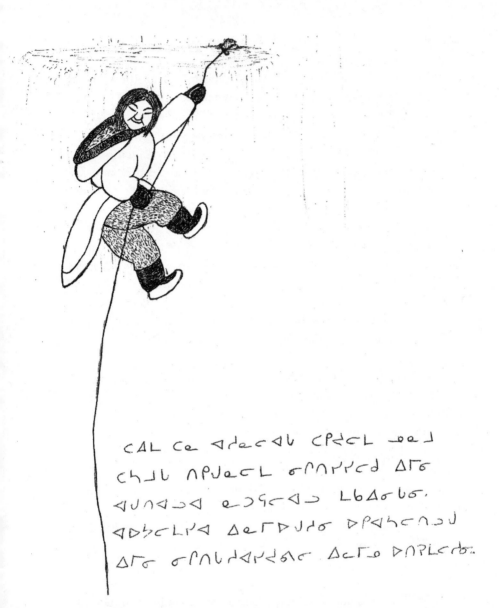

ᑕᐊᐃᒪ ᑕᓇ ᐊᑐᓇᐊᓕ ᒐ ᑕᑭᔪᐊᓕᕐᒪ ᓄᓇᒧᑦ
ᑕᔅᒧᖓ ᑎᑭᒍᓇᓕᕐᒪ ᓂᖏᑎᑦᓯᓕᖅ ᐃᒥᓂᒃ
ᐊᖑᑎᐊᓗ ᓇᑦᑐᕋᓕᐊᓗᒃ ᒪᖄᓂᖓᓂ.
ᐊᐅᔭᓕᕐᒫᑦᓯᐊ ᐃᓇᒥᐅᖑᑦᓂ ᐅᑭᐊᒃᓴᓕᕐᑎᓗᒍ
ᐃᒥᓂᒃ ᓂᖏᑎᒐᓱᐊᓯᔪᕕᓂᖅ ᐃᓚᒥᓄ ᐅᑎᕈᒪᓕᕐᓱᓂ.

FIGURE 20. The eagle husband's wife quickly escapes from the home, using a rope of caribou sinews. The Inuktitut text says: *Taima taanna atsunaalianga takijuulirmat nunamut tasamunga tikigunnalirmat ningititsisiliqquq imminik angutialua natturalialuk maqainningani. Aujalirmaatsiaq innamiungutsuni ukiaksalirtilugu imminik ningitigasuasijuviniq ilaminut utirumalirsuni*—Because this woman's rope is very long she is able to reach the ground down there because she lowered herself while her eagle husband was away hunting. The entire summer through into the fall she lived on the cliff but she is able to lower herself, thus returning to her kin. From a drawing by Paulusi Sivuak, 1973.

happens. She unwinds the rope to the sea and takes so long to lower herself that she scrapes off all of the skin on the palms of her hands. Nonetheless, she manages to get away in the boat with her kinfolk (Rasmussen 1929, 284). In *Kupaaq*'s story, she simply lowers herself down to her kinfolk's camp, which is at the cliff bottom.

When it got back home, the eagle husband realized that its wife had gone down the cliff. It began to hover above the camp, almost causing the tents to be blown away because of the air moved by its wings.

As similarly described in Chapter 5 with the fulmar, the Inuit way of thinking links the eagle's great wingspan to its power to stir up a violent wind.

The girl's father said to the eagle, "Hover slowly at a man's height, and I'll love you like I would a son-in-law."

Frightened by the eagle's strength, the girl's father opts for cunning. This is an effective weapon for the small or the weak when confronted by a superior force. The man here tries to convince the eagle by playing on its feelings. In *Ivaluarjuk*'s variant (Rasmussen 1929, 284), the eagle raises a storm, and the men of the camp call up to it with words of flattery:

"Eagle, let us see what a handsome fellow you are; spread your wings wide!"

Kupaaq, for his part, finishes the episode this way:

The eagle wanted to be loved, so it flew down to a man's height and was struck by an arrow just under its wing (Figure 21). It fell and the dogs ate its flesh. Under one of its wings, a female dog had pups. This gives an idea of its wingspan.

The bird's great wingspan is striking for Inuit, all the more so because they seldom encounter eagles. According to *Ivaluarjuk*, a female dog has her litter in the shelter of the eagle's skeleton once all of the flesh has been eaten (Rasmussen 1929, 284).

ᑕᐃᒪ ᏟᏋ ᔪᑐᖅᏟᐊᓗ Ꮯᑯᒡᐅᑲ ᔪᐁᏟᑐ ᏁᏢᐅᏁᏟᐅᑐ
ᏁᏢᐅᏁᏟᏟᏒ ᐊᔪᏁᏟᐊᑐᏟᐅᓂᐊ Ꮯᑯᒡᐅᑲ ᐊᔪᏁᓂᐅ. ᏟᏟᓂᐅ
"ᐊᐊᏟᏋᏋ ᏟᑯᏟᐅᑐᏋᏟᏁᓂᐅᏘᐅᏒᐅᐸ? Ꮯᑯᐊ ᐊᔪᏁ Ꮯᐅᐅᐁᑕ ᐊᐅᏒᎢ
ᏝᏅᏟᐊᓂᐅ "ᓂᏟᐅᐁᏁᓂᐅᐊᏟᏋᏟᏁᏢ ᐃᏟᏟᏟᏋᏁ" ᏟᏟᐅᓂᐅ
ᐊᐊᏟᏋ Ꮯᑯᐊ ᐊᔪᏁ ᏟᏋᏟᐅ ᐃᏟᏟᏝᏁᏟᐅᏟᐊᓂᐅ ᏢᏁᏟᏟᏘᏁᐅᐁᐅᐅ.

FIGURE 21. The eagle husband is killed by the family of the young girl it has abducted. The Inuktitut text says: *Taima taanna nakturalialuk taakkununga nunalinnut tikiutilirniquq. Tikiutilirami, apirijualuulirtuviniq taakkuniinga angutiinnik latsuni : "Aipparalii takulauratannginivisiuk?" Taakkua angutiik paniup anigik kiujuviniik: "Ningautaarinialiratigit isaangalirit" Lajuviniik. Asuilaa taakkua angutiik qulaani isaangasilirtuviniq pitittaugiirsunilu—* Then this large eagle arrives at the camp and upon arriving asks the man saying, "Have you not seen my spouse?" That man responds to his daughter's spouse, "Because I will have you as my son-in-law spread your wings." Then that man shot a bow and arrow up into its wings. From a drawing by Paulusi Sivuak, 1973. Made by Johanne Lévesque. Archival fonds of B. Saladin d'Anglure.

The Sculpin Husband

This episode is the most mysterious one and the hardest to interpret. Analysis of *Ivaluarjuk*'s variant reveals hardly any more details, other than that the girl is taken away by her sculpin husband and stowed away under a stone (Rasmussen 1929, 283). She is never found again.

The girl with a *kanajuq* [sculpin] husband never came back. People would see her at low tide, but lost her from view when they tried to catch her.

These details make sense when one knows that sculpins are caught in summer at low tide, in tide pools. They hide under stones, which you have to lift to catch them. Presumably, the girl has been turned into a sculpin.

Here too, the ending is sad. The girl is gone, like her petrified playmate. She has disappeared through a change of scale, having been reduced to a sculpin's infra-human scale. She does not have the luck of her two playmates who are scaled up to the world of eagles and bowhead whales. It is worth recalling that in the Inuit way of symbolic thinking, a bowhead whale and a sculpin are the same animal but on different scales of existence. Only a shaman could transcend such differences in size. This was undoubtedly why he would call them by one word alone: *taakslaingiq*. This term belongs to the language of shamans and means "he whose name must not be mentioned" (Rasmussen 1930b, 79). We have a good example of different scales in a myth told to me and illustrated by Daividialuk Alasuaq of Puvirnituq, of a giant walking in the sea with a club. He is hunting sculpins, and he clubs any sculpin whose head appears at the surface. Then suddenly, Inuit in kayaks are hunting and harpooning the same animals, which for them are bowhead whales (Figure 10).

The myth of the four girls shows that marriage is not a choice for girls and even less a game. It also shows that the names of animals, and of any other entity possessed by a master spirit, cannot be uttered carelessly, for the spirits see, hear, sense, and feel with greater acuity than do humans. A spirit responds to anyone who has uttered its name or who, above all else, has used its name to make a wish. Because these four girls ignored that rule, two of them are cast out of the human world, and the other two bear the stigma of this experience on their bodies.

CHAPTER 8

A Battered Wife Chooses to Be Reborn in Animal Forms, Then as a Man

The myth of this chapter is known throughout the central portion of the Inuit homeland.[1] I gathered three variants in Igloolik: one personally from *Iqallijuq* and the other two from her son-in-law *Kupaaq*. One of the latter variants was told to me in an interactive setting with several of *Kupaaq*'s children questioning him. It is thus richer than his mother-in-law's variant and will be used here as the basic text.

Life as a Battered Wife

This wife, so it is said, was always the target of her husband's anger. He often abused her, punching her and even hitting her with a stick. He was bad-tempered, as is the case with some. He would pick a quarrel with her at the first opportunity, as many are prone to do with children. She soon had enough of being mistreated this way and began to wish for death.

The theme of a battered or abused wife is recurrent in Inuit oral tradition. This variant does not tell us the reason for the abuse. We know she was childless, a failing most often blamed on the woman and a cause for reproach and mistreatment. In the two variants published by Rasmussen

(1929, 59–60; 1930b, 41–45), the story begins with the wife's miscarriage. She hides it from friends and family, she throws the fetus to the dogs, and its soul is reincarnated in a dog before passing on to other animal species. Boas (1901) also has two variants: in one, a woman is abandoned by her campmates and metamorphoses into various animals; in the other, an old woman dies, her corpse is pecked at by a raven, and her soul enters the bird before migrating to several other species.

In historical times, suicide was a socially accepted way out of dire straits. Inuit considered it a beautiful death, especially when the motive was altruistic, like an old man wishing in a time of famine to be no longer a burden on his family. Elders were nonetheless highly esteemed, being respected and listened to if one wished to reach their age. Suicide might have been a likelier option for women, their circumstances being in general more difficult than those of men (Saladin d'Anglure 1977b, 1978a).

One evening, when her husband came back from hunting and again got angry at her and again began to beat her, she had the idea of metamorphosing into a dog as she slipped under the caribou-skin blanket on the sleeping platform to escape his punching and beating. But he didn't calm down and kept hitting her. She began to cry without uttering the slightest word. Pounding at her fiercely through the blanket, he managed to injure her, making her want to moan with pain, but instead the yelping of a dog was heard. The yelping continued. Suddenly, a dog's muzzle appeared at the edge of the blanket. Then the animal leaped to the door and ran out. She had turned into a dog.

Although animals metamorphosing into humans and humans into animals belong to a mythical reality going back to the dawn of time, this reality is still nearby. It hovers in the background, close to empirical reality. It is part of the largely invisible world of spirits, who rule over the elements, the animals, and the dead. In normal times, only shamans had access to that world through their close ties to helping spirits. Nonetheless, an abused human could likewise cross the boundary separating that world from the human world to visit the dead and the great spirits or to enter the animal world. A human could also be taken across this boundary for a serious breach of group rules, as shown in the previous chapter.

In most variants of the myth, the battered wife opts for a dog's life as her first metamorphosis. This choice can undoubtedly be linked to two characteristics of a sled dog (*Canis familiaris*). First, it is the closest animal to humans and the only one to receive a personal name (Chapter 5); it is also the only animal that is domesticated and works for humans. Second, it is harshly disciplined and made to obey through regular whipping. When Inuit women refer to the way they lived in the past, they sometimes compare it to a dog's life (Saladin d'Anglure 1977b).

Here, the metamorphosis is gradual. The battered wife stops talking, and you can hear crying, moaning, and then the yelping of a dog. For a man, a dog is a pet that belongs to his home space. His wife's metamorphosis is equivalent to being reborn in this space and, like a baby, she has no experience with her new life.

Life as a Sled Dog

The vicious husband quickly took possession of the woman who had turned into a dog, and he added her to his dog team. He even made her his lead dog because once harnessed, she began to pull with lots of zeal.

Inuit often choose a female dog to lead a dog team. They claim it pulls better, obeys orders better, and pulls along the other dogs. By choosing to become a dog, the battered wife does not have to move far away. She remains in the home space she knows, while sharing the collective life of the dog team. She nonetheless escapes the loneliness of a wife abused by her husband.

When she, the lead dog, was pulling, she didn't know how to guide the other dogs when her master wanted to change direction. Whenever he tried to make her turn and she didn't understand, he would whip her. He would thrash about, shout a lot, and beat her to make her change direction.

Brought up as a woman, she has learned to serve her man and meet his needs. So it is not hard for her to obey once she has become a dog. For these reasons, she soon proves herself on the dog team and is made the lead dog, without the least training to be a sled dog. Now, a lead dog's most important quality is to understand its master's orders quickly, especially orders to move forward, to stop, and to change direction. This ability to understand is learned through lengthy training. The problem, evoked in the next passage, is the dog team's trouble when moving ahead on fore-shore ice, amid the icy slabs broken up by the tides. The dogs must follow their driver's orders to the letter. This is easier on areas of flat, smooth ice and on large snow-covered expanses.

Because she was often beaten, she asked an old dog that had previously been the lead dog, "I wonder why I'm so often beaten, even when I'm pulling good and hard?" It answered, "If he wants to turn and you turn in the same direction as he does, you won't get beaten. Similarly, when you come to icy patches full of bumps and holes, if you try to avoid them and go over the *manirait* [flat areas], you won't get beaten." She followed this advice and was no longer beaten. When she no longer knew what direction to go in, she would turn to her master and try to follow his instructions, and that way she no longer was beaten.

In the beginning, humans and animals spoke the same language, shared the same human appearance, were able to live the same lives, and married each other. One group could be told apart from the other by its accent, by some aspects of its way of life, by some of its eating habits, and by its man-ner of dress. Mythical history tells how humans gradually differentiated from animals, the former becoming hunters and the latter becoming game (Chapter 6). Shamans, as we have seen earlier, still enjoyed the power to go from one world to the other and to return to the enchanted universe of the dawn of time. Their helping spirits, whose form they sometimes took, were often predatory animals.

She was often very thirsty and would rush back to camp with the intention of going to lick the *kaugarsivik* [a container in which people would pound seal blubber to extract lamp oil]. She loved to lick the oil, the only way she could quench her thirst. When she didn't reach the *kaugarsivik* fast enough and still had her harness on her back, she would lick oil residues that had spilled from the lamp around the igloo, so thirsty she was. One day, again leading the dog team back to the igloo and being very thirsty, she took a shortcut—a straight route home to get there faster. She went by a place where no one had the habit of going. Her master tried to make her change direction, but she disobeyed, obsessed with her idea of getting home faster, and she was beaten again. As she hadn't been beaten for a long while, she had forgotten how dogs yelp with pain. Thus when being hit again and again she involuntarily began to moan like a human: *"A'aa!"* ["Ow, ow!"].

When a dead person's name-soul is reincarnated in a baby, it needs time to get used to its new state, notably during the neonatal period—as we saw in the first chapter, with *Iqallijuq*'s story. This transition is a time of some confusion, between the habits acquired during the last life and those to be acquired in the new one. It is not unusual for a baby during this time to commit acts or utter words that were those of its dead namesake. Similarly, during her metamorphosis, the battered wife's name-soul wavers between the habits of her previous human life and those of her new canine life. There is an inverse symmetry between the first episode of the story, when the abusive husband strikes his wife and she yelps like a dog, and this second episode, when he strikes his dog and it moans like a human. The first case was a prelude to a metamorphosis about to begin; the second, a prelude to the end of this metamorphosed life.

The man then decided to kill the woman-turned-lead-dog because she had moaned like a human. Because his igloo had no porch, only an entrance, she clearly heard him say he wanted to kill her. He said he'd make her come in three times to be fed, and once she had eaten her fill he'd kill her with a blow from a snow stick. Although she had become a dog, she understood all that he said, and she knew he wanted to kill her.

Just as *Savviurtalik*'s name-soul understood all that was said around her when she lived in the womb and could even, without words, influence the humans around her, the battered wife's name-soul understands all that her ex-husband says and thinks, even though she now lives in a dog's body. She goes along with being killed—and even wishes for death—because it is the only way to escape her life as a domestic dog, which is hardly more satisfying than hers was as a battered wife.

He made her enter the igloo and gave her a first morsel of meat, which she seized with her teeth and began to eat. When she was done, he gave her another morsel, which she seized again with her teeth and ate. When he offered her a third one, she didn't seize it right away with her teeth because she knew she'd get hit with a snow stick. So she closed her eyes for a moment and only then did she bite into the meat. At that moment, he dealt her a blow with the snow stick and killed her. When she was dead, he took her corpse out of the igloo. He took it far away because he no longer wanted to see her—she who had been first his wife and then his sled dog. He went very far away to lay it down on the plain. There, she was soon eaten by an *amaruq* [wolf], and she herself became a wolf.

With this second metamorphosis, the battered wife enters a savage, predatory world, and also a spirit world. Inuit call it *tumitaittuq* ("where there are no traces of footprints"), in opposition to *tumitaqartuq* ("where there are traces of footprints"); that is, inhabited space, which is daily used and has many tracks left by humans and dogs (Saladin d'Anglure 2004). Her new life as a predatory wolf is in stark contrast to her old one as a beaten dog. In passing, we will note that the battered wife's soul goes from the dog's body to the wolf's when the wolf devours the dog's corpse. She becomes the wolf's new soul, as if being ingested were equivalent to being reborn.

Life as a Predatory Wolf

Having become a wolf, she observed that her companions would very often pursue *tuktuit* [caribou]. She tried to follow them, but they outdistanced her each time because she tired very quickly. She was very hungry, and began to lose more and more weight. Since she wanted to eat, she made great efforts to run like the others, but to no avail. This wasn't surprising. She had no experience living as a wolf. When the wolf pack was pursuing caribou, she managed to catch up to them only after they had finished devouring their prey. She was much too slow.

Arctic wolves (*Canis lupus*) or *amaruit* live in packs and follow migrating caribou, their main food source (Randa 1994; Anand-Wheeler 2002). They are free, but unlike Inuit, who divide up catches among themselves, wolves observe the rule of first come, first served. Too bad for latecomers! This is disconcerting for the wolf woman, who is used to the practice of everyone getting a share of the game meat as long as they have taken part in the hunt. She is also used to the practice of the needy getting a share back at the camp.

She then asked an old wolf, "How is it that when I'm galloping with all of my strength the others always outdistance me, and I catch no prey?" It answered, "If you're very hungry, you must, when galloping, throw your forefeet as far ahead as possible and your hindfeet behind, stretching them as much as possible, as if you want to touch both ends of the world [of the horizon]. You'll then catch up to the other wolves." This was what she undertook to do, but being inexperienced she succeeded only after several fruitless tries.

Among humans, as among animals, elders are a fount of knowledge. Throughout this story, the heroine asks elderly individuals to initiate her into the secrets of survival, after she becomes one animal species or another. She will question an old caribou and an old walrus for the same reason.

Finally, she could run as the old wolf had told her, and she caught up to the others. She was now able to eat a few caribou rumens and crunch some bones. Her strength came back. Little by little, she managed to run as fast as the others and catch up to them when they were still devouring their prey, and thus get better portions of meat. She became faster and faster and, when galloping the way she had been told, she soon no longer had any trouble keeping pace with the other wolves. And so she managed to surpass them. One day, she even succeeded in being the first to get to the caribou, before the other wolves could kill them.

Inuit think she-wolves are faster than males. A myth tells how one of them kills the father of her cubs because he leaves them nothing to eat after killing his prey (Mitiarjuk 2014).

But she was clueless as to how to immobilize and kill her prey. She got near a caribou and tried to bite it, but it delivered a hoof kick right in her face, knocking her out.

ᑲᓇᒍ ᑐᑐ ᐊᒪᑭᒥ ᐅᑕᑭᔾ ᐊᒪᑭᑭ ᑐᑐᒥ ᐊᔪᐊᕐᒻᑅ
ᑐᑭᔪᒍ ᑐᑐᐅᑲᐅᑲ ᑲᕆᓯ ᐊᓂ ᓂᑦᒥᕆ.
ᑲᐊᒪᒍ ᑐᑐᐃ ᐊᓂᑕ ᐊᒪᑭᒥ ᑐᑯᑲᐊᕕᓂᒥᐅᒻᒪ ᑲᐅᕿᒪᔪᐊᕝ.

FIGURE 22. The beaten woman, reincarnated as a wolf, is knocked out with a hoof kick by a caribou she has just caught. The Inuktitut text says: *Taannaguuq tuktu amarurmik utaqqijuq. Amaruruuq tuktumik anguilirmat. Tukitsugu tuqutauvuq qaritangit anitisugit. Taimaguuq tuktuit ilangat amarurnik tuquraisuuviniummat qaujimajauvutt*—They say that the caribou waited for the wolf because the wolf overtook the caribou. They say it was killed by stomping out its brains. Thus some caribou know how to kill wolves. From a drawing by Paulusi Sivuak, 1973. Made by Johanne Lévesque. Archival fonds of B. Saladin d'Anglure.

FIGURE 23. The battered woman, reincarnated as a wolf, succeeds in killing her first caribou. From a drawing by Paulusi Sivuak, 1973. Made by Johanne Lévesque. Archival fonds of B. Saladin d'Anglure.

It is known that a large male caribou can kill a wolf with a hoof kick (Figure 22) or an antler jab. For this reason, wolves prefer to attack young fawns or sick individuals.

Feeling dejected, she again questioned the old wolf, "How is it I can't immobilize any caribou? I often try to bite them, but I don't know what to do to kill them. I can't kill them." It answered, "Whenever you catch up to a caribou, keep right near one of its hindfeet. Then bite its *kimmiqquaq* [Achilles tendon], and rip it out. That way, you'll immobilize it on the spot. Next cut its throat out by biting through its *tuqqujaaq* [larynx], thus causing its death. If you do this, you'll become a true caribou killer, a true wolf." This was how she learned to kill caribou all on her own to feed herself, and she soon gained weight.

The old male wolf is teaching a hunting lesson. When you are faced with an animal larger than yourself, and a fast one armed with hooves and antlers at that, the first goal is to immobilize it, and the second is to strike at a vital part of its body without endangering yourself. Biting the Achilles tendon of a hindfoot will throw the animal off balance (see the murder of the special dwarf, *Naarjuk*'s father, in Chapter 3). The larynx (*tuqqujaaq*), with the carotid artery and jugular veins, is certainly the body part where a caribou is most vulnerable to lethal bites (Figure 23).[2] The wounded animal no longer has any defence, and the wound will soon lead to death.

When she grew old for a wolf, she became tired of this way of life and let herself die on the ground. While she lay on the plain, a caribou passed over her corpse, and she took the opportunity to enter it.

The contrast is again very stark. She will soon live the life of her prey of yesterday. Her metamorphosis once more takes place metonymically, by simple contact, her soul going from a wolf body to a caribou body. She is again as inexperienced as a baby.

Life as a Hunted but Happy Caribou

She thus became a caribou and now had to feed on what grew on the ground. Despite her grazing, she couldn't gain weight. She even became very lean because she ate withered noxious plants, which are called *niqqarittualuit.* So she asked an old caribou, "How is it I can't fatten up when eating what grows on the ground?" It answered, "If you eat only ordinary plants, you won't be able to fatten up. To fatten up, you'll have to eat white lichens, which caribou call *ursuq* [fat], and also red and black *quajautit* [rock mosses], which grow on stones and seem stuck to them." So she began to eat lichen and mosses and soon gained weight.

Although food has been a recurring leitmotif from one metamorphosis to the next, it has previously been meat that humans, dogs, or wolves may eat. Here, the food is meant for herbivores. Although Inuit sometimes eat roots, buds, seaweed, or Arctic dock, plants make up only a tiny proportion of their diet. True, they do not mind eating predigested plants from the small intestine of a white-tailed ptarmigan or a ringed seal or the contents of a caribou's rumen, but such food becomes available very sporadically. Caribou feed on plants and lichens that humans find indigestible and unfamiliar.

After spending some time with the caribou, she noticed they were often anxious. They felt threatened, though unable to identify the danger. She herself was unafraid because she didn't know what they feared. When they were in this state, they would first turn in all directions and then stop to listen. As soon as one of them sensed something, it would run away with its head held upright.

Although caribou lack good eyesight, they have highly developed senses of smell and hearing. They are always on the lookout, and the slightest thing out of the ordinary will make them flee.

While remaining motionless, one of them said, "May the *qulalik* [female that has calved], she who this year first became a mother of a *Pisugasuasarnaaq* ['A little one that is trying to walk'], perform a divination by lifting her foot so that we may know the nature of the danger."

Inuit had a custom of honouring first-time achievements over the life cycle, such as the first game animal someone ever killed, or over the yearly cycle of activities, such as the first kill of the year. Such achievements were major rites of passage in social life (Saladin d'Anglure 2001b [2000]). The same custom is here transposed into the animal world, which is conceived as sharing the same humanity as the Inuit. Calving takes place during the moon of May (*Nurrait*, "the moon of fawns") in the Igloolik region (Saladin d'Anglure 1993a [1990b]; Randa 1994). It is a key time in the seasonal reproductive cycle of species hunted by Inuit. The cycle begins in March for ringed seals and continues into April for bearded seals, into May for caribou, and finally into June, the moon of eggs, for migrating birds. For caribou, May is the first calving of the season; for humans, it is the first caribou meat of the season.

In the social life of caribou, the *qulalik*—the first female to calve that year—is endowed with magic powers; here, the power of divination.[3] Inuit call this practice *qilaniq*, which is performed by shamans and, in emergencies, by the uninitiated. A strap is used to feel the weight of the foot or head of someone stretched out on the ground. Questions are then put to the spirit that is believed to have entered that part of the body. If the foot or head feels lighter, the answer is negative. If heavier, the answer is affirmative. Finally, we should note that the caribou are speaking a language related to that of shamans and therefore somewhat divergent from everyday speech. Such language is used by certain great mythical characters, by spirits, and by animals when they talk among themselves or appear in human form.

Indeed, caribou are very afraid of humans. They fear them a lot. Because they were very afraid, the female that had first calved that year obeyed and lifted her forefoot and struck the ground with her hoof. After discovering where the danger came from, she went off in the opposite direction, while singing the following chant: "*Takkuungaang najuukkaavuut tumaakkaavuut tautaqa&irpuruuq, inuktaqaa&alirpuruuq nainasuattaliirittii qinirasuattalirittii.*" "Over there, I see people who visit our homes, who follow our tracks far away. They're humans. They're hunters. Try to smell them. Try to locate them."

Caribou have poor eyesight, as mentioned earlier. This handicap can be offset by divination. The oracle encourages the other caribou to use all of their senses to locate the danger.

While they sang, many caribou had fled to a lake. The woman-turned-caribou did as the others, but having found a companion, the two of them dawdled on the way there and grazed where lichen was plentiful. When done grazing, they caught up to the bulk of the herd, which had been moving farther ahead, and they arrived near the lake.

The action is in late summer or early autumn, when caribou gather in large herds to migrate to winter pastures. This migration will require swimming across some lakes and rivers. Meanwhile, the Inuit have come and are lying in wait with their kayaks, which are faster on the water than these animals are. It is the time of year when caribou fur gets dense enough for making warm winter clothing. This hunt will also provide large stores of meat for winter, when game are scarce and hunting difficult (Saladin d'Anglure and Vézinet 1977).

Her companions then said, "Now we're going to cross by kayak!," and they advanced to the shore of the lake. She first thought they were talking about kayaks, like the ones used by the Inuit, and that she would have the caribou who accompanied her as her kayak companion. When they got to the water's edge, they explained to her that the kayaks were actually their own chests and the paddles their own feet. So they began to paddle, caribou-style, to the other side of the lake.

Inuit conceive a kayak as a body with a backbone. It has a spinal column (the keel), to which are attached ribs (planking) and a penis (bow).[4] When a caribou swims in water, it is like an Inuk moving forward in a kayak with a double-bladed paddle; the caribou's feet act like paddles. Misunderstandings still plague the woman who has metamorphosed into a caribou. She interprets what the caribou tell her as a human would. This episode brings to mind the one about the loon that becomes a hunter in a kayak.[5]

She trailed behind, trying to cross the lake by doing as they did. Unknown to her, some Inuit [humans] were approaching. When she noticed them, it was already too late, and she was met by Inuit in kayaks. The Inuit went into action and pursued them, feverishly attacking the ones they caught up with and running them through with their spears one after another. Some caribou tried to flee back the way they came, but the Inuit pursued and killed them in turn. The woman-turned-caribou imagined that getting speared would hurt a lot, but she felt only a nice tickling as the spear went through, for it had been well-sharpened. And now she too was killed.

For the first time in this myth, the narrator sees things from the animal's viewpoint, as a victim of humans. We thus come to a sort of "hunting morality," that is, the rules a hunter should obey not only to prevent the hunted animal from suffering but also to make it feel some pleasure when killed. For this to happen, it must be killed properly. We will see in a later episode that the hunter's weapon penetrates the animal as a man's penis penetrates a woman. A poorly honed weapon is painful to the animal. Conversely, a well-honed one is pleasurable and causes a nice tickling sensation.

When all of them were killed, the hunters tied them up and towed them to shore with their kayaks; there, they hauled them ashore and skinned them by making a cut in the skin on the mid-chest. The woman-turned-caribou again thought this would be painful, and when a hunter began to skin her she felt an intense pain in her chest because the knife was poorly honed. She cried out in pain, "A' aa!," and hoped the man would sharpen his cutlass; this he did, before continuing to cut all the way down the skin of her chest. The feeling was now nice. She felt only a slight tickle, and during the end of the skinning she no longer cried out in pain. When her skin was removed, the hunter cut her up and put her in a stone cache, where she was left as a stock of meat for winter.

This passage illustrates the power of spirits to act on living things by the simple force of a tacit wish or desire (Chapter 1). This power of thought was also available to humans through magic spells and incantations (*irinaliutiit*) or mere wishes, such as the ones made by the girls who played at having a husband (Chapter 7).

After killing a caribou, the hunter had to remove its skin, gut it, cut off its head and feet, remove the upper hamstrings (the ones that contain the sinews used for sewing thread), cut out the two haunches, and place them

FIGURE 24. The battered woman, reincarnated as a caribou, is speared as she crosses the ford. From a drawing by *Juanasialuk*. Engraving on stone. Federation of Cooperatives of New Quebec. Made by Johanne Lévesque.

inside the carcass. The carcasses were then put in stone caches, on which were placed the antlers to act as landmarks whenever snow covered the caches.

After a long while in the stone cache, she began to suffer from being unable to change position. She had been placed under the others, and the part of her that sat on the ground was in great pain because it bore her full weight. So she impatiently waited for someone to come and take her out, for she found the waiting very long. Try as she might to change position, she couldn't.

Her name-soul, having become a caribou, is still bound to that identity even after being killed, cut up, and cached. She continues to feel the same sensations as when the animal was alive, hence the painful cramp due to her forced immobility.

A soul could remain bound to its body for up to six months until the next spring equinox, which marked the change of season. Inuit were then freed from the winter prohibitions that existed to leave the souls of killed land or sea animals in peace and thus give them time to undo their ties to existence as live animals.

When winter came, she heard a crunching of footsteps on the snow outside, and when someone began to dismantle the stone cache she felt overcome by joy. She was soon removed from the cache, and the pain-stricken part of her body was finally pulled out. She no longer suffered in pain. The man loaded the pieces onto his sled to take them back to his igloo and thaw them out. While being taken away, she began to think about the unwelcome prospect of being eaten by a postpartum woman who would be subject to many restrictions. Now, no sooner had she been taken to the igloo than a postpartum woman came by and asked for the woman-turned-caribou as her share of the meat. At the last moment, she was given another piece. The woman-turned-caribou was glad to be eaten by another person, who wouldn't be under the postpartum dietary taboo. Once all of her flesh had been eaten, her bones were thrown outside onto the shore ice, on top of some walrus bones. When summer came, the ice melted, the tide covered the bones, and she who had been a woman before being a caribou entered a walrus bone that came back to life. She became a walrus.

The story now comes to a key stage in the transmigration of the woman's name-soul: going from land to sea. All of the dictates of Inuit tradition converged on the need to keep the two worlds apart. On any given day, it was forbidden to eat the flesh of animals from both worlds. So human mediation is doubly needed here before the human soul of a caribou body can enter a walrus body. The change of body is also helped by the change of season—the transition from winter, when taboos are strict, to summer, when they are much weaker.

Humans killed and ate both walrus and caribou, leaving only the bones, that is, the most lasting part of an animal and the part that best identifies a species (Chapter 7). Since bones are completely "dead," the name-soul can safely go from the bones of a caribou to the bones of a walrus (*Odobenus rosmarus*) or *aiviq*. Contact with water then brings the ensouled bones to life. Similarly, in some circumstances, people would bring together the different parts of a marine mammal's skeleton and throw them into the sea so that these parts could come alive as an animal of that species.

An Irksome Life as a Walrus

Having become a walrus, she had to get what walrus feed on, *ammuumajuit* [truncate softshell, *Mya truncata*], a sort of clam, which she had to look for at the sea bottom while not suffocating [when submersed]. But she couldn't dive that deep. Whenever she tried, she risked dying of asphyxia. For this reason she asked an old walrus for advice, "How does one dive down to the bottom of the sea? I try, but I never manage to touch bottom. How do you go about getting food for yourself?" It answered, "You must first aim upwards, to the middle of the sky above and then act as if you want to go there. Finally, you abruptly change direction and, with a running start, dive as fast as possible down to the sea bottom, which you will bump into with your tusks. You'll then go about feeding on clams."

Walruses love clams or, more exactly, truncate softshell clams. After killing a walrus, Inuit remove its stomach contents, in this case predigested clams with the shells removed. They then make a stew they are very fond of. In the variant gathered by Comer and published by Boas (1901), the woman, now a walrus, cannot eat the clams because they shut their shells when they see her. The old walrus tells her to cry out *"Uuurq! Uuurq!"* to make them half-open their shells for her to eat their flesh. Clams are found at the bottom of the sea and on sandy beaches. The latter have to be dug up, as one does with cockles.

She did what she had been told. She aimed for the sky, took a running start, reversed her position, and dove down to the bottom, but failed to reach it despite the downward thrusts she made with her tusks. In her haste to do everything right, she hadn't inhaled enough air and had to go back to the surface. She was quite disappointed. She tried again and, with a determined second try, succeeded in collecting clams and eating plenty of them, thus fattening herself up. She discovered that walruses liked to kiss each other by rubbing snouts with their very prickly whiskers when they hadn't seen each other for a short time. It hurt her when she tried to kiss that way, and she didn't like it at all, even though her companions were openly very affectionate toward her. She lost all desire to be a walrus and let herself die.

Walruses have whiskers with large, thick, and dense bristles. They rub each other's snouts while groups of them frolic in the sea. This is always a point of amazement for Inuit, who kiss similarly by sniffing each other and rubbing one face against the other. In the variant gathered by Comer (Boas 1901), the woman-turned-walrus complains that her snout is completely inflamed by the countless kisses she has to endure.

The corpse floated for a long time at sea and began to swell and smell bad. With its foreflippers angled forward, it drifted to shore where it washed up. She [her name-soul] then wished to be pecked at by a raven and become a raven.

The word *silu* was used for the corpse of a marine mammal that had washed ashore. If it washed up head first, it could be eaten. The reverse position was interpreted as a bad sign, and neither humans nor dogs could eat the corpse. Only scavengers, like ravens, would. In this episode of the myth, a metamorphosis again happens by ingestion, and again because of a tacit wish expressed by thought.

Life as a Scavenging Raven

When a raven began to peck away, she [her name-soul] entered it and became a raven. She was hungry and began to look for food as a raven would. She began to look for food with another raven while flying above a frozen bay, with a very cloudy sky and a fine powder snow blowing over the ground. Winter had come, food was scarce, and the two ravens began to fly in different directions, looking for anything to eat.

The common raven [*Corvus corax*] or *tulugaq* is, with the white-tailed ptarmigan and the snowy owl, one of the few birds that overwinter in the Arctic. It can be seen flying in the sky around camps in search of garbage. Inuit liked to use its skin with the feathers still on to wipe their babies clean and to make them their first clothes, as we have seen previously (Chapter 2). The raven also holds a key place in their cosmology, as a demiurge among the Inuit of Alaska or as the creator of daylight among the Inuit of the Central and Eastern Arctic (Kleivan 1971).

When one of the two found something, it cawed, and the other would come over. So she who had been a woman began to caw to her companion, because she had just spotted a *nanuq* [polar bear, *Ursus maritimus*] eating the corpse of a *nattiq* [ringed seal, *Phoca hispida*]. She thought they would both have food to eat. She arrived before the other raven did and began to pick through what remained of the *nanuq*'s meal. She ate its leftovers by drawing near and hopping from one side to the other. At a given moment, however, misjudging the condition of the ice and having alighted on the sea ice, she slid and fell with her feet spread apart. The polar bear seized the opportunity to bite and kill her. The woman-turned-raven fell onto the *nattiq* [ringed seal], the same bear having killed both of them. She then decided to become a ringed seal.

This is the second time since the story began that the transmigration of the name-soul has been doubly mediated. The operation is difficult. The name-soul has to go from the raven's aerial world to the ringed seal's aquatic world. The mediator is a *nanuq*, a polar bear, an amphibious animal. It has a special mediating role in the system of representation of the Inuit, in their mythology, and in their shamanism (Saladin d'Anglure

1990a [1980]). It is the most human-like of all animals, hunting seals, living in a snow house, and standing on two feet. Some Inuit even claim that its flesh tastes the same as human flesh (Chapter 14). The Moon Man, one of the most powerful spirits, who endows shamans with clairvoyance, has a dog team of polar bears (Chapter 9).

Life as a Ringed Seal, with Men Lying in Wait

Having become a *nattiq* [a ringed seal], she discovered that seals had *agliut* [breathing holes] in the ice. The breathing holes were very bright when looked at from below, through the dark water. She also noticed that many ringed seals would jostle each other for access to the bright holes, to be the first one out to breathe. But whenever the sound of footsteps was heard in the vicinity of a hole, they'd dive back underwater and look for another bright hole. Holes watched by waiting Inuit hunters looked dark when seen from below. Seals spotted them easily. She who had been a raven was overtaken by the other ringed seals racing to the bright holes, and to keep from suffocating she had to resign herself to going to a dark hole to breathe.

Two logics face off here. The first is the logic of survival: a *nattiq* (ringed seal, *Phoca hispida*) is looking for bright breathing holes, which the hunters are not watching. The second is the logic of sacrifice: the seal wants to be killed. It wants to offer itself to a good hunter who sharpens his weapons properly, who obeys the rules of the great spirits and the shamans, and who respects game animals. The seal's soul will thereby reincarnate in another animal of the same species. The second logic is implicit throughout the myth, whereas the first one is explicit. In other variants, the logic of self-sacrifice is stated more clearly. The seals assign each other the dark holes in order to be killed and showered with fresh water by Inuit who observe the customary rules. The seals will stay away if hunters at the holes are negligent or show no respect for the rules.

When she came to the hole, she glimpsed above her a drop of water about to fall on her from the snow that covered the hole. She tried to avoid it, but in vain, and she felt a tickling sensation in her head. The drop of water was actually the point of a harpoon that had struck her in the head.

There is a twofold reality here. She is thirsty for fresh water but tries to avoid the drop of water about to fall on her. She fails to avoid it, but instead of discomfort she feels pleasure, a tickling sensation. The sexual symbolism of hunting is omnipresent. Evidently, she has been harpooned by a hunter who honed his weapon very well.

She tried to escape but was firmly grabbed and hauled up through the narrow hole, and she even received blows to her body. That made her angry, for she had been a human.

The ringed seal remembers her previous lives as an abused wife and as a beaten dog. She does not appreciate the blows from the hunter at all.

When the hunter hauled her up onto the ice, she suddenly discovered that the man who had harpooned and struck her was her own brother, the brother she had when she was still human and suffered her husband's anger.

Events have taken a dramatic turn for this woman in a ringed seal's body, the result being a reversal of circumstances. This man is dear to her. He is her own brother.

The hunter, that is, her brother, was unable to have children—or rather his wife had been pregnant several times, but each pregnancy had ended in miscarriage, and she had lost all of her unborn infants.

The woman-turned-ringed-seal knows that her brother is childless and would like to have children. Her soul knows about his wife's repeated miscarriages and sees an unhoped-for end to her wanderings from one animal species to another in search of a better life.

While he loaded the ringed seal onto his sled to take it back to his igloo, the soul in the seal began to hope that a woman, her brother's wife, would cut her up, and that the woman's trouser belt would be loosened.

Her name-soul is now fully aware of the situation and is regaining full power to act on her future by the power of thought. Still incarnated in the seal, she expresses her desire to reincarnate again, but this time as her brother's child.

The man who had harpooned her took her to a spot near his igloo. He then went in and took his boots off, leaving his wife with the job of bringing the seal inside and cutting it up. She (the wife) did so, dragging the body into the igloo and beginning to cut it up. While she worked, her loosened trouser belt brushed against the seal's corpse, as [the name-soul] had wished, by the power of thought.

The sexual division of labour varied from one Inuit group to another. Bringing the animal's body inside and cutting it up could sometimes be done by the man, but usually his wife did it. Here, the wife has to do it because the woman's name-soul in the seal is weary of her animal metempsychoses and now wishes to become a human fetus in her sister-in-law's womb.

She who had been a woman, before becoming a seal, promptly seized the chance to haul herself up along the belt to the interior of her brother's wife, and she became a human fetus.

A loosened belt is synonymous with openness and is also a means to change one's state of being—from a soul, here incarnated in a freshly killed seal, to a human fetus in the womb of her brother's wife (Chapter 1).

Life as a Human Fetus

Sometime after, the [brother's] wife realized she was pregnant and began to cry. She fervently wished to have a child, and since all of her preceding pregnancies had miscarried, she thought this one would too.

Being a barren woman or one who repeatedly miscarried was a difficult situation for Inuit and caused great distress (Chapter 1). A miscarriage was more painful to live through than complete sterility. On top of her emotional distress, the woman had to endure long, severe restrictions on her life, and she would be tempted to keep it secret. This is in fact the starting point for one variant of the myth.

Now inside, she who had become a fetus was aware of everything that happened outside. She felt very uneasy, hearing her brother's wife crying, and she no longer wished to stay in her; however, when the woman stopped crying, the fetus decided to stay. She stayed for a long time as a fetus. She knew that the woman on waking up early in the morning would go outside and that she would also rush out whenever men came back from hunting. She did this so that her baby would be born faster and would later succeed in hunting.

Everyone knew and followed these rules. By encouraging the fetus to become rapid and by going outside whenever it wanted, an expectant mother would help it become a boy. This was what people said. This was also why a pregnant woman would welcome hunters and travellers. Everyone sought rapidity: men, to succeed in hunting; women, to give birth to boys who would be future hunters or to girls who would be skilful sewers and have many sons (Chapters 1 and 3).

She who was now a fetus wished to go outside. Her little home had become too confined and uncomfortable. A large pool of water was forming at the end of the home. The time had come for her to go out.

Here we see the immediate effect on the fetus of the expectant mother's compliance with the ritual injunctions. We again see the image of a womb-igloo that melts with the coming of summer, an image already encountered in *Iqallijuq*'s memories from the womb (Chapter 1) and in those of *Uumarnituq*'s first child in the variant published by Boas (1907) (Chapter 2).

On her way out, she saw on each side of the exit a woman's knife [*ulu*] on her right and a harpoon point [*sakku*] on her left. She wanted to take the *ulu* to be born a girl [*arnaq*] and then changed her mind, grabbed the *sakku* to become a boy [*angut*], and on coming out became a baby boy. Her sex had been changed by the choice she had just made.

This passage shows the Inuit theory of *sipiniuniq* (change of sex): a fetus or baby can choose a sex other than the one of the person it is reincarnating (Chapters 1 and 2).

Aumarjuat Is Reborn as a Hunter after a Woman's Life

It was very cold, and a thick cloud of fog surrounded the boy because of his birth in the bitter cold.

This is the same scenario as in *Iqallijuq*'s memories of birth (Chapter 1). Fog is a source of danger and is caused by postpartum bleeding. It is visible to a baby, to animals, and to spirits. Because of this danger, the new mother will be secluded until her period of confinement is over.

The membrane [amniotic sac] that covered him was removed. He wanted to speak and recount his experience in the womb, but out of his mouth came only a baby's wailing, "*Ungaa, Ungaa.*"

The transition from fetal life to human life and to an infant's first moments leads to ambiguities: here, the baby's thwarted desire to be articulate and to express his thoughts very clearly. He still thinks like a fetus while speaking like a baby (Chapters 1 and 2).

The baby grew and grew and remembered more and more of his life in the womb. Later, when he grew even more and became a little boy, he could finally recount all of his memories. It is said he even composed the following song: "*Nukaapaqqaamimmaa nuliangaagullii aniigiaramaa ungaa&artungaa ungaa&artungaa ungaajajaa*" ["When I came out of my younger brother's wife, I began to wail, '*Ungaa, ajaaja Ungaa ajaaja*'"].

In the variant gathered by Rasmussen (1929, 60), the child grows up to become a skilful hunter. He is so strong that his sealing float is made from the whole skin of a bearded seal, and he easily captures animals of all species. He cares for his parents and brings them food until the end of their days. This variant also tells us he is named *Aumarjuat* ("Big Ember"). This presumably was already the battered wife's name at the beginning of the myth.

Besides its sociological dimensions, this myth has an ontological and cosmological dimension.[6] It is about kinship ties: the marital problems of a childless wife; the violence inflicted by her husband; the delight of brother-sister relationships; and the joy of son-parent relationships. The myth is also about relations of sex and gender: the difficulty of being a woman; and the possibility of changing sex and going from female to male activities. It explains rules about human-animal relations by reversing perspective—to use Piaget's expression. We are initiated into the life of each kind of animal, whether predator, game, or scavenger, whether living in the air, under the water, or on the land. Through this myth we learn about Inuit hunting knowledge, as do Inuit themselves (Saladin d'Anglure 1977b, 57). Through it we also discover the logic that justifies boundaries between humans and game animals, an ambiguous logic of desire and pleasure, which an animal feels when choosing to be killed and eaten, as if its desire and pleasure were sexual. The animal wants love and respect from the hunter while he penetrates and cuts it up with a well-honed weapon.

CHAPTER 9

Kaujjajjuk, a Mistreated Orphan Rescued by the Moon Man

This story is about *Kaujjajjuk* (literally "He who receives walrus skin" [to feed on]) and the Moon Man, who rescues him and helps him get back at his oppressors.[1] Known throughout most of the Inuit homeland, the story centres on a recurring mythological theme: the revenge of a mistreated orphan. Until the mid-twentieth century, many Inuit children were orphans because so many adults died during hunting accidents or complications of childbirth. Their situation was unenviable when no close kin were around to care for them.

In Igloolik I heard this myth as two distinct stories.[2] Most of the elements of both appear in a single story collected by Boas (1901, 186–88) from Cumberland Sound and by Rasmussen (1929, 151–53) from *Ivalvarjuk*, on the west coast of Hudson Bay. This chapter will feature the two stories told by *Kupaaq* (1972), which I will compare with variants from other regions of Canada's Central Arctic.

ᐸᐃᒪᐊᑦᖐ ᐃᑦᐊᕆᕆᐳᐹᑦᖐ ᐊᓂᖅᕐᓗ
ᑐᕐᔾᒥᐅᑕᕆᐳᐸᐸᕼᖅᒐᖅᑐᐊᖐ ᐊᐅᒻᒥᑎᖃᕋᓂ.
ᐊᐅᒻᒥᑎᖃᕐᖓᒥ ᑭᒥ ᐃᒻᒪᐊᖐ ᓯᓂᒃᐸᑐᐊᖐ ᑐᕐᒥᐅᑕᐅᑦᖐ.
ᑭᒻ ᐅᖅᖁᒍᑎᒋᑦᖐᒋᑦ ᖁᐊᕆᒃᑯᑎᓐᓂᒋᑦ ᓯᓂᒃᐸᑐᐊᖐ.
ᐅᓪᓚᒪ ᐸᐃᒪᕋᐅ ᐱᓇᑦᐅᐊᑎᐊᐅᐸᑐᐊᖐ ᐊᐳᓯᕇᑎᑎᑕᐅᑦᖐ.
ᐸᐃᒪᐊᑦᖐ ᑲᐅᔾᔭᕐᔪᐊᕐᓗᒻᒥᒃ ᐊᑎᖃᕐᑎᑕᐅᐸᕐᓚᑦᑕᓂᕐᒥᔪᖅᑦ.

FIGURE 25. The orphan Walrus-Skin is forced to sleep in the igloo entranceway with the dogs. The Inuktitut text says: *Taimaitsuni iliarrurijautsuni anirraminut tuursumiutarijauvalirattatuviniq aummitiqarani; aummitiqannginami qimmiit immuani sinikpaktuviniq tuursumiutautsuni. Qimmiit uqqugutigitsugit quarikkutinngisugit sinikpatuviniq. Ullulimaat taimaraaluk pinasuartitauvaktuviniq apusiriititititautsuni. Taimaitsuni kaujjajuarjualugmik atiqartitauvallirattanirmijuq*— Then being an orphan he was sent out to live in the entrance porch without any bedclothes. He slept curled up with the dogs as bedclothes in the entrance porch. The dogs kept him warm [and protected him] against the cold while he was sleeping. Every day the snow tried to cover him over. Because of this he was usually named Big *Kaujjajjuk*. After a drawing and text by Paulusi Sivuak, 1973. Made by Johanne Lévesque. Archival Fonds of B. Saladin d'Anglure.

Walrus-Skin, a Victim of Abuse

The myth of Walrus-Skin is exemplary in the way it shows how an orphan can cope with extreme situations and thrive with outside assistance. Here is the first story that *Kupaaq* told me:

Kaujjajjuk [Walrus-Skin] was an orphan mistreated by his campmates [Figure 25]. This abuse included being forbidden to sleep in a home.

Inuit hospitality was legendary, and so we can understand the tragedy of a child being forbidden to sleep and eat with other people in a home. This social exclusion threatens the child's life. *Ivaluarjuk*, in his variant, said the boy is mistreated because he is still little (Rasmussen 1929, 151). Other variants give other reasons: he is treated this way either because he is made to do tasks forbidden to boys or because his mother has broken taboos.

He had nowhere to live. He slept in entranceways with the dogs. To get a bit of warmth, he would sleep on a dog and, thus, off the ground. He would also have a dog for a pillow, a dog under his feet to keep them warm, and a dog on top for a blanket. This was how he slept, completely surrounded by dogs.

Traditional homes, whether igloos or semi-subterranean houses, included, in addition to the living area, a double-door entry and an entranceway. In winter, the dogs slept in that enclosure. Walrus-Skin's friendship with dogs shows an interesting side of relations between Inuit and their sled dogs. This animal being gregarious by nature, a small hierarchical social unit would form among dogs on the same team and from the same household. Moreover, commensalism and sometimes even affective ties would develop between dogs and some household members, especially children. A puppy could be given to a child and named after him or her (Saladin d'Anglure 2015a).

People fed the boy pieces of walrus skin. When the dogs were fed, he would eat with them.

The worst kind of mistreatment is to deny food to a needy person. To make this boy eat with the dogs is to show an extreme desire to humiliate and reject him. The skin of a walrus (*kauk*) is too tough for anyone to eat except during famine, when people will eat anything. It has to be chewed in small raw morsels for a long while before swallowing. Dogs have no problem because of their sharp teeth. *Ivaluarjuk*'s variant adds that the orphan received strips of walrus skin to chew over and over, as women do with a piece of hard dry leather—by moistening it with their saliva to make it more pliable.

An old woman was kind to Walrus-Skin, but she didn't dare show him affection. She was afraid of the other people. She gave him a very small blade to wedge between his teeth so that he could eat faster while chewing walrus skin. The blade would cut through that skin, and he could get a second helping before the dogs had gone through all of the food.

Compassion is a key value of Inuit culture, although in times of scarcity and famine the dominant adults would favour productive over non-productive individuals. According to *Ivaluarjuk*, the old woman feels pity for the young boy and secretly cuts up small morsels of walrus skin for him to swallow more easily. She also gives him a stone blade small enough for him to hide in one of his ears, or under his foreskin (Rasmussen 1929, 89). This detail brings to mind the sexual symbolism of a detachable harpoon point.

But the sudden rapidity with which he now ate aroused the suspicions of his campmates. The people searched him and discovered the blade between his teeth. They took it away. He had to go back to eating only with his teeth and so his portion was no longer enough. The dogs had tougher teeth than he did, and they finished the food before he could.

One can speak here of relentless sadism. His campmates want him to wither away and die of hunger, insidiously and without apparent violence.

Assistance from the Moon Man (Moon Brother)[3]
In *Kupaaq*'s variant, a new episode of the myth now begins:

One evening, while trying to go to sleep, he heard someone shouting to him, "*Kaujjajjuk*, come out!"

Ivaluarjuk's variant has more details: One night *Kaujjajjuk* is sleeping in the entranceway of a home and beams of moonlight come down to illuminate him. Other variants describe a full moon in the sky;[4] *Kaujjajjuk* then awakes to the sound of a sled skidding over the snow, and he hears the voice of a man ordering his dogs to halt and calling each of them by name: *Tiriatsiaq*! ("Pretty Ermine"), *Kajurjuk*! ("Big Red"), and *Nalupiritsuq*! ("Mud Trudger") (Rasmussen 1929, 89).[5]

He didn't want to go out. So he said to one of the dogs, "I won't go out! You, the dog that acts as my blanket, go out!" The dog on top of him went outside. But the person shouted to him again, "*Kaujjajjuk*, come out!"

A long exchange ensues, creating suspense in the narrator's audience. The listeners hang on to each word he speaks, even if they all know the story already. They want to hear what comes next:

He said to another dog, "I won't go out! You, at the end of my feet, go out!" The dog at his feet went outside. "*Kaujjajjuk*, come out!" shouted the voice again from outside. "I won't go out!" he replied. "You, the dog by my side, go out!" The dog by his side went outside. Only two dogs remained to keep him warm. But he didn't want to leave, and he kept making the dogs go outside. The person outside shouted to him again, "*Kaujjajjuk*, come out!" *Kaujjajjuk* said, "I won't go out! You, the dog who acts as my pillow, go out!" The dog under his head went outside. Again, someone shouted, "*Kaujjajjuk*, come out!" There remained only the dog under him. He answered, "I won't go out! You, who acts as my mattress, go out!" His mattress dog went outside. There were no longer any dogs in the entranceway. The person calling to him shouted again, "*Kaujjajjuk*, come out!" There was no longer anyone to send outside, so he went. He saw a big strong man, very well-dressed in new caribou-skin clothes, with a new whip in his hand. The man walked over to *Kaujjajjuk*, grasped him by the hand, and took him far away.

According to *Ivaluarjuk*, the Moon Man takes *Kaujjajjuk* to a place where no human footprints are to be seen (Rasmussen 1929, 89), that is, to a place conducive to dialogue with spirits.[6] Spirits leave no footprints, and such places are their realm. Shamans go there when they want to enter into contact with spirits quickly. The new caribou-skin clothes are a sign of opulence, and they contrast with the rags of Walrus-Skin (*Kaujjajjuk*). The whip is a symbol of masculinity. In Iglulik, whenever a young man made his first kill, he would be given a whip with a handle made from a polar bear's penis bone, in recognition of his new role as a provider (Saladin d'Anglure 1990a [1980]).

The Training of Walrus-Skin

They went far away and stopped on a slope. The man released the boy's hand and whipped him for the first time. Then he pushed him, and *Kaujjajjuk* [Walrus-Skin] slid to the bottom of the slope. Whenever he fell, the man would whip and push him. His clothes, which were in tatters, had been stuffed with old head hair and old caribou hair to keep him warm. The man treated *Kaujjajjuk* so harshly that the stuffing of his clothes began to fall out.

According to *Ivaluarjuk*, Walrus-Skin begins to vomit, and from his clothing fall out piles of women's hair combings and scraps of caribou fur from women's trousers. These are cast-offs and discards from women (Rasmussen 1929, 89). In *Naukajjik*'s variant, two women would give him their old caribou-skin shorts to chew on (Rasmussen 1930b, 52). Young boys were forbidden to look at women combing their hair, and women's shorts were likewise subject to many prohibitions because they could be soiled with menstrual or postpartum blood.

When no more [stuffing] remained, the man kept whipping him and told him to try to lift a stone stuck to the ground. He couldn't, and the man whipped him a bit more and then told him to try again, and this time he managed to lift the stone. The stones he had to lift were bigger and bigger. If he failed to lift one of them, the man would push and whip him, and that made him stronger. The man then told him to lift a very big stone. He couldn't, and the man whipped him again, and Walrus-Skin finally managed to lift it. When he became so strong that he could lift stones solidly stuck to the ground, the man stopped whipping him.

This episode inspired the Inuit makers of the film *Atanarjuat* in the scene where the older brother *Aamarjuaq* is making his younger brother lift heavy stones and shoving him to make him stronger (Chapter 13). Walrus-Skin's initiation is over. He has passed all of the tests and been transformed little by little into an adult with uncommon strength. He can now defend himself against all of his oppressors.

His clothes were so old almost nothing remained after the whipping. The man with the whip gave him his own new clothing and his whip.

A gift of new clothing accompanies the major transitions of life and the transition to a new annual cycle. Here, it accompanies a series of tests, and the physical and psychological transformation of little Walrus-Skin. This theme also appears in the myth of *Atanaarjuat* (Chapter 13). The hero's wife, a victim of mistreatment by their campmates, finds her husband again after a long absence, and he gives her a new, richly decorated garment. In the case of Walrus-Skin, the clothing he receives has not been made by human hands. He is instead given the Moon Man's own clothing.

The man told Walrus-Skin to go to the rear of the camp and wait for the others to wake up. When the people began to get up, Walrus-Skin would then whip the ground three times. Once he had struck the ground three times with the whip, the Moon Man, who had made him into a man and who exercised control over animals, would then send three polar bears to earth.

It is known in oral tradition that the Moon Man's sled dogs are polar bears. Previously, Walrus-Skin lived on the infra-human scale of existence because of his small size and the mistreatment he suffered. Now, with the Moon Man's help, he has risen to a supra-human scale. He once lived with dogs; now he is a friend of polar bears. The Moon Man himself was once a teenager oppressed by his mother and kept by her at a childlike stage (Chapter 4). So he decides to help Walrus-Skin overcome the insurmountable obstacles that his campmates have placed in his way. The little oppressed orphan has become a being above the others and feared by them.

Walrus-Skin's Revenge

When the people woke up, Walrus-Skin struck the ground three times with his whip, and three polar bears came from the moon and headed for the camp. When the people discovered there were polar bears in the camp, they were very excited, and one of them shouted, "But where is Walrus-Skin?" The man's idea was to get the bears to attack the boy and thus give the men time to kill the bears. Someone again shouted, "Where is Walrus-Skin? He has to help us catch the polar bears. We'll use him to distract the polar bears." This was when Walrus-Skin began walking to the camp, singing, "Here's Walrus-Skin! I'm just right for distracting polar bears. I'm useful. I'm very, very useful." Several children had gone looking for Walrus-Skin, as they had known him previously with his old ripped clothing. When one of the boys spied him, he cried out, "Here's Walrus-Skin, the good-for-nothing!"

The adults of the camp have picked on Walrus-Skin so much that even boys his own age insult him. His vengeance will be all the more unforgiving.

Walrus-Skin went to the child who had seen him, and he whipped him. He then grabbed the child's head and twisted his neck. When he met people along the way he twisted their necks and killed them. He was still walking to the camp and singing, "Here's Walrus-Skin! I'm just right for distracting bears. I'm useful. I'm very, very useful." He then saw a man come to him, and he went to him while singing, "I killed your child. I twisted his head around, and the back of his neck snapped! I'm useful. I'm very, very useful. I was good for nothing. Now I'm very useful." He approached the man and killed him. When he saw another man come to him, he said, "What are you doing here? Are you trying to come and get me?" Then he whipped, struck, and killed him. He next came to the camp, where the men had gone out to try and catch the bears. They still hoped to use him to distract the bears. As soon as he approached them, they grabbed him and threw him to the polar bears, but the polar bears didn't pounce on him. He got up, began to grab hold of the men by their legs, and then threw them to the polar bears, which killed them. The women then began to come out. Because they had likewise been unkind to him, he also threw them to the polar bears, and everybody was killed [Figure 26].

FIGURE 26. Revenge of Walrus-Skin, the mistreated orphan, who kills his adversaries thanks to the polar bears that the Moon Man sent him. After a text and drawing by Daividialuk Amittuq Alasuaq, Povungnituk, 1971. Made by Johanne Lévesque. Archival fonds of B. Saladin d'Anglure.

In his variant *Ivaluarjuk*, much more than *Kupaaq*, stresses the women's malice toward *Kaujjajjuk*. They begin to sing derisively while he is still being looked for: "Where is *Kaujjajjuk*, *Kaujjajjuk*, miserable wretch? Not too good to frighten bears away! Not too good to make a morsel for the bears! Well and good, let him tease them! Well and good, let them eat him up!" So sang the women (Rasmussen 1929, 90). They were always the cruellest to Walrus-Skin.

There remained only an old woman, the one who had been kind to Walrus-Skin. The old woman was so afraid that Walrus-Skin discovered her trying to hide under the dogs' feeding trough. Walrus-Skin approached her and told her that he didn't want to kill her and that she need not fear him. He said to her, "You took good care of me when I needed help. I'm not going to hurt you now." They were the two sole survivors of the camp.

Ivaluarjuk adds (Rasmussen 1929, 90):

Afterwards he (*Kaujjajjuk*) married the old woman who had always sided with him. That was his way of thanking her. So the miserable *Kaujjajjuk* became a strong man and a great fighter, because the Moon Spirit came to him as the Lord of Power and cleansed him from his mother's breach of taboo.

In the second variant told by *Kupaaq*, Walrus-Skin has a somewhat older sister and an adult brother, *Igalaaq*. This brother sends them to get seawater, and to do so they have to walk over the fast ice. The ice breaks away, and Walrus-Skin and his sister are taken far off to the south on the drift ice. After several days of drifting, the ice floe comes close to shore, and they manage to get to a camp where they are welcomed. Afterwards, however, they suffer all kinds of abuse. Here is the second story that *Kupaaq* told me:

Lost on the Ice

Kaujjajjuk was a little boy. He had an older sister and an adult brother. *Kaujjajjuk*'s big brother went hunting for *nattiq* [ringed seal] at the breathing hole, and he caught one. *Kaujjajjuk* was happy when his brother came home with the ringed seal. He went to meet his brother and said to him, "*Igalaaq*, did you catch a ringed seal?" His big brother said to him, "I intended to catch a ringed seal, and I got one! If you're not tired, go and get some salt water."

When Inuit killed a seal and wanted to make stew, they salted it with seawater. To get seawater they often went far away on the ice and collected it from crevasses or at the edge of the fast ice, where open water appears.

"Isn't it wonderful, *Igalaaq*, that you've caught a ringed seal!" *Igalaaq* again replied, "I intended to catch a ringed seal. I got one! If you're not tired, go and get some salt water."

Authority was assigned hierarchically among the Inuit by generation, by relative age, and by gender. Forebears had authority over their descendants, and within the same generation men had authority over women and older people over younger people.

His big brother wanted him to get salt water, so he headed to the edge of the ice with his sister. They had only a small shoulder blade from a ringed seal to collect salt water. They had to go and get some from the sea. While they were at the edge of the fast ice, the ice broke away, and Walrus-Skin and his sister began to drift on their little island of floating ice. They couldn't get back to the coast, and the ice they were on drifted to the other side of the sea and reached the coast of the Uqqurmiut ["The people of the lee side"].

This kind of accident was fairly common on the coasts of Inuit country. Hunters would disappear when the ice they were hunting on broke away and drifted off. *Ivaluarjuk*'s variant identifies the Uqqurmiut ("The people of the lee side") as being the Sallirmiut, the inhabitants of Southampton Island (Rasmussen 1929, 151–53). Since the prevailing winds were from the northwest, this location seems credible from the standpoint of people living in Iglulik or Aivilik territory.

ᑕᐊ ᑲᐅ�᙮ ᐱᐊᒋᓂ ᒪᐅᐊᒥ ᑲᓯᐸᐸᖃᒋᑎ᙮
ᒪᐅᐊᒋ ᑲᓯᑲᕚᐊᒪ ᑭᐱᕚᒍ ᑭᐊ᙮ ᑲᓯᓐᑕᐸᖃᐊᒋ᙮
ᐸᐱᒪᐊᓂ ᑭᐱ ᓴᐊᐃᓴᐅᐊᐊᒋ᙮
ᐱᐊᖁᐅᑕᐊ ᑲᓇᐊ(ᐱᐱᒐᑌ) ᒪᐅᐊᒥ ᑲᓯᕚᐊᐊᒋ᙮

FIGURE 27. The nasty girl lifts the small Walrus-Skin by his nostrils to bring him into the igloo. The Inuktitut text says: *Tanna Kaujjajuk pivitsuni manuamit qavvirunnapanningituq. Manuarmit qavviqajairmat qingangittigut kilutsugu qavvititauvattuviniq. Taimaitsuni qingangik nirittuniulirtuviniik. Piaraumullu kaamullu (pirlimut) manuamik qavviqajairpatuviniq*—This *Kaujjajjak* is unable to climb up the doorstep. Because climbing up the doorstep is like [climbing] a mountain, he is lifted up to the back of the house. He is infertile and hungry (from deprivation), not being able to climb up the doorstep. After a text and drawing by Daividialuk Amittuq Alasuaq, Povungnituk, 1971. Made by Johanne Lévesque. Archival fonds of B. Saladin d'Anglure.

The Hard Lives of Two Lost Children

They found some Inuit and went with them to their camp. There, they began to live among them. Walrus-Skin, the little boy, was mistreated by these people.

According to *Ivaluarjuk*, the people starve the two children and give them the roughest and most wearisome tasks (Rasmussen 1929, 151).

Whenever the young boy tried to enter the igloo, two nasty, almost adult teenage girls would hoist him inside using a hook made of two polar bear canines, which they would slip into his nostrils (Figure 27).

This detail struck the Inuit imagination, for it appears in all variants of the myth. To enter the main living area of the igloo, you had to step up to the floor of that room, which was higher than the floor of the entranceway. The sometimes large difference in floor level kept heat inside the igloo. To bring Walrus-Skin across this threshold, the two teenage girls pull him up by his nostrils.

The dwellers used Walrus-Skin's sister to weave caribou sinews. Her fingers were worn almost to the bone from this work. Not much flesh remained on her fingers.[7] Her thumbs, forefingers, and middle fingers eventually lost all of their flesh, and the bones appeared.

Such hard work was usually done by experienced women who protected each finger with a small leather cylinder. They were thus protected from getting hurt. These thimbles were indispensable for sewing waterproof seams, lapped seams with very tight stitching, tents, boat covers, and waterproof boots.

The camp dwellers mistreated Walrus-Skin and his sister because they knew the two children were far from home and separated from their family. The two nasty girls spared no pains to make him suffer by hooking him by his nostrils when they wanted to hoist him up into their home.

Ivaluarjuk adds two details. Walrus-Skin's chores include having to empty leather pails of urine, and he tells his persecutors, "Do not be so cruel to me. You had better not go too far, for my brother is a great sha-man!" (Rasmussen 1929, 151).

Assistance from His Brother, the Shaman

Here, the role of shaman (*angakkuq*) is played by the older brother (*angajuq*),[8] while in the last story this role was assigned to the Moon Man.

But Walrus-Skin's brother *Igalaaq* ["The windowpane"][9] was worried about his little brother and his little sister. Being a shaman, *Igalaaq* began to look for Walrus-Skin and his sister using his shamanic powers, and he found them among the people of the lee side.

A great shaman's performances included his flight through the air (*ilimmaqturniq*). He could fly through the sky and go far away to look for game animals or a lost traveller or to catch up on news from family and relatives at a distant location.

Igalaaq made a very fast boat and went looking for Walrus-Skin and his sister. Summer was in full swing when he came to the camp of the people of the lee side. It being summer, they were playing inside a semi-subterranean house. Out of malice, they would never let Walrus-Skin take part in their games. They burdened him with work, like emptying the urine pails once the men had relieved themselves before playing. Walrus-Skin found the pail very heavy to carry and had to use his teeth to take it outside. The people would then smear the rim of the pail with excrement.

Games were played mainly in winter, when there were fewer hunting activities. This was the season when people built large ceremonial snow ig-loos (*qaggiq*). Nonetheless, after community hunts for large marine mam-mals, feasting would often be held in a large semi-subterranean house. In his variant, *Ivaluarjuk* has the people organizing games in a feasting house in honour of their visitor. They are happy to welcome him and are getting ready to sing and dance in the feasting house. They ask Walrus-Skin to work hard at pounding old chunks of bearded seal blubber, the toughest they can find, to extract lamp oil. This is very hard work for the young boy (Rasmussen 1929, 151–52).

When *Igalaaq* arrived at the camp, Walrus-Skin and his sister recognized their big brother and wanted to stay near him, but *Igalaaq* told them to keep away, so that people wouldn't know he was their big brother. Soon after he arrived, the games began inside the feasting house. People called for Walrus-Skin, and the two nasty girls hoisted him inside, hooking him by his nostrils on polar bear canines while *Igalaaq* looked on.

The plot takes shape, and the protagonists are brought together: *Igalaaq*, as the guest for whom the feasting has been organized; *Kaujjajjuk*, as the orphan made to do the dirty work; and the men of the camp, who suspect neither their guest's identity nor his intentions.[10] Again, cunning is used to counter the malice of an entire group. The two nasty girls play a very ambiguous role. On the one hand, they are protective; on the other, they are sadists who hoist Walrus-Skin by his nostrils with polar bear canines whenever he wants to enter the home. So his nostrils become excessively wide. We will later see the fate that awaits the two nasty girls in some variants.

The men relieved themselves in the pail to get ready for playing, and they told *Igalaaq* to do the same, which he did. They then coated the rim of the pail with excrement and told Walrus-Skin to go and empty it outside, but *Igalaaq* spoke up and said, "Let me do it. I'm stronger!"

Magical Vengeance

Walrus-Skin left the semi-subterranean house, and *Igalaaq* got ready to go out and empty the pail. But before he went outside he spilled its contents in the feasting house. Inside, the people were covered in urine and excrement because everything was spilled all over the floor. They were wearing their loveliest boots for the games and began to walk on tiptoe, trying not to soil them.

Inuit with the means to do so would get their wives to make ceremonial clothing (*qaliruat*) out of shorthaired caribou hides with very contrasting colours: dark brown with white inserts. The hides were from females killed in midsummer, after the moult. Such clothing was worn by the caribou man who asked for *Uinigumasuittuq*'s hand in marriage (Chapter 5).

Boots, too, were finely decorated. The higher the status of an individual (a shaman, a great hunter, an artisan, a wrestler, a singer, or a chief of a powerful family), the more decorated his ceremonial clothing.[11]

All of the people who were inside rushed outside. Meanwhile, *Igalaaq* and Walrus-Skin rushed back into the feasting house to keep away from their adversaries. Once outside, the people decided to wall up the entrance to the feasting house by piling up stones against the door, so that *Igalaaq* and Walrus-Skin could no longer get out. Walrus-Skin and *Igalaaq* had forgotten that their sister too was in the camp. She was lynched by the men.

So dies the sister of Walrus-Skin and *Igalaaq*. This horrible lynching is missing from all other variants of the myth except for *Ivaluarjuk*'s, in which the camp dwellers hang the girl from a drying frame (Rasmussen 1929, 152). Such a fate was usually reserved for dangerous dogs that had bitten or killed someone. Hanging was also a way to commit suicide.

There was a hole on the side of the hut, but it wasn't big enough to let anyone through and, the door being blocked, there was no longer any possible way out for Walrus-Skin and *Igalaaq*.

Alone against everyone else, *Igalaaq* and his younger brother now have to summon means beyond the reach of ordinary humans. Shamanism is a level of power that requires assistance from great spirits like Moon Brother, *Kannaaluk*, or *Naarjuk*, or from humans chosen by the spirits to be custodians of such power. In this sense, both of the Walrus-Skin stories may be considered the same story about an oppressed little boy's initiation into the ways of shamanism.

When an old woman passed near the hole, *Igalaaq* called out to her and told her there was an ermine skin under the seat of his boat. He added he wanted her to give it to him. *Igalaaq* was a shaman, and he wanted the ermine skin as an aid for his shamanic work.

The "old woman" character is very common in Inuit myths. She is sometimes wicked (Moon Brother's unworthy mother) and sometimes compassionate, a figure who can oppose the injustices of dominant adults (Chapter 2, the old woman who took in a bear cub). In both of the stories told by *Kupaaq*, a helpful old woman assists Walrus-Skin. When, in Inuit society, an old woman had lost all of her close kin and required care by another family, her precarious situation resembled an orphan's. She was nonetheless often said to have magic powers. Being no longer subject to the taboos that limited the lives of women between puberty and meno-pause, she could care for dying people, women in childbirth, newborn ba-bies, and anyone else subject to ritual injunctions. She had little to lose by opposing injustices, for she was unafraid of death. When an old woman's condition became too difficult or when the group's survival was at stake, during a famine for example, she could decide to end her life. Such a sui-cide would ensure her a happy place in the hereafter (Chapter 8).

The old woman brought the skin, and *Igalaaq* chewed on it to remove the blubber still attached. He then softened it and breathed life into it with his mouth. The skin inflated and could now breathe. He brought it back to life.

In Chapter 11, we will see the magic power of air from the body, and how it can heal a sick person or make an enemy run away. In the variant of this story told by *Naukajjik* (Rasmussen 1930b, 55), Walrus-Skin's older brother takes the ermine skin and washes it in the urine pail, the one into which he has peed, thus giving life back to the animal. This is shaman-ism. The animal's skin represents the animal, which acts as the shaman's helper. In this relationship, the animal usually infuses the shaman with its life force, but here we see the reverse: the shaman gives life to the animal. He breathes his vital energy into it and soaks it in his fresh urine. *Iqallijuq*, the creator of Atlantic salmon and Arctic char (Chapter 6), likewise gives life to wood chips by smearing them with his sperm. The scatological side of this story, with urine and excrement being spread around, may refer to the ermine's very strong and foul smell. Even animals like a dog or a wolf will not eat an ermine's flesh when they kill one (Freuchen 1935). Another myth, the one about a man married to a fox woman (Chapter 6), is simi-larly scatological, with a wolverine and its turd wife. Wolverines likewise have a reputation for smelling very bad (Randa 1994).

He then made the ermine go out through the remaining hole on the side of the feasting house, and when the people noticed, they chased after to kill it. The ermine took refuge under a rock, and a man bent over to kill it, but it slipped into his mouth, and he died.

In *Ivaluarjuk*'s variant, he tells us that the ermine skin is *Igalaaq*'s amulet. This means he has a very close relationship with this animal. Its skin might even have been used to clean his body at birth. He has only to keep the dried ermine skin and breathe life into it whenever he wants and needs its help (Rasmussen 1929, 152). When Inuit wish to skin an ermine, they do so as one would a rabbit in Western societies. This method fully preserves the skin, and its only openings are those through which the animal's body is pulled out, that is, a rear opening and three for the mouth and the eyes. By breathing into the rear opening, *Igalaaq* gives the animal his force. Here we find the magic power of breath, already mentioned in Chapter 3 with regard to *Naarjuk*, and which we will again discuss in Chapter 11.

Inuit believe this small predator can penetrate a human through the mouth and come out through the anus, after devouring the body from inside. This deadly route can also be followed in the other direction. In Chapter 6, an ermine comes out of the mouth of the woman who cheated on her husband.

This was a shaman's performance—*Igalaaq*'s. He had used the ermine to kill a man. The ermine went back into the feasting house, and the men were unable to find it. One of the ermine's whiskers was a bit bloodstained because of its bloody route.

Ermines (*Mustella erminea*) are plentiful in the Arctic. They are highly agile and even reckless with humans. Adults and children chase them frantically, but they usually escape. In terms of size, they are to humans as humans are to polar bears, the two animal species being seen as symbolically equivalent. In the language of shamans, both have the same name (*uqsuralik*). Inuit say the two species have the same skeleton. When children make a little replica of a camp on their scale, they place beside the little toy tent or semi-subterranean house an ermine skull to represent a polar bear skull, just as they use lemming skins to represent caribou hides.

I previously established another symbolic equivalence between the polar bear and the sled dog, from the Moon Man's standpoint, that is, from the standpoint of spirits and entities belonging to a larger scale of existence where wild animals are domesticated and where polar bears are the Moon Man's sled dogs.

An ermine is the helping animal of *Igalaaq*, Walrus-Skin's older brother, and is also in a domestic relationship with this shaman who keeps its skin as an amulet. Walrus-Skin thus has two analogous allies. His older brother has a pet ermine, and the Moon Man is assisted by his polar bears, one of which is called Pretty Ermine. These are the two heroes who right the wrongs in the two variants of the Walrus-Skin story told by *Kupaaq*.

Igalaaq again made the ermine go outside, and the people began to chase it again. The ermine took shelter under a rock, and two men tried to catch it, but, while bending down, they were killed on the spot and never got back up. The ermine returned to the feasting house, and its two whiskers were now bloody. *Igalaaq* sent it outside again, and the number of those who died while bent over kept growing. Finally someone said, "Those who are inside may be responsible for what's happening to us." When they found out *Igalaaq* was killing them, they took away the stones that blocked the entrance and let the two come out. *Igalaaq* and Walrus-Skin remained together, for *Igalaaq* didn't want to abandon his little brother. He thought that if he abandoned him the people might kill him. The people then began to treat Walrus-Skin with deference because they feared his brother.

Kupaaq's story ends here, but *Ivaluarjuk*'s story and the ones reported by Boas have an additional episode. According to *Ivaluarjuk*, *Igalaaq* makes peace with the camp survivors and decides to go away with his younger brother. They remember their sister but discover too late that the people of the camp have hanged her. *Igalaaq* seizes the two nasty teenage girls who used to hoist Walrus-Skin by his nostrils and gives them to his younger brother. But first he wants to train his brother by beating him. Bit by bit the boy grows and becomes very strong. Once he is fully grown and has an adult's strength, he receives the two nasty girls as wives. Now is his chance for vengeance. He tolerates no negligence from either and demands total obedience. When they have trouble following him, he beats them until one of them dislocates a shoulder and the other loses an eye. In the Cumberland Sound variant, one of the women has a left shoulder lower than the right because her husband strikes her so often on that side, while the other wife squints because she is always looking stealthily in his direction (Boas 1901).

The two stories told by *Kupaaq* are similarly structured. Both teach us that orphans and defenceless children deserve respect and that disrespect may lead to terrible revenge. Nor should such people suffer abuses of power or inhumane treatments. Both stories also show injustice being fought by individuals with superhuman powers, such as the Moon Man or the shaman who is Walrus-Skin's older brother. These stories are from Igloolik but have variants in other regions, where the respective episodes become so entangled that they form a single myth. Such regional variations show how myths are perpetually being reconstructed and rearranged.

CHAPTER 10

The Danger of Being Impregnated by a Spirit When You Have a Jealous Husband

Here we have the theme of a battered childless wife, already encountered in Chapter 8. This time, she does not seek to escape her human fate by trying different animal incarnations. She instead resorts to the supra-human power of the Moon Man, who protects women in distress.

A Battered Wife Beseeches the Moon Man for Help

Kupaaq (1972) told me a variant fairly close to those of Boas and Rasmussen.[1]

This woman was continually being beaten by her husband and had enough.

Ivaluarjuk, in his variant (Rasmussen 1929, 87–88), tells us more about the causes of the wife-beating than does *Kupaaq* (1972) or the informant of Boas (1901). In the evening, when the wife is getting ready to go to bed, her husband makes her leave the igloo because he wants to sleep with other women. When no other woman wishes to sleep with him anymore, he becomes even more cruel toward his wife. He strips her clothes off and leaves her outside, naked, whatever the weather. We also learn that the couple cannot have children. This may explain the husband's harshness.

> One night, when she had been beaten again, she left the igloo and went away from the camp to a place where the snow had no footprints [*tumitaittuq*].

She is seeking to enter into contact with the spirit world. According to *Ivaluarjuk*, she has decided to leave her husband for good (Rasmussen 1929, 87).

> She didn't have to go very far. She squatted on the snow, pulled her hood down over her head, bent her face to the ground and said, "*Taqqiq!* [Moon Man], come and get me!"

This was the ritual posture for going from one level of reality to another or for making a request to a spirit.[2] *Ivaluarjuk* gives us more details on how and where this ritual is carried out:

> It was the full moon, and very light. She went over to a place where there were no footprints, where no one had trodden the snow, and here she began walking backwards, very slowly, while wishing for the Moon Spirit to come and carry her off (Rasmussen 1929, 87–88).

Both ways of praying, either out loud or silently, are acceptable to spirits if done properly in such places without footprints. Walking backwards is tantamount to not leaving footprints, since the backward-pointing tracks look like they come from nowhere. This clever ploy opens the way for her to enter sacred space. I know of no other description of this procedure. *Kupaaq*'s story continues:

> She saw nothing, for she had her hood pulled down over her head and her face turned toward the ground.

A lowered, hood-covered head was required in several circumstances, notably to avoid the dangerous gaze of tabooed women or to summon a spirit. Here, it enables the invisible spirit world to show itself. The woman's posture is like that of someone learning to be a shaman and waiting for the *qaumaniq* (inner light) of shamanic vision. It is also like the posture of a shaman getting his soul ready to fly into the great heavenly beyond, while he remains concealed behind a skin curtain. *Ivaluarjuk* mentions in his account that the woman feels the Moon Man coming nearer and nearer but is careful not to look up (Rasmussen 1929, 87). *Kupaaq* adds:

> She soon heard the sound of a dog team trying to stop nearby: "*Uuaauu! Pualukittuq!* [He who has little mittens[3]], *Uuaauu! Arjiq!* [unknown meaning], *Uuau! Tiriattiaq!* [Pretty Ermine]." The Moon Man was calling his dogs by name to bring them to a halt.

The woman's request has been heard, and she learns by her sense of hearing, with her head hood-covered and facing the ground. The three names she hears are those of the Moon Man's sled-dogs—actually, polar bears, as mentioned in the last chapter.[4] Here again there are three bear-dogs. One of them, *Tiriattiaq* ("Pretty Ermine"), has a highly suggestive name because of the symbolic equivalence between the ermine and the polar bear. The same name appears in a variant of this myth published by Boas (1901) and in several other variants about *Kaujjajjuk*, that is, the ones published by Boas (1888) or told by *Ivaluarjuk* (Rasmussen 1929, 87).[5] The two other bears on the team have different names: *Nalupiritsuq* ("Mud Trudger", a black dog according to *Ivaluarjuk*) and *Miglialik* (perhaps *Migslialik*, "which has an umbilical cord").

A Heavenly Journey

The Moon Man told the woman to sit on his sled and close her eyes when she no longer heard the sound of the dog team moving forward on the snow. Above all, she shouldn't open her eyes, or else she would fall off. When they started on their way, she closed her eyes. She still heard the sound made by the dog team on the snow, but it gradually died down and completely disappeared.

When the dogsled is sliding over frozen snow, it makes a very characteristic squeaking (*kalirraq*), which stops when the sled leaves the ground and rises into the air. The consequences can be dire if she opens her eyes when going from one world to the other. The dogsled may be halted in its ascension into the sky and fall back to earth, or more probably she will be ejected.

She half-opened one eye but saw nothing, and one of her mittens fell away.

The temptation to do what is forbidden is part of Inuit reality. In a variant told by *Panniaq*, a younger brother of *Kupaaq*, we learn that the woman almost falls off the dogsled and loses one of her mittens after half-opening one eye. We also learn that the dogsled likewise squeaks when going over clouds (MacDonald 1998).

When she again heard the sound of the dog team moving over the snow, the Moon Man told her to open her eyes. She saw they were now on an *igliniq* [trail], which reflected the light from igloo windows. One of the ice windows shone brighter than the others.

The other worlds are in the image of the world of humans. We are here in the world of the Ullurmiut ("The people of the Land of Day"), where Moon, Sun, and Star Beings live. An igloo window is made from a piece of translucent lake ice that has been shaved thinner.

The Moon Man told her this was where they were going. Once they got there, and as she entered, she would have to turn her head away because of the strong light from the side room [of the igloo], and above all not try to look [at the light source], even from the corner of her eye, or else it would burn her.

Igloos often had a side room or *qariaq* that could be used to put up close kin—here, the Moon Man's sister, the Sun Woman. This woman keeps her solar appearance when confronted by strangers, while assuming her human appearance for family members.[6] In *Ivaluarjuk*'s variant, the Moon Man warns:

I live in a double house; be careful not to look into the room next to mine. The sun [Siqiniq] lives there, and she will burn you.

When they arrived at their destination, they were greeted by people whose hoods had a trimming of short-haired fur. These were Star Beings.

Stars, like other heavenly bodies, live in the upper world, where the souls of some of the dead are also found. Several myths tell how some humans fled into space and formed the different constellations. The fur trim on their hoods seems to represent the bright beams of light that radiate outward from these heavenly bodies. The radiating beams from a star are like the hood's fur trim around a face.

A Visit to the Moon Man's Home

When they halted in front of the window that shone the brightest, the Moon Man told her to go inside. She went in, but she had forgotten what he had advised her to do. From the corner of her eye, she looked at what there was in the room next to his, and her eyelashes were burned immediately; she then turned her head away and no longer had to suffer. The one sitting in the next room was indeed Siqiniq, Taqqiq's sister. The woman was asked to sit on the right side of the sleeping platform, and there she sat. There were also two tall girls seated at the back of the platform. They were almost adult, and their knees were folded against their bodies, for they had both been disemboweled.

Women are not the only ones to get disembowelled in Inuit myths. Men, too, suffer this fate if they have broken taboos, as in the story about two hunters who lose their entrails while asleep on the edge of the ice, this being forbidden to them (Rasmussen 1929, 83–84). As a result, they are quickly sent to the Land of the Dead and will no longer be providers of meat.

They had been inside for a good while when the Moon Man told her that Ululijarnaat ["She who is armed with an ulu"] was about to arrive [Figure 28]. He warned her about this woman. She was an utterly titsinnartuq [grotesque] being who tried to make others laugh. "When she tries to make you laugh," he said, "and you can no longer hold it in, you

FIGURE 28. *Ululijarnaat*, the grotesque being who lives in the heavenly world, tries to make the humans nearby laugh in order to eviscerate them. From a drawing by Karali Andreassen, Greenland, 1906. National Museum of Denmark, Copenhagen. This character is known in West Greenland under the name of *Nalikateq*.

must slip your hands under the front of your parka and poke them out through the neck, under your chin. Then place them in front of your mouth and pretend to blow." One of the two young girls seated at the back of the platform, with her knees folded against herself, began to talk, "It's because we laughed that we are this way!" The other agreed. Both of them had been disemboweled because they couldn't restrain their laughter. They had burst out laughing and been disemboweled by *Ululijarnaat.*

Laughing uncontrollably was considered dangerous in a culture that valued self-control, particularly with respect to laughter. Inuit feel that white people laugh uncontrollably, like children. Behind the symbolism of laughter and the openness it signifies, one might see in the appearance of these disemboweled young women the image of an empty woman who cannot have children. The test that the human female will undergo, while visiting the Moon Man's home, will determine her future childbearing.

Ululijarnaat surely best incarnates satirical comedy in Inuit mythology. Greenlanders depict her in high spirits, with a mouth split open from ear to ear, hopping about, with a knife in one hand and a dish in the other, her only clothing being a pair of dog-skin shorts from which hangs, between her legs, a live dog's head (Figure 28, and Saladin d'Anglure 1994b [1986]. *Panniaq's* variant adds that her bootlaces are untied and that her boots fold like accordions (MacDonald 1998).[7]

Ululijarnaat puts human visitors to the laugh test, whose outcome is life or death. Anyone who fails is condemned to the Land of the Dead. Children are taught at a very early age to control their emotions. It is not good to laugh out loud or to get angry. A group game, called *arsiq*, requires its players to remain straight-faced as long as possible while watching someone make faces and ham it up. The first player to break out laughing takes the other person's place, and the game starts over. During the community celebrations of the winter solstice called *Tivajuut*, two grotesque, cross-dressed shamans similarly try to get spectators to laugh in the community feasting house (*qaggiq*). It is said that those who cannot hold back their laughter will have their lives shortened (Saladin d'Anglure 1993b [1989]).[8]

In the Cumberland Sound variant (Boas 1901, 198), the Moon Man says to the earth woman:

"Do not laugh at anything she may do, else she will cut out your intestines. She is very fond of such food. If you feel that you cannot help laughing, put your left hand under your knees, and then raise it with all the fingers bent down from the second joint except the middle finger, which you must extend."

As we will see further on, the woman will create the impression of being a polar bear by pointing her middle finger at *Ululijarnaat* and blowing between her hands, thus making the terrible *Ululijarnaat* run away. But back to *Kupaaq*'s story:

After some time, an Arctic fox without its skin came in and went back out. It had come for a quick look.

A skinned animal, like a disembowelled woman, is an inverted image of earthly reality. It is an animal without identity. In the animal world, the skin—the body's envelope—is what identifies the species of a living animal. When an animal is dead, its skeleton identifies its species. Disembowelled humans will pass on neither their ancestors' identities nor, in the present case, their own, since they will have no descendants. Personal identity is passed on via the names given to newborn babies (Chapter 1).

This bizarre intrusion, which heralds the coming of *Ululijarnaat*, seems intended to unsettle the human visitor and weaken her resistance to laughter. The fox has been stripped of its outer envelope and belongs to *Ululijarnaat*, like a pet. It feeds on fresh, live guts, which it tears out of humans. In the human world, Arctic foxes plunder meat caches at night.

When it was gone, a dish with a whetstone and an *ulu* [a woman's half-moon knife] were thrown into the igloo.

Again, suspense is maintained in the telling of the myth. The dangerous *Ululijarnaat* is coming, and her long-announced arrival will become one of the major events of the woman's heavenly journey. Either the earth woman will pass the test and be impregnated by Moon Brother, the ultimate goal of her journey, or she will fail, be disembowelled, and become a dead soul.[9]

The Disemboweller and the Laugh Test

A person whose face was covered with *tunniit* [tattoos] came in right after. She took her knife and began to sharpen it. She danced and sharpened her knife while saying, "Look at the tattoos on my face, *ihii ihii!* Look at the tattoos on my forehead, *ihii, i!*"

The dreadful *Ululijarnaat* has arrived, a terrifying sight to unarmed humans with her sharpened knife, her tattooed face, and her solitary dance—a prelude to human sacrifice. In Igloolik, people said women had to be tattooed to be beautiful.[10] In Nunavik, girls who refused facial tattooing were told that after death their faces would be stained with tar from the Sun Woman's lamp and burned by the sun's rays.

Ululijarnaat's mouth is split wide open, giving the impression that she laughs all the time. This adds to her grotesqueness and androgyny. Indeed, a laughing mouth is a man's mouth in Alaskan symbolism. A woman, on the other hand, is always portrayed with a sad mouth (Saladin d'Anglure 1993b, 84, Figure 13a and 13b [1989, 53, Figure 13a and 13b]). As for the live dog's head, mentioned above, this image brings to mind the penis/dog's head that we encountered in *Iqallijuq*'s memories from the womb, in Chapter 1.

She turned around and the earth woman was on the brink of hysterical laughter. She who was dancing said, "Look at *Ululijarnaat* ['She who is armed with an *ulu*'], *ihii i!* Look at the tattoos on my face, *ihii i!* Look at the tattoos on my forehead, *ihii i, paammajaa, paammajaa!*" The woman, unable to hold back her laughter, slid her hands under the front of her parka, poked them out through the neck, placed them on her chin, and pretended to blow loudly. *Ululijarnaat* right away took her dish and threw it outside, saying, "They've been helped by *uqsuraliit* [polar bears]! They've been helped by polar bears!" She left the woman who pretended to blow and never came back.

Polar bears have a habit of blowing loudly, especially when annoyed, and Inuit imitate this characteristic. By blowing between her hands, the woman makes herself seem to be a polar bear in human form. We saw in the Cumberland Sound variant that the human female, after sliding her left hand under her knee, closes her fingers except for the middle one, which she points at *Ululijarnaat*. The effect is immediate, and the disemboweller cries out, "I am much afraid of that bear!" (Boas 1901).

By imitating the blowing sound of a polar bear, named *Ursuralik* ("he who has fat") in the language of shamans and spirits and a powerful male symbol, the woman is able to fend off the power of *Ululijarnaat*, who can present only her *ulu* (woman's knife), her skinless fox, and the live dog's head hanging between her legs—this is in the variant of the myth from Ammassalik, where she is named *Nalikateq* (see Figure 28). These are certainly polar bear counterparts, but on a smaller scale of existence.[11] Clearly, *Ululijarnaat* is outclassed by the Moon Man and his polar bear "dog."[12] In another myth published by Boas (1888), a shaman tells how he goes to the Moon Man by making a shamanic flight with the assistance of his helping spirit, a polar bear. He reaches the upper world, is put to the test of laughter, and escapes only with its help.

Another detail, implicit in *Kupaaq*'s variant but explicit in *Ivaluarjuk*'s (Rasmussen 1929, 85–88), is that the human female during her heavenly stay has sex with the Moon Man and soon becomes pregnant by him. She feels very comfortable in his home and appreciates him caring for her.

The Earth Seen from the Moon

Near the sleeping platform, there was a caribou shoulder blade placed beside the oil lamp. He told her to lift it, and [when she did] she saw a hole. She looked through the hole and right away caught sight of her home camp, down below.

Spirits have such keen senses that they can perceive faraway people or objects as if these were up close. The Moon Man and the Sun Woman can thus see and hear from their home everything that humans do and say. This is confirmed by another myth, reported by Rasmussen (1929, 86). In it, *Inukpasujjuk* states that the inhabitants of heaven see what happens inside homes as if there were no roofs. Inuit think that *Kannaaluk*'s home in the lower world has no ceiling and that, symmetrically, she can likewise look up and see what humans do and say.

The people were playing the game of *amaruujaq* ["imitating a wolf"], and she recognized her husband standing nearby. The fur trim of his hood was covered with frost because he had been standing still.

The wolf game (*amaruujaq*) is much liked by Inuit on long winter nights. The woman's husband is the only one not joining in. *Ivaluarjuk*'s variant places him near his meat stand, sorrowful and with bowed head (Rasmussen 1929, 87). The variant published by Boas (1901, 198) provides an explanation: the husband's clothing is covered with ice and snow because he has come back from seal hunting and has just learned that his wife is gone.

She was asked to spit through the hole, and this she did. The Inuit down below then cried out, "A star has defecated! A star has defecated!" Her spittle shone as it fell to earth.

"Shooting stars" or meteorites are seen especially in winter, when the sky is very dark. Inuit interpret them as being star excrement or spittle. On hearing her campmates and on seeing her husband saddened by her absence, the woman feels so homesick for her community, her friends, and her neighbours that she forgets the abuse she often suffered.

Because she missed being back home, the Moon Man said to her, "Once you're back home, don't eat game meat brought back by your husband. Or else you'll die!"

In *Kupaaq*'s variant, melancholy makes the woman want to go home after she sees her people playing the wolf game, as if she were there. Her husband's sorrow also moves her. In *Ivaluarjuk*'s variant, the Moon Man takes the initiative of sending her back to earth (Rasmussen 1929, 88):

The time came when she was ready to bring forth, and the Moon Spirit now thought it better that she should go down to earth and give birth to the child in her own place. And so he drove her home and built a little house for her.

This detail is significant. Humans cannot give birth in other worlds, only on earth. The Moon Man nonetheless imposes on her many limitations to preserve the exceptionality of the child he has fathered. Because of the intimate bond that now joins her to him, a bond that will become tangible with the child's birth, she must now consume only food provided by her heavenly lover. He provides a secret way for her to tell him when she needs food or oil. The details are in *Kupaaq*'s variant:

> He added that if she lacked blubber for her lamp, she should place it upright and it would fill with blubber coming from above. When the blubber was falling down, she should spread it with her hand and cut it up into pieces with the *taqqut* [poker] of her oil lamp. When hungry, she should tell him by taking hold of her *ulu* [half-moon knife]; she would then receive food. By brandishing her half-moon knife, she would make her hunger known.

In the hands of the monstrous *Ululijarnaat*, in the great heavenly beyond, a woman's half-moon knife (*ulu*) is an instrument for disembowelling human visitors. On earth, it becomes a means to get food from the Moon Man.

The Earthly Birth of the Moon Man's Child

> Now back in her community, she grabbed her half-moon knife, and a great noise could be heard, as if something had fallen outside. Then someone entered with a big piece of meat.

We see the Moon Man supplying another human female with food in another myth, *Tutukatuk* (Rasmussen 1929, 85–86).[13] But back to *Kupaaq*'s story:

> Initially, her husband didn't get angry at her, but when she refused to eat meat from his own hunting he got angry.

According to *Ivaluarjuk*, the husband is jealous of the Moon Man for fathering a child with his barren wife. Whenever the moon spirit brings the wife meat, the husband smears it with tar residue from the lamp, making it inedible.[14] His wife must now consume meat from animals he has killed. As a result, the Moon Man stays away from her and never comes to her again. This story ends with her husband repenting of his cruelty and feeling kindly toward her (Rasmussen 1929, 88).

A Difficult Covenant with a Heavenly Spirit

The other variants, especially *Kupaaq*'s, have a more tragic ending:

> She told him she wasn't allowed to, but fearing his anger she eventually ate meat from the animals he had caught. When she ate this meat, she died. This is the end to the story I heard.

In the Cumberland Sound variant (Boas 1901, 200), the wife agrees to eat seal meat brought by her husband. From that time on, the Moon Man stops supplying her, and she no longer receives caribou meat or lamp oil. Soon she becomes sick and dies, as does her baby. The story adds that the child dies because of the change from a caribou-meat diet to a seal-meat diet. We have already seen that it was forbidden to mix land food with sea food, so as not to offend the animal master spirits.

This myth shows how hard it is for ordinary individuals to be equally intimate with spirits and humans. The ways of life are not the same in the two worlds, nor are the codes of conduct. There is a danger in straddling boundaries and a risk of antagonizing both worlds. Not until the development of shamanism did it become possible for some individuals, whether men or women, to assume a mediating role between humans and spirits, and to run the risk of having close ties with both worlds in order to resolve problems in either one.

CHAPTER 11

Itirjuaq, the First Woman Healer

The myth of *Itirjuaq* is included here because of its uniqueness. It tells the story of an orphan girl, completely destitute in life, who discovers the power of healing with the help of her deceased grandparents. Thanks to this gift, she manages to stand up to the macho violence of a "Big Man" in her group and leads the way for female shamanism.[1] The story is like the one about *Kaujjajjuk*, another orphan, whose miserable conditions of life arouse the compassion of the Moon Man, who gives him strength and power.

I have two variants of this myth: one from *Iqallijuq* and another from her son-in-law *Kupaaq*. Here, the basic story will be *Iqallijuq*'s. It is the most consistent variant, and I will compare it with *Kupaaq*'s and the one from Boas (1901, 245–46). *Itirjuaq* was, according to *Iqallijuq*, the first woman healer.[2] Rasmussen (1929, 110) does not mention the myth, but he does allude to some beliefs that help explain several episodes, as in the following lines:

Human beings have always been afraid of sickness, and far back in the very earliest times there arose wise men who tried to find out about all the things none could understand. There were no shamans in those days, and men[3] were ignorant of all those rules of life which have since taught them to be on their guard against danger and wickedness. The first amulet that ever existed was the shell portion of a sea-urchin (*itiujaq*, "which resembles an anus"). It has a hole through it, and is hence called *itiq* (anus) and the fact of its being made the first amulet was due to its being associated with a particular power of healing.

Why did Rasmussen's informants not tell him the story of *Itirjuaq* (Big-Anus)? It is still known in Igloolik, and it supports and illustrates the above comments. At least one of the Iglulingmiut still had that name when Rasmussen visited, thus keeping the memory of the myth alive. Might this silence be due to the almost indecent form of the story? Might it also be due to its "feminist" perspective, as seen through the puritanical lens of reason that held sway over the West in the late nineteenth and early twentieth centuries? This was the "reason" that surprised the Inuit when they made their first contacts with Europeans and North Americans. Such puritanism was subsequently promoted, of course, by various missionaries and the nascent field of anthropology; early anthropologists would bowdlerize their texts before publication or translate offensive passages into Latin, as seen in early publications by Boas (1888, 1901).

The hypothesis of male-centred reason might also explain why this myth was played down by male informants, in particular leading shamans, and by anthropologists who took an interest in Inuit mythology from the Central and Eastern Arctic and who were almost exclusively men (Rink, Boas, Rasmussen, Holtved, Savard, Oosten, Blaisel, Laugrand, etc.).

A Miserable Orphan Girl Makes an Amulet Out of a Sea Urchin

Here is the story that *Iqallijuq* told me (1977, 1979):

Itirjuaq didn't know how to scrape skins; nor did she know how to cut them up to make garments or how to sew.

Scraping skins to remove any remaining fat, drying them by stretching them on the ground with wooden or bone stakes, buffing them with a burnishing stone, cutting them up with a half-moon knife (*ulu*) after taking measurements with one's arms, hands, and fingers, and finally sewing them with caribou sinews and a bone or ivory needle—these were the tasks that a woman of marriageable age was supposed to know how to do. Without these skills she was doomed to singlehood, dependence, and public scorn. This was the case with *Itirjuaq*.

Why did *Itirjuaq* fail to learn these life skills from the people around her? *Iqallijuq* explained to me in her comments that *Itirjuaq* lost her parents at a very early age. Her grandparents then cared for her, but they were destitute and died when she was still very young. *Kupaaq*, for his part, added that she would go begging for food from others. He also included this detail:

Nor could she have children.

This was an additional handicap for a woman, especially an orphaned woman. The alternative of adoption was available mostly to women in large families.

But she benefitted from a special protection from her deceased grandparents, who had been quite attached to her when they were alive. After their death, they gave her a power to understand things.

Clairvoyance (*qaumaniq*) was a gift. Among the Inuit, it was gained during one of the first stages of learning to become a shaman (Rasmussen 1929, 112–13; Saladin d'Anglure 1988a, 2001a). In historic times, several accounts confirm that some individuals gained clairvoyance on their own, and without being taught, after a serious illness, a terrible bereavement, or an accident. Given the pre-shamanic setting of this myth, we are probably looking at a case of this sort. The little orphan girl's poverty and distress were undoubtedly necessary but insufficient conditions for gaining this clairvoyance. The rest may be explained by assistance from her deceased grandparents.

[Thanks to this gift], she began to look for a helping spirit and, having found an *itiujaq* [sea urchin's shell] on the shore, she made it into an amulet and inhaled [its power] through its opening. She thus became a shaman.

We know how one became a shaman from accounts left by early ethnographers and by former shamans. Once the novice received clairvoyance, an aura (*qaumaniq*) would emanate from his/her body and attract helping spirits (*tuurngait*) looking for a shaman to be with.

In *Itirjuaq*'s case, her *qaumaniq* makes her go to the shore to pick up the shell of a sea urchin (*Echinoidea*), and then makes her put it to her mouth and inhale the air inside. The air flows through her body, and she discovers its power. To understand this newfound healing power, recall the discussion, begun in Chapter 3 of this book, on *Naarjuk*—the Spirit Master of the atmosphere, of the cosmos, and of body exhalations that contain part of his power.

Sea urchins are found in Arctic waters, especially in the polynya zones where tides and ocean currents combine to maintain open areas of water surrounded by ice. In some regions, like the Belcher Islands or Inukjuak (Nunavik), Inuit collect sea urchins and eat them. Elsewhere, one mostly comes across empty sea urchin shells with two openings, one for the mouth and one for the anus. These shells are called *itiq* (anus) or *itiujaq* (anus-like).[4] The egg shape of an empty shell may also bring to mind the bubble (*pudlaq*) that contains a living person's soul, a bubble said to be lodged in the groin, according to Rasmussen's informants (1929, 58). *Itirjuaq* thus discovers the power of body breath and flatulence, a power activated here by possessing a sea urchin shell and inhaling the air inside.

The Magic Power of Body Exhalations

Ijituuq, an Inuk from Igloolik, told me that in childhood his shaman grandfather had given him a sea urchin amulet to protect him from danger. To this end, he had to clench it in his left hand (the hand used by shamans to operate) and fart in the direction of the danger. One day a polar bear confronted him, and he thought about using his amulet. He was too afraid, however, and did not have enough time, so he preferred to run away (Saladin d'Anglure 2001a).

> She became able to heal sick people by letting go with a fart in their direction.

A fart (*niliq*) is considered to have healing power in all of the early accounts published by Rasmussen (1929) or collected by Comer on the west coast of Hudson Bay (Boas 1901).[5] In fact, Rasmussen, when doing fieldwork among the Iglulingmiut, had in hand the following observations by Comer:

> It is also said that long ago there were no *angakkut* (shamans). When a man was sick, his friends would send for a man who knew how to blow off the disease. He would blow at the invalid and poke him. The person who blew at the sick one did not speak. He simply blew, touched the patient, and went out. Those who were left with the patient would say, "Come out of him," meaning that the sickness should come out of his body, while they blew at the same time to remove the smell of the person who had blown first (Boas 1901, 133).

Rasmussen (1929, 110) wrote:

> When a man fell ill, one would go and sit by him, and, pointing to the diseased part, break wind behind. Then one went outside, while another held one hand hollowed over the diseased part, breathing at the same time out over the palm of his other hand in a direction away from the person to be cured. It was then believed that wind and breath together combined all the power emanating from within the human body, a power so mysterious and strong that it was able to cure disease.

Back to *Iqallijuq*'s story:

> She [*Itirjuaq*] had two husbands, who adored her and whom she loved a lot. They hunted caribou, and she was never short of food.

Here, *Itirjuaq* is clearly a paradoxical character. In traditional Inuit society, no man would have married a woman who could neither sew nor have children, and yet she had two husbands.

Knud Rasmussen encountered at most two cases of women with two husbands during the Fifth Thule Expedition (1921–24), which took him from one end of the Inuit homeland to the other. When I questioned elders on these cases of polyandry, they responded with embarrassed laughter that in the one case they knew the two husbands shared their wife's bed in the same igloo. The idea seemed to them completely incongruous. In her comments, *Iqallijuq* insisted that the husbands were very much in love with *Itirjuaq* and pampered her. In the Boas (1901) variant from Baffin Island, the heroine named Eterseoot (*Itirsiut*) likewise has two husbands, this being stated at the outset. Polygamy was traditionally reserved for men whose social position was higher than average. Such men were very good hunters who could feed a large family, or they were shamans or great singers who could win song tournaments.

She thus healed one of her husbands, who had become ill, and then one of her brothers and several members of her family.

Itirjuaq's success as a healer strengthens her ties to her husbands and to other family members. She gains a degree of authority seldom acknowledged in an orphaned woman.

The people heard about her and began to ask for her help when they were ill. In return, they scraped the caribou skins brought to her by her husbands. They would cut up and sew the skins, thus making beautiful jackets and coats for her and her husbands.

The Art of Healing, a New Power for Women

Here we have the key to *Itirjuaq*'s success. Her art of healing and her clairvoyance have market value in this generalized trading system, similar to the ones now flourishing again in the West under the name of LETS (Local Exchange Trading Systems). Her exceptional powers offset her shortcomings in an economy based on the sexual division of labour. In addition, because of the life-saving importance of her services, people make her the loveliest garments, a service usually reserved for families of Big Men.

In the Boas (1901) variant, *Itirsiut* does not know how to sew but knows how to scrape and cut up skins. She then puts them under her bed, and the next day, thanks to her shamanic powers, she finds sewn clothing. On the other hand, no allusion is made to her healing ability:

She was also given children to adopt.

Her last handicap, her sterility, is also offset when her patients give her children. She can thus not only join the group's system of production/

reproduction but also hold a social position above that of ordinary women. She rises to a rank equivalent to that of a Big Man.

But an arrogant man with two wives began to hate her for no other reasons than that she didn't know how to do anything and that, while having two husbands, she was a good-for-nothing.

For *Itirjuaq*, everything is fine with her husbands, her family, and her neighbours until intransigent opposition to her arises in the form of the local Big Man. He has never required her services and sees her as a good-for-nothing. Actually, he is jealous of *Itirjuaq*'s reputation and the social standing she is gaining with her healing power. This is an affront to his own authority and to his rank of *isumataq* ("wise man") or *angajuqqaaq* (chief).[6]

In the Boas variant (1901, 245–46), the man is a widower who wrongly accuses *Itirsiut* of having killed his wife. He wishes to avenge her death and even announces his intention to kill *Itirsiut*. *Iqallijuq* describes his vengeance as follows:

One day, when her two husbands were hunting, he entered her home and killed her with a blow to her head. He then went looking for walrus meat in one of his caches, thinking ahead to the prohibition on all activities after someone dies.

So the murder of *Itirjuaq* is premeditated. Traditionally, an Inuk would often get back at someone by surprising and killing that person while in a position of weakness. Afterwards, the killer was supposed to refrain from work for the next four days if the victim was a woman or the next three days if a man (Boas 1907).

But then, while again walking by her home, he saw her, and she was shouting to him, "Me too, me too! I want a portion of meat!" Putting down his load, he ran toward her and again killed her by striking her on the head. He then used snow to wall up the door and entranceway to her igloo. But when he left again, she was once more standing and calling out to him the same way.

The Healing Woman Wins Out over the Big Man

Without bothering to go and meet her, and without turning around, he went home, and having scarcely arrived, came down with a splitting headache and went to bed. That evening his pain got worse, and one of his wives left with a gift [*tunijjuti*] to go to *Itirjuaq*'s home and ask her to heal her husband.

If one abused an innocent person or unfairly tried to cast a spell on a shaman, the elders would say the abuse or spell would likely boomerang. To ensure that *Itirjuaq* will provide help, her assailant's wife gives her a special gift (*tunijjuti*) for her helping spirit. It was customary to give a gift to a shaman who was being asked to treat a personal illness. This had to be done beforehand to ensure the spirit's benevolence and thus assist the healing.

Seeing that she was being called to her assailant's bedside, she went there and began to sing to him, "So this is the big man! So that's what happened yesterday, when in broad daylight he hit *Itirjuaq*'s head again and again, but that hitting has now come back against his own head."

Kupaaq's variant describes what *Itirjuaq* says on entering:

"This big man is no longer anything now!" He replied, "Her big anus has gone to her head!" She left without saying a word, and he died.

In the variant published by Boas (1901, 245–46), the assailant, whose name is Kowertse (*Quvirti*), stabs the female shaman *Itirsiut* to death, only to become ill when he gets home. *Itirsiut* is not dead. She calls for help and is taken home, where she revives little by little until it seems as if nothing happened. She no longer has the slightest trace of the blows she received. She is then called to her murderer's bedside. *Itirsiut* sits alongside the sick man and whispers in his ear:

"*Quvirti* [Kowertse], what ails you?" and he did not respond. Then she repeated, "What ails you?" Still, he did not respond. Then she said, "Yesterday you were dreadful. You cut me, and tried to kill me. My name means 'backside.' I am sure you have cut your own backside." Then she went home and told the people that she thought *Quvirti* would soon die.

She said, "He cut me with his knife, and still I am alive and whole; but he is sick, although he has not been cut or scratched." Very soon he died.

Iqallijuq's variant uses almost the same language:

She then went away, and he died. He who had hit her head again and again died. *Itirjuaq* was alive, loved and respected by all. She was the first woman to heal the sick.

One senses in *Iqallijuq*'s comments some identification with the leading character of the myth. As an atypical woman, *Iqallijuq* had likewise been brought up as a boy and was better at tracking game animals than at sewing. Only as an adult did she learn women's work on her own, and not without some hardship. At the end of her life, she could nonetheless take satisfaction in being recognized and honoured by everyone.

This myth invites several comments. First, *Itirjuaq* is an exemplary figure for the study of Inuit gender relations. She is a model of the emancipated woman: a female healer initiated into a primary level of shamanism that has undoubtedly been passed on, discreetly, from one woman to another.

Second, *Itirjuaq* is an unusual character. She stakes out a middle ground in the sexual division of labour and in the social definition of gender categories. She stands apart from other mythical figures of atypical women, like the one who refused to marry (Chapter 5), or the one who tried different animal lives before living as a man, namely her own brother's son (Chapter 8). *Itirjuaq* is original because she has discovered and appropriated the basics of shamanism, thus earning recognition as a healing woman. This status transcends the sexual division of labour and offers women an original way to affirm their identity.

Third, *Itirjuaq* is not a hunting woman—a role that offers women another way to affirm their identity in Inuit society and is exemplified by *Iqallijuq* in Chapter 1, the favourite wife of a polygamous great hunter. Nor does she call for the Moon Man's assistance, as does the battered wife of Chapter 10. *Itirjuaq*'s success is expressed through polyandry; she has two devoted husbands at her beck and call in an essentially monogamous society dominated by polygynous Big Men. Her victory over the local Big Man asserts the supremacy of female shamanic power over this type of macho leader.

Can this healing art be a form of shamanism? The Boas text answers in the affirmative, but not the accounts reported by Rasmussen. At most, they describe a mythical age when everyone knew how to heal in the manner of *Itirjuaq*—although her name goes unmentioned—at a time when there were still no shamans (Rasmussen 1929, 110).[7]

The problem, then, is how we define shamanism. We may formulate the hypothesis that *Itirjuaq* is considered a shaman in the Inuit way of thinking because she was the first to treat illnesses by calling on a cosmic power that exists in any living body: the magic power of breath and flatulence. This calls to mind old folk beliefs from Europe (Gaignebet and Florentin 1974). Among the Inuit, such power is associated with the soul and with *Naarjuk*, the spirit of the atmosphere (*Sila*), the winds, and the motions of the cosmos (Chapter 3).

CHAPTER 12

The Strange Man and His Whale

To continue in the same vein as the *Itirjuaq* myth, I would like to present an Alaskan myth that seems to explore the same themes but with a male character. It comes from another island with a strong storytelling tradition: St. Lawrence Island, at the far west of the Inuit homeland just south of the Bering Strait, between Siberia and Alaska. This is close to where the ancestors of today's Inuit began to spread eastward 1,000 years ago. In their dialect its inhabitants call themselves Yupiit (a dialectal variant of the term Inuit).[1] It is a place where bowhead whales are still hunted, a place that takes us back to the origins of Inuit culture. The myth of "The Strange Man and His Whale" deals with gender identity, the sexual division of labour, and the relationship between hunting and procreating.

A Transgender Man Stays Home and Does Women's Work[2]

The story was taken down, transcribed in the Yupik language, and translated into English by Grace Slwooko (1979), a Yupik woman from Sivuqaq (Gambell) on St. Lawrence Island, Alaska:[3]

For us, in the Eskimos' (Yupiit) belief, there is another sex between man and woman. In other places, they might be referred to as people with dual sex characteristics.

The narrator is alluding to expressions that some Amerindian authors or organizations have adopted to replace the anthropological term *berdache*. These expressions most often stress the duality of such people ("Two-Spirits").

But Eskimos here in this area of Siberia and St. Lawrence Island have great consideration for this kind of person because he can't help his nature. We look at this mostly in the way a person dresses and not in the way he acts. When a man with a mustache is dressed like a woman, we are careful not to make fun of him as instructed by our elders. The elders would say that such people were protected by the Maker of All. So to laugh at him would bring a curse to the thoughtless ones.

Cross-dressing has been observed in many Siberian peoples, notably the Chukchi—who live the closest to the Yupiit of Siberia and St. Lawrence Island. It has also been practised by their Amerindian neighbours in mainland Alaska and the Pacific Northwest. Study of this subject is usually biased. Cross-dressed individuals were long believed to be homosexual, but only a tiny minority actually were. In fact, they should be viewed through the lens of gender rather than sexual orientation. When Jane Murphy (1974, 64) conducted research among the Yupiit of St. Lawrence Island in the mid-1950s, she wrote that "sexual deviance was not, however, ignored in their system of morals.[4] Homosexuality, for example, was severely disapproved of even though the transgender shamans who sometimes practiced homosexuality were thought to be the most powerful."[5]

Traditionally an Inuk from Canada's Central Arctic could not choose to live with someone of the same sex to form a family. Family formation had to be with someone of the opposite sex. Same-sex relationships were one of several workarounds for single men and women, a kind of palliative sex before marriage or after the loss of a spouse. Other workarounds included zoophilia and incest, which were considered deviant.

Cross-dressing most often involved children who at birth had received the name and identity of a deceased person of the opposite sex. This would be done either to fulfill a wish that the person had made while alive or after death, by appearing in a dream to one of the future parents, or to protect the baby from lethal forces that had made the mother miscarry several times before. The new identity, so it was thought, would protect the baby from evil spirits. This was the case with *Iqallijuq* (Chapter 1).

Another pre-birth scenario involved the *sipiniq*, a fetus who decided before leaving the womb to change sex and choose the tools of the opposite sex, laid out near the exit to the small womb-igloo (as with *Iqallijuq* in Chapter 1 and *Aumarjuat*, "Big Ember," in Chapter 8). A shaman could also authorize a gender change to heal a seriously ill child. The child would receive a new name and identity from someone of the opposite sex or even from one of the shaman's helping spirits to prevent evil spirits from recognizing the child. Again, this was the case with *Iqallijuq* (Chapter 1).

Murphy (1974, 63) provides further information on the therapeutic aspects of this shamanic ritual. Normally, a childhood illness would be blamed on an evil spirit stealing a child's soul. The shaman would then send his helping spirit to look for the child's soul in the other worlds, and his spirit would bring it back. If the illness re-occurred or if the ritual failed, the shaman could choose another ritual to protect the child by means of a new name-soul. People described the second ritual as a way of "changing everything and making everything right." If the child were a girl, her hair would be cut like a boy's, and she would be made to smoke a pipe, wear boy's clothing, and associate with groups of boys. If the child were a boy, he would have to wear girl's clothing and adopt girlish behaviour (Murphy 1974). *Ujarak* had been cross-dressed this way as a child (see Introduction).

Who is the Maker of All and the protector of transgender people? He is the spirit known in Canada's Central Arctic as *Silaap Inua*, "the master of the atmosphere" (or *Naarjuk*, "Big Belly," in the language of shamans). There is thus a spiritual dimension to cross-dressing, since this cosmic spirit protects transgender people.

So when we see a man dress like a woman he is showing respect to his nature and we are not to laugh at him or hurt his feelings. So there was one like that in this story. The man in this story dressed like a woman and never wanted to go hunting, but stayed home and sewed. He was the eldest of four brothers.

The strange man is the oldest of four brothers. In the past, such an un-balanced sex ratio among sibling children often led to one being assigned the role of the opposite sex. I had an opportunity in Alaska to meet a Yu-pik woman from the Siberian side of the Bering Strait who was the oldest of four daughters and who had been raised as a boy. She knew all about hunting, which she had often done while assisting her father. Such life stories were common among the Inuit of Nunavut and Nunavik, where I knew many cross-dressed young people.

The situation in this myth differs, however, from the one that could be seen in Canada's Central Arctic. The strange man from St. Lawrence Island remains transgender in adulthood and does only women's activities, whereas any cross-dressing among Canadian Inuit stopped habitually at puberty. A cross-dressed boy would then give up his braids and girl's cloth-ing and kill his first big game. A cross-dressed girl would start wearing women's clothing right after her first period, get her face and part of her body tattooed, and prepare for home life as a wife and mother. Such peo-ple went through a real identity crisis, which might lead some to become shamans. In any event, their inverted socialization marked them for life. Their gender would still be altered non-visibly and symbolically by the terms used to address them: "mother," "father," "sister," "brother," and so on—the same terms people had used to address their namesakes of the op-posite sex. There was also a custom of betrothing a young cross-gendered boy to a young cross-gendered girl, thus striking a new balance that often reversed the rule of patrilocal residence after marriage. The new son-in-law would move in with his wife's family and help them out with male tasks. We know that shamans did practise a form of adult cross-dressing in Canada's Central Arctic, although we know little about the subject.[6]

The Transgender Man Is Resented by His Younger Brothers

It happened that the youngest brother, when they got whales and walruses out on the ice and sea, would get upset about meat taken to the eldest brother who didn't go out hunting at all. The youngest brother would complain, "Why do we have to take meat to our eldest brother when he doesn't work out on the cold moving ice and sea like us?" (Slwooko 1979)

The sexual division of labour required boys to learn how to hunt and how to participate in all of the community's hunting activities. Each participant was entitled to a share of the meat, even if he had not personally taken part in catching the animal. If a man refused to join in a community hunt for no valid reason, he would not get his share of the meat. If he repeatedly refused, he would be expelled from the group. As for the girls, they had to learn how to sew, how to process hides, how to cook, and how to take care of the home and children. These skills were taught by the midwife with help from women elders, and these people would tell the group all about the children's first-time achievements.[7]

In this story, the youngest brother does not wish to accommodate his oldest brother's identity; nor does he think about the cosmological dimension of this life choice. He tries to persuade the other brothers to make their oldest brother help them. In very clear-cut language, he invokes the rule that only those who participate in the hunt are entitled to a share of the meat. In doing so, he violates the Inuit shamanic tradition of assigning the fate of transgender people to the spirits.

When the strange acting man heard about this, he went out to the shore. He buried his face in his parky[8] sleeves and the large ruff which were made like women's clothing, and cried because the brothers hurt his feelings. There he cried and cried.

The Maker of All Comes to Rescue the Female Man

Soon a voice was heard asking, "Why is the woman crying?" It was the voice of the Maker of All. In answer, the strange man said, "My brothers complained about me not being out on the ice and sea with them at the hunts. I am unable to go. I can't! I can't! I'm like a woman. How can I when I'm made like this?" he sobbed on as he poured out his grief. So the voice answered, "All right, I'll see to it that you'll get something." So very much comforted, the strange man went home. It wasn't long when he felt that he was getting big like a woman that was going to have a baby! He got bigger. Boy, the poor strange man was frightened. "If I'm going to have a baby, how will it ever be delivered?" he moaned to himself. But the voice soon talked to him again asking, "Why is the woman crying again?" For an answer, the strange man asked, "If I'm going to have a baby, how is it going to be delivered?" "You go down to the sea and bury your face in your sleeves and ruff and rest there on the sea. You won't sink," the voice answered. So the strange man hurried down to the sea in his parky made like that of women and got on the sea and buried his face with his sleeves and large ruff made of black dog skin. This was the women's original parky. There he floated around as he cried.

The Transgender Man Gives Birth to a Baby Whale

Somehow a little whale is born.

The Maker of All could have supplied the strange man with meat, as the Moon Man regularly did for the woman who bore his child (Chapter 10). He could have also met the strange man's need for food, as did the protective spirits of *Itirjuaq* (Chapter 11) by giving her two caring husbands and generous patients. Or, finally, he could have transformed the strange man so that he could manage on his own, as the Moon Man did with Walrus-Skin (Chapter 9).

Yet the Maker of All solves the strange man's problem in a subtler way that is better suited to his special situation. The creator is acting here as the spirit of *Sila* would—as one who commands life and the motions of the cosmos. The strange man is neither a bullied orphan nor a barren or battered wife. He has a man's body, while affirming his feminine side by cross-dressing and by choosing women's activities. The Maker of All therefore makes him give birth to a baby whale that will lure other whales and provide the Yupiit with meat.

Like a woman, the strange man gives rather than takes life, but some masculinity remains in him, and this is why he gives birth to an animal son. This fact elevates him to a special category above that of ordinary humans: he is neither a reproducing, childbearing woman nor a producing, meat-providing man, but rather a transgender man who gives birth to an animal son—a lure for whales and thus a boon for hunters in the community.

FIGURE 29. The strange man of St. Lawrence Island with the whale calf he has just birthed. From a drawing by J. Leslie Boffa (Slwooko 1979).

When his baby was born, it was not like the humans. Instead, it was a little whale! The strange man picked up the tiny whale and took it home. He loved it so dearly that he carved a large wooden bowl and put water in it for the whale to swim in [Figure 29]. The whale was getting big fast so that in no time he had to carve another bowl. When the whale got too large to be kept in the house, the man took him to the sea. He stayed at the waves for some time. While he was at the waves, the little whale would come ashore many times to be with his mother.

This episode harks back to the story about the old single woman who adopts a bear cub and raises it as her son (Chapter 2).

When he [the whale] was grown up, the strange man made a marker for his son. He made holes at his nose and put a reddened baby seal skin on his nose to mark him. So the little whale would play out in the sea.

This is a wise precaution. All animals are potential game unless they are distinctively marked or set apart by their size, coat colour, or behaviour. I mentioned in Chapter 3 that the term *Silaat* ("children of *Sila*") is used for unusual-looking animals. They should not be killed, for that would bring misfortune. Nor should they be eaten, for their meat would kill anyone who ate it.

The Whale Son Provides Meat

There were times when he got as far as the horizon. He got to going so far away that he would bring another whale along when he came home. So the younger brothers of the strange man would go out and kill the one he brought. He brought home many whales and the brothers were getting rich. The people of the village also became good whalers because of the whales which followed the man's special whale given him by the Maker of All. They were not short of meat and oil. They had plenty of bones for housing poles and for other uses. That was the way the strange man was comforted.

To explain the symbolism of this birth of a baby whale, I will discuss a ritual observed among the Iglulik Inuit of Nunavut. When a girl with a female identity had her first period, she would be sent to each household of the camp with a leather cup. Whenever she entered a home the women would pour a little water into her cup and say, "Good for you, you had a son!" Thus, the blood from a girl's first period, a sign that she was now fertile, would be associated with childbearing. On the other hand, when the girl had a male identity and been cross-dressed as a child, she would be told in the same circumstances, "Good for you, you cut up a whale!" She was congratulated on being a good hunter. Having a son, killing a whale, and cutting it up were considered symbolically analogous.

When the strange man gives birth to a baby whale, his position is symmetrical and opposite to that of a girl who has a male identity and is having her first period. A woman is expected to give birth to future hunters, and a man is expected to kill game to feed his family. In the myth, however, the strange man performs none of these traditional roles. He instead gives birth to a special whale that lures other whales ashore to become meat for his brothers.

In fact, he is performing the role of a shaman—a mediator who, straddling the boundary of gender and sex, can straddle other boundaries between the human and animal worlds, and between the spirit and human worlds. Among the Yupiit of Alaska, childhood cross-dressing was often a prelude to the child becoming a shaman (Murphy 1974). As noted earlier, shamans used to be cross-dressed in northeastern Siberia, which is home to the Chukchi—the Yupiit's neighbours. I have recorded several accounts about male shamans cross-dressing when they had to officiate. With some success, I have confirmed the same pattern among the Inuit of Nunavut: childhood cross-dressing paved the way for life as a shaman (Saladin d'Anglure 1994b [1986], 1988a), and there was a physical or symbolic gender change of any male or female shaman with a helping spirit of the opposite sex.[9]

The Whale Son Is Murdered

Then one day, his whale didn't come home. The strange man waited at the shore very anxiously and he was very worried. He waited and waited, but no whale came. Another day passed on, still no sign of his whale. Then finally he got into his parky and buried his face in his sleeves and the large ruff and cried. He cried and cried, and soon he heard a voice asking to know why the woman was crying. The strange man poured out his sorrow in answer. So the voice said to him, "You go out to the sea in your parky as you always do until you stop but you will still be moving." The man did as he was told. Out there on the ocean he moved along but he did not see where he was going.

The strange man is like a shaman travelling to another world in the heavens or under the water, or flying through the air to get news about travellers on their way home. Interestingly, whenever the Maker of All intervenes on his behalf, the strange man buries his face and does not look, in the same way as the battered wife whom Moon Brother takes away on his sled to his heavenly igloo (Chapter 10). In both cases, the human enters a level of reality that is specific to spirits and shamans.

When he stopped moving, he got his head up from his parky and what a strange place he was coming to! Where was he? The strange man wondered and tried to figure it out. Soon he found out that he was coming to a different village.

The Maker of All has led him far from his familiar landscape, far from the hunting grounds of the people of his village, hence his feeling of disorientation and strangeness. This does not bode well for his whale son.

As soon as he came to the coast he skipped along to the shore. He walked up to the beach. At the beach, what tragedy met his eyes! There was the marked head of his son! Just the head. Where was his body? In vain he ran around the large head to see the body, but it was gone. His son was killed!

One cannot help but think of the myth about the old woman who adopts a bear cub and raises it as her son until the day comes when her campmates want to kill it and divide the meat among themselves. They could have instead used it to procure meat (Chapter 2).

He could see that there was a village close by. He followed the path to a house. When he got there, he found out that it was the home of a crew that got his son. The people were getting together there to tell stories to celebrate the event or honor the catch. The people humbly welcomed the strange man and asked him if he had a story to tell as they were doing this to show their thankfulness for a great event that had been given to them.

Hunting exploits often gave rise to long stories or songs to liven up the community feast.

The Rules Are Broken, and Heaven's Wrath Is Brought Down

The strange man replied, "I am coming to tell a story for I certainly have one." He started, "There is a man who was born to be unable to go hunting for whales and all animals like others do. When he was accused, he cried to the Maker of All, and he was given a strange and powerful son, a whale. What a heart lifter he was. He got many whales for the village so the man, or his parent, was not helpless anymore. Very proudly he raised his son. He was a joy to him. So he put a marker on him, a beautiful piece of work on him, a reddened baby seal skin of great prize. To the parent's great sorrow, however, his son was killed when the poor ambitious child got too far from home. They should have left him alone as he had markings, but they have killed him anyway. This is a tragedy to his parent. That is my story." With this, the sorrowing mother [of the whale son] left the place in tears. There was a terrible silence after he left. The people tried to understand what he meant and they thought about killing a whale with reddened skins on his nose.

This story is made all the more dramatic by its modest tone and moving content. In very simple language, the strange man points to a very simple rule of Inuit morality: the importance of respecting a distinctively marked animal. He ends his story by bursting into tears. This, together with his being protected by the Maker of All, immediately sets in motion the melting away of those who have caused his sorrow.

A terrible and horrible thing happened after the strange man left the place. The crew of the boat that killed the whale with the reddened baby seal skin on its nose started to sweat! The men sweated and sweated.

Terrified by their appearance, the men looked at each other. They got smaller and smaller until they all turned to liquid.

The strange man's impregnation happened through tears and seawater, as did his whale son's delivery and birth. Again, it was by tears and seawater that the Maker of All took him on a search for his missing son. Now, when his son's killers are confronted with their responsibility for murder, they break out in a sweat so profuse that their bodies gradually turn to liquid. All of these fluids—tears, seawater, and sweat—share one thing in common: saltiness. What began in tears ends in sweat, as if to show the fragility of human life and its submission to the rules of the cosmos. It would have been simpler at the outset if the younger brothers had kept supplying the strange man with meat.

They say that every time someone got a seal or some other animal which looked strange, usually some sorrow would come to the family that happened to get it. I guess this was because that animal was marked as belonging to someone and that it should never have been killed.

Let us come back to the strange man. He seems to be a male replica of Big-Anus (*Itirjuaq*). Both of these heroes, in their own way, cannot do the tasks usually assigned to their gender. Both straddle the gender boundary, and both can provide a kind of mediation that no ordinary human can. *Itirjuaq* mediates between her patients' ill bodies and *Naarjuk*, who commands the atmosphere, the motions of the cosmos, and the movements of life. The strange man mediates between the hunters, their game animals, and the Maker of All. Both express differing but complementary facets of Inuit shamanic mediation. At the same time, by straddling the boundaries laid down by social rules, these go-betweens irritate some of their fellow humans and arouse their anger—the Big Man's anger toward *Itirjuaq,* and the younger brother's anger toward the strange man, his eldest brother.

CHAPTER 13

Atanaarjuat, the Fast Runner: A Mythical Hero

With this chapter we come to another type of story, one in which a lo-cal historical figure has turned into a mythical hero (see also Chapter 14). Such transformations have undoubtedly occurred in the mythologies of all peoples but are not always easy to identify because the process began so long ago. I already touched on this point in Chapter 5 when discussing *Uinigumasuittuq* ("She who refused to marry"). *Atanaarjuat* belongs to a different category of hero whose epic adventures are still very much re-membered in the oral tradition of the Iglulingmiut and the Inuit of neigh-bouring regions (Arctic Bay, Pond Inlet, Clyde River, Repulse Bay, Rankin Inlet, and Arviat).

In its different variants, the story refers so precisely to where things happened that we can locate it in the Igloolik region. The references to bowhead whaling could place the story in a rather distant past, since such hunting came with the Thule people, the direct ancestors of today's Inuit. Yet this past must still be relatively recent because some of the action oc-curred at the camp on Qikirtaarjuk ("The little island") when this place had already become a headland (Chapter 5). So *Atanaarjuat* is historical. This is the story that Igloolik Isuma Productions chose to make into its first full-length fiction film.[1]

The story of *Atanaarjuat* may be thought of as both a myth and a historical epic. It has elements of both. On the one hand, it is structured like a myth and as such resembles several of the myths presented in this book. On the other, it took place in the pre-colonial historical past on a clearly identified territory. It was then passed down via oral tradition over many generations.[2]

The story can be dated to about five centuries ago, when the slow uplifting of the earth's crust (postglacial rebound) turned Qikirtaarjuk from an island into a headland. When the glaciers over this region melted 7,000 years ago, the ground was no longer depressed by the huge mass of ice and slowly began to rebound to its former level (Chapter 5).

A variant of this myth was first transcribed in the last years of the nineteenth century by whaling captain George Comer (Boas 1901). As with Lyon's mention of the two brothers (1824), Comer's variant places the action in Amittuq, the name the Iglulingmiut gave their territory. This variant has many elements that round out and clarify *Kupaaq*'s variant (1972), which I will use for my analysis.

Another variant was published in English by Rasmussen (1929, 298–99), who took it down from *Inukpasujjuk*, a Netsilik immigrant among the Aivilik Inuit of Repulse Bay. It is sketchy and clearly not from a native of the Amittuq region. While leading the Fifth Thule Expedition (1921–24), Rasmussen found at least one person named *Atanaarjuat* among the Iglulingmiut and several others with this as a second name among the Aivilingmiut.[3]

This myth was also mentioned, in syllabics this time, by Jimmy Ettuk of Arctic Bay in the comments he made on the back of a drawing of three scenes from the myth (Figure 30). He provided few details, however.[4] His comments will be discussed further on.

In 1972, in Igloolik, I recorded an Inuktitut variant of the myth from *Kupaaq*. It will be the main reference for this chapter. In the early 1990s, the same narrator recounted several other variants to the local cultural association Inudlariit. Some years later, Igloolik Isuma Productions took down several more variants from village elders when it began working on a full-length feature film about the myth of *Atanaarjuat*. Two of them will provide me with information missing from *Kupaaq*'s variant. They are from François *Quassa* and Hervé *Paniaq*, who is *Kupaaq*'s younger brother. Because another family adopted *Paniaq* at a very early age, he had access to other sources than his original family.

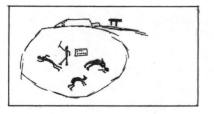

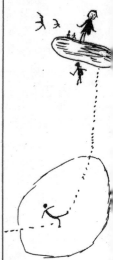

FIGURE 30. Three episodes of the epic of *Atanaarjuat* (clockwise from bottom left): 1. The killing of the brother; 2. The flight of *Atanaarjuat*; 3. The revenge of *Atanaarjuat*, who kills his opponents. From a drawing by Jimmy Ettuk (Blodgett 1986).

The Two Brothers and Their Difficult Childhood

Comer provides the variant that tells us the most about the childhood of *Atanaarjuat* and his younger brother *Aamarjuaq*:

> At Amitoq [Amittuq] there once lived a man and his wife. The man wished his children to be very strong. For this reason he made the mother, after each child was born, sit on the floor of the hut with her feet raised to each side of the doorway. In this position she had to eat, taking a large piece of half-cooked meat in both hands, and tearing off pieces with her teeth, while the fat ran down her arms. While she was doing this, her husband remained in the entrance-way and kept off the dogs with his whip. This made the children exceedingly strong. One of the sons of this couple was named *Armackjuark* [*Aamarjuaq*]. He came to be a very strong man. His wrists were as thick as the legs of a bear. He had one brother, who was called *Artinarkjuark* [*Atanaarjuat*], and one half-brother (Boas 1901, 328–31).

To make his sons stronger, the man chooses a seemingly strange procedure: he puts his wife through terrible ordeals. Eating requires much physical effort without the support of your back and with your legs outstretched and raised to each side, instead of being folded underneath in the usual position. Here, the effort is all the more strenuous because his wife has to tear off mouthfuls from a large piece of half-cooked meat by using her teeth, like a dog, a bear, or some other carnivore. People believed that the behaviour of a pregnant woman or of a mother who had just given birth would directly affect her child.

Paniaq's variant (1997) likewise provides some details that are missing from *Kupaaq*'s. The father wants his sons to be stronger than himself, having been a poor hunter mistreated by his hunting friends. His children further develop their muscles because of the hardships imposed on their family by camp neighbours. Since their father often comes home from hunting empty-handed, the children get only a few walrus ribs as their share of the game meat. They never eat their fill.

To understand how this Spartan diet helped the two sons, we must keep in mind how boys were supposed to be raised. Mothers were told that their boys should never eat their fill and should eat sparingly in order to become strong, tough, and able to withstand the difficult hunting life.

A minimum of clothing was also recommended to make them resistant to severe cold snaps and bad weather (Chapter 9).

Jealousy, Hostility, and Domestic Violence

When the two brothers had grown up, they were able to feed their entire families. They usually lived here, in this region [Iglulik]. While living at Pingiqqalik,[5] with families who felt animosity toward them, they went by dogsled to Ugliit Island to bring back walrus blubber they had left in stone caches. While they were trying to find their caches, some of their campmates, jealous of their hunting success, made off with the dogsled and fled to the camp. *Atanaarjuat*, who was an unbeatable runner, caught up to them, overtook the dogs, and forced them to stop, thus enabling his brother *Aamarjuaq*, known for his physical strength, to catch up in turn and throw the robbers off the sled. Having taken back control of their dog team, the two brothers returned to Pingiqqalik, leaving their foiled assailants far behind on the ice (Paniaq 1997).

The variant taken down by Comer puts more stress on domestic disputes, primarily between *Aamarjuaq*'s two wives:

He [*Aamarjuaq*] had two wives—*Ecootlikechark* [*Ikullikisaq*] and *Arknuckkaark* [*Arnakkaaq*]. The former was thin and lean, while the latter was very stout. *Ikullikisaq* was jealous of the other wife, and used to taunt her, saying that she had large hips and did not look well; while *Arnakkaaq* would retort that the other one had legs as thin as the pieces of bone which are used to dig marrow out of broken bones (Boas 1901, 328–29).

Kupaaq confirms that the two brothers were polygynous, and he describes the complex relationships between them and their in-laws in the neighbouring camp:

Atanaarjuat and *Aamarjuaq* were brothers, and *Atanaarjuat* was the younger one. They lived at Iksivautaujaak, not far from Iglulik. They each had two wives. Each brother had a wife from nearby Iglulik camp. This was the camp of the other hunters, the ones who were jealous of the two brothers' great hunting success. Both women very often went there to visit and even stay for a while. In the spring, their families plotted to kill the two brothers. They knew that once the ice was gone the brothers would go back to bowhead whale hunting, which they were especially good at.

Comer spoke of *Aamarjuaq*'s success in hunting bowhead whales:

Armuckjuark [*Aamarjuaq*] was a successful whaler.[6] He liked best to go off in his kayak when a strong southeasterly wind was blowing. He would go out alone, carrying a large float made of the skin of a ground-seal;[7] and when he had killed a whale, he would leave it, and the whale would soon drift ashore. Between times he used to go home and tell the people to be on the lookout for a whale (Boas 1901, 329).

Kupaaq, too, describes how the two brothers would go whaling:

When *Uannaq* [the northwesterly wind] began to blow from inland, the two brothers would go kayak hunting for bowhead whales. They would each use a float made from the skin of a big bearded seal and let it drift at sea with their catch when they had harpooned a bowhead whale. When the wind changed and *Nigiiq* [the southeasterly wind] began to blow, they went back to the camp, letting the wind and the currents push their catches ashore. The floats were made of bearded seal skin. A person on shore could thus see their catches arrive. The other people found these brothers very skilful. They each had a big stone for a seat, at the place where they kept watch for whales. This is why the place is named Iksivautaujaak ["which looks like two seats"], to the left [west] of Iglulik [the old site].

One of the two stones is still visible at the place named Iksivautaujaak (Photo 14), and the other one is believed to have rolled down and onto the beach. Today the sea is much farther from the shore of that time. The above hunting strategy is original and does not seem to have been mentioned elsewhere, although it is known that a fatally wounded bowhead whale always ends up washing ashore, being pushed there by winds and tides.

The variant taken down by Comer describes the different characters of the two brothers, with *Aamarjuaq* having Herculean strength and a very bad temper. Here is how the narrator described him:

He [*Aamarjuaq*] was not a good caribou-hunter, however, because he could not paddle on the lakes as quickly as others. His uncle, particularly, used to pass by him in his kayak and kill the caribou before he could reach them..One day when the caribou were crossing a lake, he [*Aamarjuaq*] asked his wives to bring him his paddle. It was so large that it required both of them to carry it. He took his brother *Atanaarjuat* into his kayak and started. His uncle followed him, and soon passed him. This enraged *Aamarjuaq*, who, with a powerful stroke of his paddle, made the water whirl so rapidly that his uncle was capsized and drowned. *Atanaarjuat* did not like the way in which his brother was acting, and as soon as they reached the shore he jumped out of the kayak and went to his tent (Boas 1901, 329).

Aamarjuaq is portrayed as conceited. He is the very image of abusive brute force. His younger brother, whom the other variants describe as the faster runner—this is, incidentally, the meaning of his name—is conversely portrayed as kind and respectful of others. He is nonetheless bound by ties of fraternal solidarity to his older brother, whom he respects and obeys. Comer's variant next reports a terrifying example of *Aamarjuaq*'s violence, which also appears in some of the more recently gathered variants:

Later in the winter the people went to fetch some caribou-meat from their caches. When they returned, *Ikullikisaaq* [the jealous woman, and *Aamarjuaq*'s wife] distributed it. Soon she returned and told her husband that she had met his half-brother in one of the entrance-passages, and that in trying to pass her he had tried to overcome her. In fact, they merely happened to meet, and in trying to pass each other had always moved to the same side. *Aamarjuaq* believed his wife. The next morning he arose early, went to his half-brother's house, and said that he was going to kill him. His half-brother said, "Wait until I am dressed." He got up, and as soon as he was dressed, *Aamarjuaq* stabbed him with his knife. Then their mother began to cry. She was sad over the loss of her child, and told *Aamarjuaq* that his wife had deceived him, and had lied in regard to his half-brother, and ended by saying that she hoped *Aamarjuaq* would not die if he should be stabbed by the other people. *Aamarjuaq* returned to his house. Early the next morning he asked *Ikullikisaaq* which way the wind was blowing. She retorted that he might find out by going out himself. Then he took hold of her hand with both of his, pulled her fingers apart, and split her hand and arm up to the elbow. She gave a wild shriek and died. He knew now that she had lied, and he felt sorry for having slain his half-brother (Boas 1901, 329–30).

Quassa's variant (1998) very similarly describes how *Aamarjuaq* murders one of his wives. Each of the two brothers has a bad-tempered wife who is so unruly that each brother prefers to stay longer with his other wife. One morning, *Aamarjuaq's* defiant wife goes out for a few moments after waking and then comes back. He questions her about the weather outside, and she impertinently tells him to go and look for himself. He then asks her to hold out her hand. He grabs her fingers with both of his hands and, with two of her fingers in each hand, he pulls them apart in opposite directions and splits open first her hand and then her arm up to her elbow. She screams so loud in pain that she almost seems to convulse with laughter. The murder stirs up very hard feelings against the two brothers among her relatives. This tragedy, according to *Quassa*, leads to plans to kill both of the brothers.

A Murderous Ambush

Here is *Kupaaq's* description of the ambush set for them:

One spring day, while the two brothers were out hunting some distance away on the ice, they saw human outlines hopping like ravens, on the horizon, on a large rock overlooking the camp of their enemies. On their return they asked their wives to go and visit there to find out what was happening. They then went to bed and fell asleep, tired by the day spent hunting. The two wives made a long visit to the other camp, and there they were told to place caribou-skin stockings outside the tents, against the tent walls, to indicate where each of the two brothers slept. They then went home late at night. They did what they had been asked to do, and they too went to bed. While everyone slept, the people of the other camp came to kill the two brothers.

The variant taken down by Comer provides many details about the attack:

At dark the people attacked them. By far the greater number assailed *Aamarjuaq*'s tent, while only about half that number attacked *Atanaarjuat*'s tent. They jumped on top of the tent-skins, so that the tent fell down, and they tried to stab the inmates. As soon as *Aamarjuaq* felt the tent falling down, he arose on his hands and feet, and crawled in this way quite a distance, carrying tent and men along; and finally he was despatched. The other men broke down *Atanaarjuat*'s tent; but one of their number pitied him, and, while the others were trying to kill him, he shouted, "*Aamarjuaq* is coming!" Then all the men jumped up from the tent, and *Atanaarjuat* took this opportunity to escape; but blood was flowing from his wounds. Finally he came to a stream, and by wading in it he covered his tracks (Boas 1901, 330).

Kupaaq's variant is fairly close to this one, with a few differences:

They leaped onto the tents, which fell down under their weight, and they began to make stabbing thrusts through the walls. *Aamarjuaq* was killed by a stab through his tent. But a little old woman standing not far away cried out, "*Atanaarjuat angajuata arpapaasi!*" ["*Atanaarjuat*'s older brother is coming to attack you!"]. On hearing her words, the men atop *Atanaarjuat*'s tent leaped to the ground and, overcome with fright, turned to look around themselves for several moments. This was when *Atanaarjuat* crawled out from under his tent, stark naked, and fled. *Atanaarjuat* ran naked to the sea ice and began to run away. The people took off after him, but he leaped over a wide crevasse in the ice, and they were unable to do likewise. They went to the end of the crevasse to walk around it and came back on the other side looking for his tracks. They found them easily, for the flesh of the soles of his feet had been scraped raw from running on the bare sea ice. He went to Siuraq to get himself some clothing. An elderly couple lived there with their granddaughter. They were there to trap eider ducks, which they caught with snares, and also to collect the eggs.

According to *Kupaaq*, eider ducks would come in droves to nest on the island. Today, it is mostly a nesting site for common terns. The snares were made out of baleen bristles from bowhead whales. At that time, people used eider skins with the feathers still attached to make warm clothing when caribou skins were lacking. This skill is no longer known to the

Iglulik Inuit, but the sketches in Captain Lyon's book show Iglulik hunters in eider-skin clothing (Figure 5).

When he arrived, they cut out the snow with his footprints and put it back upside down to conceal his bloody trail. The old man then gave *Atanaarjuat* his *nattiq* [sealskin jacket] and his *nattiqutiik* [sealskin trousers] for him to wear. He had no other clothes; they next helped him go to a place on the shore where there were large piles of seaweed, and they hid him underneath.

In his comments, *Kupaaq* adds that one can still see these seaweed piles, which are formed by the currents, the wind, and the tides. According to *Quassa* (1998) and Comer (Boas 1901, 330–31), *Atanaarjuat* instead goes to his parents' camp. This is what Comer wrote down:

Then he travelled on until he came to the place where his parents lived, near a point where they were catching ducks with whalebone snares. They dressed his wounds and gave him new clothing. On the following day the people who were pursuing him came to the tent. Then his mother made him lie down on the ground, and covered him up. The people asked the old couple if they had seen any one coming that way. They replied that no one had come, and invited them to rest, and gave them to eat. Soon the people left, believing *Atanaarjuat* to be dead.

These details agree very much with *Kupaaq*'s variant:

When his pursuers arrived, they asked the old couple if they had seen anyone. They had seen no one that whole spring, they answered. They then offered their visitors food—eider duck stew.

To allay suspicions, feed your enemies to their heart's content. This is a good strategy in war, and *Atanaarjuat* will use it at the end of this story.

The people left them to go home because they had failed to find the man they had been looking for.

The Making of a Hero

Atanaarjuat, the fastest of all runners, has foot wounds so bad he can no longer walk. His situation is like a baby's. He depends entirely on his host family, and in the following episodes we will see his rebirth as a hero.

After the pursuers left, the old couple kept watching the vicinity to see if anyone was coming. They took care of the injured man by applying blubber to his wounds and keeping the blubber in place with an eider-skin bandage. At the approach of summer, when the wounds healed, they all left for the mainland to take up residence at Tasiujaq. *Atanaarjuat* then left the old couple, and went away with their granddaughter to Tasirjuaq in order to hunt caribou.

They leave the small island of Siuraq for Baffin Island, on the other side of Fury and Hecla Strait. They go to Tasiujaq, where the old couple pitch their camp. From there *Atanaarjuat* borrows his host's kayak and, accompanied by the old couple's granddaughter, goes inland to Tasirjuaq ("The very big lake"). This lake has a *nalluk*, a narrow part that caribou swim across during their autumn migration.

When winter came, he built there a home made from blocks of ice. He sprinkled water on the ground all around to make it slippery. He also made himself ice cleats out of a caribou antler so that he wouldn't slip, and finally a club out of a *narruniq* [the part of a caribou antler attached to the animal's head]. He also made caribou-skin clothing for himself and for one of his wives.

Atanaarjuat has had time to think about the tragic events he has lived through. One of his wives stayed faithful to him and the other betrayed him. He is coldly preparing his vengeance and his return to his family.

After he finished all of that, he came back to Tasiujaq and the old couple's camp. There, he waited for an ice bridge to form over the *ikiq* [narrows] that separated him from Igloolik Island, his old campsite. He then placed a roll of caribou skins on his back and set off on the way home.

This ice bridge is very well-known to the Iglulingmiut. It forms each year after a period of intense cold, usually in mid-winter.

While he was still some distance away, the people saw him coming. One of his wives cried out immediately, "There is only *Atanaarjuat* who comes that way!" and she rushed forward to meet him. When she got to him, he exclaimed, "I don't remember having made you wear such wretched clothing!" He ripped up her old clothes and offered her the new ones he had made for her.

We see here the role of clothing in showing social status, especially the two extremes: being deprived and forced to wear old, tattered clothes, and conversely being rewarded with new, lavish clothes (Chapter 9). Most people wear ordinary clothing.

When his other wife came in turn to meet him, he ripped up her trousers and simply gave her a caribou skin so that she could make a new pair of trousers. He told her to go back to her family. He had no intention at all to keep her as a wife.

In the comments that Jimmy Ettuk (1964) wrote for his drawings about this myth, *Atanaarjuat* decides to get back at his faithless wife by splitting open her hand and arm up to her elbow. This vengeance appears above in Comer's variant but is carried out by *Aamarjuaq*.

The variant taken down by Comer is closer to *Kupaaq*'s and includes a few more details:

During this time he made a beautiful set of clothing for himself, and one for a woman (one of his wives). In winter he went back to his own village, and when the people saw him coming they recognized him at once. The man who had stabbed him in the side, and who thought that he had died of his wound, had carried a charm as a protection against *Atanaarjuat*'s spirit. When he saw *Atanaarjuat* alive, he dropped the charm when no one was looking. *Atanaarjuat* now called his wives, one of whom came quickly. He asked her to take off her old duck-skin suit, which he tore to pieces, and gave her the beautiful clothes which he had made. He would not have the other woman because she did not come at once when he had called. He then challenged two men who had stabbed him, and slew both of them. Then he left the village with his wife, and lived happily ever after (Boas 1901, 331).

This is where Comer's variant ends. *Kupaaq*'s version continues with additional episodes:

Once he had settled in, he invited the men who had tried to kill him to come and eat caribou in his ice house. They accepted and followed him there. He then treated them to plenty of caribou meat. Hardly had they finished than he brought them more. When he offered them even more, they told him they were full. He then left, claiming he wanted to relieve his bladder. So he left, put on his caribou-fur stockings, and attached the antler ice cleats he had made. He then grabbed the club and went back in. He began to strike at the men with his club. Some of them tried to get out, but they slipped and played dead while lying flat on the ground. He took their pulse and killed them too. This is how he killed all of those who had tried to kill him.

His vengeance was cruel. According to Inuit tradition, a blood crime has to be avenged by the same shedding of blood.

Eradicating a Wrong at Its Roots and the Wish for Vengeance

This is where the story ends in all but one of the variants. *Kupaaq*'s variant has an additional episode:

He afterwards returned to the camp [Iglulik] with his wife. He brought four boys and told them he had killed their fathers. He wanted the boys to kill him once they had become adults. One of them would grab him, another would lift him up, a third would throw him to the ground, and a fourth would stab him with a knife.

This seems at first to be a humanitarian gesture. Indeed, custom had it that a murderer should take care of his victim's wife and children. Murder leads to vendetta, however, and custom also had it that the victim's children should be brought up with a desire for vengeance. Paradoxically, *Atanaarjuat* will provide the four children of his victims with such an upbringing.

> When they became adults, he wanted them to try to kill him. The one who was supposed to grab him did so, and the second one lifted him up. The one who was supposed to throw him to the ground began to do so, but he caught him by the legs and threw him to the ground. The boy's head rolled away far from his body. The one who was supposed to stab him tried to do so, but he caught him by the wrist and stabbed him with his own knife. He killed all four of them. I think this is the end.

Here, *Atanaarjuat* is a superhero. Even when confronted by four younger opponents, he prevails and kills them. In this, he may be fulfilling a threefold wish: eradicate a wrong at its roots; end an interpersonal conflict that extends in the myth across three generations; and start anew with a clean slate. He could have just as easily killed the children instead of taking them in, but he wanted to give them a chance, thereby proving that tolerance and reflection are worth more than impulsiveness and violence. This ending differs considerably, however, from the ending of the film *Atanarjuat*, where the hero spares his enemies and lets the village elders merely ostracize them. Christianization has left a profound mark on the minds of today's Iglulingmiut. When the village elders were consulted about the film scenario, they unanimously asked that the ending be more merciful.

This myth is also about all sorts of problems with family life and interfamily life. It comes down hard on mistreatment of poor hunters and physically weak individuals, like the parents of the two brothers. We have already addressed this theme in previous chapters. The myth warns against vengeance if used unwisely and stirred up by badmouthing. It also condemns abuse of physical strength, which cost the life of the bad-tempered and arrogant *Aamarjuaq*, who can be likened to the Big Man of Chapter 11. Finally, it shows how polygyny threatens household peace because the wives are jealous of each other. Kinship ties become hard to manage when a dispute between wives degenerates into a clash between in-laws.

Through his tests of strength and endurance, *Atanaarjuat* symbolically dies and rises from the dead. He thus becomes a shaman, although this is not explicit in the different variants of the myth we have examined.

This mythical epic has one major theme that may tell us a lot about its audience and its popularity—a love of speed. The leading character, *Atanaarjuat*, has been conditioned from birth to become the fastest of all hunters, a destiny charted in advance by his name and by his childhood upbringing, thanks to a father anxious to protect his son from malevolent neighbours. Love of speed was pervasive in Inuit culture. Young boys were trained to outrun animals on land, especially caribou and also wolves (Saladin d'Anglure 2001b [2000]). Later, as men, they had to be fast kayakers—to bring meat home after hunting at sea. Meanwhile, little girls were taught to sew and work fast—to become appreciated wives and give birth quickly to sons who would become adept hunters or to daughters who would become skilful sewers. . . . The same leitmotif comes up again and again throughout this book. Speed, pushed to an extreme, gives the hero his aura. Indeed, he is not only as fast as predators like wolves or polar bears and valued prey like caribou but also as fast as spirits like the *Ijirait,* who are said to be so quick-footed they can outdistance caribou. This gift explains how *Atanaarjuat* became the patron spirit of the whole region, if Lyon (1824) is to be believed, and a powerful helping spirit for shamans.

In almost every region of the Inuit Arctic, oral tradition preserves the memory of an ancestor who was reputedly the fastest runner and capable of outrunning land animals. Such was the case on the Belcher Islands, where the new village was named Sanikiluaq after a forebear of the leading local family, a man as fast as wolves and caribou and even able to catch up to them (see Chapter 15).

CHAPTER 14

Ataguttaaluk, the Cannibal Forebear (or The Birth of a Myth)

This tragic story is set in the winter of 1905 in the Igloolik region, and I have chosen to present it here because it is becoming a founding myth and an event to be commemorated by the main heroine's descendants. Rasmussen (1929, 29–32) published the first detailed version after he took it down in 1922 from *Tagurnaaq*, who helped rescue *Ataguttaaluk*. Father Guy Mary-Rousselière recorded another version in 1968 from *Atuat*, who was *Tagurnaaq*'s adopted daughter and who witnessed the event. He published a somewhat abridged French translation (1969b) while providing me with the original Inuktitut version, which I was able to transcribe and translate in full. I had an opportunity to meet *Atuat* in 1974 and likewise record her version, as well as a version told by *Iqallijuq* (1979), who had heard it from her mother-in-law—*Ataguttaaluk* herself.[1]

This tragedy had two groups of actors: those who were starving, and those who rescued the sole survivor. The first group encompassed four families who lived in the Pond Inlet (Tununiq) region, in north Baffin Island. They were closely related to the Iglulik Inuit.[2] The first group's main family was headed by *Qumangaapik* and his wife, *Ataguttaaluk* (the sole survivor), both of whom had lost their first spouse. They were accompanied by *Kunnuk*, the teenaged son of *Qumangaapik*, and his first wife. With them were their four children: the older daughter *Atagullik*, the younger daughter *Niviatsiarannuk*, their son *Angiliq*, and a male baby whose name is not given. The second family comprised *Piugaattuq* and his wife *Tatiggak*, a first cousin of *Ataguttaaluk*. There were also two younger couples: *Aksarjuk*, another cousin of *Ataguttaaluk*, and his young wife *Sarpinaq*, who had often quarrelled with her husband; and finally *Sigluk*, a nephew of *Piugaattuq* and his wife *Ittukusuk*.

The rescuers were the second group: *Padluq*, a shaman of mature years; his older wife *Tagurnaaq*, who had led a troubled married life with several ex-husbands and who had shamanic powers; and their adopted daughter *Atuat*, who was eleven at the time (1905). She was the biological daughter of the shamans *Ava* and *Urulu*, who in 1922 would be Rasmussen's hosts and informants.

In the spring of 1905, *Padluq* decided to go by dogsled with his family from Iglulik to Tununiq (Pond Inlet) in northern Baffin Island to get ammunition from the little whaling company store. The previous summer he had hunted caribou near Kangirslujjuaq on Baffin Island and left several meat caches there. His dog team had only three dogs, so he needed to borrow one from the old *isumataq* (chief, "wise man") of Iglulik, *Amarualik*, who decided to accompany him with a second dog team and help him take apart his caches and bring some of the provisions back to Iglulik camp. It had rained that year in mid-winter, and the old chief saw this as a bad omen. A hunter must have lost his life. Heavy rain means that the master spirit of *Sila* is mourning an accidental death, for this entity shares the life breath of every human (Chapter 3).

So begins the story that *Atuat* (1974) told me in Igloolik, after being invited through the intermediary of her younger brother *Ujarak*, who had been working with me for four years. I have divided her story into five episodes, following the division published by Father Guy Mary-Rousselière (1969b). I draw primarily on the first oral version told by *Atuat* (1968) to him and the version of her adoptive mother *Tagurnaaq* (Rasmussen 1929, 29–32). For some episodes I use later material I recorded from *Atuat* (1974) and from *Iqallijuq* (1979), who heard these facts from her mother-in-law *Ataguttaaluk*, the sole survivor of this famine and the main participant and witness.

Padluq and the Portents of Tragedy

These four versions—the one told by *Tagurnaaq* (Rasmussen 1929), the two told by *Atuat* (1968, 1974), and the one told by *Iqallijuq* (1979)—are reconstructions twenty-four years, sixty-three years, sixty-nine years, and seventy-four years after the events. They are replete with seemingly trifling details that provide insight into real life and which position the narrator as an actor in the story. All of the portents of the tragedy contribute to giving the travellers a role as rescuers, as predetermined.

This is what *Atuat* told me in 1974:

My story begins when we left a place called Kangirslujjuaq. There was my mother *Tagurnaaq*, my father *Padluq*, and myself. We had only three dogs, three males. One of the dogs was old and not a good sled dog, but the other two were very good dogs. I was only a little girl at the time, and that spring I had gone to see my "uncle" *Nataaq*, who wasn't walking yet.

Kangirslujjuaq camp is across from Igloolik on Baffin Island. This is where one leaves the coast to follow the inland route to Tununiq. In the story, this is where *Amarualik* has left the travellers to return to his camp at Iglulik. When *Atuat* talks about her uncle *Nataaq*, she is referring to her biological brother. She calls him "maternal uncle" because of their respective names and because of the kinship ties that existed between their namesakes.

I don't remember how many times we slept on the route after leaving Kangirslujjuaq. I often had to walk while my parents helped the dogs pull the sled until we halted near the place called Nirivviujut ("The place where humans were eaten")[3] to spend the night.

Despite his shamanic powers, *Padluq* has a weak dog team. He is down to three dogs: two adult males and a young pup. So he has to harness himself to the sled with his wife to go uphill. In *Atuat*'s first version (Mary-Rousselière 1969b), the sled intriguingly stops sometimes on flat ground or even when going downhill, as if someone wants to immobilize it. After several days of travel, they halt one evening and pitch their skin tent to spend the night.

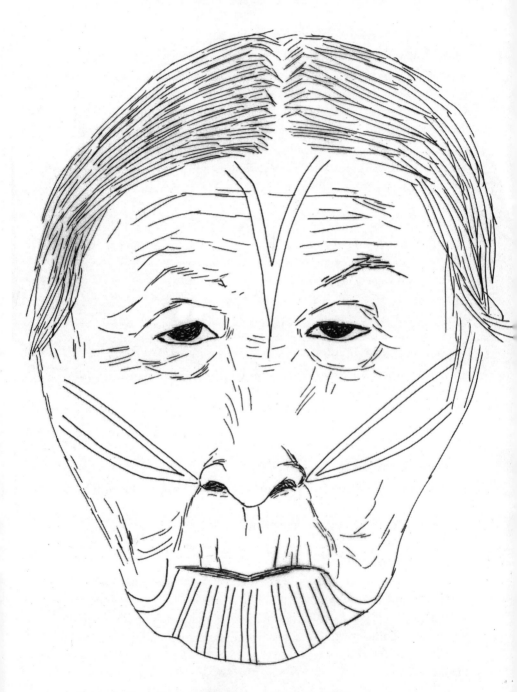

FIGURE 31. Portrait of *Atuat*. Drawing by Leah Idlout, Igloolik, 1974. Archival fonds of B. Saladin d'Anglure.

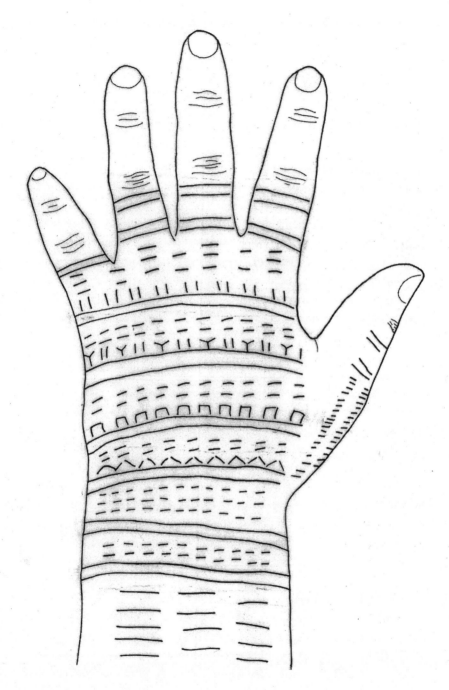

FIGURE 32. *Atuat*'s tattoos. Drawing of her left hand by Leah
Idlout, Igloolik, 1974.

We then saw an *aqiggiq* [rock ptarmigan] coming from the place toward which we were supposed to go. It flew above the stones that surrounded our tent. It was a male ptarmigan, and while it flew around our tent, you'd have thought it was saying human words. It landed in front of our door and then flew off in the direction it had come from. "Oh!" said my mother, "that's a very bad omen!"

According to *Tagurnaaq*, they see the rock ptarmigan on the morning of the third day (Rasmussen 1929, 29) while camped at a site named Aunirit ("The place where the snow has melted"). She tries to hit the bird by throwing a walrus tusk and then an axe, but in vain. Unknown to them, *Qumangaapik* (*Ataguttaaluk*'s husband) has died of hunger shortly before. At birth his body was wiped with a rock ptarmigan's skin, and he used the skin as an amulet, the bird thus becoming his guardian animal. Only later will the meaning of the omen become clear to them. In her first version, *Atuat* has the bird cackling at the top of its voice and walking around the tent on the stones that hold down the edge of the sealskin (Mary-Rousselière 1969b).

When my father woke up, he told us he had been dreaming. In his dream, a dog was galloping in our direction, but just before coming to the big stone that anchored the guy rope of our sealskin tent, it disappeared into the ground with its harness and the tether attached to it. My father added that this was a very bad omen.

According to *Atuat*'s first version, *Qumangaapik* (*Ataguttaaluk*'s dead husband) has sent this sign to alert them to come and rescue his wife (Mary-Rousselière 1969b). According to *Tagurnaaq*, *Padluq* has the gift of clairvoyance and can predict the future. He dreamed about a friend being eaten by his closest kin (Rasmussen 1929, 29).

We then got on our way again and came to a place where the snow was soft and deep, thus making our progress very difficult. My father wanted to carry our luggage to our destination, the idea being that we would get there the next day. But my mother, who was older than my father, said to him: "*Uumaq!* [This is how they would call each other reciprocally.] Let's all go ahead first, and you'll come back for the luggage. That way, it'll be easier for you to travel by following our footprints. If you try to carry our luggage by going first, you won't succeed in getting there all by yourself."

Tagurnaaq had been married several times before moving in with *Padluq*. She is a wise woman who does not hesitate to speak her mind. Her opinion here is a very sound one.

A Starving Survivor

After casting aside our luggage we reached a lake, and without stopping to rest we crossed the frozen lake. When we got to the other side I tried to follow my mother on foot, by walking in her footprints, but I very soon got tired because of the deep snow. While we were walking I suddenly heard the sound of a voice and said, "I think I heard an Arctic fox or a wolf or a wolverine."

Some other details were provided by *Tagurnaaq*, her adoptive mother, when questioned by Rasmussen (1929, 29) fifty years before *Atuat*'s account:

Then we heard a noise. We could not make out what it was: sometimes it sounded like a dying animal in pain, and then again like human voices in the distance.

Atuat (1974) continues her story:

But there wasn't the slightest footprint around us. My parents, who were pulling the sled, didn't even stop. The sound of a voice could again be heard; this time, it seemed nearer. On hearing it they stopped. They had harnessed themselves to the sled, and when they stopped they looked at each other. The voice could now be heard, and it didn't sound like a human one. It said, "I don't deserve to live anymore!" Then it fell silent. The person who spoke saw us, but we didn't see him or her, for it was snowing; everything was white. It was spring. The person was watching for the slightest sign of travellers and had just seen forms that moved, being sure the forms were a dog team. That was why this person had shouted, "I don't deserve to live anymore!" and this person was now shrieking with whatever strength remained. My father said to his wife, "*Uumaq*! This is a person who has eaten human flesh! What a horrible thing! I wonder whom that person ate."

There was a very strict rule against eating human flesh. Unfortunately, in more than a few cases starvation forced people to eat the corpses of campmates who had died of hunger.

We kept on advancing toward the voice, and it was at that moment that I first began turning things over in my mind. Because I was only a child, I thought the person had removed a human thigh, and, biting into it, made this special noise . . . that's what I thought. When we got close to the voice, we saw an igloo with a form that moved.

According to *Tagurnaaq*, it was more like a little shelter with a piece of a skin rug partly covering it. It lay half-hidden in a drift (Rasmussen 1929, 30).

Before dying of hunger, the person's husband had asked her to stick his spyglass and his gun into the snow, outside the igloo. These are the words he had said, "While you're still able to walk, go and stick my spyglass and my gun into the snow. We have many relatives, and if someone comes by here, he'll notice the gun and the spyglass and will find you."

In a snow-covered, white, and treeless environment like the Arctic tundra, anything upright and dark-coloured will stand out against the flat horizon and be seen from afar.

This was what he had told his wife, and she had carried out his wish. There were small blocks of snow around the hole where she took shelter. When she stood up to scan her surroundings her head appeared, and when we saw her we first thought she was a dog. Getting closer, we saw the spyglass and the gun, but again we thought these were dogs. We then realized these were a spyglass and a gun. We had also thought we had seen an igloo, but it was only a collection of blocks of snow, which surrounded her. The wind had piled up snow around her, and she had cut out small blocks that she had arranged around the hole where she had taken shelter.

In the spring it is hard to measure the size, shape, or distance of what you see. You sometimes think you see a polar bear moving through the snow, and you find an Arctic fox. Seagulls standing on snow-covered ground may be taken for a dog team. Besides the lack of vertical landmarks, the spring sun also produces optical deformations and mirages by causing columns of warm air to rise from the snow surface.

When we stopped right near the place where she was, my parents went to see her, and I heard them talking for a long time with her, to try to find out who she was. My mother shouted to me, "*Aniksaannuk!*" ["Sweet little adopted brother"]—that was how she would address me. She had given me the name of her brother *Atuat* after he had been murdered.

At that moment, according to *Atuat's* first oral version (Atuat 1968), her mother stops her from walking farther, saying:

"Don't follow us any farther! When we've finished hearing what has happened you may come! . . . *Aniksaannuk!* Your *illuannuk* ['sweet little girl cousin'] has been eaten by her mother! What a terrible misfortune!"

This was *Atagullik*, the oldest of *Ataguttaaluk's* daughters, and *Atuat* calls her by that name. In *Atuat's* first version, *Atagullik* was her friend (Mary-Rousselière 1969b). They were the same age and used to play with dolls together when they lived in the same camp.

This was horrible. I suddenly had the impression of no longer knowing where I was going. When I got there I clung to my mother's clothes (Mary-Rousselière 1969b, 14).

Atuat's 1974 version describes what she saw:

I managed to make out a human form that really looked like a bird embryo still in its egg, with its head, wings, feet, neck. . . . She had cut her long hair, and when I saw her I really thought she was a bird embryo. All three of us had the same thought. We had trouble recognizing her as a human being. Her jacket no longer had any sleeves or panels; she had eaten them. She had cut her hair, and her skin no longer looked human. It's unbelievable! A human being can resist death and survive, even when skin and bones, as long as he or she isn't stricken by illness. I now know this by experience (Mary-Rousselière 1969b).

Here, *Atuat* is consistent with what her adoptive mother *Tagurnaaq* told Knud Rasmussen (1929, 30) nearly sixty years earlier:

We saw a human being squatting down inside, a poor woman, her face turned piteously towards us. Her eyes were all bloodshot, from weeping, so greatly had she suffered. . . . There was nothing of her but bones and dry skin, there seemed indeed hardly to be a drop of blood in all her body . . . and when we looked in, there lay a human skull with the flesh gnawed from the bones.

Atuat adds in her 1974 version:

My parents finally recognized her when she mentioned the names of her husband and her children and when they saw the tattoos on her face. My father, who thought she was going to die from one minute to the next, went to get our tent from the sled, and he put it up to provide her with a shelter; he then anchored the base of the tent with stones.

Tagurnaaq gives us the first words she said to her rescuers.

She recognized *Padluq*, who she knew well. They reciprocally called each other by the pet name *Kikkaq*, which literally means "you, my gnawed bone."[4] So she called out to him, saying: "*Kikkaak* [vocative form], I have eaten my elder brother and my children." "My elder brother" was her pet name for her husband. . . . "*Kikkaak*! I have eaten your fellow-singer from the feasting, him with whom you used to sing when we were gathered in the great house [*qaggiq*] at a feast." My husband [*Padluq*] was so moved at the sight of this living skeleton, which had once been a young woman, that it was long before he knew what to answer. At last he said: "You had the will to live, therefore you live." We now put up our tent close by, and cut away a piece of the fore curtain to make a little tent for her. She could not come into the tent with us, for she was unclean, having touched dead bodies. When we went to move her, she tried to get up, but fell back in the snow. Then we tried to feed her with a little meat, but after she had swallowed a couple of mouthfuls, she fell to trembling all over, and could eat no more. Then we gave her a little hot soup, and when she was a little quieter, we looked round the shelter and found the skull of her husband and those of her children; but the brains were gone. We found the gnawed bones, too. The only part she had not been able to eat was the entrails. We gave up our journey then, and decided to drive back with her to Iglulik as soon as she felt a little stronger (Rasmussen 1929, 30).

Atuat, the adopted daughter of *Padluq* and *Tagurnaaq*, adds a few details in 1968 (Mary-Rousselière 1969b):

Padluq used the piece of tent we had cut away to make a roof for the little snow shelter he built for the survivor.

Her 1974 version continues as follows:

My mother wanted to carry the woman, but she began to crawl ahead by herself on all fours. Her throat and neck were only skin on her bones. She made headway by herself, and the dogs began to bark on seeing her. When we saw her this way, she looked like a human being. She settled into the tent, on the skins that had been used to cover our load.

The shelter is precarious, being a circular snow wall covered by a piece of the tent. The groundsheet is a sealskin that protected the load on the sled. The caribou furs to be used as a mattress were unloaded with much of the luggage when the travellers made their last halt (Mary-Rousselière 1969b).

We had with us, as provisions for the trip, a *pangniq* [big male caribou] that had been killed during the autumn and kept in a stone cache for the whole winter. My father removed a piece of it, while my mother looked for her oil lamp. While doing so, she moved something on the ground and uncovered human guts, the guts of *Ittukutsuk* [the last person to die]. *Ataguttaaluk* had covered them over, but because they couldn't dry out they had turned a blackish colour.

This detail raises the first suspicion about *Ataguttaaluk*. According to *Atuat*, she tries to conceal the fact that a few days previously she killed and ate the last person to be with her, *Ittukusuk*. Little by little, other details will strengthen this suspicion, which is missing from *Tagurnaaq's* story fifty years earlier.

We had arrived not long after *Ittukutsuk's* death. When my mother found her oil lamp, she put oil in it and lit it. My father took a piece of seal blubber and said to his wife, "I'm going to give her only small pieces to eat. If she eats too much, she may die, and if she dies, people will blame me because I have no kin."

Padluq knows that *Ataguttaaluk* has many powerful kin, so he must be doubly careful. He is right about the risks of overeating after a starvation diet, and this remark is in line with traditional knowledge handed down from generation to generation.

"No! Let her eat, and when she's had her fill she'll no longer want to eat. I've found human guts, including some parts that have been eaten. I know full well she's not telling the whole truth," said my mother. She had indeed known *Ataguttaaluk* long before these events. We had lived in the same camp as she had, and she would often tell false things. My mother added, "I know she's been getting food!"

Atuat is voicing her mistrust of *Ataguttaaluk*. *Atuat's* biological parents, *Ava* and *Urulu*, were not always on the best of terms with *Ataguttaaluk's* family, especially after the tragedy—when *Ataguttaaluk* remarried with *Iktuksarjuat* and converted with him to Catholicism. *Atuat* and her family lived mainly in the region of Arctic Bay (Tununirusiq), where Anglicanism prevailed. Of all the versions of the tragedy I have found, hers is the one that judges the survivor the most harshly. Her first version (Mary-Rousselière 1969b) is even harsher than her second:

"You can give her lots to eat," said my mother. "She's lying. She has always been a liar. *Ittukutsuk*'s guts are still there, and there are still scraps of food. She says she's eaten nothing for five days, but that's not true. Even if she does eat, she won't die from it. Go ahead, give her enough to eat!" Evening fell, and *Ataguttaaluk* was numb with cold. She ate and tolerated the food well. She had been feeding herself, from time to time. She was close to death, and her eyes were beginning to swell up. Had she not taken a bit of food, she wouldn't have survived.

The Story Told by *Ataguttaaluk*, the Survivor

We will now hear the version told by the survivor herself, as reported by *Atuat* (1974), who evidently tends to doubt its credibility. By that time *Atuat* was the sole remaining witness. Despite some circumspection, due to the people sitting next to her and listening, her scepticism is obvious:

After they had given her food, she told my adoptive parents what had happened, but I don't know what she told them.

This 1974 account partially contradicts *Atuat*'s 1968 account (Mary-Rousselière 1969b, 16), in which she says the following about *Ataguttaaluk*:

What she said, I haven't forgotten. I was beside my mother when *Ataguttaaluk*, having finished eating, began to recount all that had happened.

In 1974, *Atuat* was surrounded by her cousin *Iqallijuq* (*Ataguttaaluk*'s daughter-in-law), by her younger brother *Ujarak*, and several of *Ataguttaaluk*'s grandchildren. She was thus more cautious, knowing that her listeners had for the most part heard the story in person from the survivor. In 1968, she had been telling it only to the Catholic missionary and his tape recorder. She had also passed on hearsay, which does not have the same value for Inuit as an eyewitness account. She was less responsible for its truthfulness.

This is what I was told later: when *Ataguttaaluk*'s husband understood they couldn't survive for long, he told her that, having still enough strength to walk, he wanted to go and hunt seals. It was autumn, and the sea was frozen. They hadn't gone far inland, and he could still walk down to the sea to go sealing. But *Ataguttaaluk* had kept him from going, fearing she'd be attacked by wolves while he was gone. He wanted to go sealing to get food to eat, but his wife wouldn't let him.

This is a backhanded accusation. The implication is that *Ataguttaaluk*, by refusing to let her husband leave, is responsible for his death and the deaths of the others in the group. This accusation runs counter to the account by *Atuat*'s adoptive mother *Tagurnaaq* (Rasmussen 1929, 30–31), who gave the following details:

They had gone up country hunting caribou, but had not been able to find any; they then tried fishing in the lakes but there were no fish. Her husband wandered all about in search of food, but always without success, and they grew weaker and weaker. Then they decided to turn back towards Iglulik, but were overtaken by heavy snowfalls. The snow kept on, it grew deeper and deeper, and they themselves were growing weaker and weaker every day; they lay in their snow hut and could get nothing to eat. Then, after the snow had fallen steadily for some time there came fierce blizzards, and at last her husband was so exhausted that he could not stand. They kept themselves alive for some time by eating the dogs, but these also were wasted away and there was little strength in them as food; it simply kept them alive, so that they could not even die. At last the husband and all the children were frozen to death.

Other accounts, taken down by Guy Mary-Rousselière (1969b, 7), tell us that of the four families who together went caribou hunting, two made it back to Pond Inlet:

The first to go were *Piugaattuq* and his wife *Tatiggaq*, accompanied by *Aksarjuk*, *Piugaattuq*'s nephew, who had decided to leave behind his wife *Sarpinaq*. When he reached his destination, *Piugaattuq* borrowed a dog team and went back to bring help to the rest of the group. Meanwhile a shaman from a neighbouring camp heard crying and wailing in his trances from a place inland, and he concluded that *Qumangaapik*'s band was in trouble, so he sent *Apitak* to bring them help. *Apitak* reached the group of starving people and brought back *Sarpinaq*, the woman left behind by her husband. *Ataguttaaluk* had by then lost her youngest child to illness. When *Piugaattuq* reached *Qumangaapik*'s camp, he tried to convince *Qumangaapik* to leave with him, but he refused to go away from his youngest child's grave. *Piugaattuq* left with *Sigluk* and his wife *Ittukusuk*, but *Sigluk* fell victim to serious frostbite, and they turned back. *Sigluk* then fell ill and died in the camp of starving people. According to *Atuat*, he suffocated on caribou fur while trying to eat an old hide. All of *Piugaattuq*'s sled-dogs were eaten, but the young man nonetheless decided to reach the coast on foot. It is said that he was then murdered by *Kuatsuk*, *Ittukusuk*'s brother, who was furious because he didn't bring back his young sister.

Qumangaapik's camp is now reduced to *Qumangaapik*'s family minus their youngest child plus *Ittukusuk*, *Sigluk*'s widow. We continue with *Atuat*'s account (1974):

When he sensed his coming death, *Qumangaapik* said to his wife, "It has already happened in the past, in times of starvation, that people survived by feeding on human flesh. When I die, I want you to eat my body to survive, for you have many relatives."

The allusion to *Ataguttaaluk*'s numerous kin is a good argument to convince her to agree to eat her husband's corpse and survive. Both of them know that her kin will help her build a new life.

She refused his offer, but he insisted, "Please, you'll have to eat me!"

Collective morality tolerates breaking the rule against cannibalism in cases of acute starvation. One must then perform very strict propitiatory rites and compensate the families of the dead.

When *Qumangaapik* died of exhaustion, his widow, his son [*Kunnuk*], and *Ittukusuk* tried in vain to move his corpse.

They discuss among themselves what they should do, and little by little the widow's refusal gives way to doubt and then to resignation. According to *Atuat*'s first version (Mary-Rousselière 1969b, 16), *Ataguttaaluk* spoke these words:

> "He's dead now, he who wanted so much to be eaten. Well, let's put him on the ground and cut him up. His wish was to be eaten!" Then all three of them again joined forces to move the corpse and put it on the ground, and now it had become a lot lighter.

In her second version, *Atuat* (1974) reported the following:

> They tried again subsequently and easily managed to put him on the ground. This was because he was dead, and they were thinking very keenly about his desire to be eaten.

This opposition between lightness and heaviness (*uqinniq/uqumainniq*) has a primary meaning that is physical and a secondary meaning that is symbolic. The secondary meaning concerns what a spirit wishes. Thus, in the *qilaniq* divination ritual (divination by means of a strap), a person uses a leather strap to weigh a patient's head or leg while calling on a spirit to penetrate the patient's body (see above, in Chapter 8). This penetration makes the head or leg heavier. When asked a question, the spirit answers affirmatively by increasing the weight on the strap and negatively by decreasing the weight. *Ataguttaaluk* has shamanic powers and knows this technique well. She interprets the impossibility of lifting the corpse as expressing the dead man's wish to be eaten.

> *Kunnuk*, the dead man's son, began to cut up his father's corpse, addressing him by the term *aniannuk* ["sweet brother"] and saying, "I am cutting up my *aniannuk!*"

The term he uses for his father, "sweet brother" (a kinship term used normally by a sister), is one that his deceased namesake used in the previous generation for *Qumangaapik*. In her first version (Mary-Rousselière 1969b, 16–17), *Atuat* added:

Having opened up his father's body, and trying to cut the head off, he began to howl and weep with horror over his dismemberment of his own father's body.

Atuat herself wept when giving these details.

After eating it, they also ate the frozen corpses of *Ataguttaaluk*'s children, who had died of hunger one after another. *Sigluk* had suffocated to death after eating a caribou hide from which he had removed the fur, and his corpse had been taken outside, [and put] alongside the other corpses—I saw the place where the corpses had been put. They ate him too.

Iqallijuq (1979) told me something *Ataguttaaluk* had confided in her about the first mouthfuls of human flesh she had ingested. The flesh had, she said, the same taste as polar bear meat. Because of this similarity she was thereafter forbidden to eat any meat of that animal.

In this way, *Kunnuk, Ataguttaaluk*, and *Ittukusuk* ate the flesh of the frozen corpses. *Kunnuk* in turn died of hunger, leaving *Ittukusuk* the sole survivor with *Ataguttaaluk*. The dome of their igloo had caved in when the temperature had warmed up. This was when *Ataguttaaluk* offered to remove the lice from *Ittukusuk*'s hair.

A Fatal Delousing

Mutual delousing was common among the Inuit, as it was among most Indigenous peoples of the Americas, and undoubtedly elsewhere around the world, in the days when hides were the main materials for clothing. It was even part of lovemaking. A girl could quite often be seen removing lice from a young man, with his head resting on her knees in total abandon, or vice versa. The best way to kill a louse was to crush it between your teeth. It was a rather paltry source of food. The head louse (*Pediculus capitis*) or *kumaq* was a major figure in Inuit mythology and shamanism. A shaman had to untangle and delouse the hair of *Takannaaluk*, the mistress of marine mammals, who had lost her fingers and thus could not do this task on her own. The lice in her hair were the marine mammals she held back when humans had broken her rules. In addition, when shamans flew through the sky they saw caribou as "giant lice" (*kumaruat*), the word in their language for caribou.

Ataguttaaluk recounted first of all that after a while she noticed that *It-tukusuk*'s head was no longer moving, as if she were dead. She then examined her face and discovered a bit of blood below her nose. She was dead. Much later, she finally recounted what really happened with *Ittukusuk*: "*Ittukusuk* wouldn't stop saying that lots of people were dying just about everywhere and that she'd like to be able to eat them. She also thought it would get harder and harder to kill animals. . . . She was very young; she was *Kuatsuk*'s youngest sister."

These details show us the state of mind of *Ataguttaaluk*'s last campmate, whose cannibal longings are beginning to bother *Ataguttaaluk*. She is young and has a keen desire to live. We have seen that her brother is the same *Kuatsuk* who killed *Piugaattuq* when the latter was trying to reach Pond Inlet after bringing aid to the camp of starving people.

At that moment, *Ataguttaaluk* thought *Ittukusuk* wanted to kill her, all the more so because she had tried to take the knife of her dead husband [*Qumangaapik*]. So she hid the knife (Atuat 1974).

Although this version by *Atuat* judges *Ataguttaaluk* more harshly, it is not necessarily the less likely version. Let us hear more of what *Atuat* had to say:

So that's what happened: *Ataguttaaluk* offered to remove the lice from *Ittukusuk*'s head in order to kill her by thrusting a meat spike into her ear. . . . For a while, she hid this fact, but she would be heard singing and recounting all by herself what really happened. My mother [*Tagurnaaq*] knew right away that *Ataguttaaluk* was hiding some details about what had happened.

If one accepts this hypothesis, it is possible to piece together the sequence of events by putting oneself in *Ataguttaaluk*'s place. The two widows have eaten the corpses of their respective husbands. They are without food, have had no means of travel ever since their dogs were eaten, and cannot walk through the deep snow made soggy by the warming spring weather. They can only wait for some travellers to pass through with their dog team. Delousing is a way to keep busy and kill time; it is also an affectionate gesture of solidarity when survival itself has become problematic. Undoubtedly, they have often indulged in this little mutual pleasure during the long weeks of waiting.

Ataguttaaluk can be easily imagined sitting on her heels, carefully separating her young campmate's strands of hair while on the lookout for any little parasite. Whenever her scrawny fingers flush one out, she squashes it between her teeth and tries to savour the taste of this last miserable bit of food, the only food remaining. She begins to dream . . . if only she were further along in becoming a shaman and could fly through the air (*ilimaqturniq*), she would not be looking for these thin little lice; she would instead be pursuing "giant lice" (*kumaruat*, "caribou" in the language of shamans) while flying over the plain. Or if she had been initiated into undersea diving (*nakkainiq*), she would be diving down to see *Kannaaluk* ("The great woman down below") to free "sea lice" (marine mammals) that the uncontested mistress of marine mammals is holding prisoner in her hair . . .

Ataguttaaluk snaps out of her daydream and makes a quick decision. She is like a hunter who comes face to face with a big predator—which arouses not only fear but also craving for food—and she has to think fast. The young shaman sees her semi-drowsy campmate and acts fast by driving a meat spike through her ear and into her skull. She keeps up the pressure until her campmate's body no longer shows the slightest sign of life. A trickle of blood flows from the victim's nostrils and then nothing more.

Ataguttaaluk is now alone with the shame of her atrocious act. Yet at the same time the fresh blood and the flesh she touches awakens in her an even greater feeling of ravenous hunger. She has made her choice. And there were only three possible ones: dying of hunger together; being killed without warning by her young campmate and then getting eaten by her; or killing her to survive.

The Cannibal Woman Is Confined and Made to Atone

This is the remainder of the story that *Atuat* (1974) told me:

> Because *Ataguttaaluk* had eaten human flesh, she had to be isolated from other people.

Those who have eaten human flesh are forbidden to do certain things, just like a person who has handled a human corpse or recently lost a close family member. These prohibitions are food-related. One must eat apart from others, and one must eat well-cooked foods. These prohibitions also apply to sex. One must abstain from all sexual intercourse. One must shun all contact with other people, their weapons, and their tools. One may not even speak to others, except for minors and postmenopausal women—such people may act as go-betweens.

In the present case, it would have been very difficult for *Atuat*'s family to continue the original trip. That would have involved going from one territory to another, and each territory is controlled by a spirit they must avoid irritating.

> So we turned back and went to Qikirtaarjuk camp [on Igloolik Island] where old *Amarualik* lived with *Uuttukuttuk*, his adopted son.

This was where *Padluq* and his family began their trip to Baffin Island and overland to Pond Inlet to get ammunition. *Ataguttaaluk* has two brothers at Iglulik camp, *Ungalaaq* and *Nutarariaq*, and another, *Inuaraq*, at Pond Inlet. According to *Atuat*'s first version, *Padluq* wants to continue his trip because they are about halfway there. *Ataguttaaluk* is opposed because she fears meeting up with *Kuatsuk*, the older brother of her victim *Ittukusuk*, whom she has eaten (Mary-Rousselière 1969b).

> My parents had to pull the sled for most of the way. *Amarualik* saw us from afar with his spyglass and decided to come and meet us. *Padluq* saw him too and walked in his direction, while *Ataguttaaluk* began once more to whine, saying, "I don't deserve to live anymore!"

Ataguttaaluk wants to forewarn any newly encountered person about her state of impurity and repentance. She wishes to prevent *Amarualik* from having to live with the prohibitions she has to live with. Her words also suggest she is asking for his indulgence.

On meeting *Amarualik*, my father told him what happened, and *Amarualik* seemed frightened. He asked for the victims' names. He was an old man, and he looked nervous. He was worried about his daughter-in-law (Atuat 1974).

This is the same *Amarualik* who interpreted the unusually mild weather in winter as a bad sign. He sensed the coming of the human tragedy and is now anxious to know the names of the dead.

All the while on the way back I didn't eat. I wasn't hungry at all. My mother did tell me to eat, but I answered, "I'm fat, and that woman has only skin on her bones. I'm not hungry. I can't stop thinking about my cousin who was eaten." When we got to the camp, the camp dwellers behaved toward *Ataguttaaluk* as one usually does with the dead. They walked around her as one would walk around the grave of someone who has just died. They did so because she had eaten human flesh and also for those she had eaten. My parents didn't know, but they ought to have walked that way around her each morning after waking up, once we had found her. People acted as if she were dead, for she had eaten dead people. We began to practise that custom only after the elders had informed my parents. That lasted the whole time we stayed in the camp. *Ataguttaaluk* then left to live at her brother's place. She stayed with him all summer long, until early autumn, until *Iktuksarjuat* married her (Atuat 1974).

The great shaman *Iktuksarjuat*, the most famous hunter of the region, is not unknown to *Ataguttaaluk*. He has just lost his wife *Qattalik*, and to take care of his children he has married *Kalluk*, the sister of *Qumangaapik*, who was *Ataguttaaluk's* dead husband. He is also her uncle by marriage, his sister *Qatturaannuk* being the second wife of *Paulak*, *Ataguttaaluk's* father.

We went inland for caribou hunting, and when we came back she was remarried to him.

For several months, the propitiatory rite is performed every morning to appease the souls of the dead she has eaten, and also to mollify the powerful mistress of marine mammals *Kannaaluk*, who, according to the myths, lived right here at Qikirtaarjuk at the dawn of time (Chapter 5). Children are frightened by the survivor, who is now called *niqiturniq* or *inukturniq* ("man-eater"). She shrieks whenever strangers come to the camp, to keep them from getting close. Her lips and mouth have turned a dark colour, as is the case with *taaqtut*, man-eaters who do not confess to their crimes. Yet she has confessed to everything, except—if *Atuat*'s account is to be believed—to *Ittukusuk*'s murder, which she will talk about only later, during a public confession at a shaman's request. Bear meat is forbidden to her for the rest of her days. As we have seen, that kind of meat has the same taste as human flesh (Saladin d'Anglure 1980a).

Little by little, *Ataguttaaluk* gets her strength back in her new family. The winter tragedy has severely tested this family. *Iktuksarjuat* has lost his much-loved young brother *Piugaattuq*, whom *Kuatsuk* executed close to Pond Inlet. *Iktuksarjuat*'s brother-in-law *Iqipiriaq* is mourning the death of his son *Sigluk*, who was *Ittukusuk*'s husband. Although *Iqipiriaq* gave *Sigluk* up for adoption to *Pittaaluk*, the brother of his wife and *Iktuksarjuat*, he still considers the boy to be his and cannot bear learning that his son has been eaten. Here is what *Iqallijuq* (1979) told me. She was *Ataguttaaluk*'s daughter-in-law and lived with her for some twenty years:

> *Iqipiriaq* waited for the passing of the first few days of confinement that had been imposed on the man-eater, and entered the woman's tent with a knife in his hand. Guessing his intentions, the poor, grief-stricken woman stood defenceless before him, burst into tears, and said, "Kill me. I'm not worthy of living anymore when all who were dear to me are now dead!" This plain-spokenness and spontaneity in the depths of despair moved the great shaman, who spared her life.

She will be grateful for his clemency and will make it a point of honour to pay the price of blood, by giving up one of her children. No punitive expedition will go north to try to avenge the murder of *Piugaattuq*. *Iktuksarjuat* has married the woman who killed the murderer's sister, thus cancelling, so to speak, the blood debt. The elders say it is better to replace a dead person than to avenge his death. One should listen to them, for they know the secrets of life.

At *Ataguttaaluk*'s request, people no longer ask her questions. She will tell everything, she says, as and when the terrible memories come back to her, adding that it will be mortally dangerous to question her unduly. Her adventure was out of the ordinary in two ways. On the one hand, it was exemplary and outstanding, proving her courage, resistance, and will to survive. On the other, it was horrendous because she had to eat her own children, her husband, and her fellow travellers. She has thus become a being unlike any other, a person both young and old who has come back from an "other" world. This ordeal has aged her psychologically, putting her in the same class as elders and "those who think" (*isumataq*). Many years later, the white people will give her the title Queen of Igloolik. Among the Inuit, people older than oneself are not asked questions. Moreover, her ordeal has made her shamanic power stronger, and a feeling of fear surrounds her. Someone who has seen death so closely and eaten human flesh must be treated carefully. She cannot be bothered without risk.

Debts of Blood, Gifts of Children, and Reincarnation

Ataguttaaluk's remarriage is followed by a year of many births, including many baby boys. One is born to *Iqipiriaq*'s sister and is named *Sigluk* after *Iqipiriaq*'s dead (and eaten) son. *Iktuksarjuat*'s sister likewise has a boy, who is named after their murdered brother *Piugaattuq*.

Ataguttaaluk, too, is pregnant, as is her co-wife *Kallu*, who is the first to give birth . . . to a boy. Because this child is the first to be born after the death of their co-wife *Qattalik*, and after the death of *Qumangaapik*, who was *Kallu*'s brother and *Ataguttaaluk*'s unfortunate husband, the boy receives a double identity and is named after both of the dead people. When *Ataguttaaluk* in turn has a son, she gives life back, through him, to the oldest of her dead children, the little girl *Atagudlik*, who died under such harsh conditions and whom she had to eat. This son is also named after *Piugaattuq*, the murdered uncle. *Iktuksarjuat* will again have his dead brother living nearby.

Three years later, *Ataguttaaluk* gives birth to a daughter named *Niviarsiaraannuk*. This is the name of her former second child, who died and was eaten in the tragic adventure. The baby is given to *Akpalialuk*, the daughter of *Pauttuut*, who is *Iktuksarjuat*'s sister. Childless, she has remarried with *Iqipiriaq*. The famine survivor's third child is a son, whom she offers to *Iqipiriaq* to replace the son she ate. The baby receives the name of the dead son *Sigluk*. *Ataguttaaluk's* fourth child is another son and is named *Angiliq*, the name of her former third child, who died of hunger and was eaten. This young son will stay home and take care of his parents until they die (Iktuksarjuat in 1944, Ataguttaaluk in 1948). When *Ataguttaaluk* gives birth to her last child, her daughter *Niviarsiat* (born in 1915), she offers her to *Kallu,* her co-wife and the sister of her dead first husband, *Qumangaapik.*

So it has taken *Ataguttaaluk* ten years to pay off the debts of blood she contracted in the tragic circumstances we have described. She has given up for adoption three of the five children from her remarriage with *Iktuksarjuat.* With her "creditors" she has forged a web of social bonds: *qiturngaqatigiit* ("those who have a child in common"); child sponsorship and interfamily fellowship; and *nuliksariit* ("those whose children are promised in marriage") or child betrothal, as in the case of *Niviatsiaq*, who is promised at birth to *Iqipiriaq's* grandson. This giving and receiving of children often leads to further exchanges of food, goods and services, and even other children.

Ataguttaaluk nonetheless keeps two of her sons. The oldest son re-incarnates her husband's murdered brother *Piugaattuq* and her daughter *Atagullik,* who is the oldest daughter from her first marriage and who died and was eaten during the famine. Her youngest son *Angiliq* replaces another of her children who died in the same conditions and had the same name. She can thus live in peace with herself and with the souls of her victims, who are now satisfied and reincarnated by having their names passed on to a new generation. She has observed the custom of satisfying the souls of the dead by giving their names once more to the first children born in a family.

When the rules are broken, game animals disappear and other misfortunes arise. Conversely, when the rules are followed, the life of the group is brought back into balance. The cycle of life begins anew, as *Ataguttaaluk* confirmed to Peter Freuchen (1935) in 1923:

I got a new husband, and I got with him three new children. They are all named for the dead ones that only served to keep me alive so they could be reborn.

FIGURE 33. The underground house (*qarmaq*) of *Iktuksarjuat* and *Ataguttaaluk* with its inhabitants. After a drawing by Suzanne *Niviattiaq*, daughter of the couple, 1970. The characters shown are: 1. *Iktuksarjuat*; 2. *Ataguttaaluk*; 3. *Piugaattuq*, the eldest son of the couple; 4. *Angliliq*, the youngest son of the couple; 5. and 6. The respective wives of the two brothers; 7. Michel *Kupaaq*, son of *Piugaattuq*; 8. *Aaluluq*, daughter of *Piugaattuq*. *Niviattiaq*, having been adopted by the second wife of *Iktuksarjuat*, lives in another dwelling.

Speaking the Unspeakable to Avert Death and Famine

Several years after Rasmussen and Freuchen passed through the Igloolik region, *Iqallijuq* became the wife of *Ukumaaluk*, *Ataguttaaluk*'s son-in-law, and moved to the same camp as her mother-in-law's. She thus had an opportunity to get to know her and to hear her talk about the tragedy that had marked the first part of her life, at the dawn of the century. One day, *Ataguttaaluk* told her something in confidence: after each of the few times she had told her story, significantly more game animals were caught and significantly more sons were born. The former shaman, then about to convert to Catholicism with her husband and her entire family,[5] even added that the effects would be the same if someone in the future told her story, as heard from herself, without changing any details.

Iqallijuq twice told the story before letting me record it in 1979. Each time, according to her, the predicted effect took place over the following year. The same thing happened again after she told me the story. That is what she said when I came back to see her the next year, in 1980. Therefore, speaking about these unspeakable events, which so contravened the socially accepted rules of human life and the commandments of the great spirits, had the power not only to bring death and misfortune to nosy people but also to undo misfortune by bringing life. These tragic experiences have a strength and power going far beyond their telling in words. They have exemplary value and a moral that justifies their being remembered and even commemorated.

History, Myth, and Commemoration

In May 2004, more than 100 Inuit—all of them descended from *Ataguttaaluk* and native to the Igloolik region—decided to go to Inukturvik (or Nirivviujut) on Baffin Island, where their forebear had been found a century earlier after almost miraculously surviving the deaths of all her loved ones. Her story became a myth in her lifetime and has spread beyond the Igloolik region through the many offspring of her remarriage with the old *Iktuksarjuat*. After she died in May 1948, many babies born that year were named after her, thus reviving her presence and her memory. In the late 1960s a large school was built in Igloolik and named after *Ataguttaaluk*.

Such tragedies have been remembered and mythologized in other regions. In Nunavik, the inhabitants of Kangiqsualujjuaq (George River) preserve the memory of an ancestor who sacrificed herself so that her off-spring could survive. I was told this story by her great-grandson George *Annanak*, whose father *Annanak* faced starvation when his parents and his paternal grandmother were in the valley of the Kuurujjuaq River (which empties into Ungava Bay) while on their way to the Labrador coast. They had used up all of their reserves of food, and the grandmother convinced her family to let her die and then eat her to ensure their survival. She told them that if they respected her wishes, they would have a very abundant posterity who would preserve her memory. After she died they reluctantly ate her, and her grandson (*Annanak*) survived. In the mid-1960s more than 300 Inuit were descended from this heroic forebear. A provincial park is to be created around the Kuurujjuaq River, and there are plans to commemorate this outstanding event.

Both stories are becoming myths. In both, the rule against cannibalism was broken in order to perpetuate one's lineage. In the first story, a man, sensing his coming death, asked his young wife to feed on his corpse so that she might survive until help came. In the second story, a grandmother asked her grandson to eat her to ensure their posterity.

In the first few chapters of this book, we learned about the origin myths and the strict rules they laid down for relations between the Inuit world and the animal world. Henceforth, Inuit shall eat animals. The corollary is that Inuit shall not eat each other and that animals shall no longer be potential spouses, as they had been in the early times of humanity. Because of the vagaries of life, some humans will kill other humans and may have to eat their flesh, while others will succumb to the temptation of zoophilia. Both transgressions threaten the fragile balance between the elements of the cosmos and, above all, the continuity of the cosmic cycles that ensure the reproduction of life.

CHAPTER 15

Qisaruatsiaq: Back to Her Mother's Womb

In 1971, I began studying womb memories, a narrative genre of Inuit oral tradition (see Chapter 1). This was at Sanikiluaq on the Belcher Islands, and I was collecting Aani Qitusuk's memories of her birth. Thirty-two years later, in June 2003, I had an opportunity to return for the first time.

Back in 1971, the village was still named Qurlutuq ("waterfall") after a river that drops abruptly into the sea. At that time the south end of the Belcher Islands had another camp, called South Camp in English, but the Canadian authorities later forced its inhabitants to move to Qurlutuq, which became the only village on the Belchers. It was then renamed Sanikiluaq after the father of several elders of that time. *Sanikiluaq* had traditionally hunted there and been the fastest man on the east coast of Hudson Bay before marrying on the Belchers and settling there for good. He could outrun wolves, according to some, or caribou, according to others. His reputation had spread beyond the limits of the region, making him a sort of *Atanaarjuat* of Hudson Bay's east coast and nearby islands (Chapter 13).

In June 2003 there remained alive very few of the elders I had worked with between 1968 and 1971, and the teenagers I had known were now the village leaders. Much had changed for the local Inuit, there being now a large school, a small airport, a co-op, and many services. My visit aroused much curiosity. Right away, on the day after my arrival I was asked to appear on a Saturday morning radio call-in show that reached all of the village households. It gave me an opportunity to explain the reason for my trip, to talk about my memories, and to take questions from listeners— entirely in the Inuit language. I was interviewed by *Qisaruatsiaq* ("Pretty Rumen"), this being her traditional Inuit name.[1] She worked for the high school, was proficient in English, and seemed very much at ease behind her microphone.

After I presented my research and answered many questions, a female voice called in to ask whether I recalled my visit to her family and my work with her father. The woman was Aani Qitusuk. I remembered her very well and even recited to her the names of her entire kin group, whose genealogy I had studied back then.

After she hung up, the call-in portion of the show came to an end. I briefly talked with my interviewer, telling her my recollections of Aani Qitusuk, who in 1971 had recounted her birth to me when I was investigating beliefs about pregnancy and birth with her parents. I added that while passing through Igloolik several months later (December 1971) I had recorded memories of life in the womb from another Inuit woman, *Iqallijuq*, who had just died in 2002. Right then *Qisaruatsiaq*'s face lit up, and she asked in Inuktitut, "Do these things really interest you?" "Of course!" I answered. "Well," she said, "I too have memories of my life in my mother's womb and my birth, and I can tell them to you." She then said that in the past she had never told anyone other than a few elders who were now gone, for fear that people would make fun of her. Several weeks earlier in a speech to high school graduates, she had nonetheless chosen to tell them about her memories in the hope of encouraging them to respect the fetuses they would carry as future mothers. At that time she had written a short text in English, which she promised to show me.

She gave it to me several days later and agreed to my filming her story in Inuktitut. She wanted no other witnesses, fearing people would tease her. I returned to see her in the spring of 2004, and she made some new comments about the text and her childhood.[2]

Womb Memories

This is *Qisaruatsiaq*'s story:

> I remember when I was still in my mother's womb. It was the most comfortable place you can imagine or possibly can be. I remember being happy and so comfortable. It was warm and secure, no worry in the world. I used to feel what my mother was feeling. I had a terrible feeling when she was sad or when she was scared, but still secure. I used to be really happy when she was eating because I would not be hungry. I was hungry when she was hungry. [3]

A fetus feels this symbiotic oneness. The unborn *Qisaruatsiaq* feels hungry when her mother feels hungry, and full when her mother feels full. For Inuit, "being hungry" essentially concerns traditional food: meat from wild animals and local fish.

> I was excited when I felt my mother happy while eating. When she ate, it was as if I too were eating, and whatever she ate, it was as if I too were eating it. When she was sad, for whatever reason, I too was sad. I felt each of her emotions. One time she started coughing, and something terrible went into my place and I couldn't breathe. It was so smelly, and it was like that for a while. I was sick. What is that smell? It was in fact the smoke from the burning brushwood over which she was making a meal. She was coughing because she had inhaled a bit of smoke while making a meal.

After the sense of taste, the sense of smell is now evoked through an experience so unpleasant that *Qisaruatsiaq* said she still reacts negatively to the smoke and smells from the cooking fire when she goes camping. She then added:

> There used to be some noises coming from somewhere. Some of them used to be so good to hear. My mother used to hum a lot of hymns that still hit home, in particular, "Amazing Grace."

The hymn is Anglican and very well-known. It was taught to the Inuit by the first missionaries and by the Inuit catechists they trained. When

Qisaruatsiaq heard it after her birth, she recognized it, and she still likes to listen to it or hum it.[4]

I used to be scared when I heard another voice that was not familiar. I started to notice that the place I was in was getting smaller and it was kind of getting crowded. There was less room to move around to stretch around. I used to try and push the wall, but it couldn't stretch anymore. I had a strange feeling that something was happening and there was pushing. It was so uncomfortable being pushed around like that.

These remarks are consistent with what *Iqallijuq* told me (Chapter 1). As the fetus grows, it has the impression that its home is shrinking. For a traditional childbirth two women usually accompanied the mother-to-be, who would sit on her heels with her thighs spread apart. One of the women would sit behind and grasp her around the waist with both arms, to exert pressure on the womb to help the fetus come out. The other woman would place herself in front of the mother-to-be and eventually pierce the amniotic sac and grab the head of the baby being born.

Then my comfortable home was no longer comfortable. My warm swimming place was going out through a small hole. I tried so much to stay in, but something or somebody was trying to get rid of me, so I was fighting. I didn't want to go out. My head was being pulled into the little hole.

Unlike *Iqallijuq*, who really wanted to leave once her womb shelter no longer had enough room, *Qisaruatsiaq* wishes to stay inside.

Memories of Birth

The narrator now addresses her listeners to explain the meaning of her memories.

When the waters broke, the tepid water escaped from my first home by the little hole, and when I was born I was pushed the same way out. Then, I was so scared, and the first thing I noticed was [that] this was a cold place that I went into. Why did they do that? What place is this that is so cold? I was born, in fact, in a tent in October 1956. That was why it was so bright and so cold.

At that time Inuit no longer used sealskin tents but tents of white canvas, which the women would cut up and sew by themselves. The women would get it at the Hudson's Bay Company store. The tent is so bright because its canvas lets daylight pass through at a time of year close to the fall equinox. The brightness of the tent is in stark contrast to the darkness of the womb.

That was how my life began, outside my first, warm home. It was so cold . . . and there was, most of the time, so much light that I couldn't easily open my eyes . . . And there was so much noise. Then I noticed some creatures, and one of them just pulled my feet and slapped my behind, and I had no choice but to cry out. What kind of cruel place and creatures are these? The people I saw at that moment were some of the women present at my birth. One of them slapped me on my bum, as is usually done with newborn babies. Then all of a sudden, one of these creatures cut off my lifeline (umbilical cord). Just cut off my lifeline; how am I going to eat now, without an umbilical cord? I will always remember the woman who cut off my lifeline and tied a knot where it was! One of the creatures, the one who had cut my umbilical cord, was Hannah Uppik. I hated her for doing that, until I discovered that she was the one who had delivered me.

For Inuit, the person who ties and cuts the umbilical cord is the child's second mother—she who made the child (*pimaji*). This woman will later play a key role in the child's development and upbringing as an intermediary between the child and the group. The child will gradually join the group through one new achievement after another (Saladin d'Anglure 2001b [2000]). Each first-time achievement (*pigiurniq*) gives rise to a more or less elaborate rite presided over by the woman who tied the child's umbilical cord. This was the case with *Iqallijuq*, whose midwife *Uviluq* accompanied her first moments of life (Chapter 1). On each of these occasions, the child's family offers the midwife a gift, a *qillaquti* (gift for tying the umbilical cord).

On the Belcher Islands, however, where *Qisaruatsiaq* was born, and in groups living on the east coast of Hudson Bay (the Itivimiut), the custom differs from what is seen elsewhere in the Inuit homeland. The "cultural mother" role is played not by the person who cuts and ties the umbilical cord but rather by the one who gives the newborn baby its first clothes. Because Anglican missionaries had converted these groups by the second half of the nineteenth century, this difference may reflect the influence of Christian birth rites (baptism, godfather, godmother) (Guemple 1969; Saladin d'Anglure 2001b [2000]).

Niceness and Nastiness of Newborn Life

These creatures were so noisy. I was wrapped in something, but before I was wrapped, there was this crazy creature that was so rough in handling me and maybe she was mad or something because it was making a lot of noise. The crazy person who callously wrapped me up was Suapik Uqait-tuq. She was the one who had ripped open and drained my first wrapping. She didn't wish to do the job of dressing me, but with no one else available she was the one who became my *Sanajiar'uk* [midwife-dresser]. I didn't like this place. I was just terrified and I couldn't stop my crying until there was a familiar voice and I was in warm and loving arms. But before I could do anything, there was something being put in my mouth! What is this? First they slap me, then this? I was fighting and crying because I didn't know what this thing was. It was being forced into my mouth! Still I was fighting. Then I was so tired I gave up fighting. I let that thing into my mouth. Wow, this is good! It was like food, but coming from this thing in my mouth. I sucked all I could. So this is food, *wai*, this is how I am going to eat. . . .

So, this life outside of my warm place began. It was so cold and bright I could hardly open my eyes most of the time, and it was noisy. These creatures were heartless and rough. I used to wish that my mother would be available and take care of me all the time because when someone else was taking care of me they were ruthless and rough. I didn't know what was going to happen next! I used to be so scared that they were going to drop me, and I didn't like to be wrapped up so tight because I couldn't move my arms when I was scared. I used to fight and cry hard when I was being wrapped up and I couldn't talk, just cry. There were a lot of things that I wanted to say but couldn't. My mother knew best but she was always busy.

Being near her was so precious. I used to look forward to my feedings, as she would hold me lovingly, I used to like that a lot. I couldn't sleep, being wrapped up so tight. I was too hot. I began to cry because I couldn't tell anyone that I was hungry, that I was too hot, that I was in a very uncomfortable situation, that I was farting, or that I was ill. The only thing I could do was cry and cry, until someone finally paid attention to me.

The reader is struck by the power of the sensations expressed by *Qisaruatsiaq*. With astonishing ease, she changes perspective from her life as a fetus to her life as a newborn baby.

Most of the time, someone other than my mother took care of me because my mother was too busy with women's work. When someone else took care of me, I was afraid. I didn't know what was going to happen, while with my mother I had absolute trust in her acts and felt my life was safe. My mother was the one who best understood me, but she was always busy. It was so important for me to be near her. I gladly waited for her to feed me, and also to hold me with affection. That made me so happy. Once in a while, there would be a rough face looking down on me and *kuunik* [kiss] me on the cheeks and that was my father. I feared my father because my mother had feelings of fear toward him when I was still in her; my father was indeed a very severe person. I felt these feelings for some time. Then my memories clouded over until I was two years old. But that's another story.

When I asked *Qisaruatsiaq* about the meaning of the last remark, she told me she had been taken away at two years of age to a hospital in the South, after being diagnosed with early tuberculosis during an annual medical visit by the government icebreaker. This was a terrible shock, and when she finally came back to her loved ones, several years later, she no longer spoke a word of Inuktitut. She experienced her return as a new birth and had to relearn her language and culture. This traumatizing experience might be related to the quality of her memories from the womb and newborn life.

In her speech to the high school graduates, *Qisaruatsiaq* wanted to add a few remarks and recommendations she thought would help them in life:

I feel for the unborn babies when I see their mother smoking. Just a little bit of smoke can choke you when you are inside the mother's womb, because you have no choice but to take it because the mother is taking it. The smoke doesn't go anywhere. It stays in the womb. I feel for the babies that are being handled roughly by the parents. They feel everything that the mother is doing, her every feeling, whatever, whenever, anytime and each time, every feeling that the mother is feeling. You name it, the baby feels it. Young mothers, please be aware of what you are doing to the baby. One fine day, they will grow up like we did, and they will become parents, too. And we all want to have kids that are well cared for and well-behaved.

Delighted to find an attentive and trustworthy listener, *Qisaruatsiaq* told me she had long believed that her memories were dreams until some elders, now dead, reassured her otherwise. She was neither the only one nor the first to remember her life in the womb and her birth.

Thus, in two Nunavut villages 1,500 kilometres apart, two women, *Iqallijuq*, born in 1905, and *Qisaruatsiaq*, born two generations later in 1956, vividly recollected their lives in the womb, at birth, and during early childhood. Both of them went through hard times of losing or being separated from their loved ones and being exposed to the problems of life. They nonetheless pulled through, thanks to their strength of character and tenacity. They were also highly attuned to the world around them. People said they had the gift of clairvoyance and the ability to foresee the future.

Both were practising Christians, the older one Catholic and the younger one Anglican. The older one knew the era of shamanism and was married to a shaman. She saw the first white people come and move into her community: traders, missionaries, and government agents. Finally, her people were relocated to a large year-round settlement, a village designed by white people. The younger woman spent several years in hospitals in the South, learned English, and later worked full-time in an educational institution. Both of them were a part of their day and age and saw all the problems of their communities: drug and alcohol abuse, domestic and family violence, and youth suicide.

When *Iqallijuq* passed away in the year 2000, surrounded by her loved ones, she was ninety-five and had many descendants. She and her loved ones attributed her longevity to the special conditions of her birth and her identity. She freely admitted to one thing: had her mother not become a widow, and had she not subsequently been baptized into the Catholic faith, she would have become a shaman. The same might be said about *Qisaruatsiaq*.

In telling these stories, both narrators show a remarkable ability to go from one scale of existence to another and to see things from the perspective of someone within a womb, a fetus. A fetal perspective comes up time and again in the different myths of this book. The ability to change your scale of existence, and therefore your vantage point, seems to be key to decoding the symbolic systems at work in the oral traditions and rites of the Inuit. Finally, these stories clearly confirm the hypothesis I advanced nearly thirty years ago: that womb memories are for Inuit a narrative genre that transcends the generations and the great changes their society has undergone. Such memories tap into the core of their value system—the reproduction of life.

1. The three shaman brothers Rasmussen met in the region of Igloolik: on the left the eldest, *Ivaluarjuk*, great storyteller and talented singer, in the center *Ava*, father of *Ujarak*, and, on the right, the youngest, *Pilakapsik*.

2. The storyteller and shaman *Urulu*, the wife of the shaman *Ava* and mother of *Ujarak*, c.1921–24.

3. The great storyteller *Ivaluarjuk*, 1922. Brother of *Ava* and uncle of *Ujarak*, one of Saladin d'Anglure's main informants.

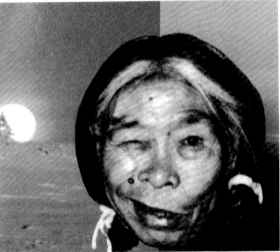

4. *Inukpasujjuk*, a storyteller from the neighbouring Natsilik region, one of Rasmussen's main informants, 1922.

5. The Caribou Inuit shaman *Igjugaarjuk* from Yathkyed Lake, wearing Greenland clothing he received from Rasmussen, 1922.

6. Knud Rasmussen (1879–1933) was responsible for the Fifth Thule Expedition, which spent nearly two years in the Igloolik area in 1921–1922 and 1922–1923.

7. *Iqallijuq* in Igloolik making a mocking grin in the sun (half-sad, half-laughing), when she reappears for the first time, in mid-January, after two months of absence. On the left, the circumpolar moon, due north and on the right, the sun, facing south.

8. *Iqallijuq* preparing seal skins to make a tent. Igloolik, 1973.

9. The caribou is a land animal that provides skin, sinews, antlers, and flesh for the Iglulingmiut. Land animals should never come in contact with marine animals.

10. The walrus is one of the most important marine resources for Iglulingmiut. In the winter they smash through the ice to breathe.

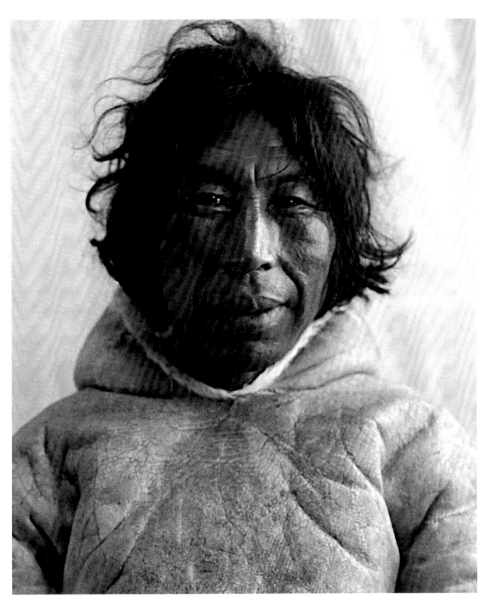

11. Michel *Kupaaq*, the main narrator of the myths and legends in this book, photographed in Igloolik in 1974.

12. *Pitsiulaaq* in his seal-skinned kayak near the shore of Igloolik Island, 1973.

13. *Arnainnuk* and *Kupaaq*, with *Qaunnaq*, their adopted daughter, in a semi-subterranean house. Igloolik, 1974.

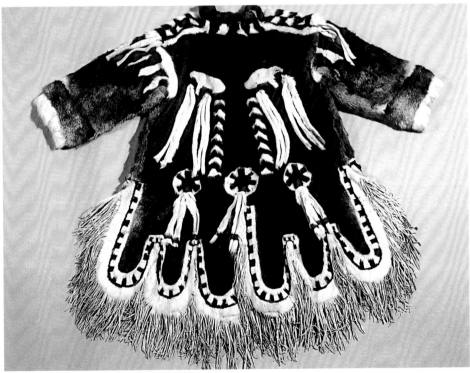

14. The stone that, according to oral tradition, *Atanaarjuat* sat on watching whales, when the sea level was much higher. Ungaluujaak Camp, Igloolik Island, 1988.

15. Replica of the shamanic cloak (seen from the back) made of caribou skin by *Qingailisaq*, *Ujarak*'s grandfather, and bought by Captain Comer at the end of the nineteenth century.

16. *Kupaaq* wearing a replica of *Qingailisaq*'s shaman coat, made by his wife, great-great-granddaughter of *Qingailisaq*. Igloolik, 1983.

17. Michel *Kupaaq* in the early 1990s in Igloolik.

18. Alexina *Kublu*, daughter of *Kupaaq* and granddaughter of *Iqallijuq* (*Kublu* is the name of *Iqallijuq*'s father-in-law). In her arms, her granddaughter who received the name *Iqallijuq*. Alexina served as Languages Commissioner of Nunavut, and earlier as Senior Justice of the Peace for the territory.

19. *Iktuksarjuat*, the shaman nicknamed by the whites the "king of Igloolik." He took *Ataguttaaluk* as his second wife after her cannibal adventure and was one of the main leaders of the region.

20. *Ataguttaaluk*, nicknamed "Queen of Igloolik" by the whites. She is the shaman who survived the famine of 1905–1906 by eating the corpses of her husband, her children, and her camp companions who died of hunger.

Conclusion

The year 1971 marked a turning point for me. In particular, I had learned about the existence of womb memories from several Inuit informants, as related in the first and last chapters of this book. These accounts made me rethink the Inuit notion of personhood and its relationships to cosmology and mythology. I realized that cosmogenesis was seen as a form of onto-genesis and that, conversely, the reproduction of life was seen as a process of elements being recomposed in the same way that the universe progres-sively differentiated and took form at the dawn of time.

This rethinking took place in a very stimulating intellectual setting: the Laboratory of Social Anthropology of the Collège de France. It was headed by Professor Claude Lévi-Strauss, who had invited me to join in 1964, when I became a researcher at the CNRS (the French National Cen-tre for Scientific Research). Each year researchers were asked to talk about the progress of their work at a seminar hosted by Claude Lévi-Strauss. Be-cause I was leaving in 1971 on a long research mission to study the Inuit of Canada, my presentation was scheduled for January 1971.

In previous years, I had spoken about kinship and marriage and the Inuit system of personal names and place names. But I had never discussed how Inuit represent reproduction, pregnancy, and birth—all of which seemed increasingly key to the study of Inuit symbolic systems. So I chose to address that theme under the title "From Delivery [of a baby] to Docking [of a kayak]," in other words, the rites of passage that mark human development from fetal life and birth to a man getting his first kayak or a woman having her first period—the last two events marking one's entry into the category of adult producers/reproducers. In passing, I stressed the symbolic equivalence of the womb, the igloo, and the vault of the heavens (Figure 34).

Lévi-Strauss closely followed my presentation and made several constructive remarks and suggestions. He noted that the Inuit conception of the reproduction of life uses the same model on different scales of existence or in different ontological, sociological, and cosmological settings. He also suggested that the concept of "reversibility of perspective," which the psychologist Jean Piaget (1971 [1947]) had devised to explain child development, was especially relevant to Inuit, who very easily change perspective both in social life and in myths. The last (fourth) volume of Lévi-Strauss's *Mythologiques* series came out in French that year (1971) and in English in 1981.

In the audience, my colleague Nicole Belmont (1971), a researcher in the same laboratory, showed much interest in my presentation and suggested that as part of my next fieldwork I include questions on childbirth positions, the subject of her newly published doctoral dissertation. Many years later I joyfully accepted her offer to publish the French edition of this book on Inuit oral tradition. I acknowledge here my intellectual debt to these two anthropological colleagues and friends who later continued to give me advice and encouragement.[1]

Let us come back to the present book and its content. Our circular journey through the heart of Inuit oral tradition began with *Savviurtalik*'s recollections from beyond the grave at the dawn of the twentieth century (Chapter 1) and ended with *Qisaruassiaq*'s memories from the womb at the dawn of the twenty-first (Chapter 15). While on this journey we encountered a recent epic-like myth (*Atanaarjuat*) and a true story (*Ataguttaaluk*) that is now becoming a myth. Both are rooted in the land and memory of the Iglulingmiut and were still being told in the 1960s during long evenings with the entire family in a tent or igloo. We also encountered myths about the genesis of human life (Chapter 2), the ambiguous relationships of humans with animals (Chapters 2, 5, 6, 7, and 8) and with

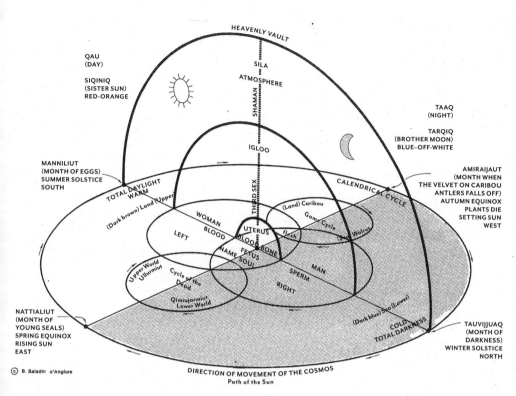

FIGURE 34. Summary schema of the fetus, the calendar cycle, and the three scales of Inuit symbolism: the womb (intra-human world), the igloo (human world), and the vault of the heavens (supra-human world). Designed by B. Saladin d'Anglure and made by Olivier Breton.

heavenly spirits (Chapters 6, 9, and 10), and the origins of shamanism and religious mediation (Chapters 11 and 12).

Mediation is a means to resolve the great contradictions or paradoxes of human life, as expressed in the different myths. This oral tradition tells us that humans were initially, and still are, faced with five major contradictions:

1. The Sex Difference. Why do we need women, when there could be only men? Were not the first two humans a pair of male adults who had come from the ground? The myths give a very clear answer: we need women so that humans can increase their numbers faster. The first two men explored the possibility of male pregnancy but came to an anatomical impasse—no birth canal. *Aakulujjuusi* had to use a magical incantation to create a vagina in the body of his companion *Uumarnituq*, thus turning him into a woman and making possible the birth of their first child. Male pregnancy also appears in the myth of the strange man (Chapter 12), but in a very different setting, and it does not lead to a human birth.

2. Sterility or Infertility of Couples. Why cannot some women procreate, when others can very easily? The Inuit, like many other peoples, blamed the woman for the sterility of a couple. The myths first offer this solution: go and harvest babies who emerge from the ground as the first two humans did. This solution, which leads to adoption, sometimes meant looking for a long time, as we saw in Chapter 2, or even, for some women, failing to find any babies at all. Inuit still commonly practise adoption. The other solution was to exchange partners with another infertile couple.[2]

3. The Existence of Animals, which are so closely akin to Inuit. In the myths, animals could turn into humans (Chapters 5, 6, and 7), just as humans could reincarnate as animals (Chapter 8) or turn into animals. This close kinship led to humans adopting animal babies (Chapter 2) or marrying animals (Chapters 5, 6, and 7), not to mention giving birth to them, like the man who had a baby whale (Chapter 12). Unfortunately, such intimate ties come to a tragic end in the myths. Despite being close kin, animals were also the main food source for humans in a land where very little food could be grown. Because Inuit forbade the eating of human flesh (Chapter 14)—

unlike many other Amerindian groups—they chose to exclude animals from their ties of kinship and marriage, thus making it easier for them to hunt and eat animals and use their hides, sinews, or bones. All sorts of precautions were needed. The hunter–game animal relationship was fragile and required the goodwill of the spirit masters of different animal species and collaboration with them.

4. *Ageing.* Why do we grow old? Life is so wonderful when we are young and in full possession of our physical powers. This question was answered during the mythical times before the present age of short lifespans. The answer was to somersault into youth: an old man would become a young adult again by somersaulting head first from the edge of his sleeping platform and onto the floor of his dwelling. A strange age pyramid resulted from this interesting custom, as described in Chapter 2. Parallels may be drawn between this ritual of starting life anew late in life and the Inuit custom of elder suicide—old men and women choosing to die because they no longer wanted to be a burden on their loved ones and wished to reincarnate in the bodies of newborn children. This brings us to the topic of death.

5. *War and Death.* Why do we have war and death? We live by exchanging and sharing, we need so much time to learn to live, and we often have so little time to enjoy life before death ends it all. The myths answer this question through the words of a woman, in all likelihood the first woman, *Uumarnituq*. She called for war and death so that overcrowding would not totally extinguish humanity on the island of the first humans. When the island began to tip over, threatening to submerge everybody, *Uumarnituq* understood that survival required dispersal to other lands and shorter lifespans. Despite *Aakulujjuusi*'s opposition, the woman's wishes prevailed. Human life was shortened, and war appeared. To regain the lost continuity of human life, the Inuit had to give up their expanding population of mythical times and embrace a simpler reproductive ideology. Life now continued after death in two ways: your name-soul would reincarnate in a newborn body, and your double-soul would survive as an ethereal, weightless entity in the hereafter.

These myths do not exist solely to answer the great existential and ontological questions of humans in daily empirical reality. They also serve to stig-
matize certain behaviours that run counter to social rules, like a young girl
refusing the spouse her parents have chosen for her (Chapter 5), or the idea
that a girl can choose her husband or treat marriage like a game (Chapter 7).

These myths are about female lives in a society where men, as hunters,
dominate the life of the group (Chapters 2, 4, 8, 10, and 11). There are few
means of escape for the battered wife, the orphaned girl, the sister raped
by her own brother, the wife who is barren or repeatedly miscarries, the
elderly widow who lives alone, or the female survivor of starvation. The
means are not only few but also risky. A woman might escape by becoming a man in another life (Chapter 8), by getting impregnated by a spirit
(Chapter 10), by adopting an animal (Chapter 2), by escaping to another
world (Chapter 4), by eating her dead kinfolk (Chapter 13), or finally by
gaining a woman healer's powers (Chapter 11).

These myths also explore the problems of male lives. An old man
wants to escape the dangers of hunting (Chapter 1). A son is kept at a
childlike stage by an abusive mother (Chapter 4). An abandoned baby boy
with an erection is mocked (Chapter 3). A husband has a cheating wife
(Chapter 6). An orphan boy is abused (Chapter 9). A husband is a victim
of his scheming wife (Chapter 13). A transgender man is disowned by his
own brothers (Chapter 12). Again, the means of escape are few and risky.
A man might escape by being reborn as a woman in another life (Chapter
1), by fleeing to another world, by avenging himself and killing an abusive
parent (Chapter 4), by looking for a wife in the animal world (Chapter 6),
or finally by running away and preparing his revenge (Chapter 13).

To resolve these crises and conflicts, Inuit oral tradition counsels the
blurring of boundaries between opposing worlds: male and female; human
and animal; the living and the dead; ordinary humans and great spirits;
the visible and the invisible. Such blurring brings back the undifferentiated
universe of primeval times and is expressed in shamanism. Inuit oral tradition affirms a close relationship between shamanism and all of the great
figures: spirits like Big Belly, Moon Brother, or the headstrong daughter
and mistress of marine mammals; the first woman healer, Big-Anus; the
shaman *Ataguttaaluk*; the strange transgender man; and—why not?—the
storyteller *Iqallijuq*. Transgenderism makes sense in shamanism, as does
marriage across boundaries. A shaman may marry an animal helping spirit

and it will incarnate in him or he in it, or he may marry a great heavenly or underwater spirit or a dead person. By these means a shaman can solve problems that ordinary humans have trouble coping with, and such problems are numerous because life itself has grown much more complex since primeval times. Meaning is thus given back to life.[3]

Afterword

I would like to pay a special tribute here to the great anthropologist Claude Lévi-Strauss, who passed away on 30 October 2009. I am greatly in debt to him for my career as an ethnographer and above all as an anthropologist. When he learned in April 1963 from Alfred Métraux—one of my PhD professors—that I had collected astonishingly complex fieldwork data on Inuit kinship practices,[1] he asked me to present my findings to his seminar at the École Pratique des Hautes Études – Section VI (Economic and Social Sciences) in October of that same year.[2] My presentation took place over three sessions, after which he encouraged me to submit my candidacy to the CNRS (the French National Centre for Scientific Research) and offered me, if successful, a place in his Laboratory of Social Anthropology. I thus joined his laboratory in late 1964. For the rest of his life, Lévi-Strauss never stopped offering me his advice—and friendship—on my research projects, my work, and my career choices, whether in France or Canada. His preface to the French edition of this book attests to our special relationship.

In 1966, Jean Pouillon, the editor-in-chief of the journal *L'Homme*, based at the Laboratory of Social Anthropology, launched a project to publish a Festschrift in honour of Claude Lévi-Strauss[3] and sent me an invitation to contribute while I was on my first CNRS mission to Kangiq-sujuaq (Arctic Quebec).[4] This village was home to *Mitiarjuk* Nappaaluk, an exceptional Inuit woman who was so key to my learning the language, culture, and social life of the Inuit. She was a good mother and an excellent hunter. Though never formally educated, she had learned the syllabic writing system that Methodist missionaries had invented in the late nineteenth century for the Cree, and which the first Anglican missionaries and then Catholic missionaries had adapted several years later to the Inuit language. She had no brothers and a father in frail health. She thus knew the Inuit language extensively because her parents, having no son, had taught her how to do both men's work and women's work.

In the 1950s *Mitiarjuk*'s linguistic skills had caught the attention of Father Robert Lechat, then in charge of the Oblate mission, who wished to become more proficient in the Inuit language. In 1953 he asked her to write down sentences with as much vocabulary as possible and a wide variety of grammatical structures. She soon grew tired of this exercise. Bringing together her childhood memories and stories about her grandparents, she began to describe the life of *Sanaaq*, an Inuit woman who had lived in that region when the first white people arrived in tall ships during the second half of the twentieth century. She thus reinvented the novel at a time when Inuit knowledge was still being passed down orally. Enough was written to fill three large school notebooks, which she gave to the missionary. Father Lechat was soon transferred several hundred kilometres away to the new village of Kuujjuaq, which was taking shape near a military landing strip built by the Americans during the Second World War, and which would become the capital of Arctic Quebec. I met him there in early winter 1956, during my first winter stay in the Arctic. He read to me and translated several pages of this fascinating manuscript.

I met *Mitiarjuk* in 1961 and provided her with a new notebook to write down what she knew about her forebears, my intention being to make her unfinished manuscript the centrepiece of my doctoral dissertation. At that time Father Lechat gave me a copy so that I could go and work with her in the field and encourage her to complete it and comment on it. So began a long working relationship with her. She finished the episodes that several hospital stays in the South had interrupted. During the winter of 1965–66 I spent hours interviewing her almost every day. I transliterated the syllabics into standard Latin script, translated the text word for word, and had the translation read by the new missionary at Kangiqsujuaq, Father Jules Dion. Between 1966 and 1967, the text took on the appearance of a novel.[5] *Mitiarjuk* had so much to say that I gave her more notebooks to write down whatever she felt had to be passed on to new generations of Inuit. Little by little she wrote for me a sort of encyclopedia of around 400 pages.

I owe a lot to *Mitiarjuk*, who was the first to speak to me about the existence of *sipiniit*, those babies who, according to Inuit, changed sex during birth. She told me the importance of personal names, which most often came from people who had died or were about to die and who wished to reincarnate as newborn babies. She inspired most of my research and later work.

A Festschrift

The Festschrift in honour of Lévi-Strauss ran to 1,452 pages and was published in 1970 by Mouton (The Hague, Paris) with eighty-six contributions in two volumes under the title *Échanges et Communications, mélanges offerts à Claude Lévi-Strauss à l'occasion de son 60ème anniversaire*. Its eight sections chronologically follow Lévi-Strauss's main publications, beginning with his ethnography *La vie familiale et sociale des Indiens Nambikwara* (1948) and ending with *Mythologiques* (1964–68).[6]

My contribution (2:1013–39), "Nom et parenté chez les Esquimaux tarramiut du Nouveau-Québec (Canada)," was placed in the seventh section about *La pensée sauvage* (1962), one of Lévi-Strauss's most philosophical works in the sense that it unveils—to paraphrase Jean Pouillon (1970, 1:v)—the meaning of "primitive" classifications made by Indigenous logicians. I supported my text with several quotes from *Mitiarjuk*'s writings. In the second footnote, I also noted that methodological choices may explain why authors interested in Inuit (Eskimo) personal names have often misunderstood the effects of namesaking on kinship practices. On the one hand, these authors are much more interested in terms of reference than in terms of address (*tuqsurauti*) within the informant's family group. On the other hand, they do not bother to investigate terms of address for non-kin (friends) who belong to the territorial group or even to neighbouring groups. Only by studying all inter-individual relationships among members of a regional group can we measure the meaning, scope, and effects of namesaking, such as generational or gender reversal (in cases where the name belongs to the opposite sex) with visible cross-dressing until puberty. When such individuals were cross-dressed as children, they would remain symbolically transgendered their entire lives in the terms that they used to address others or that others used to address them.

Mythologiques and Inuit Mythology

In Paris, I had the good fortune to take several courses and seminars that Lévi-Strauss taught at the Collège de France, notably the ones that gave rise to his multi-volume *Mythologiques*.[7] This experience was what likely led me to collect several dozen myths in Igloolik from the mouth of my friend *Kupaaq*—the group's best storyteller—as well as from several elders of both sexes during my many interviews in that village on various themes, over the next thirty years. Many of these myths and their local or regional variants are included in this book. In their own way, these myths illustrate Inuit cosmogenesis: from Chapter 2, when the first two humans appeared, to Chapter 7, which deals with the reproduction of human life and the impasse of intermarriage with animals. Central to the book is Chapter 8 with the myth of *Arnakpaktuq*, the woman who is beaten by her husband and who turns first into a sled dog, then a wolf, then a caribou, then a walrus, then a raven, and then a ringed seal, which is harpooned by her own brother (a human) and cut up by his wife, whose womb is then penetrated by the woman's wandering soul. She develops in what seems to be a small igloo and then, before being born, chooses to change sex and becomes her brother's son. When the son becomes a teenager named *Aumarjuat* ("Big Ember"), he will teach Inuit hunters the unique knowledge he gained about each species he incarnated in prior lives and became the best hunter of his group.

Then come three more chapters. Chapter 11 tells the story of a young orphan girl who is barren and knows nothing of women's work. She is also polyandrous and becomes the first Inuit healer, receiving in exchange for her services the children she wishes to adopt and the clothes she needs. Chapter 12 is unlike the others in the sense that it was collected and translated by a Yupik woman from St. Lawrence Island in the Bering Strait and off the southern Alaskan coast. It contains a myth that seems to me inversely symmetrical to the previous one. Several brothers hunt bowhead whales, except for the oldest one, who refuses to hunt and prefers to dress as a woman and do women's work. The day comes when the master spirit of the cosmos hears his complaints and takes him to the seashore and into the water, from which he emerges pregnant. He eventually gives birth to a baby whale. He raises it in the seawater until it is strong enough to swim out to sea and lure wild whales that will keep its hunting uncles happy with plenty of meat. But the story ends tragically.

Chapter 13 is about a historical myth set nearly five centuries ago in the Igloolik region. This is the story of *Atanaarjuat*, which was made into a leading film (*Atanarjuat: The Fast Runner*) that won an award at Cannes in 2001. Chapter 14 features a "myth in progress" with the story of *Ataguttaaluk*, who survived by feeding on the flesh of friends and family who had died of starvation. Once saved, she went about having children and giving a child to each family that had lost someone in the tragedy.

Chapters 2 through 14 are bookended by an initial chapter and a final one that both exemplify the same narrative genre: memories from the womb. Two women from different generations, thirty years apart and in Arctic locations several hundred kilometres apart, recount their memories of life in the womb in almost the same terms.

The main theme running through this book, therefore, is that Inuit cosmogenesis is viewed through the lens of ontogenesis, or vice versa, in a circular vision of life and its reproduction on three different scales: at birth, with changes of sex (illustrated by the myth of Chapter 8); before puberty, with cross-dressing of children who have been named after persons of the opposite sex; and in adulthood, with shamans who cross-dress in their rituals when their namesake of the opposite sex becomes their helping spirit, or when they have any helping spirit of the opposite sex. This theme is echoed by the title of this book: *Inuit Stories of Being and Rebirth: Gender, Shamanism, and the Third Sex.*

Inuit Stories of Being and Rebirth

In the early 2000s France's leading publisher Gallimard chose my colleague Nicole Belmont, a longstanding associate of Lévi-Strauss, to be the editor of a new series: Le langage des contes (The Language of Tales). She had closely followed my various publications and asked me to write a book about Inuit oral tradition for the series, which resulted in *Être et renaître Inuit, homme, femme ou chamane* (2006b). Belmont knew about my many articles on womb memories, birth, namesaking, and reincarnation, and the basis of these phenomena in myths. She also knew that at the request of Professor Yves Bonnefoy (Collège de France) I had contributed an article to the *Dictionnaire des Mythologies et des Religions des sociétés traditionnelles et du Monde antique*: "Esquimaux : La mythologie des Inuit de l'Arctique central nord-américain" (1981),[8] later published in English as "The Mythology of the Inuit of the Central Arctic" (1994a). The article recounted the cosmogenesis of the present world when the first two Inuit emerge from a clod of peat. Both are adult males, and one of them impregnates the other and turns him into a woman by means of a magic chant. They are the ancestors of all humans, and this magical creation of the first woman from a man can be compared with the belief, still present among the Inuit, that a fetus can choose to change sex during birth if such is the desire of the ancestor it is reincarnating.

The Inuit Logic of the "Included Middle"[9]

In 1971, on the eve of my departure on a new CNRS mission to the Igloolik region, which Knud Rasmussen had earlier visited as head of the Fifth Thule Expedition (1922–23), I was preoccupied with the question of cross-dressing of young Inuit and change of sex at birth (*sipiniuniq*). I had learned about these practices at Kangiqsujuaq from *Mitiarjuk* and, in the case of cross-dressing, had personally observed them. Neither was mentioned by Rasmussen when discussing the practices or beliefs of this group in his monograph (1929). I arrived at Igloolik in early December 1971, during the polar night that lasts two and a half months. There, I met two elders who had been cross-dressed as children. Juanasi *Ujarak* was a respected man and a son and brother of shamans. He had worn braids and female clothing until puberty, when he killed his first fawn with an arrow, having been helped by an uncle who guided his hand. There was also Rose *Iqallijuq*, who had changed sex at birth and been cross-dressed and brought up as a boy because she was the reincarnation of her maternal grandfather and was the oldest sibling. They became my friends and initiated me into the symbolism, myths, beliefs, and ancestral rules of the local Inuit. With *Ujarak*, I discovered through a shaman's song that an igloo's ceiling was also a smaller version of the sky and the cosmos. I filmed their accounts and immersed myself in the Inuit system of thought, whose elements I collected year after year, until their deaths in 1985 (*Ujarak*) and 2002 (*Iqalliuq*).

Meanwhile, I tried to show the existence of an Inuit "third gender." This gender was defined structurally by overlapping of the boundary between the two other genders, and functionally by mediation on the three major scales of existence where human life is socially reproduced: the infra-human scale (fetuses, dwarves, and small animals); the human scale (sexual division of labour and learning about this sexual division, which involves Inuit adults and adolescents and their typical game animals); and the supra-human scale (shamans, animal masters, souls of the departed, and also very large game animals and major mythical figures). First, I wished to show the centrality and character of this "total social fact," which ethnography, ethnology, and anthropology had until then either ignored or considered to be atypical, exceptional, or marginal.

Second, I tried to nail down the reasons for this ignorance or marginalization. I pondered the theoretical framework and the methodological tools that I would need in order to recognize how the various components of the third gender fit together and form a coherent whole.

Anthropologists ignore or marginalize the social phenomena that I have grouped together under the term "third gender" primarily because of the almost exclusively masculine perspective that has long pervaded the scientific process, beginning with the stage of data gathering, and because of the depreciation of the sex/gender variable in the Judeo-Christian tradition that has been the ideological horizon for Western science, especially with regard to phenomena that this tradition has condemned (such as cross-dressing) or which are not part of its value system. Comparative study of religion and especially of shamanism could have given rise to a positive third gender approach, as suggested in studies by Fraser (1926), Czaplicka (1914), or Sternberg (1925). It seems, however, that the research bias I have just deplored has been so strong since the 1930s that Eliade (1964) completely disregarded the problem and ignored it, despite the extensive and easily accessible literature on the subject, as attested by the many references in his classic work on shamanism.

Another reason why these phenomena have been ignored or marginalized is the frequent confusion between the theme of sexuality, under which they have been classified too often, and the theme of gender, where they are more meaningful.

Finally, and above all, there is the predominance of binary logic in the social sciences. With respect to sex/gender categories, binary logic has made marginal or exceptional any behaviour that does not fit the mutually exclusive norms of masculinity and femininity, in keeping with the long-established principle of the excluded middle. Binary logic furthermore preserves these same categories by allowing exceptions. I am levelling this criticism at both marginalist and flexibilist anthropologists, regardless of whether they are men or women and whether or not they adhere to feminism.

Among the authors I have in mind, let me first mention those who have looked into the sexual division of labour and have considered exceptional those cases that fall outside their categories. These authors include Margaret Mead (1935), with her category of "atypicals"; Naomi Giffen (1930), with her "exceptions"; and William Willmott (1960), Jean Briggs (1970, 1974), and Lee Guemple (1976), with their concept of "flexibility." I will also mention those who have used a binary approach to analyze sex/gender categories with respect to religious and political organization and have construed such concepts as "inversion" whenever observed practices deviate from the usual norms (see R. Bradbury 1966; C. Geertz et al. 1966, G. Balandier 1974). S. Tcherkézoff (1987 [1983]) and E. Corin (1986) have made an interesting criticism of the binary approach to inversion.

In addition to the problems that anthropologists have had in addressing this kind of problem, as evident with the Inuit, there are also the problems that anthropology has encountered, from the outset, in integrating Inuit data into its theoretical debates—with the exception, of course, of Marcel Mauss (1979 [1906]), who gave such data a key place in his essay. This situation is probably explained by the Western cultural context within which different anthropological theories have developed. In particular, the Inuit have been marginal in Western space-time, on the one hand because they occupy the northernmost margins of our inhabited world, and on the other hand because they illustrate, more than other peoples do, what may have been, at the margins of our history, the Western world's prehistoric (Paleolithic) past. This marginalization is also probably related to the astonishing finding by L. Spier (1925) and G.P. Murdock (1949), following the pioneering work by L.H. Morgan (1871), that Western societies have an Eskimo kinship system. This finding has never been satisfactorily explained, despite much research on kinship among the Inuit since the Second World War. It is paradoxical that the latest attempts to conceptualize hunter-gatherer societies, using new theoretical frameworks, have once again marginalized the Inuit, as in the book by my colleague and friend Marshall Sahlins (1968, 1976), which makes Arctic hunters in general and the Inuit in particular an exception to his view that hunter-gatherers lived a life of abundance. Clearly, by recognizing the third gender as an object of anthropological interest, we will bring the Inuit into the heart of future theoretical debates in anthropology.

To create a framework in which the third gender will take shape and meaning, I have taken a structural, holistic, and ternary approach. My structural approach has revealed the place of sexual differentiation in cosmology as a model for all other differentiations, and shown the main levels of intelligibility for expression of the Inuit third sex, namely at the ontological, sociological, and shamanic or cosmic levels. These levels mirror each other, as do the major stages of the reproduction of human life (the life of the fetus, the socialization of the child, and the mediation of the shaman).

My holistic approach is closely tied to this structural approach and is the only way to integrate the above-mentioned levels into a coherent model of Inuit thought. I have progressively developed this model by listening to my Inuit friends over the years, in line with the progress of my research. With its four dimensions of space and time, it expresses a holistic concern. Through it I have assembled the different elements of the third gender within an interconnected whole.

Finally, my ternary approach transcends the limitations of the binarism that has marginalized my subject of research and denied its reality. Based on the statistics collected in the Igloolik region by Rasmussen in the 1920s and by myself and my research team in the 1970s, it appears that in 1970 the total population had a 2 percent minority of *sipiniit* (individuals thought to have changed sex at birth) and a 15 percent minority of children or adolescents who were or had been visibly cross-dressed. In the 1920s, around 20 percent of all adults were recognized as being shamans or as having been initiated into shamanism. I advanced the hypothesis that the three categories were interlinked, and that to study them we should use an "included middle" logic and construct a triangular system of gender categories. We should not reduce the system to a simple binary opposition. No theoretical work seems to have addressed the third gender problem, as I have defined the term; certainly not coherently and satisfactorily. More than one author has used the expression "the third sex" or "the third gender," but often in different senses that notably refer to the theme of sexuality (cf. Berndt 1978; Poole 1981; Jacobs 1983; Chinas 1985; McBroom 1986). At this point, I would like to discuss three major avenues of research, each of which touches on certain aspects of my work.

The first avenue is centred on gender. This concept was developed by John Money, an American psychologist and sexologist who oversaw sex reassignment surgery and paved the way for transexulatity. He was convinced that appropriate parental upbringing could successfully change a child's gender, an idea that was later challenged. He also paved the way for gender studies and gender theory, both of which were initiated by thinkers from sexual minorities (gay and lesbian), notably Judith Butler in the United States and Monique Wittig in France. Butler wrote that the new wave of French philosophers had inspired her, particularly Michel Foucault and the post-structuralists. Feeling discriminated against because of their sexual orientation, these radical feminists challenged heteronormativity and feminist movements that confined themselves to the fight for sexual equality. Through the impetus of Butler's writings, gender studies and the newly created gender theory brought about the creation of queer movements, which have used the case of intersex individuals as a means to criticize the binary approach to the sexes and to advocate instead an approach that encompasses all forms of sexuality, thus making gender a personal choice. Aside from their critique of binarism, which I support, I totally disagree with their confusion of gender with sexual orientation.

The second avenue of research is the androgyny movement in social psychology. It too was born in California, through the writings of Sandra Bem (1978), J. Trebilcot (1986), and many other authors. Bem developed the Bem Sex-Role Inventory (BSRI 1971) for business recruiting of senior executives, a test that proved highly successful in North America.[10] She subsequently drifted toward a radical form of feminism that called for androgynous upbringing of everyone from an early age, in daycare centres, with a view to eradicating heteronormativity. This idea has been taken up by other radical feminist social psychologists. While I agree that children should no longer be brought up according to gender stereotypes in terms of toys, physical activities, and so on, it seems to me utopian to want to transform humanity by making all of us androgynous. The same criticism applies to Élisabeth Badinter (1986), who used the classical model of social evolution of Bachofen (1861)—much disputed by anthropologists—to argue that humanity adopted matriarchy after the hunting-gathering stage because only maternity could be proven. Only later were women stripped of their power by men, who then established patriarchy. Badinter thought that our societies were becoming androgynous and that a new era was coming when relations between men and women would enter into harmonious balance. This is indeed yet another utopia, judging by the persistence of flagrant inequalities after several decades of attempts in this direction. A much more liberal solution may be a social model where men and women coexist with a third gender, as the Inuit do, with the provision that androgynous individuals are not discriminated against by old binarist prejudices. Such a social model seems to me more compatible with my data, because American research on psychological androgyny has never found the populations under study to be more than 30 percent androgynous.

Overall, the androgyny movement in social psychology has one major flaw: it has never established any relationship between androgynous characteristics and family and sociocultural setting, notably birth order, sex of individuals in relation to other siblings, or familial construction of sibling identity.[11] To me, these factors play a decisive role, as shown by the Inuit example.

The third avenue of research is in anthropology. It is the holistic approach of L. Dumont (1983), who studied ideologies, that is, systems of ideas and values, through a ternary approach by analyzing them according to their hierarchical levels. Already C. Lévi-Strauss (1963 [1958]) had stressed the limitations of dualistic approaches in anthropology for study of social organization, myths, or rites. M. Douglas (1966) also doubted the applicability of binarism beyond analytical processes. Following Lévi-Strauss and especially Dumont, S. Tcherkézoff (1987 [1983]) used a ternary approach to overhaul analysis of dualistic classifications, notably those of the political Right and Left, in studying the overall system of ideology and ritual in an African society.

Toward a New Rationalization of the Social Sciences

There thus seems to be a certain convergence among different lines of academic thought and among different disciplines to broaden their field or area of study by forging new tools and methods that aim to transcend certain limitations of Western logic. In this, there is probably a real revolution in the making that I will simply outline here. Perhaps through it a new generation of anthropologists, including Inuit anthropologists, may try to unify the discipline and its different ways of thinking, which binary oppositions have too often divided. If the third gender does exist where I believe it exists and does play the role of mediation, crisis management, and change that I believe it plays, then this "total social fact," which is based in human biological nature and forms one of the axes of culture and society, will shed new light not only on social statics and their structures but also on social dynamics and social change. Solid bridges may then be built to link the works of such people as Marx, Engels, Mauss, Lévi-Strauss, Bourdieu, Dumont, Balandier, Leroi-Gourhan, Sahlins, Turner, Geertz, Foucault, and many others. If this same concept enables us to transcend the different Inuit levels of reality of dream, myth, and trance, bridges may also be built with the works of Freud, Jung, Piaget, Bastide, Rouget, and ethno-psychoanalysts. Furthermore, the different schools of feminism and gender studies could get a second wind and integrate their theoretical assets with general anthropology. There is certainly room now for a ternary school of anthropology that could make intelligible everything in the excluded middle that scientific binarism has marginalized, and which could recognize the central place of such intermediaries in human reality.

There remains the question of credibility. Some colleagues raised doubts when I published the principles of my approach and theory in several academic articles. Some objected that Rasmussen had reported nothing about a third gender; nor had any of the leading ethnographers of the Inuit. Others objected that Inuit had no concept of a third gender. Still others wondered how I had managed to collect such data while they themselves had been doing fieldwork in adjacent villages, without having observed anything comparable. Once again, everything was attributed to my imagination.

I found an answer to the question of the third gender in 2004 while compiling different sources on Inuit myths in order to have a yardstick for analyzing a corpus of myths that I had personally collected at Igloolik. The answer was in the myth of a cross-dressed man who gave birth to a baby whale. It had been published by Slwooko (1979), a Yupik woman from St. Lawrence Island (Alaska). Her account thus begins: "For the Whites, there are two sexes. For us, in Yupiit beliefs, there is another sex between man and woman" (see Chapter 12 of this book). I thought back over my life journey and recalled certain key moments. I had read a short book by Michel Serres (*Le Tiers-Instruit*, 1989 [*The Troubadour of Knowledge*, 1997]), which I found very interesting. From memory, I can quote a line by the author: "A right-handed person is hemiplegic. A left-handed person is hemiplegic if not forced to become right-handed. If a left-handed person has been made right-handed, he is a complete being." A bit further he added: "There is a hand for writing and there is a hand for caressing." Now, I am left-handed by birth (as was my mother) but was forced to write with my right hand. In this change of handedness, is there not something analogous to the change of gender among the Inuit? Do not both lead to a certain maximization of potential that makes one able to see what others do not, and able to mediate by blurring the boundary between right and left? To represent and understand Inuit imagining, should we not blur the boundary that the shaman blurs between right and left, masculinity and femininity, humanity and animality, the world of the living and the world of the dead? Should we not imagine as the Inuit themselves imagine?

Proto-Taoism and Inuit Cosmology: a Logic of the "Included Middle"

In 1985 I was invited, along with my colleague Kristopher Schipper, a specialist in Taoism and Director of Studies for Section V (Religious Sciences) of the École Pratique des Hautes Études (Sorbonne, Paris),[12] to take part with the renowned ethnopsychiatrist Tobie Nathan in a round table on "Forming Sexual Identity in the Family Space." I had just published my first article on the Inuit third gender (1985) and was the first to speak on this theme. Schipper was the second to speak and told me straight away that everything I had just said on the Inuit was Chinese proto-Taoism. I was surprised, but his remark seems to make sense when one considers that the Inuit came from Central Asia some 10,000 years ago. I understood his point much better when I learned via the Internet in 2011 about a paper by Liang Shao, a professor at the École centrale de Lyon on "Logiques du tiers-exclus et du tiers-inclus en science naturelle et dans les langues," in which he contrasted Western approaches (an excluded middle) with the Taoist approach and the Chinese language (an included middle). Suddenly, all of my previous writings on kinship, change of sex, and cross-dressing of children and Inuit shamans were now confirmed around the axis of the

Taoist *Qi* and its equivalent, the Inuit *Sila* (Saladin d'Anglure 2015b, 111–32). Increasingly, I now believe that all of the native peoples of the Americas and Oceania, likewise of Asian origin, could be similarly compared and we would get the same result, in contrast to the leading monotheistic religions, which adopted Aristotle's logic. Islam did so through Averroes, Judaism through Moses Maimonides, and Catholicism through Thomas Aquinas. This may explain why, in these three great religious traditions, we encounter the extremist temptation of radical binary oppositions. Therein lies another avenue of research for future generations of researchers in the social sciences and the humanities.[13]

Bernard Saladin d'Anglure, CM, PhD
Professor Emeritus, Anthropology
Université Laval

Glossary of Inuktitut Terms

A

A'aa! Onomatopoeia, cry of pain by a human when being struck.

Agiaq "The file," personal name (Igloolik).

Aakulujjuk Personal name and place name.

Aakulujjuusi Name of the first man to emerge from the ground, the ancestor of the Inuit.

Aamarjuaq Mythical character (Igloolik).

Annanak Ancestor of the most important family of Kangiqsualujjuaq (George River). He ate his grandmother, at her request, to stay alive.

Annanak Family name.

Aasivak Ground spider (*Alopecosa asivak*); also personal name.

Aatuat Shaman Ava's daughter, adopted by Tagurnaaq. She was one of the sled passengers who discovered Ataguttaaluk on the brink of death. Aatuat contributed to this book.

Aggiarjuit Plural of Aggiarjuk; name given to people born during the sunny season, between the spring and fall equinoxes.

Aggiarjuk Long-tailed duck (*Clangula hyemalis*).

Aglu Breathing hole for seals under the sea ice.

Agluit Plural of Aglu.

Aippaksaq Betrothed son or daughter.

Aippili Abel, pronounced in the Inuit way.

Aiviliajuk Name given to Kannaaluk, Nuliajuk, or Sedna in the writings of Lyon (1824).

Aivilik "The place where there are walruses." Name of the territory adjoining Repulse Bay.

Aivilingmiut Inhabitants of the Aivilik region.

Aiviq Walrus (*Odobenus rosmarus*).

Ajagaq Cup and ball game.

Ajaraq Cat's cradle.

Akitsiraq Inuit name of the Law School Society (Nunavut).

Akkalookjo See Aakulujjuk.

Aksarjuk Personal name (Igloolik).

Akslaak Dual form of Akslaq.

Akslaq Black bear (*Ursus americanis*).

Akslat Plural of Akslaq.

Akulivik Name of the village of Cape Smith (Nunavik).

Akuq Rear panel of a man's or woman's parka.

Akutuinnaq "A man's caribou-skin parka with a long rear panel" (Igloolik).

Alariaq Personal name: Kupaaq's mother.

Alasuaq Personal name, which has become a family name (Nunavik).

Alliit Plural of Alliq.

Alliq "That which is lower." The Netsilik Inuit name for the lower world.

Amarualik Personal name: a shaman and leader in the early twentieth century. His name has become a family name (Igloolik).

Amaruit Plural of Amaruq.

Amaruq Arctic wolf (*Canis lupus arctos*).

Amaruujuaq Game of tag. It is played in a group outside, mainly in winter.

Amaut Back pouch of a woman's parka, used to carry a baby.

Amiqslaq Northern collared lemming (*Dicrostonyx groenlandicus*).

Amittuq "The narrow"; former name of the Igloolik region, in particular the Melville Peninsula region that lies across from the village.

Amityook Old spelling of Amittuq.

Ammuumajuit Plural of Ammuumajuq.

Ammuumajuq A clam commonly called blunt gaper or truncate softshell (*Mya truncata*).

Amug-yoo-a See Aamarjuaq.

Angajuq Older same-sex sibling.

Angajuqqaak Dual form of Angajuqqaq.

Angajuqqaaq Parent, leader, store manager.

Angak Maternal uncle (Ego = male or female).

Angakkuq Male or female shaman.

Angiliq Personal name: son of Ataguttaaluk and Qumangaapik. He died and was eaten by his mother during the famine.

Angut Male, whether human, animal, or plant.

Ani Brother (Ego = female).

Aniannuk "Sweet brother"; kinship term used by a woman.

Aniksaannuk "Sweet little adopted brother" (Ego = female).

Aningaq "Favourite brother" (Ego = female).

Anirniq Breath, respiration. Name given to good or bad spirits by Christian missionaries.

Apaapa "Food" in children's language.

Apaaq Personal name, which has become a family name (Igloolik).

Apitak Personal name (Tununiq, Pond Inlet).

Aqiggiarjuit Plural of Aqiggiarjuk; nickname for all people born during the time of year when the moon is at its highest in the sky, between the fall and spring equinoxes.

Aqiggiarjuk Willow ptarmigan (*Lagopus lagopus*, Igloolik).

Aqiggiq Rock ptarmigan (*Lagopus muta*, Nunavik).

Aqsarniit Plural of Aqsarniq.

Aqsarniq Aurora borealis or northern lights, a reflection of souls kicking a ball around in the heavens.

Arjiq Unknown meaning; name of one of the Moon Man's sled dogs.

-arjuk "little," diminutive suffix.

Arknuckkaark See Arnakkaaq, second wife of Aamarjuaq, the mythical hero.

Arnainnuk "Nice woman"; personal name of Iqallijuq's daughter (Igloolik).

Arnakkaaq Personal name.

Arnakpaktuq Mythical woman who reincarnates in several animal species.

Arnaq Female human, animal, or plant.

Arnaqquaksaq Former term for a woman between two ages of life, "who is becoming old." It appears in place names. Name also given to Kannaaluk/Nuliajuk/Sedna.

Arnartaaq Personal name: female counterpart of Iqallijuq.

-arniq Suffix: "which smells or tastes like" a food or living thing.

Arraaq Placenta; personal name: literally "He who follows," "The second."

Arsiq Group game where one player after another has to say "arsiq" while not laughing.

Artinarkjuark Old spelling of Atanaarjuat.

Arviit Plural of Arviq.

Arviq Bowhead whale (*Balaena mysticetus*).

Ataata Father (Ego = male or female).

Ataatakuluk "Sweet father," kinship term.

Atagullik Personal name: older daughter of Ataguttaaluk and Qumangaapik. She died and was eaten by her mother.

Ataguttaaluk Personal name, which has become a family name (Igloolik).

Atanaarjuat Personal name: mythical hero.

Atanarjuat See Atanaarjuat.

Atiq Personal name and also a person's namesake.

Atmackjuark See Aamarjuaq.

Attana-ghiooa Old spelling of Atanaarjuat.

Atuat Shaman, Ava's daughter, adopted by Tagurnaaq. She was one of the sled passengers who discovered Ataguttaaluk on the brink of death. Atuat contributed to this book.

Atungait See Atungaq.

Atungaq Sole of a boot. Personal name: mythical hero and shaman who went around the world.

Aujuittuq "The land where the snow never melts," glaciers on Baffin Island.

Auk Blood.

Aumaq "Ember."

Aumarjuat "Big Ember," personal name. Name of mythical woman who reincarnated in various animals before changing sex and becoming her brother's son.

Aupaluk Place name, bay, and village of Nunavik.

Aupartuq "He or she is red or orange-coloured."

Auruqtuq Aborted fetus, "which has been turned into blood."

Auvvik Caterpillar (Nunavik); see also Miqqulingiaq (Nunavut).

Ava Personal name and a little female spirit of the shore. It has become a family name.

Avingait Plural of Avingaq.

Avingaq Lemming.

Avvajjaq Place name: old winter camp in the Igloolik region. This is where the first Catholic missionary became established.

D

Dalasi Dalassie, first name.

Davidialuk "Big David."

E

Eccootlikechark Personal name; see also Ikullikisaq.

Eskimo English adaptation of the French spelling Esquimau/x.

Esquimau/x Former name given to the Inuit by Western Europeans and Algonquins.

Eterseoot Old spelling of Itirsiut.

Ettuk Jimmy, family name of an Arctic Bay artist who made drawings of various episodes of the myth of Atanaarjuat; see also Ittuq.

H

Hila See Sila (Caribou Inuit).

I

Ia-a-a-a! Onomatopoeia of a fulmar's cry. It sounds like a human sniggering.

Igalaaq "Windowpane of ice or skin"; personal name: mythical figure, name of the shaman older brother of Kaujjajjuk II (Igloolik).

Iggarlik "Which wears goggles," the northern fulmar (Igloolik).

Igjugaarjuk Personal name: Caribou Inuit shaman encountered by Rasmussen.

Igjugârjuk See Igjugaarjuk.

Igliaq Womb, from root word igliq: "sleeping platform in the igloo."

Igliniq Trail made in the snow.

Igloolik Official name of village on Igloolik Island (Nunavut); see also Iglulik.

Igloolik Isuma Inuit cultural production company in Igloolik.

Igloolik Nunavut Documentary directed and produced by B. Saladin d'Anglure and M. Tréguer (1977).

Iglu "Dwelling"; generic term, usually a small igloo made of snow while one is travelling.

Igluligaarjuk Place name: village of Chesterfield Inlet.

Iglulik Old winter camp discovered by Parry and Lyon in 1822. Rasmussen applied this term to the entire region stretching from Arctic Bay to North Baffin as far as Repulse Bay. The old camp is on the west coast of Hudson Bay, and this is its current standardized spelling. The older spelling survives in the official name of the village of Igloolik and the island.

Iglulingmiut Inhabitants of the Igloolik region and former winter camp of the same name; currently, the inhabitants of the village of Igloolik.

Ihii! Onomatopoeia of Ululijarnaat's laughter; the grotesque woman from the land of the Ullurmiut.

Ijiqqat Old plural form of Ijiraq.

Ijirait New plural form of Ijiraq.

Ijiraq Human-looking spirit that can make itself invisible or assume the form of a caribou. It lives inland.

Ijituuq Personal name; originally a nickname, "he eats an eye," which has become a family name (Igloolik). Agiaq's older brother. He contributed to this book.

Ikajurti Assistant, name given to a midwife.

Ikiq Place name: narrow stretch of sea that in winter becomes an ice bridge (Igloolik).

Ikpiarjuk Place name: "The little bag." This is the name of the cove where the village of Igloolik is located.

Ikradliyork Way of pronouncing Iqallijuq in French.

Iksivautaujaak Place name on Igloolik Island: "The two stones that look like seats."

Iktuksarjuat Personal name: great shaman and chief of the Iglulingmiut (d. 1944). It has become a family name.

Ikullikisaq Personal name: one of the two wives of Aamarjuaq, the mythical hero.

Iliarjugaarjuk Personal name: mythical orphan who was chased into the sky by an old man and became the star Muphrid.

Ilimmaqturniq A shaman's flight through the air.

Illuannuk "Sweet little girl cousin," name used by children for a cross-cousin (offspring of one's father's sister or mother's brother).

Illuinanganik qungaujaqpuq "He laughs with half his face." Provocative grimace made at the sun when it returns in January.

Imaruittuq Personal name, which has become a family name (Igloolik).

Ingiaqqaqattauk "They are competing against each other," implicitly the moon and the sun. Name of the lunar month of January.

Innaarulik Personal name: "It has a cliff." Said of an island or a shore.

Inua Literally "his master," his master spirit.

Inuaraq Personal name: Ataguttaaluk's brother. It has become a family name.

Inugagulligaarjuk Legendary "little dwarf" (Nunavut).

Inugagulligait Legendary "dwarf" (Nunavik).

Inugagulligarjuit Plural of Inugagulligaarjuk.

Inuit Plural of Inuk, "humans."

Inuk A human.

Inukpasujjuk Legendary "giant" (Nunavut); personal name of Rasmussen's storyteller and informant.

Inuksugaq Pile of stones, small cairn.

Inuksuk Human-shaped stone cairn, personal name: Inuk from Igloolik who contributed to this book. It has become a family name.

Inuktitut "In the Inuit manner"; Inuit language.

Inukturniq Man-eater; see also niqiturniq.

Inukturvik Place name on Baffin Island, "The place where someone ate human flesh," where Ataguttaaluk was found.

Inullariit "Authentic Inuit," name of a cultural association in Igloolik.

Inummariit "Real Inuit," name of a former cultural association in Igloolik and name of a former cultural magazine of this association.

Inuusiq Portion of life attributed at birth to an individual.

Iqallijuq Personal name (Igloolik): Inuit woman who greatly contributed to this book. This is also the name of the creator of Arctic char, Atlantic salmon, and other salmonids; a mythical character.

Iqaluit Plural of Iqaluk. Place name: capital of Nunavut, "The salmonids," formerly Frobisher Bay.

Iqaluk Generic term for a salmonid, like the Atlantic salmon (*Salmo salar*) or the Arctic char (*Salvelinus alpinus*). It has become a family name.

Iqalukpik Arctic char (*Salvelinus alpinus*).

Iqipiriaq Personal name: biological father of Sigluk, young man who died of hunger and was eaten by Ataguttaaluk.

Iqqiliit "Those who have nits of head lice," name given by the Inuit to the Chipewyan.

Iqqut Dog's name; fixed frame for (skin) windowpane of a semi-subterranean house.

Irinaliuti Magical song, magic spell, charm.

Irnivik Small hut for childbirth.

Irqaviaq Personal name.

Isuma "Thought, intelligence"; see also Igloolik Isuma.

Isumataq "Wise man, chief."

Itirjuaq "Big-Anus," heroine of a myth, the first woman healer.

Itiq Anus, sea urchin; see also itiujaq.

Itiqanngittut "Those who have no anuses," human-looking mythical spirits without anuses.

Itirsiut Another name given to Itirjuaq (Baffin Island).

Itiujaq "Which looks like an anus," sea urchin.

Itivimiut "The inhabitants of the other side," term used by the Inuit of Ungava Bay for those living on the east coast of Hudson Bay, or by the Inuit of Kangiqsujuaq for inhabitants of summer camps on the other side of the small peninsula formed by the south shore of Kangiqsujuaq Fjord.

Itsuti Arctic white heather (*Cassiope tetragona*), very good fuel for a fire.

Ittukusuk Personal name (Igloolik): Kuatsuk's younger sister. She was killed and eaten by Ataguttaaluk.

Ittuliaq Personal name: Iqallijuq's father and shaman.

Ittuq "The old one," meaning grandfather. It is also a personal name and has become a family name.

Ivaluarjuk "The little sinew"; personal name: Ava's older brother, shaman, storyteller, and singer, one of Rasmussen's main informants. It has become a family name.

Ivujivik Place name: "The place where the ice floes move (Nunavik)."

J

-juk "Fat" or "big," augmentative suffix (Igloolik).

K

Kajuji North American brown lemming (*Lemmus trimucronatus*).

Kajurjuk "Big Red," name of a dog that became the star Aldebaran and was used as a sled dog by the Moon Man.

Kalirraq Squeaking made by a sled's runners on the snow.

Kallu Thunder. Personal name.

Kanajuq Sculpin, Cottidae family (*Oncocottus hexacornis*, Nunavik; and *Myoxocephalus scorpioides,* Igloolik).

Kananniq Northeasterly wind that usually blows in the spring (Igloolik).

Kangiqsualujjuaq Place name: "The very very big bay" (Nunavik).

Kangiqsujuaq Place name: "The very big bay" (Nunavik).

Kangirslujjuaq Place name: "The very big bay" (Nunavut) on Baffin Island. Caribou are plentiful there and are hunted.

Kangirsuk Place name: "The big bay" (Nunavik).

Kannaaluk Mythical character: "The great woman down below" (Igloolik); also called Nuliajuk or Sedna.

Kannaaluuk "The two great ones down below," mythical characters Kannaaluk and her father.

Kappianaq Personal name (Igloolik). It has become a family name.

Kaugarsivik A stone or a bowhead whale vertebra that is used to pound pieces of blubber to extract oil.

Kaujjajjuk "He who receives walrus skin," name of mythical orphan (Nunavut).

Kaujjajuk Another name (Nunavik) for the character of Kaujjajjuk.

Kauk Walrus skin.

Kayak See qajaq, boat used by a Inuit hunter.

Kiiguti "Support," shamanic term for someone's namesake.

Kiigutigiik Two people with the same name: the namesake and the person given that name; a shamanic term.

Kijjaq Very short-haired fur above a wolf's forehead.

Kikkaak Vocative form of Kikkaq.

Kikkaq Meaning unknown. Term that two people call each other.

Kimmiqquaq Achilles' heel.

Kinaalik Caribou Inuit female shaman, encountered by Rasmussen.

Kinerto Place name: old spelling of Kiniqtuq.

Kingulliq "The second," that which comes after. Name also given to the star Vega.

Kiniq Front panel of a woman's parka.

Kinirvik Skin or snow shelter where a mother, after giving birth, is secluded with her baby as long as she is bleeding.

Kitturiaq Mosquito, Culicidae family; also a personal name.

Kiviuq Mythical hero.

Koonooka Personal name, old spelling.

Kopârk Old spelling of Kupaaq.

Kowertse Personal name, old spelling of Quvirti.

Kuatsuk Personal name: Ittukusuk's older brother and presumed murderer of Piugaattuq, Iktuksarjuat's brother.

Kublu Personal name: "Thumb." It has become a family name.

Kukiligaatsiat Human-looking spirits with long claws (Nunavik).

Kukilingiattiaraaluit See Kukiligaatsiat.

Kukiliqatsiait See Kukiligaatsiat.

Kumaruaq "Giant louse," shamanic term for a caribou.

Kunnuk Personal name: Qumangaapik's son, eaten during the famine. His name has become a family name.

Kunuk Personal name (Igloolik). It has become a family name.

Kupaaq Personal name (Igloolik): Ataguttaaluk's grandson. He contributed to this book, and his name has become a family name.

Kusugaq Personal name, which has become a family name (west coast of Hudson Bay).

Kuurujjuaq River, whose source is not far from the Labrador coast and which empties into Ungava Bay a little northeast of the village of Kangiqsualujjuaq, in the heart of Kuurujjuaq National Park.

L

-lik Suffix: "which has . . ."

Lumaajuq "She who says lumaaq," mythical woman who was turned into a beluga and cries "Lumaaq."

Lumaaq Onomatopoeia of the cry of the mythical woman who was turned into a beluga (Nunavik).

M

Maktaaq Edible skin and blubber of the beluga and narwhal.

Maktajaq Nickname of a woman whose lips looked like *maktak*, the skin and blubber of a bowhead whale.

Maktak Edible skin and blubber of a bowhead whale.

Mamaqpuq "It's good" or "He's good." Said when speaking about a food one likes or a person one likes to make love to.

Maniraq Plain, a flat, open area.

Mauna! "Over here!"

Midliqjuaq Place name, island in Hudson Strait.

Mig(s)lialik Meaning unknown, probably "the one with the umbilical cord" name of one of the Moon Man's sled dogs.

Miksliaqatigiit "Those who share the same umbilical cord," offspring of the same mother.

Minguliqtiqutiqarvik Small leather cone into which food is placed for a baby's dead namesake.

Minguttinaaqtuq Caribou-skin parka of a young teen girl.

Miqquliit A man's caribou-fur boots.

Miqqulingiaq Furry chrysalis of a moth or butterfly, fuzzy caterpillar (Igloolik); see also Auvvik (Nunavik).

Mitiarjuk Personal name: Inuit woman from Kangiqsujuaq, author of the novel *Sanaaq*.

Mitiik Dual form of Mitiq.

Mitiit Plural of Mitiq.

Mitiq Eider duck (*Somateria spectabilis*).

Mitligjuaq See Midliqjuaq.

N

Naarjuk "Big Belly," shamanic term for Silaap Inua, "the master of the cosmos."

Naaq "Belly."

Naja "Sister" (Ego = male).

Najaannuk "Sweet sister," kinship term used by a man.

Najangaq "Favourite sister," kinship term used by a man.

Najannaaq "Favourite sister," kinship term used by a man.

Nakkainiq A shaman's journey into the lower world, at the bottom of the sea.

Nakturalik "Which has a hook, a hooked bill," Greenlandic white-tailed eagle (*Haliaetus albicilla groenlandicus*).

Nakturaq Hooked bill of an eagle, a hook.

Nalupiritsuq Meaning unknown; name of one of the Moon Man's sled-dogs.

Nanuq Polar bear (*Ursus maritimus*).

Nanurjuk Giant polar bear; also Alcyone, a star of the Pleiades.

Nappajuk Name given to Nuliajuk's father, alias Kannaaluk, or Aiviliajuk in Lyon's writings.

Nasuk Personal name (Igloolik): former Anglican minister. It has become a family name.

Nataaq Personal name (Igloolik): older son of Ava and Urulu. It has become a family name.

Natijjat Lunar month when ringed seals (nattiit) give birth, March, spring equinox.

Natsirutiik Dual form: waterproof sealskin trousers, which a hunter will put on in the summer to go hunting in a kayak.

Nattiaviniit Plural of Nattiaviniq.

Nattiaviniq Young ringed seal that is one year old.

Nattiit Plural of Nattiq.

Nattiq Ringed seal (*Phoca hispida*), also a waterproof jacket made from ringed seal skin (Igloolik).

Nattiquti Sealskin trousers for kayaking (Igloolik).

Naukajjik Personal name: one of Rasmussen's storytellers and informants.

Netsilik Name of a territory and Inuit group adjacent to the Iglulik Inuit. "The place where there are ringed seals." It should be written as Natsilik.

Niaquqtaak Dual form of Niaquqtaq.

Niaquqtaq Small head-shaped mound of sod (origin of the first men).

Nigiiq The gentle, female southeasterly wind (Igloolik).

Niliq Fart, flatulence.

Ningiuraaluk Old mythical woman who pursued her grandson (Iliarjugaarjuk) across the sky and became Vega.

-nippuq suffix: "which smells or tastes like" a food or a living thing.

Niqiturniq Man-eater; see also inukturniq.

Niqqarittualuit Dried, inedible tundra plants.

Nirivviujut Another name of the place where everyone except Ataguttaaluk starved to death; see also Inukturvik.

Nirliik Dual form of Nirliq.

Nirliit Plural of Nirliq.

Nirliq Canada goose (*Branta canadensis*).

Nirralajuq Person born facing upwards, the traditional birth position of Inuit babies.

Niviarsiarannuk Personal name: second daughter of Ataguttaaluk and Qumangaapik. She died and was eaten by her mother.

Niviarsiat Daughter of Attaguttaaluk and Iktuksarjuat, adopted by co-wife Kallu.

Nuili! Imperative of nuivuq, "may it appear."

Nuliajuk "The great wife," mythical figure also known by the names of Kannaaluk or Sedna.

Nuliaksaq Betrothed girl.

Nuliksariit The two couples whose children are promised in marriage.

Nuna The earth.

Nunavik Administrative region formerly called Nouveau-Québec.

Nunavut Territory created (1999) out of the northeastern part of Canada's Northwest Territories.

Nungak Personal name, which has become a family name (Nunavik).

Nurrait Plural of Nurraq.

Nurraq Newborn fawn of a caribou (Tuktu).

Nutaraaluk Personal name: son of the shaman Alariaq who lived in Nunavik and Cape Dorset. Also the name of Kupaaq's mother who lived in Igloolik.

Nutarariaq Personal name: Ataguttaaluk's brother. It has become a family name (Igloolik).

Nuvalingaq Personal name (Sanikiluaq), which has become a family name.

Nuvvijaq Personal name: Iqallijuq's mother (Igloolik).

O

Omerneeto Old spelling of Uumarnituq.

Oo, oo! Onomatopoeia, uu'uu! (modern spelling). It expresses a baby's desire to drink.

Ouyarak Old spelling of Ujarak, personal name (Igloolik).

Owmirneto Old spelling of Uumarnituq.

P

Paammajaa! Meaning unknown, refrain from the song of Ululijarnaat, the mythical woman who tried to make human visitors laugh.

Padluq Tagurnaaq's husband.

Pangniq Large, old male caribou (Tuktu).

Panikuluk "Sweet daughter," affectionate kinship term.

Panniaq Personal name (Igloolik), which has become a family name.

Papa See apaapa.

Paulak Personal name (Igloolik): Ataguttaaluk's father.

Pauttuut Personal name (Igloolik).

Pigiurniq First-time performance, to achieve something for the first time.

Pingiqqalik Place name: camp (Igloolik region).

Pisugasuarnaaq In the language of the caribou, means a young fawn.

Pitsiulaaq Personal name (Kinngait): a famous Cape Dorset artist. It has become a family name.

Pittaaluk Personal name (Igloolik): Sigluk's adoptive father and Iktuksarjuat's brother. It has become a family name.

Piugaattuq Personal name (Igloolik): elder who contributed to this book. It has become a family name.

Pualukittuq Dog's name: "He who has little mittens," name of one of the Moon Man's dogs.

Pualuuk Dual form: pair of mittens.

Pudlaq Bubble that is embedded in the body and contains the soul.

Pukiit Plural of Pukiq.

Pukiksait Plural of Pukiksaq.

Pukiksaq White egg, bigger than a goose egg, which emerges from the ground and hatches into a Pukiq.

Pukiq White female caribou that hatches from an egg that emerged from the ground. It has magic powers. The term also means the ventral part of a caribou's skin, which is covered with white fur.

Pulamajuq "It disappears as if falling down a hole," said of an eclipsed sun or moon.

Putulik "The one with a hole" or "The hollow man." Personal name: mythical tube-man, creator of the salmonids; see also Iqallijuq. It has become a family name.

Puuq "Bag, container"; means a woman in shamanic language.

Q

Qaaq Exclamation; onomatopoeia describing the noise of something bursting.

Qaggiq A festive gathering place, a large igloo for playing games, or a stone circle used in summer.

Qajaq Inuit term for a one-man boat, a kayak.

Qaliruaq Ceremonial caribou-skin garment with hand-sewn designs.

Qaliruat Plural of Qaliruaq.

Qallunaaq "He who has large eyebrows," a white person.

Qallunaat Plural of Qallunaaq.

Qaqsauq Red-throated loon (*Gavia stellata*).

Qaqsaut Plural of qaqsauq.

Qaqulluk Northern fulmar (*Fulmarus glacialis*).

Qariaq Side room added to a dwelling.

Qarii! Cry made by a Canada goose.

Qarliik Dual form: shorts, trousers.

Qarmaq Semi-subterranean dwelling made of sod, stones, and bones.

Qatiktalik Place name: Cape Fullerton, Iqallijuq's birthplace.

Qattalik Personal name (Igloolik): Iktuksarjuat's first wife.

Qatturaannuk Personal name (Igloolik): Iktussarjuat's sister.

Qau Daylight, the forehead.

Qaujimaniq Knowledge.

Qaumaniq "The shaman's second sight," brightness, light, aura.

Qauruti A woman's forehead tattoo.

Qavvik Wolverine, lynx (*Gulo gulo luscus*).

Qijuttaq Fuel for a fire, comprised of Arctic white heather and other dwarf shrubs.

Qikirtaarjuk Place name: "The little island." It is currently a headland that forms part of Igloolik Island.

Qilalugait Plural of Qilalugaq.

Qilalugaq Beluga or white whale (*Delphinapterus leucas*) and also narwhal; see tuugalik.

Qilaniq Divining technique where a leather strap is used to lift a limb, a head, or an object.

Qillaquti Gift to a midwife as thanks for tying the baby's umbilical cord.

Qimiujaq The lower world, under the sea.

Qimiujarmiut The souls of the living dead in Qimiujaq.

Qimmiq Sled dog, Canadian Eskimo dog (*Canis familiaris borealis*).

Qingailisaq Personal name (Igloolik): shaman famous for his decorated coat.

Qingarniit Plural of Qingarniq.

Qingarniq Invocation to the spirits in places without footprints.

Qiqpaujaq A man's caribou-skin parka.

Qisaruaq Rumen of a caribou (tuktu).

Qisaruatsiaq Personal name: "Pretty Rumen" (Sanikiluaq and Nunavik).

Qitsuajuit plural of Qitsuajuk.

Qitsuajuk Human-looking mythical spirit with long claws (Nunavik).

Qittuarjuit Plural of Qittuarjuk.

Qittuarjuk "Like a Qitsuajuk" (Igloolik).

Qiturngaqatigiit "Those who have a child in common." The term encompasses adoptive parents and biological parents.

Qitusuk Personal name (Sanikiluaq).

Quajautik Red and black moss on rocks. Edible.

Quajautit Plural of Quajautik.

Quassa Personal name. Also a family name.

Quijaturvik Small hut used as a toilet.

Qulalik Female caribou that has just calved.

Qulissiaq "The top" (of the door), or the stew being boiled "over" the oil lamp.

Qulittalik Personal name (Igloolik).

Qumangaapik Personal name (Igloolik): Ataguttaaluk's first husband. He asked her to eat him after his death.

Qupiqruit Plural of Qupiqruq.

Qupiqruq Insects, generic term for larvae, worms, sand hoppers, maggots of the fly *Calliphora*.

Qupiqruqtaujuviniq "She who was devoured by maggots," mythical character (Igloolik).

Qurlutuq Place name: "waterfall."

Quvirti Personal name: mythical figure of the Big Man who tried to kill Itirsiut, the first woman healer.

S

Saittuq Personal name: a shaman of the early twentieth century (Iglulik).

Sakaniq Shamanic séance during which the shaman's helping spirit intervenes.

Sakariasi Inuit spelling of Zaccharias.

Sakiattiat The dogs of the bear hunters (Ullaktut). The dogs became the six Pleiades, and the bear became Alcyone (Nanurjuk).

Sakku Harpoon point (Igloolik), also rifle bullet.

Sallirmiut "The inhabitants of Salliq," on Southampton Island (Nunavut). There are, however, many places called Salliq in the Inuit-inhabited Arctic.

Salunippa "Bad smell."

Sanaaq Personal name; title of Mitiarjuk's novel (Kangiqsujuaq).

Sanaji "He or she who works," name given to a midwife; see also Ikajurti.

Sanajiar'uk Woman who offers a newborn baby its first piece of clothing (Sanikiluaq); see also Sanaji.

Sanikiluaq Personal name, and current name of the village on the Belcher Islands (Nunavut).

Sanna "The great woman down below," mythical character; see also Sedna, Kannaaluk, or Nuliajuk.

Sarpinaq Personal name (Igloolik).

Savviurtalik Personal name (Igloolik): Iqallijuq's maternal grandfather, a great bowhead whale hunter and shaman.

Sedna Old spelling of Sanna, mythical character; see also Nuliajuk and Kannaaluk.

Siarnaq Dog's name: "Grey"; name of the dog that became Uinigumasuittuq's husband in the myth.

Sigluk Personal name (Igloolik): he died of hunger and was eaten by Ataguttaaluk.

Siksik Arctic ground squirrel (*Citellus parryi*), small Arctic rodent.

Sila The atmosphere, the cosmos, the outside, intelligence, reason.

Silaaksait Plural of Silaaksaq.

Silaaksaq Egg that emerges from the ground and hatches into a Silaaq.

Silaap Inua The master of the Cosmos; see also Naarjuk.

Silaaq "Sila's child"; giant, brown caribou with magic powers.

Silaat Plural of Silaaq.

Silaga nauk? "Where is my Sila?" i.e., the weather on the day of my birth.

Silaittuq Unreasonable, foolish.

Silaluttuq A person born on a day of bad weather. Such a person can cause bad weather, like Kiviuq the mythical hero.

Silapaak A man's outer trousers.

Silattiavak A person born on a day of good weather and who can calm a storm.

Silatujuq Reasonable, wise.

Silu A dead animal that has washed ashore.

Sipiniit Plural of Sipiniq.

Sipiniq Individual who changed sex while being born.

Siqiniq Sun; Sun Sister, mythical character.

Siuraq "Sand," name of a sandy island off Igloolik.

Sivulliit Name of the stars Muphrid and Arcturus, in the mythology of Igloolik.

Slwooko Personal name (St. Lawrence Island, Alaska).

Suapik See Uqaittuq.

Suluvvaut Hair tied up in a topknot above the forehead, worn by a caribou that has turned into a man.

-sunniq Suffix: "which smells or tastes like" a food or living thing.

T

Taaq Darkness.

Taaqtuq "The darkened one," nickname given to a man-eater whose mouth has been completely blackened on the inside.

Taaqtut Plural of Taaqtuq.

Tadluruti Tattoo on a woman's chin.

Tagurnaaq Personal Name (Igloolik): Rasmussen's informant. She was one of the sled passengers who discovered Ataguttaaluk on the brink of death.

Takannaaluk See Kannaaluk.

Taktuup Inua Master spirit of the fog.

Taktuup nuliirpara "I've taken the fog's wife!"; charm spoken during a ritual to dissipate the fog.

Taptaqut According to Nellie Kusugaq, all of the Inuit named Taptaqut also had the name Atanaarjuat.

Taqqiapik Personal name: "Little moon" (Nunavik).

Taqqiq Moon or male spirit of the moon.

Taqqut Stone or wood poker to adjust the flame of an oil lamp.

Tarniq A person's double-soul, which leaves the body at death and goes into the hereafter.

Tarramiut Inhabitant of the shade, of the North, of the south shore of Hudson Strait.

Tasirjuaq "The very big lake," place name: very big lake on Baffin Island.

Tasiujaq Place name: "Which looks like a lake." Bay that turns into a marine lake at low tide.

Tatiggak Personal name: "Sandhill crane" (*Grus canadensis*).

Tautunngittuq "He cannot see," he is blind or suffers from snow blindness (Igloolik).

Tauvijjuaq "The great darkness," name of the lunar month of December in Igloolik.

Tiriaq Ermine, stoat, or short-tailed weasel (*Mustella erminea*).

Tiriatsiaq "Pretty Ermine," name of one of the Moon Man's dogs; in fact a polar bear (Nunavik and South Baffin).

Tiriattiaq Same meaning as Tiriatsiaq, but in the Igloolik dialect.

Tiriganniaq Arctic fox (*Alopex lagopus*).

Tiriganniasunniq Arctic fox smell, urine smell.

Titsinnartuq Grotesque, which makes people laugh. Said of the mythical woman Ululijarnaat, who lived in Ullurmiut country.

Tivajuut Ritual celebrations at the winter solstice with two masked, transgender shamans.

Tuktu Caribou (*Rangifer tarandus*).

Tuktuit Plural of tuktu.

Tulimaq Animal or human rib. Name of the shaman who befriended Lyon in 1822, in Iglulik.

Tulugaq Common raven (*Corvus corax*).

Tulugaqtuuti "What used to be a raven"; amulet made from a raven skin, mythical reference.

Tumitaittuq "Area without footprints on the snow"; where one meets spirits.

Tumitaqartuq "Area with footprints on the snow."

Tuniit plural of Tuniq.

Tunijjuti Gift to a shaman who is asked for a consultation with his helping spirit. The gift is for the spirit.

Tuniq Inhabitant of the Arctic who preceded today's Inuit. A person of the Dorset culture, according to archaeologists.

Tunniit Facial tattoos of Inuit women.

Tunnu Caribou suet, particularly fat from the back near the loins.

Tununiq Name of the Pond Inlet region (Nunavut).

Tuqqujaaq Larynx of humans and other mammals, with the carotid artery and jugular veins.

Tuqsluqausiq Term of address for speaking to someone.

Tuqsluqausit Plural of Tuqsluqausiq.

Tuqujuq "He/she is dead, numb, lifeless."

-turniq Infix: the fact of consuming something or someone for food or for sex.

Tutukatuk Mythical character: a woman who committed a transgression and was taken away by the Moon Man to be admonished.

Tuugalik Narwhal, nickname given to this mammal to distinguish it from the beluga. Both species are called Qilalugaq.

Tuulliq Personal name: "Big loon" (*Gavia immer*).

Tuurngait Plural of Tuurngaq.

Tuurngaq Shaman's helping spirit, also a large human-looking spirit that lives inside rocks.

U

Uannaq The cold, male northwesterly wind (Igloolik).

Uggussuk "I'm sorry" in the language of the Qittuarjuit mythical spirits.

Ugliit Plural of Ugliq.

Ugliq Island, where walruses haul out to rest on dry land.

Uhuu! Onomatopoeia of a giant crying to his wife for help, in the myth.

Uik Term used by a woman for her husband, or to address him.

Uiksaq Betrothed (future husband).

Uinigumasuittuq Mythical character: "She who refused to marry." She became Kannaaluk, alias Nuliajuk, alias Sedna.

Uirniq "That which lifts itself onto," meaning the upturned front of a sled's runners or the xiphoid process of the sternum. The term is constructed from the root "uik," meaning "husband."

Ujarak "Stone," personal name: shaman Ava's son, who contributed to this book.

Ujarasujjuit Plural of Ujarasujjuk.

Ujarasujjuk Erratic, a fairly large block of stone.

Ujarasujjuuk Dual form of Ujarasujjuk.

Ujjuk Bearded seal (*Erignathus barbatus*).

Ujuu Onomatopoeia that may be translated as "phew!" (sigh of relief).

Ukiujuittuq "The land without winter": in the myths, the country where migrating birds come from.

Ukkusiq Traditional Inuit stone (steatite) cooking pot for making stew.

Ukpik Snowy owl (*Nyctea nyctea*). Alternate spelling, uppik.

Ukpiit Snowy owls, plural.

Ukpikarniq Ritual of a perilous somersault to renewed youth; when one changes territory.

Ukumaaluk Personal name (Igloolik). Iqallijuq's deceased husband.

Ullaktut Orion's Belt, "Those who run," the three mythical bear hunters who became stars.

Ulluqarvik "The place where daylight appears," the eastern sky.

Ulluriaq Personal name, "Star" (Igloolik): old woman shaman who died at a very old age in the 1930s in Igloolik. She claimed to have known Hall, Parry, and Lyon.

Ullurmiut "The people of the Land of Day": the heavenly hereafter of double-souls.

Ulu A woman's knife shaped like a half moon.

Uluaruti Tattoos on a woman's cheeks.

Ululijarnaat Female mythical character who lived on the moon and eviscerated with an ulu human visitors who laughed when seeing her.

Umiaq Large multi-passenger boat with skin stretched over a wooden frame and propelled by a sail or paddles.

Umiat Plural of umiaq.

Unaliq Personal name.

Ungaa Onomatopoeia for a baby's cry.

Ungalaaq Personal name, Ataguttaaluk's brother.

Ungaluujakuluk "Little Ungaluujaq," area on the Melville Peninsula across from Ungaluujaq.

Ungaluujaq Place name: "Which looks like an igloo base."

Ungava Name of an Inuit territory in northeastern Nunavik and by extension, a large bay of the same name; eastern part of Hudson Strait.

Ungirlaq Laced caribou-skin children's underwear. Naarjuk wore one.

Unngiqsaq The sinew belt holding up a pair of pants.

Uppik Snowy owl (*Nyctea nyctea*), personal name; see also Ukpik.

Uqaittuq (Suapik) Name of Qisaruatsiaq's midwife/dresser (Sanikiluaq).

Uqi Character in the legend of Atanaarjuat, who under this name played the role of the jealous bad guy in the film.

Uqinniq Lightness, a negative sign when one is divining by weighing.

Uqqurmiut "The people of the leeward side," those who inhabit a region sheltered from the prevailing wind.

Uqsuraliit Plural of Uqsuralik.

Uqsuralik "He who has fat," a shamanic term for either a polar bear or an ermine.

Uqumainniq Heaviness, a positive sign when one is divining by weighing.

Uqumiagait Plural of Uqummiagaq.

Uqummiagaq Residue of chewed blubber from which oil is extracted.

Ursuriaq Place name: "Marble Island," off Hudson Bay's west coast.

Urulu Personal name: female shaman, Ujarak's mother and Rasmussen's informant.

Usuk Penis of a man or other animals.

Usuujaq "That which looks like a penis": bow of a kayak.

Utuqqalualuk Mythical old man who became the star Arcturus.

Uuaauu! Cry of a dog-team driver to halt his sled dogs, here the Moon Man.

Uuau! See preceding entry.

Uumaq Reciprocal term of affection between the spouses Padluq and Tagurnaaq.

Uumarnituq Name of the first mythical woman, the ancestor of the Inuit. She was a man who had changed into a woman.

Uuttukuttuk Personal name: son adopted by the old chief Amarualik.

Uuurq! Uuurq! Onomatopoeia imitating the bellowing of a male walrus calling to a female.

Uviluq Blue mussel (*Mytilus edulis*); personal name: Iqallijuq's midwife (Igloolik).

Y

Ya, yaa Refrain accompanying the song of a husband looking for his Canada goose wife.

Yupiit Plural of Yupik, the self-designation of the Inuit who live south of the Yukon River, on St. Lawrence Island, and on the Siberian coast.

Yupik Singular of Yupiit.

Notes

Foreword

1   The current freeze-up keeps large ships from using this strait to go farther west. The Arctic's gradually warming temperatures may make it navigable in the foreseeable future.

2   Iglulik is the transcription in standard spelling (adopted by Nunavut authorities) of the name of the very old Inuit winter camp at the southeast end of the island, which Inuit still inhabited when Parry arrived. This is the spelling that Rasmussen used when studying the local Inuit in 1921–24. In its English form of Igloolik, this place name has been applied both to the whole island and to the permanent village where the island's population has been settled since the mid-1960s, some fifteen kilometres west of the old site. When speaking of the village, I will use the term Igloolik. On the other hand, when speaking of the regional group and culture, I will use Iglulik and Iglulingmiut (for the inhabitants of the Igloolik region).

3   Traditionally, Inuit had only personal names from dead or living ancestors or from the helping spirits of shamans. With Christianization, they were given Christian first names, frequently taken from the Bible if they were Anglican or from the Catalogue of Saints if they were Catholic. In 1970, the government of the Northwest Territories decided to give all Inuit of the territories last names, this being done in some confusion. In day-to-day family life, the system of personal names still prevails (Chapter 1), but for administrative purposes last names have become common usage. To distinguish these two levels of naming, personal names will be italicized in this book, as will be terms used only in Inuktitut, whereas last names will be transcribed normally, as well as village names that Canadian authorities have officially recognized.

4   These collections include a very richly decorated caribou-skin shaman coat that belonged to the shaman *Qingailisaq* of Iglulik.

5   The Tarramiut Inuit dialect is spoken on the south shore of Hudson Strait from the village of Akulivik on the west to Aupaluk on Ungava Bay on the east. I had learned it while staying in that region between 1955 and 1971.

Introduction: *Iqallijuq, Ujarak, Kupaaq*, and the Others

1 The nineteen-year cycle is also named the Metonic cycle, after the Greek astronomer Meton, who in 432 BC discovered that nineteen solar years equal 235 lunar months. Therefore, every nineteen years the phases of the moon fall on the same dates of the same months. In 1990 I went back to Igloolik to verify this and to see, with my own eyes, that the full moon circled around the sky without setting.

2 The names *Iqallijuq* and *Ujarak* are pronounced *Ikradliyork* and *Ooyarak*.

3 The name *Kupaaq* is pronounced *Koopârk*.

4 In 1930, twenty Inuit from Iglulik, for the most part closely related to the old couple, had already been baptized there.

5 Inuktitut is the name of the Inuit language. It literally means "in the manner of an Inuk person."

6 Because he was a first-born child, his grandparents kept him with them during the summer so that his parents could go inland and hunt caribou. They thus adopted him as a servant.

7 I made 16-mm colour films on four subjects: *Iqallijuq*'s memories from the womb; the song of the shaman *Saittuq*, sung and commented on by *Ujarak*; the myth of *Uinigumasuittuq* ("She who refused to marry") as told by *Kupaaq*; and the making of a sealskin tent and a semi-subterranean house, with *Iqallijuq* and the family of *Arnainnuk* and *Kupaaq*. Excerpts from the films were inserted into a two-hour documentary I co-produced with Michel Treguer (1977), titled *Igloolik Nunavut*, which aired on the French TV network FR3 in 1977 and can be downloaded for free from the Isuma TV website: http://www.isuma.tv/fr/bernardsaladindanglure (French and English subtitles).

8 With regular and appreciated support from the Canada Council for the Arts and others; see www.artcirq.org.

9 Father Louis Fournier helped the Inuit create a local co-op and then the Inummariit Cultural Association, which from 1972 to 1977 produced a magazine with the same name as well as occasional publications in the Inuit language.

10 John MacDonald, who has long managed the Igloolik Research Laboratory.

11 See the Igloolik Isuma Productions website at www.isuma.ca.

12 The Canada 2011 Census found 45,000 Inuit in Canada. At that time, Greenland's Inuit population was estimated at 55,000 people and Alaska's at 51,000. In addition, there were around 2,000 Siberian Inuit. Thus, in total, there are over 150,000 Inuit. The mean natural increase is currently 2 percent.

13 This was the case with at least most of the inhabitants of what would become Nunavut and Nunavik. In the eastern reaches of the first territory, and in the western reaches of the second, the Latin alphabet had already been introduced either by whalers or by Moravian missionaries. Syllabics, invented by Wesleyan missionaries in the mid-nineteenth century for the Cree, was adapted to the Inuit language by the Anglicans and then taken up by the Catholics. It is a sort of simplified shorthand.

Interlude 1: Song of *Saittuq*

1 Bernard Saladin d'Anglure filmed *Saittuq* while he sang and pointed at the different parts of the igloo. This film may be viewed on the Isuma TV website.

2   *Igliq* is a sleeping platform covered with caribou and bear skins. It is often likened to the land.

3   *Natiq* is the ground, the floor of an igloo. It is likened to the sea.

4   *Sikuliaq* is the new ice that has formed on the sea. In winter, families often built their igloos on the sea ice.

5   *Katak* is an opening at the far end of an entranceway. It is likened here to the moon.

6   *Igalaq* refers to the ice windowpane of an igloo. It lets in sunlight, hence the analogy to the sun.

7   *Aki* is a small platform where the provisions from the hunt are placed.

8   *Imarjuaq* is the big "sea," implicitly including marine game animals.

9   *Iglu* refers to a spiral of snow blocks that is laid upon the first circle of blocks on the ground. It forms the dome of the igloo.

10   *Silarjuaq* is "the vast universe." This is *Sila*, which has several meanings: the outdoors, the weather, the logos, the order of the cosmos.

11   *Kangiq* is a shamanic term for the air shaft of an igloo.

Chapter 1: *Savviurtalik* Is Reincarnated

1   An initial version of this story was published in Inuktitut with a literal translation in Saladin d'Anglure (1977). It corresponds to the 16-mm colour film made with *Iqallijuq* in 1973 and is included in the documentary *Igloolik Nunavut* (Saladin d'Anglure and Tréguer 1977). A second version was published in Saladin d'Anglure (1998).

2   *Iqallijuq* remembered having received at least five names, each of which gave her an identity. Her grandfather's name had the most kinship power, *Iqallijuq* the most supernatural power, and *Arnartaaq* the most life power.

3   See in Chapter 6 the encounter with the spirit *Iqallijuq*, the creator of the salmonids (Atlantic salmon, Arctic char). Also see Saladin d'Anglure (2006a [2001]) for the relationships between helping spirits and personal names.

4   When a mother has ended her time of recovery from childbirth and is again allowed to have sex with her baby's father, she must, the first time she has sex, remove the sperm that drains out of her vulva and smear it over the newborn's body to strengthen the child.

5   During the *Tivajuut* festival at the winter solstice, each person has to imitate the cry of the bird whose skin was used to wipe that person at birth.

6   Literally "my second," the one that follows me.

Chapter 2: Inuit Genesis and the Desire for Children

1   This account was from two Netsilik immigrants, *Tuulliq* and *Unaliq*, who had come from the Repulse Bay region some twenty years earlier. Rasmussen adds, however, that the story was well-known to the Iglulingmiut.

2   This is according to *Agiaq*, who places the event on Igloolik Island. He was told the story by *Ulluriaq*, a very old shaman woman from Iglulik who died in the 1930s. The characters *Uumarnituq* and *Aakulujjuusi* are mentioned in Boas (1901, 178; 1907, 483–85) and for Iglulik

in Mary-Rousselière (1969a, 114–15). Carpenter (1968) also alludes to this story with regard to the Aivilik Inuit on Southampton Island, who are very close to the Iglulingmiut.

3   This is according to my translation of an unpublished manuscript in the Inuit language from the Rasmussen collection, found in Denmark by Mrs. R. Søby, who obligingly sent me a copy. For this I wish to thank her. This version, however, does not mention the names of the first two humans. A freely written English translation is available in Rasmussen (1929, 252).

4   One is reminded of the old belief in the Western world that a baby can be born from a mandrake root.

5   The pregnant man theme is found also among the Yupiit of St. Lawrence Island. See Chapter 12.

6   For the remainder of the story, I will spell the names of the first two humans using standardized spelling—here between square brackets.

7   Food is *apaapa* in the language of children; drink is *uu'uu*.

8   See reference to Claude Lévi-Strauss in this book's Conclusion. Lévi-Strauss, who often alluded in his published writings on myths to Piaget's "reversibility of perspective," was the one who drew my attention to this concept, which he found especially appropriate for analysis of my Inuit data.

9   *Miqqulingiaq*, a fuzzy caterpillar of a moth or butterfly, according to *Kupaaq*. Its name is derived from the root *miqquq* (hair). In Nunavik, it is called *auvvik*. Boas translated the term as "chrysalis."

10   A husband who cannot yet hunt and is unable to procreate is in the position of a woman who stays home to mind the oil lamp. This is women's work in the sexual division of labour.

11   See in Chapter 12 the story of a bowhead whale fathered by an Inuk, which lures the other whales to his father's village and provides him with plenty of food.

12   The same ambiguity may be found in the French countryside, where a pig would be fattened and almost considered a member of the family until it had to be killed. All sorts of flaws would then be ascribed to it, and it would again become an animal to be butchered. See also the sacrifice of tamed wild animals by the Shipibo-Conibo of Peru's Amazonian region (Morin and Saladin d'Anglure 2007).

13   This equivalence of alternating generations is an observable social reality in many groups around the world. See the article by A. Radcliffe-Brown (1940) on joking relationships. It is found in societies with elementary kinship structures (Lévi-Strauss 1969a [1949]). It may be seen in the way identity and personal names are passed down from grandparents to grandchildren, as among the Inuit, or in the French tradition of making a grandparent a baby's godfather or godmother and giving the baby the grandparent's first name.

14   Raven is the master of daylight in the mythologies of several North and South American peoples; see especially Lévi-Strauss (1981 [1971]) for the Salish.

15   The Arctic fox (*Alopex lagopus*) lives in burrows it digs in the soil. It is known for plundering stone caches that contain stores of meat. A myth tells the story of a fox that turns into a beautiful girl after taking off its skin (Chapter 6). Fox fur is usually reserved for women's clothing.

16   The universe therefore came into existence as a human being does. Gestation begins with life in a dark womb as part of the mother's body (the earth) and ends with the baby's birth (a desired son) (Saladin d'Anglure 1977b, 1991; Bordin 2015 [2002]).

17   A well-known myth in Igloolik, the myth of *Tulugaqtuuti* tells the story of an orphan who had been clothed in a raven's skin at birth and who later managed to rid himself of his enemies with this guardian bird's help (Kupaaq 1973).

18 See Rasmussen (1929, 94–95). The lower world is called *Alliit* ("The people down below") among the Netsilik. This term is understood in Igloolik, but people prefer *Qimiujaq*.

19 With war as the organizing principle of human ecology, we are not very far from the Heraclitean principle of Polemos and an ontology of negativity along the lines of Hegel, Marx, or Marcuse. The Asian origin of the Inuit might explain this analogy with pre-Socratic thought. The question remains open.

Chapter 3: *Naarjuk:* The Giant Baby with Prominent Genitals and the Master of *Sila*

1 In an older publication (Saladin d'Anglure 1980a) on this major cosmic figure, I proposed translating *Naarjuk* as "Little Belly," confusing the two infixes *-arjuk* (small) and *-juk* (big). Since belly is *naaq* in Inuktitut, the correct infix is evidently the second one. The word comes from the language of shamans and means the master of *Sila*.

2 In the Netsilik dialect he is called *Inugpasugssuk*, just as the giant dwarf is called *Inuaruvligasugssuk* by the Netsilik. I will use here the Iglulik dialect, which is preferred throughout my book.

3   These are giant *iqaluit* (Arctic char, *Salvelinus alpinus*).

4 A special dwarf can alter himself in two ways: by becoming as big as or bigger than his opponents, as we see in Natsilik oral tradition, or by becoming physically stronger while remaining as small as a dwarf. This happens in stories about these creatures in Nunavik: the dwarf (*Inugagulligaarjuk*) can kill an adult Inuk by jumping on him and squeezing the man's neck with both legs while pressing his mouth onto the Inuk's and killing him by sucking out his breath.

5   The Inuit way of thinking, like that of all hunters, loves trickery. There may be an affinity here with the goddess Metis of Greek mythology (Detienne and Vernant 1991 [1974]).

6 One might also see here a correspondence with the Heraclitean notion of time represented by a playful child.

7 See the previous chapter for other ritualized ways of evoking one's birth to conciliate the spirit of the place.

8 "Diver" is another name for birds of the loon family (*Gavia*).

9 Oosten (2002) published a long article on the epic of *Kiviuq*, drawing on various sources, but he failed to find the link between the orphan's birth on a stormy day and his power to cause the storm by identifying himself to the master of *Sila*. For the narrators of the different variants of this myth, the link is indeed implicit, like much of the mythology, and there must be special circumstances or an exceptional narrator to make the implicit explicit. In another publication, jointly edited by the same authors (Oosten, Laugrand, and Rasing 1999), the narrator *Nutaraaluk* recounts the orphan's invocation "*Silaga nauk?*" (Where is my *Sila*, "my weather"?), but without mentioning the orphan's plaintive cry or his birth on a stormy day. None of the dozen Inuit students who conducted the interview thought to question *Nutaraaluk* about the meaning of this invocation to *Sila*. I provide these remarks to show the problems that ethnography has in revealing the implicit.

10 Ann Fienup-Riordan (1983) is one of the very few authors to mention their symbolic importance for the Yupiit of Alaska. See the myth of *Itirjuaq*, "the woman with the big anus" and the first Inuit healer, in Chapter 11 of this book. Also see analyses by Lévi-Strauss (1988 [1985]) about body orifices in mythology.

11 In the language of obstetrics one would say that for Inuit a delivery is normal when the baby's head is freed from the vulva and the occipital bone of its skull is next to the parturient woman's sacrum. The delivery is abnormal when the baby's head is freed and the occipital bone of its skull is next to the parturient woman's pubis. In the European tradition, the reverse is normal: the first presentation is considered risky, whereas the second is recommended.

12 My sincerest thanks go to John MacDonald, the former Director of the Igloolik Research Centre, Nunavut, for providing me with these excerpts. See also MacDonald (1998).

Chapter 4: Incestuous Moon Brother Chases Sun Sister

1 He is known by the name of *Atungait* in Igloolik and also in eastern Nunavik.

2 Thus, Boas (1888, 1901) published two texts under the title "Origin of the Narwhal." The first one includes the first three episodes of the present myth, and the second the first four. Neither text has the last episode about the origin of the sun and the moon.

3 *Kublu* earned a university degree and taught at various educational institutions in Nunavut, including Nunavut Arctic College in Iqaluit, where she was a professor for over ten years in the Inuit Studies Program. Christened Alexina, she received permission from the authorities to make her personal name *Kublu* her family name. Gifted with a striking personality, *Kublu* was appointed the first justice of the peace in Nunavut. She is also chair of the Akitsraq Law School Society and has published several major publications. The precise wording of her texts and their underlying logic are in contrast with the often allusive and implicit style of the myths told by the generations of uneducated Inuit who preceded her.

4 These terms of address (*tuqsluqausit*) contain the roots *ani* ("brother" when a male is addressed by his sister) and *naja* ("sister" when a female is addressed by her brother), and the suffix *-ngaq*, *-ngaat*, or *-ngaaq* ("favourite"). Thus, *Kupaaq* and his daughter *Kublu* use the form *Aningaq* in their accounts, whereas *Ivaluarjuk* (in Rasmussen 1929) and George Kappianaq (in MacDonald 1998) use the form *Aningaat* in their accounts.

5 In *Kupaaq*'s story, and in the one published by Boas (1888) on the origin of the narwhal, the two children live with their mother. In *Ivaluarjuk*'s variant published by Rasmussen (1929), they live with their grandmother. They also live with their grandmother in George Kappianaq's variant (1986, IE-071) published by MacDonald (1998).

6 The term *tautunngittuq* can mean blindness that is congenital or accidental, and permanent or temporary like snow blindness.

7 It is worth noting that these goggles were worn almost exclusively by men, who spent much of their lives outdoors. Women and children, who most often stayed indoors or around the home, did not usually wear goggles. *Aningaq*, not yet an adult but no longer a child, apparently wore none, the result being snow blindness. In the story published by Boas (1888) on the origin of the narwhal, the brother and sister have long been fatherless. The brother makes himself a bow and arrows, with which he kills birds and provides the family with food. He is then accidentally blinded, and as he can no longer hunt, his mother deprives him of food and mistreats him.

8 Except by the Inuit of the Belcher Islands, who loved puppy meat and would eat it until the mid-twentieth century. The explorer Martin Frobisher mentioned that the Inuit he met in the Baffin Island fjord that bears his name (Frobisher Bay) would raise two kinds of dogs: big dogs for pulling sleds, and a smaller kind for food.

9 This fact has been stressed by Savard (1966) and more recently by Blaisel (1994).

10 See similar transformations in Chapters 5 and 8.

11 Lyme grass (*Elymus arenarius*) is a grass that may be found in the Arctic near lake or sea water. It often grows on sandy soils. In some regions, Inuit use it for basketwork.

12 When harpooning a walrus (*Odobenus rosmarus*), another big mammal, a hunter would tie the line to a big stone. This was when such animals were being hunted on land, on the islands where they customarily hauled up to rest. Alternatively, a hunter would take the harpoon shaft and anchor it firmly in the ice when harpooning the animal from the edge of the sea ice.

13 In Igloolik, people distinguish between *maktak*, the edible skin of the bowhead whale, and *maktaaq*, the edible skin of the beluga or the narwhal (Randa 1994; and Spalding 1998).

14 The variant from Kangiqsujuaq (Nunavik) can be read in *Sanaaq*, a novel by *Mitiarjuk* (2014 [2002]).

15 In the Eastern Arctic (Nunavik) this episode belongs to the myth of *Atungaq*, and in the Western Arctic (among the Copper Inuit) to the epic of *Kiviuq* (see beginning of this chapter). In all three cases, there is an encounter with human-looking people who feed on human flesh and have long claws at the ends of their fingers. There are good grounds to believe that these represent predatory animals that have taken human form, like wolverines (*Gulo luscus*). *Kublu* calls them *Kukilingiattiaraaluit*, *Ivaluarjuk* calls them *Kukiliqatsiait*, and Taividialuk Alasuaq (Nunavik) distinguishes between two different peoples: one called *Qitsuajuit* ("Those who claw") and the other *Kukiligaatsiat* ("Those who have long claws").

16 The parka is similar to the one that *Iqallijuq*'s mother made for her daughter after her first menstruation (Chapter 1).

17 "A separate volume would be necessary to draw up a typology of these characters, who are blocked or pierced, above or below, in front or behind," writes Lévi-Strauss (1978 [1968]) in his "Origin of Table Manners" (*Mythologiques* 3).

18 The poker's phallic appearance was noted by Lévi-Strauss (1981 [1971]) in "The Naked Man" (*Mythologiques* 4) for several myths from the Americas.

19 In the variant published by *Kublu* (2000), *Siqiniq* ("Sun Sister") puts a burning wick into her cut-off breast to turn it into a torch and then cuts off the other breast, which her brother will use the same way.

20 In other words, when you face south. When you face north, the sun moves counterclockwise from right to left.

21 In Kangiqsujuaq, Nunavik, it was made known to young girls who did not want to be tattooed that after death their faces would be burned and stained by the tar that drips from the sun's oil lamp (Saladin d'Anglure 1994b [1986]).

22 Savard (1966) also mentions this inverse symmetry, which I had reported to him.

23 For the entire end of this chapter, it is worth reading the well-documented book by John MacDonald (1998), *The Arctic Sky: Inuit Astronomy, Star Lore, and Legend*, which is based on observations and accounts by Igloolik elders.

24 Migratory birds that arrive in the Arctic in late spring.

Chapter 5: A Headstrong Daughter: The Mother of All Human Races and All Marine Mammals

1   The myth has given rise to many analyses and debates by such authors as Holtved (1967), Savard (1970), Oosten (1976, 1983), Hutchinson (1977), Saladin d'Anglure (1994a [1981], 1994b [1986], Sonne (1990), Blaisel (1994), and Laugrand and Oosten (2008).

2   Sonne (1990), in a long ethnohistorical critique, rejects Savard's structural analyses of this myth and tries to prove that many variants, including those from Iglulik, were influenced by the presence of white people on the periphery of the Inuit homeland. Without denying the heuristic value of her study, which relies essentially on print sources, I find that it lacks, to say the least, support from anthropological fieldwork and is unconvincing in its critique of structuralism.

3   This island became a headland over at least five centuries of postglacial isostatic rebound. The oldest archaeological sites, i.e., Pre-Dorset, are thus the highest in altitude above the current sea level. Dorset sites are a bit lower, being younger in time, and Thule sites are lower still, being the youngest.

4   See the account by *Mitiarjuk* (1994) on this subject that I collected at Kangiqsujuaq, Taylor (1993), and Oosten and Laugrand (2007). See also Lévi-Strauss, *The Story of Lynx* (1996, 153–66) [1991, 207–24] for more about the myth of the Dog Husband.

5   This situation brings to mind *Iqallijuq*'s memories of the womb (Chapter 1). When she was still a fetus, her father fed her by entering the womb-igloo in the form of a dog penis. Since she was her own grandfather in the process of being reincarnated, the dog was in fact a son-in-law feeding his father-in-law. From this perspective, the myth of *Uinigumasuittuq* describes a sort of regression in family development by taking this development back to the stage of the daughter's gestation or childhood, when her father was her provider.

6   See Saladin d'Anglure (1978a) for the sexual symbolism of male and female tools. See also Therrien (1987) for human body symbolism, and Figure 10.

7   Lyon (1824) mentions that the daughter's dog lover had a black and white coat. Boas, however, published a variant (1885) that describes it as white and red. This contrast of colours may evoke the colours of her offspring: one with fair skin, the ancestor of the white people, and the other with darker skin, the ancestor of the First Nations.

8   According to a variant I collected in Nunavik, the *Tuniit* had fled through northern Labrador to the northeast, i.e., to Greenland.

9   Ungaluujaq is a traditional summer camp on Igloolik Island (see Figure 17). The term means "that which resembles the first circle of blocks of snow that form the base of an igloo," or "the circle of stones where one sits during festive gatherings." There is indeed at this location a large circle of stones, which people used during summer gatherings. This was where community meals would be organized after a big whale had been caught (Lyon 1824). This is a place for hunting marine mammals and also a stopover for travellers going to or coming from the mainland. In Chapter 13, we will see that *Atanaarjuat* and his family lived in a neighbouring camp (Iksivautaujaak).

10   A wolf man (*Canis lupus*) or *amaruq* can be recognized by his long nose and by his hair cut short over his forehead.

11   See the preceding chapter for the episode where *Aningaq* is taken away in a kayak by a loon man.

12   Fulmars are rare in the Igloolik region but present on North Baffin coasts. They can be sighted, however, when migrating. According to Randa (1994), who studied Igloolik wildlife, the Iglulik Inuit distinguish between two types of fulmar: a light-coloured one and a dark-coloured one. The

latter are called *iggarlik* ("that which wears goggles"). Fulmars are characterized by their special call, *Ia-a-a-a*, which Inuit hear as sniggering.

13   *Arnaqquaksaq* means "an old woman in the making" in the old language. The term is no longer used in the Igloolik region, other than as a place name. It is the name of an old camp on Igloolik Island (Figure 17). It is also the heroine's name in the Greenlandic variants of this story.

14   Literally "former baby seals" (*Phoca hispida*) that are just a few months old. They are born during the lunar month of late March or early April, which bears their name (*Nattijjat*). Their fur is longer than that of adults. Fulmars especially love to prey on them.

15   See Chapter 5, note 8.

16   A similar pursuit is recounted in Chapter 7, when a girl betrothed to a whale tries to escape from it with her father's help.

17   *Urulu*, a female informant of Rasmussen (1929), adds in her variant that the father threw his daughter into the water so that the fulmar could snatch her by itself.

18   *Urulu*'s variant (Rasmussen 1929) speaks of *Uinigumasuittuq*'s sliced finger bones turning into *nattiit* (ringed seals, *Phoca hispida*), into *ujjuit* (bearded seals, *Erignathus barbatus*), and into *qilalugait* (belugas, *Delphinapterus leucas*). This variant does not mention her eyes being punctured.

19   Sonne (1990) suggests interpreting the severed hands or their equivalents by substitution. According to her, the hands should be seen as sealskin mittens and seal flippers, and as symbols of meat sharing among food-exchange partners. Other than the fact that Sonne ignores the existence of the "daughter with her hands chopped off" motif in the folklore of many peoples, a motif well-known to European folklorists, she does not see that human hands and seal flippers are both composed of little bones.

20   See *Mitiarjuk*'s novel *Sanaaq* (2014 [2002]), which describes some of the games in detail.

21   Although many elders use the term *Kannaaluk* in the dual form (*Kannaaluuk*) to mean the father and his daughter, it is also used in the singular to mean the daughter. She had the name of *Nuliajuk* ("The great wife") among the Aivilik, the Netsilik, and the Inuit encountered by Parry and Lyon at Iglulik camp in the early nineteenth century. She is called *Sedna* (more exactly *Sanna*, which means "The great one down below," as does *Kannaaluk*,) in southern and southeastern Baffin Island.

22   This is what Savard (1966, 1970) has shown by following the path cleared by Lévi-Strauss.

Chapter 6: A Cheated Husband and Thwarted Love in the Animal World

1   Farther west among the Natsilik Inuit, these stories are integrated into the adventures of the epic hero *Kiviuq*.

2   In summer, in this treeless inland region where caribou were hunted, kindling was essentially composed of plants from the heather family (*Ericaceae*), notably Arctic white heather, *itsuti*, a small resinous plant that burns very well. Women sometimes had to go far to gather enough. They used this kindling to cook meat in their stone pots.

3   The term is always used in the dual form, so I have translated it as "trousers."

4   *Ivaluarjuk*, the informant of Rasmussen (1929, 222), adds that she let it go up into her genitals.

5   These anatomical details reflect, in the Inuit way of thinking, what Lévi-Strauss (1978 [1968]) called a "theory of orifices." According to Randa (1994), *avingaq* is a generic term for several lemming species: *Lemmus*, *Dicrostonyx*, and *Synaptomys*. The first two are found in the Igloolik region. In this myth, the species is the northern collared lemming (*Dicrostonyx groenlandicus*) or *amiqslaq*, whose skin is stretchable, unlike the North American brown lemming (*Lemmus trimucronatus*) or *kajuji*. The ermine is a short-tailed weasel (*Mustela erminea*) or *tiriaq*, according to Randa (1994).

6   The lemming's skin was used for its curative properties. It was dried and then applied to a boil to draw out the pus. It is very thin and shrinks a lot when it dries.

7   The Arctic fox (*Alopex lagopus*) or *tiriganniaq* is a small fox species the size of a hare and weighing two and a half to five kilos. It is a fairly graceful animal with very dense, fragile fur. It feeds mainly on lemmings and white-tailed ptarmigan.

8   The wolverine (*Gulo luscus*) is the largest representative of the weasel family. It is stocky like a small brown bear, has thick fur, and is an unrivalled plunderer of meat caches. It escapes from all traps and is feared by Inuit. In Algonquian languages, its name means "He who has a bad character." It is carnivorous and can attack living animals but feeds mainly on scraps of meat. It is above all a scavenger whose glands secrete a musky scent with which it marks its territory. Its sense of smell is thus highly developed.

9   The wolverine is speaking ironically here, while choosing to ignore the warning it has been given. This animal plays a trickster role in native mythology throughout North America (Lévi-Strauss 1966 [1962]). In spite of warnings, it does as it sees fit. It is in fact a cunning animal that can escape from any trap set for it and plunder the most solid meat caches.

10 Randa (1994) assigned the mosquito to the *Culicidae* family (*kitturiaq*), the ground spider to the species *Alecopesa asivak* (*aasivak*), the wolverine to the species *Gulo luscus* (*qavvik*), and the wolf to the species *Canis lupus* (*amaruq*).

11 This happens in the film *Atanarjuat* when the hero defeats *Uqi*, his opponent in the song contest. He points his index finger at him and loudly farts (Saladin d'Anglure and Igloolik Isuma Productions 2002).

12 Eider ducks (*Somateria spectabilis*) and Canada geese (*Branta canadensis*) are migratory water birds that nest in Arctic lands in late spring and leave with their young in early autumn. Nonetheless, several eider duck colonies remain active year-round in the Arctic near seawater that is always ice-free. As in the last episode with the fox woman, the man is surprised to find an animal that has metamorphosed into a woman, but this time she is nude and bathing.

13 A bowhead whale (*Balaena mysticetus*) or *arviq* can be as long as thirty or so metres and weigh up to three metric tons per metre. It is the largest animal that Inuit traditionally hunted in Arctic waters. All of the Inuit are descended from bowhead whale hunters who became established along the Arctic coasts 1,000 years ago.

14 It is distinguished from the skin of a beluga or narwhal, which is called *mattaaq* in Igloolik (Randa 1994) see also Chapter 4 n13.

15 The *ujarasujjuit* (from *ujarak*, "stone") are most often large and therefore very heavy erratics. When travelling, Inuit would often make offerings to the spirit of the block to bring good luck.

16 Lévi-Strauss (1978 [1968]) took an interest in this hollow man, or tube man, who in other variants has big testicles or a long penis.

Chapter 7: Girls Should Not Play at Marriage

1   Randa (1994) identifies them in Igloolik as the Arctic sculpin of the *Cottidae* family (*Myoxocephalus scorpioides*).

2   Inuit oral tradition identifies many sacred sites. Inuit leaders have been demanding that government authorities recognize these sites, among other demands they have been making with other Indigenous peoples at the United Nations (Geneva). See Saladin d'Anglure (2004) and Morin (2004).

3   It was a bowhead whale, also called a Greenland right whale (*Balaena mysticetus*), well-known to the Iglulingmiut, whose waters are still home to this species in some parts of their territory. Overhunted by American whalers in the late nineteenth and the early twentieth centuries, the bowhead whale almost disappeared from the waters of Foxe Basin. For this reason, the Canadian government and the International Whaling Commission prohibited such hunting and classified the whale as a protected animal species (Saladin d'Anglure 2006c [1999], 2013). With recent growth of this population, it has become possible to set aside harvest quotas for the Inuit, who, as they see it, hunt the whale for subsistence and as one of the components of their identity. They succeeded in having their right to subsistence hunting enshrined in the Nunavut agreement they signed with the Canadian government. Ever since, management of this species has been under the responsibility of joint committees that have Inuit members.

4   In Inuktitut, the eagle is called *nakturalik*, from *nakturaq*, "hook," and *–lik*, "which has." Robbe (1994) reports that during his stay the Inuit of Ammassalik killed a Greenlandic white-tailed eagle (*Haliaetus albicilla groenlandicus*). Randa (personal communication) has confirmed that it belonged to the same species known to the Iglulik Inuit.

5   Notably by Davidialuk Alasuaq of Povungnituq (Nunavik); see Nungak and Arima (1969) and Saladin d'Anglure (1978c).

Chapter 8: A Battered Wife Chooses to Be Reborn in Animal Forms, Then as a Man

1   Several variants were published by Boas (1901) and Rasmussen (1929, 59–60; 1930b, 41–45). Blaisel (1993a and 1993b) analyzed the text of *Ivaluarjuk*'s second variant, which Rasmussen (1930b) had translated line by line.

2   See Bordin (2003) for an exhaustive lexicon of human anatomy, which may be applied with a few minor changes to other mammals.

3   See Rasmussen (1929, 141–43) for a good description of this technique and also Saladin d'Anglure (2006a [2001]).

4   On the correspondence between a kayak and a human body, see Saladin d'Anglure (1978a, 2001b [2000]) and Therrien (1987). A caribou breastbone, which here becomes the bow of a kayak, is called *uirniq*. This term comes from the root *uik* (husband) and also means the raised forward portion of a dogsled, as we saw in Chapter 5.

5   See in Chapter 4 of this book the loon that turns its body into a kayak, and in Chapter 5 the fulmar that does the same.

6   See also, by Blaisel (1993a), an analysis of *Ivaluarjuk*'s variant published by Rasmussen (1930b, 41–45).

Chapter 9: *Kaujjajjuk*, a Mistreated
Orphan Rescued by the Moon Man

1   This chapter includes a variant "*Kaujjajjuk*, A Mistreated Orphan Boy, Rescued by His Brother Shaman, *Igalaaq*." The word *Kaujjajjuk* is constructed from the root *kauk* (walrus skin). To simplify, I will translate his name here as "Walrus-Skin." Its form varies from one dialect to the next: in Nunavik, people say *Kaujjajjuk*.

2   This is also true for Nunavik, with the stories told by Davidialuk Alasuaq (Nungak and Arima 1969).

3   When the moon spirit is called *Aningaq* (literally "favourite brother") as in Chapter 4, I translate his name as Moon Brother. When he is called *Taqqiq* (which means "moon") as is the case here, I translate his name as Moon or Moon Man.

4   This detail is not unimportant. Communication with the moon spirit was easier during the winter full moon. In winter, the full moon is at its highest in the sky, and the sun is absent. This was the time of year and month when shamans during their community seances would go and visit him, or he would come down to earth.

5   In the Iglulingmiut belief system, *Kajurjuk* means "Aldebaran." This star is an old red dog on the dog team of a group of bear hunters (who became *Ullaktut*, Orion's Belt); see Figure 15 in Chapter 4.

6   See comments in Chapter 8 on the opposition between a space with footprints (inhabited by humans) and a space with no footprints (the space of spirits and prayer). See also Chapter 10, the woman who calls for help to Moon Brother in a place with no footprints.

7   This detail of fingers and hands worn to the bone appears earlier in the myth about a girl who chose an eagle to be her future husband and who slid down a rope of caribou sinew (Chapter 7).

8   The etymology of the term for shaman (*angakkuq*) remains unknown. Some authors believe it is constructed from the root *angak* (maternal uncle). It seems to me more convincing to derive it from the root *anga-*, which is found in the term *angajuq* (older brother, for a man; or older sister, for a woman). The same root appears in *angajuqqaq* (which means both parents, when in the dual form, or the chief). The maternal uncle may consequently be the man who has authority on the mother's side.

9   The igloo's windowpane may be made from lake ice, from the translucent skin of a walrus penis, or from a walrus intestine.

10   In the variant gathered by Boas (1901) from Cumberland Sound, Walrus-Skin has no siblings. He is a mistreated orphan, as in the first story told by *Kupaaq*. He sleeps in the entranceway with the dogs and has to do all of the hard, dirty chores, like taking the oil lamps outside and removing all of the dirt and residues. He has to clean the lamps and the stone cooking pots with his clothes, and he also has to empty the urine pails by using his teeth (as in the present story told by *Kupaaq* and in the one told by *Ivaluarjuk*). In distress, he calls for help from the Moon Man, who will be like an older brother to him. And the Moon Man comes to his rescue, accompanied by his wife [*sic*], as if a female presence were indispensable to the story unfolding as it should.

11   Again, see the example of this custom in the film *Atanarjuat*.

Chapter 10: The Danger of Being Impregnated by a Spirit When You Have a Jealous Husband

1   This myth is known from eastern Greenland to the west coast of Hudson Bay. Boas (1901) published a variant from Cumberland Sound and Rasmussen (1929, 87–88) another from the Igloolik region.

2   See Saladin d'Anglure (1988a) to learn more about these rites and the invocations (*qingarniit*) to spirits in such places.

3   When used for a dog, the name *Pualukittuq* may mean that the tips of its feet differ in colour from the rest of its fur.

4   The great spirits used animals that humans considered wild as domestic animals. This is attested in the beliefs of other peoples of the Americas and undoubtedly elsewhere around the world. See especially Saladin d'Anglure and Morin (1998) with regard to the Shipibo-Conibo of Peru's Amazonian region.

5   See Chapter 9. The number of bears that pull the Moon Man's sled varies, being one (Boas 1888), two (Boas 1901), or three (Rasmussen 1929; Kupaaq 1972).

6   In his much more detailed analysis of the myth collected by Eric Holtved (1951) from Thule (in northern Greenland), Savard (1966) identifies two attitudes of the Sun Woman: an aggressive attitude when she burns the edge of the hood of the nosy woman, who is guilty of breaking the limitations imposed by the Moon Man; and a friendly attitude, with sharing of secrets, when the two women later become sisters-in-law and, in a way, "co-wives." In another myth from Igloolik, the story of *Tutukatuk*, the Sun Woman confides that the many scars to be seen on her knees are due to human females breaking the rule against playing cat's cradle in the sun's presence: "When I try to go around the *Sila* [the firmament] and someone plays cat's cradle," said the Sun Woman, "the game makes me stumble, and my knees bear the marks of cuts due to the string games" (Kupaaq 1973).

7   Like laughter, untied laces are a symbol of openness. We have seen this in Chapter 8. For the same reason, a woman about to give birth would be asked to untie her bootlaces and her belt and refrain from playing cat's cradle, to make delivery easier (Saladin d'Anglure 2003a).

8   See the remarks by Lévi-Strauss (1969b [1964]) on repressed laughter and on the inability to hold back laughter.

9   Rémi Savard (1966) aptly showed these structural oppositions.

10   Inuit women had their faces tattooed with a design on the chin (*tadluruti*), a design on the cheeks (*uluaruti*) extending out from the mouth, and a design on the forehead (*qauruti*) extending out from the nasal root. They were also tattooed on the shoulders and the upper back, on the upper part of the breasts, and on the thighs down to the knees. In the Igloolik region, these tattoos were made by piercing the skin. The holes were then filled with a mixture of grease and soot.

11   See Saladin d'Anglure (1990a [1980c]). In the English version of this article, I identify certain androgynous characteristics that are consistent with the polar bear's mediating role between spirits and shamans. In the same vein, see the interesting paper by C. Trott (2006).

12   The Arctic fox, an underworld animal often associated with the world of women, also has certain androgynous characteristics and mediating functions, but on a smaller scale of existence than the polar bear's.

13   The story of *Tutukatuk* is about a pregnant woman who has broken a taboo by playing with small ringed seal bones (*inugait*). The Moon Man takes her to his home to make her aware of

the seriousness of her transgression. He then takes her back to earth when the time comes for her to give birth. He similarly continues to provide her with meat and lamp oil. In return, she is no longer supposed to touch meat brought by her husband, who becomes so resentful of his wife that she gives in to his pressuring and breaks her promise by eating his meat. Their child immediately becomes very ill. She pulls herself together quickly and henceforth scrupulously obeys all of the limitations decreed for women.

14 These tar residues, which could be used for tattooing, were symbolically considered to be the lamp's excrements.

Chapter 11: *Itirjuaq*, the First Woman Healer

1 Although women were a minority of all shamans—on average, one woman for every five men in the early twentieth century—female shamans did play a key role in Inuit society, according to the elders we interviewed (Saladin d'Anglure 1988a).

2 *Itirjuaq* appears under a somewhat different name, *Itirsiut*, likewise constructed from the root *itiq* (anus), in a Cumberland Sound myth published by Boas (1901). Boas did not speak the Inuit language and was helped by the Anglican missionary for translation.

3 This text was originally written by Rasmussen and then translated into Danish. Whenever he uses the word "man" or "men," I believe it would be better to translate as "human" or "person" in the singular and "humans" or "people" in the plural. There were men and women alike among shamans in all Inuit communities.

4 All of the elders I interviewed in Igloolik in 1972 used the term *itiujaq*. Randa (1994), who studied animal taxonomy in Igloolik, said Inuit now use the term *itiq* for a sea urchin.

5 Lévi-Strauss (1981 [1971] and 1996 [1991]) briefly mentions the power of farting in Amerindian myths but not its healing power.

6 An *isumataq* is a respected chief who is endowed with *isuma* (intelligence). An *angajuqqaaq* is a chief who is feared, i.e., someone who imposes himself by virtue of his authority, his physical strength, or his standing as an elder or forebear.

7 Some haziness nonetheless persists around the character *Itirjuaq* (described by *Iqallijuq* and *Kupaaq*) or *Itirsiut* (described by Boas). *Iqallijuq* uses the term *angakkuq* (shaman) when speaking of *Itirjuaq* and the term *tuurngaq* (helping spirit) for her sea urchin shell, which is identified at other times by the term *arnguaq* (amulet). *Kupaaq* speaks of *sakaniq* ("conducting a shamanic seance") for her healing operations.

Chapter 12: The Strange Man and His Whale

1 The Inuit of St. Lawrence Island belong to the Inuit Circumpolar Conference, like other Inuit groups elsewhere in the Arctic, and thus self-identify politically as Inuit. In their local speech, they call themselves Yupiit (plural of Yupik), which has the same meaning as Inuit (humans).

2 The section titles of this chapter were composed and inserted by Saladin d'Anglure to help guide the reader for comparisons with the last chapter and to add comments.

3 Grace Slwooko died on 14 March 2013, at the age of ninety-one. In 2004, I met her nephew Chris Petuwak Koonooka, a teacher of Yupik language and culture at Gambell High School, on St. Lawrence Island (Alaska). He was quite familiar with this myth and a Siberian variant.

4   At the same time, I was conducting my first fieldwork among the Inuit of Canada, several thousand kilometres to the east.

5   After administering Rorschach tests to Chukchi and Yupiit children in Chukotka, Jean Malaurie (1992), who seemed unfamiliar with Murphy's work, thought he could see a serious problem of doubt in the children's choice of sexual identification. He thought he could "observe traits relating to intrapsychic conflicts, linked very probably to repressed homosexuality." This conclusion is astonishing coming from a social science researcher who glosses over the distinctions between gender and sex, and between symbolic gender change and sexual orientation.

6   See the woman's parka that belonged to the shaman *Qingailisaq* from Iglulik, in Boas (1907) and Saladin d'Anglure (1986).

7   See Saladin d'Anglure (2001b [2000]) for first-time rites.

8   The term "parky" is a variant of the better known "parka" and was introduced into the Aleut language by the Russians, who in turn had adopted it from the Nenets. It originally meant any kind of fur coat, but among the Aleuts it referred to a kind of long shirt that went down to below the knees, with a standing collar and narrow sleeves. It was made from bird or seal skin and could be used both as clothing and as bedding (see Korsun 2013, 169–81).

9   Sternberg (1925) was the first to back up this hypothesis with Siberian data. See also Czaplicka (1914).

Chapter 13: *Atanaarjuat*, the Fast Runner: A Mythical Hero

1   Igloolik Isuma Productions is Canada's first independent Inuit film production company.

2   The heroes of this story, the two brothers—*Atanaarjuat*, the younger brother, and *Aamarjuaq*, the older one—were first written about in a book by Captain Lyon (1824), who, under the orders of Captain Parry, took part in an expedition to look for the Northwest Passage to the Far East, in 1821–23 (see Foreword). In his journal, Lyon lists the ten helping spirits of a shaman, *Tulimaq*, who became his friend during the long time he spent overwintering in the coastal ice floes of Igloolik Island. These spirits included "*Amug-yoo-a* [*Aamarjuaq*] and *Atta-na-ghiooa* [*Atanaarjuat*], two brothers, and as far as I can learn chief patrons of the country about Amityook [Amittuq]." The two brothers had therefore already become local heroes by that time. Amittuq does indeed mean the Igloolik region, in particular the part of the Melville Peninsula that faces Igloolik Island from the west.

3   The significance of these facts escaped Rasmussen's notice. In 2003, I learned from Nellie *Taptaqut* Kusugaq, in Rankin Inlet, that she was also named *Atanaarjuat* and that all of the *Taptaqut* of the region were *Atanaarjuat*. It may be that many of the Iglulingmiut (who lived farther north at the time of Parry and Lyon's expedition in 1822) later moved south to regions that whalers would visit and which had the first trading posts. They probably wanted easier access to imported Euro-American products, which they had discovered through contacts with explorers and then whalers.

4   These drawings and the English translation of the comments were gathered by T. Ryan in 1964 and published in Blodgett (1986).

5   Pingiqqalik is a hunting camp on the Melville Peninsula, a bit south of Igloolik Island. Ugliit is the name given to the islands where walruses had a habit of hauling themselves up when going from one place to another.

6   Referring to the bowhead whale (*Balaena mysticetus*), or *arviq* in Inuktitut. It can weigh as much as a metric ton for each foot of its length.

7   Bearded seal (*Erignathus barbatus*), or *ujjuk* in Inuktitut. This marine mammal can easily weigh as much as 250 kilograms.

Chapter 14: *Ataguttaaluk*, the Cannibal Forebear (or The Birth of a Myth)

1   As with the other stories in this book, I will primarily use the variants I have personally gathered and flesh them out with the other variants.

2   As noted previously in this book, Rasmussen (1929) believed they belonged to the same large group. I use the spelling Iglulik when talking about the old traditional camp and Igloolik for the new village that developed in the 1960s, about ten kilometres from the former site (see the Foreword of this book).

3   In Igloolik, this place is now more commonly called Inukturvik ("The place where someone ate human flesh"). Both names were obviously given after the events.

4   This was the term used by meat-sharing partners when they visited each other. It meant that when the hunter of one of the families killed a seal, he would give a bone with meat on it to his partner's family. This partner would reciprocate.

5   French missionaries propagated the Catholic faith to the far reaches of Iglulingmiut territory (Laugrand 2002).

Chapter 15: *Qisaruatsiaq*: Back to Her Mother's Womb

1   *Qisaruaq* is the name for a caribou's rumen, and the suffix *-tsiaq* means "beautiful" or "pretty."

2   I wish to thank *Qisaruatsiaq* for letting me use her account here.

3   This is undoubtedly the ground zero of sensory experience. Fetal life is generally experienced in terms of comfort, happiness, well-being, and a bit more specifically of warmth, safety, and carefreeness. There is a mixture of sensations (touch) and feelings.

4   The first verse is: "Amazing Grace, how sweet the sound, that saved a wretch like me. I once was lost but now am found, was blind, but now I see." This hymn is characterized by its serious tone and very harmonious melody.

Conclusion

1   I would also like to mention the names of several other colleagues and friends who later provided me with their support and with opportunities to discuss the progress of my research: Evelyne Lot-Falck, Françoise Héritier, Maurice Godelier, and Roberte Hamayon, not to mention my colleagues at Université Laval, where I continued my research from 1972 onward, notably Louis-Jacques Dorais.

2   See Saladin d'Anglure (1994b [1986]) on networks of spouse exchange among the Iglulingmiut during the first half of the twentieth century.

3   See Saladin d'Anglure 1994a (1981), 1994b (1986), 1988, 2001a, 2006a (2001), 2006b, 2015b, on shamanism and the "third gender" among the Inuit.

NOTES TO PAGES 291–296

Afterword

1   Five years earlier, C. Lévi-Strauss had written in the French introduction to his book
    Anthropologie structurale: "The Eskimo, while excellent technicians, are poor sociologists; the
    reverse is true of the natives of Australia" (1963 [1958], 3). As we have seen throughout the
    present book, there is an Inuit belief that ancestors can reincarnate when their names are given
    to newborn children. Such "namesaking" can reverse generations, and even genders, contrary to
    Freudian orthodoxy and Cartesian logic.

2   In 1975, it became the École des Hautes Études en Sciences Sociales (EHESS).

3   Pouillon undertook the Festschrift with the assistance of Canadian anthropologist Pierre
    Maranda, a fervent structuralist, who taught for two years at the Université de Paris X (Nanterre)
    and later became my colleague and friend in the anthropology department at Université Laval
    (Quebec City).

4   Twenty-four years later, Jean Pouillon, who had become my friend, met with me at the
    Laboratory of Social Anthropology shortly after the publication of my paper "The Inuit Third
    Gender" (2006d [1992]). He asked me, "Have you thought about applying your model to
    the boss?" He was pointing his finger at Claude Lévi-Strauss's office in the library mezzanine.
    I answered, "Yes, but I know nothing about his private life or his siblings." "He's an only
    son!" Pouillon exclaimed. To this I said, "Then I presume there's a good chance he belongs to the
    third gender. He has an androgynous first name, and he must have received a twofold investment
    from his parents, as the son they wished to have and as the daughter they didn't have." "You
    should talk to him about that!" he replied. I waited several months before doing so (cf. Afterword
    n11).

5   In 1984, with funding from the Service du Patrimoine autochtone of Quebec's Department
    of Cultural Affairs and Association Inuksiutiit Katimajiit Inc., a non-profit organization, I
    successfully published *Mitiarjuk*'s original *Sanaaq* manuscript in syllabics (1984), after offering
    her a standard author's contract that would provide her with royalties from her novel and from
    translations into other languages. My French translation was published in 2002 by Éditions Alain
    Stanké. For that version, I added a foreword (5–11), an afterword (279–286), and a glossary
    (287–301). It was a bestseller. In 2014, *Sanaaq* was also published in English by University of
    Manitoba Press.

6   In 1970, only the first three volumes of *Mythologiques* had come out in the original French, the
    fourth and final volume being in press (vol. 1, 1969b [1964]; vol. 2, 1983 [1966]; vol. 3, 1978
    [1968]).

7   Lévi-Strauss's courses fascinated and certainly influenced me, but I had more trouble with
    his books, which were incredibly rich in detail and unusually perceptive but at the same time
    crammed with tables and graphs from logic and mathematics, which were beyond the more
    classical education I had received. My disinterest was all the more justified because I heard Lévi-
    Strauss several times criticize how young researchers—including the ones in his own laboratory—
    felt obliged to go about proving their arguments the same way, rather than doing more in-depth
    ethnographic fieldwork and using the facilities available to their generation.

8   The leading Paris daily *Le Monde* reported on the originality of my article in its weekly
    supplement *Le Monde Campus*.

9   This section includes much of the keynote speech I presented at the 16th Inuit Studies
    Conference, University of Manitoba, Winnipeg, on 23 October 2008. After my presentation,
    my colleague and friend Dr. Christopher Trott, Warden and Vice-Chancellor of St. John's
    College, and David Carr, Director of University of Manitoba Press, offered to publish an English

translation of my book *Être et renaître Inuit, homme, femme ou chamane*. I wish to thank them here very much for this offer. Thanks also to Peter Frost, who agreed to translate the original French version.

10   Bem discovered that men or women who scored high on indices of both femininity and masculinity, whom she called androgynous, were better qualified than others to fill these positions because they were more flexible and better able to resolve conflicts. Her early papers appealed to me, but they were later severely criticized for their theoretical and methodological weaknesses.

11   When I questioned Claude Lévi-Strauss about the Inuit third gender and its probable existence in all societies, he answered right away, "But there aren't three genders. There are four: men who express strong masculinity; women who express strong femininity; men who express both masculinity and femininity; and women who express both femininity and masculinity." I countered, "I would classify your last two categories in the same category because both have an 'androgynous' profile that overlaps the gender boundary." I then asked him about the question I had raised with Jean Pouillon (cf. Afterword n4), and he replied, "That question should have been put to my mother, who died several years ago. . . . My first name is androgynous, and I'm a little like an *epikleros*." In ancient Greece, an *epikleros* was a daughter who inherited her father's estate because he had no son. I added that he had a woman's great sensitivity, as attested by the great importance he gave in his *Mythologiques* to the categories of the human senses, but he often concealed this sensitivity behind mathematical formulas. He smiled and said nothing more. In 2005, when Nicole Belmont provided him with the proofs of my book and asked him if he would agree to write a preface, he accepted. When she gave me the preface to read, I did not hide my joy. I saw therein his subtle agreement with my concept of a third gender associated with shamanism, and an answer to my investigations of the previous years. Was he not a great shaman of anthropology in the twentieth century?

12   Sorbonne, Paris, was where I had been invited to teach during the year 1980–81 on Inuit cosmology and shamanism.

13   In October 2016, I received an invitation from Cheng Du University (China) to accompany a Canadian delegation led by my colleague Marie-Françoise Guédon from the University of Ottawa [whom I thank here] to a symposium on ethno-cultural minorities. My paper was titled "The Ternary Logic of the Included Middle Present among the Inuit and the Taoist China, Opposed to the Binary Logic of the Excluded Middle of the Western Mind and Science." It aroused great curiosity on the part of graduate students and Chinese colleagues, who listened to it with great attention and asked me many questions.

Bibliography

Anand-Wheeler, Ingrid. 2002. *Terrestrial Mammals of Nunavut*. Government of Nunavut.

Atuat. 1968. Unpublished manuscript transcribed by Rev. P. Guy Mary-Rousselière and recounted to him by *Atuat* about the death by starvation of a party of Inuit travelling through Baffin Island and the sole survivor, *Ataguttaaluk*.

———. 1974. Entrevue en langue inuit. Interviewed by B. Saladin d'Anglure. Recording kept at Université Laval, Quebec City.

Bachoffen, Johann. 1861. *Das Mutterrecht*. Stuttgart: Krais and Hoffmann.

Badinter, Élisabeth. 1989. *Man/Woman: The One Is the Other*. Collins Harvill Press. Originally published in 1986 as *L'un est l'autre. Des relations entre hommes et femmes*. Paris: Odile Jacob.

Balandier, Georges. 1974. *Anthropo-logiques*. Paris: Librairie Générale Française, coll. Livre de poche.

Bastide, Roger. 1973. "Comportement sexuel et religion." In *Encyclopédie de la Sexualité*, 468–79. Paris: Éditions Universitaires.

Belmont, Nicole. 1971. *Les signes de la naissance. Étude des représentations symboliques associées aux naissances singulières*. Paris: Plon.

Bem, Sandra L. 1978. "Beyond Androgyny: Some Presumptuous Prescriptions for a Liberated Gender Identity." In *The Psychology of Women: Future Directions in Research*, edited by J.A. Sherman and F.L. Denmark, 1–23. New York: Psychological Dimensions.

Berndt, Catherine H. 1978. "Digging Sticks and Spears, or, the Two-Sex Model." In *Woman's Role in Aboriginal Society*. Australian Institute of Aboriginal Studies 36, Social Anthropology Series 6. Canberra.

Blaisel, Xavier. 1993a. "Trajet rituel: du harponnage à la naissance dans le mythe d'Arnaqtaaqtuq." *Études/Inuit/Studies* 17 (1): 15–46.

———. 1993b. "La chair et l'os: espace cérémoniel et temps universel chez les Inuit du Nunavut (Canada), les valeurs coutumières inuit et les rapports rituels entre humains, gibiers, esprits et forces de l'univers." PhD diss., EHESS, Paris.

———. 1994. "La logique du don dans le mythe inuit de la lune et du soleil." *Religiologiques* 10: 111–41.

Blodgett, Jean, ed. 1986. *North Baffin Drawings: Collected by Terry Ryan on North Baffin Island in 1964.* Toronto: Art Gallery of Ontario.

Boas, Franz. 1888. *The Central Eskimo.* Sixth Annual Report of the Bureau of Ethnology, Smithsonian Institution, Washington. Reprinted in 1964, Lincoln: University of Nebraska Press.

———. 1901. *The Eskimo of Baffin Island and Hudson Bay.* Bulletin of the American Museum of Natural History 15:1. New York: American Museum of Natural History.

———. 1904. "The Folklore of the Eskimo." *Journal of American Folklore* 17: 1–13. Reproduced in Franz Boas, *Race, Language, Culture,* 1955.

———. 1907. *The Eskimo of Baffin Island and Hudson Bay.* Bulletin of the American Museum of Natural History 15:2. New York: American Museum of Natural History.

———. 1910. "Ethnological Problems in Canada." *Journal of the Royal Anthropological Institute of Great Britain and Ireland* 40: 529–39.

Bordin, Guy. 2003. *Lexique analytique de l'anatomie humaine – Analytical lexicon of human anatomy: Inuktitut-Français-English.* Louvain and Dudley, MA: Peeters.

———. 2015. *Beyond Darkness and Sleep: The Inuit Night in North Baffin Island.* Leuven: Peeters. Originally published in 2002 as "La nuit inuit. Éléments de réflexion," in *Études/Inuit/Studies* 26 (1): 45–70.

Bradbury, R.E. 1966. "Fathers, Elders, and Ghosts in *Edo* Religion." In *Anthropological Approaches to the Study of Religion,* edited by M. Banton, 127–74. London: Tavistock.

Briggs, Jean L. 1974. "Eskimo Women: Makers of Men." In *Many Sisters: Women in Cross-Cultural Perspective,* edited by C.J. Matthiasson, 261–304. New York: Free Press.

———. 1991. "Expecting the Unexpected: Canadian Inuit Training for an Experimental Lifestyle." *Ethos: Journal of the Society for Psycological Anthropology* 19 (3): 259–87.

Carpenter, Edmund S. 1968. "The Timeless Present in the Mythology of the Aivilik Eskimos." In *Eskimo of the Canadian Arctic,* edited by V.F. Valentine and F.G. Vallée, 39–42. Toronto: McClelland and Stewart.

Chiñas, Beverley. 1985. "Isthmus Zapotec 'Berdaches.'" *Newsletter of the Anthropological Research Group on Homosexuality,* May, 1–4.

Corin, Ellen. 1986. "Centralité des marges et dynamiques des centres." *Anthropologie et Sociétés* 10 (2): 1–21.

Crantz, David. 1767. *The History of Greenland: Containing a Description of the Country, and Its Inhabitants; and Particularly, a Relation of the Mission Carried on for above These Thirty Years by the Unitas Fratrium, at New Herrnhuth and Lichtenfels, in that Country.* 2 vols. London: Printed for the Brethren's Society for the Furtherance of the Gospel among the Heathen and Sold by J. Dodsley.

Czaplicka, M.A. 1914. *Aboriginal Siberia: A Study in Social Anthropology.* London: Oxford University Press.

Damas, David. 1971. *Igluligmiut Kinship and Local Grouping: A Structural Approach*. National Museum of Canada, Bulletin 196, Anthropological Series 64. Ottawa: Department of Northern Affairs and National Resources.

Descola, Philippe. 2013. *Beyond Nature and Culture*. Translated by Janet Lloyd. Foreword by Marshall Sahlins. Originally published in 2005 as *Par-delà Nature et Culture*. Paris: Gallimard.

Detienne, Marcel, and Jean-Pierre Vernant. 1991. *Cunning Intelligence in Greek Culture and Society*. Translated by Janet Lloyd. Chicago: University of Chicago Press. Originally published in 1974 as *Les ruses de l'intelligence. La métis des Grecs*. Paris: Flammarion.

Dorais, Louis-Jacques. 2010. *Language of the Inuit: Syntax, Semantics, and Society in the Arctic*. McGill-Queen's Native and Northern Series. Montreal: McGill-Queen's University Press. Originally published in 1996 as *La parole inuit. Langue, culture et société dans l'Arctique nord-américain*. SELAF 354, collection Arctique. Paris: Peeters.

Douglas, Mary. 1978. "Judgments on James Frazer." *Daedalus* 107 (4): 151–64.

Dumont, Louis. 1986. *Essays on Individualism: Modern Ideology in Anthropological Perspective*. Chicago: University of Chicago Press. Originally published in 1983 as *Essai sur l'individualisme. Une perspective anthropologique sur l'idéologie moderne*. Paris: collection Esprit, Éditions du Seuil.

Eber, Dorothy H., and P. Pitseolak. 1975. *People from Our Side*. Montreal: McGill-Queen's University Press.

Eliade, Mircéa. 1964. *Shamanism: Archaic Techniques of Ecstacy*. Princeton, NJ: Princeton University Press. Originally published in 1951 as *Le chamanisme et les techniques archaïques de l'extase*. Paris: Payot.

Ettuk, Jimmy. 1964. Comments for drawings about the epic of *Atanaarjuat*. Gathered by T. Ryan in 1964 and published in Blodgett (1986).

Fienup-Riordan, Ann. 1983. *The Nelson Island Eskimo: Social Structure and Ritual Distribution*. Anchorage: Alaska Pacific University Press.

———. 1994. *Boundaries and Passages: Rule and Ritual in Yup'ik Eskimo Oral Tradition*. Norman: University of Oklahoma Press.

Fitzhugh, William, and Susan Kaplan. 1982. *Inua: Spirit World of the Bering Strait Eskimo*. Washington, DC: Smithsonian Institution Press for The National Museum of Natural History.

Frazer, James G. 1907. *Adonis, Attis, Osiris: Studies in the History of Oriental Religion*. London: MacMillan.

Freuchen, Peter. 1935. *Arctic Adventure: My Life in the Frozen North*. New York: Farrar and Rinehart.

Gaignebet, Claude, and M.C. Florentin. 1974. *Le carnaval, essai de mythologie populaire*. Paris: Payot.

Geertz, Clifford. 1966. "Religion as a Cultural System." In *Anthropological Approaches to the Study of Religion*, edited by M. Banton, 1–46. London: Tavistock.

Gessain, Robert. 1978. "L'Homme-Lune dans la mythologie des Ammassalimiut." In *Systèmes de signes: textes réunis en hommage à Germaine Dieterlen*. Paris: Hermann ("Anthropologie").

Giffen, Naomi M. 1930. *The Roles of Men and Women in Eskimo Culture*. Chicago: University of Chicago Press.

Guemple, Lee. 1969. "The Eskimo Ritual Sponsor: A Problem in the Fusion of Semantic Domains." *Ethnology* 8 (4): 468–83.

———. 1976. "The Institutional Flexibility of Inuit Social Life." In *Inuit Land Use and Occupancy Project: A Report*. Vol. 2, *Supporting Studies*, edited by M. Freeman, 181–86. Ottawa: Indian and Northern Affairs.

Holtved, Eric. 1951. "The Polar Eskimos: Langage and Folklore I." *Meddellelser om Grönland*, bd. 152, no. 1.

Hooper, W.H., Lt. 1823. *Manuscript Journal 1821–1823*. Original manuscript preserved at the Royal Geographical Society, London, England.

Hutchinson, Ellen. 1977. "Order and Chaos in the Cosmology of the Baffin Island Eskimo." *Anthropology* 1 (2): 120–38.

Inuksuk, Aipili. 1991. Interviews recorded in Inuktitut by B. Saladin d'Anglure in Igloolik. Fonds BSA, Université Laval, Quebec City.

Iqallijuq, Rose. 1971–90. Interviews recorded in Inuktitut by B. Saladin d'Anglure in Igloolik. Fonds BSA, Université Laval, Quebec City.

Jacobs, Sue-Ellen. 1983. "Comment on 'the North American Berdache.'" *Current Anthropology* 24: 459–60.

Kleivan, Inge. 1971. "Why Is the Raven Black? An Analysis of an Eskimo Myth." *Acta Arctica,* Fas. 17. Arktisk Institut, Copenhagen: Munskgaard.

Korsun, S.A. 2013. "Fieldwork on the Commander Islands Aleuts." *Alaska Journal of Anthropology* 11 (1 and 2): 169–81.

Kublu, Alexina. 2000. "Aningagiik." In *Interviewing Inuit Elders: Saullu Nakasuk, Hervé Paniaq, Elisapi Ootoova, Pauloosi Angmaalik,* edited by J. Oosten and F. Laugrand, 162–81. Iqaluit, NU: Nunavut Arctic College.

Kublu, Alexina, and Jarich Oosten. 1999. "Changing Perspectives of Name and Identity Among the Inuit of Northeast Canada." In *Arctic Identities: Continuity and Change in Inuit and Saami Societies,* edited by J. Oosten and C. Remie, 56–78. Leiden: Research School CNWS, Leiden University.

Kupaaq, Michel. 1972. "Mythes et legendes d'Igloolik I." Recorded by B. Saladin d'Anglure in Igloolik, transcribed in standardized spelling, and translated into French. Manuscript. Université Laval, Quebec City, and National Museums of Canada.

———. 1973. "Mythes et legendes d'Igloolik II." Recorded by B. Saladin d'Anglure in Igloolik, transcribed in standardized spelling, and translated into French. Manuscript. Université Laval, Quebec City, and National Museums of Canada.

———. 1974. "Entrevues en Inuktitut." Conducted in Igloolik by B. Saladin d'Anglure, kept at Université Laval, Quebec City.

———. 1990. "Entrevues en Inuktitut." Conducted in Igloolik by B. Saladin d'Anglure, kept at Université Laval, Quebec City.

Laugrand, Frédéric. 2002. *Mourir et renaître. La reception du christianisme par les Inuit de l'Actique de l'Est canadien.* Québec. Les Presses de l'Université Laval.

Laugrand, Frédéric, and J.G. Oosten. 2007. "Bears and Dogs in Canadian Inuit Cosmology." In *La nature des esprits dans les cosmologies autochtones,* edited by J. Oosten and F. Laugrand, 353–86. Québec: Les Presses de l'Université Laval.

———. 2008. *The Sea Woman: Sedna in Inuit Shamanism and Art in the Eastern Arctic.* Fairbanks, AK: University of Alaska Press.

Lévi-Strauss, Claude. 1948. "La vie familiale et sociale des Indiens Nambikwara." *Journal de la Société des Américanistes* 37 (1): 1–132.

———. 1963. *Structural Anthropology*. Translated by C. Jacobson and Brooke Grundfest Schoepf. New York: Basic Books. Originally published in 1958 as *Anthropologie Structurale*. Paris: Plon.

———. 1966. *The Savage Mind*. Translated by John Weightman and Doreen Weightman. Chicago: University of Chicago Press. Originally published in 1962 as *La pensée sauvage*. Paris: Plon.

———. 1969a. *The Elementary Structures of Kinship*. Translated by James Harle Bell and John Richard von Sturmer. Edited by Rodney Needham. Boston: Beacon Press. Originally published in 1949 as *Les Structures élémentaires de la parenté*. Paris: Presses Universitaires de France.

———. 1969b. *The Raw and the Cooked*. Translated by John Weightman and Doreen Weightman. Chicago: University of Chicago Press. Originally published in 1964 as *Le cru et le cuit, Mythologiques* 1, Paris: Plon.

———. 1977a. "*Iqallijuq* ou les reminiscences d'une âme-nom inuit." *Études/Inuit/Studies* 1 (1): 33–63.

———. 1977b. "Mythes de la femme et pouvoir de l'homme chez les Inuit de l'Arctique central." *Anthropologie et Sociétés* 3: 79–98.

———. 1978. *The Origin of Table Manners*. Translated by John Weightman and Doreen Weightman. Chicago: University of Chicago Press. Originally published in 1968 as *L'origine des manières de table, Mythologiques* 3. Paris: Plon.

———. 1981. *The Naked Man*. Translated by John Weightman and Doreen Weightman. Chicago: University of Chicago Press. Originally published in 1971 as *L'homme nu, Mythologiques* 4. Paris: Plon.

———. 1983. *From Honey to Ashes*. Chicago: University of Chicago Press. Originally published in 1966 as *Du miel au cendres, Mythologiques* 2. Paris: Plon.

———. 1988. *The Jealous Potter*. Translated by Benedicte Chorier. Chicago: University of Chicago Press. Originally published in 1985 as *La potière jalouse*. Paris: Plon.

———. 1996. *The Story of Lynx*. Translated by Catherine Tihanyi. Chicago: University of Chicago Press. Originally published in 1991 as *Histoire de Lynx*. Paris: Plon.

Loyer, Emmanuelle. 2015. *Lévi-Strauss*. Paris: Flammarion.

Lyon, George F. 1824. *The Private Journal of Captain G.F. Lyon of H.M.S. Hecla, During the Recent Voyage of Discovery under Captain Parry*. London: John Murray.

MacDonald, John. 1993. "Tauvijjuaq: The Great Darkness." *Inuit Art Quarterly* 8 (2): 19–25.

———. 1998. *The Arctic Sky: Inuit Astronomy, Star Lore, and Legend*. Toronto: Royal Ontario Museum/Nunavut Research Institute.

Malaurie, Jean. 1992. "Note sur l'homosexualité et le chamanisme chez les Tchouktches et les Esquimaux d'Asie." *Nouvelle revue d'Ethnopsychiatrie* 19: 173–214.

———. 2001. *Call of the North: An Explorer's Journey to the North Pole*. New York: Harry N. Abrams. Originally published in 2001 as *L'appel du Nord: une ethnographie des Inuit, du Groenland à la Sibérie (1950–2000)*. Paris: Les Éditions de la Martinière.

Mary-Rousselière, Guy (Rév. P.). 1969a. *Les jeux de ficelle des Arviligjuarmiut*. Bulletin 233, Anthropological Series 88. Ottawa: National Museums of Canada.

———. 1969b. "L'histoire d'un cas de cannibalisme en terre de Baffin." *Eskimo* 81: 6–23.

Mauss, Marcel, with the assistance of Henri Beuchat. 1979. *Seasonal Variations of the Eskimo: A Study in Social Morphology*. London: Routledge and Keagan. Originally published in 1906 as *Essai sur les variations saisonnières des sociétés Eskimos: Étude de morphologie sociale, L'année sociologique*, published and edited by E. Durkheim. Paris: Felix Alcan.

McBroom, Patricia A. 1986. *The Third Sex: The New Professional Woman*. New York: William Morrow.

Mead, Margaret. 1935. *Sex and Temperament in Three Primitive Societies*. New York: William Morrow.

Mitiarjuk Nappaaluk, Salomé. 1984. *Sanaaq: Sanaakkut Piusiviningita Unikkausinnguangit*. Edited by Mitiarjuup Allatangit and B. Saladin d'Anglure. Inuksiutiit allaniagait 3, Inuktitut Syllabics. Inuksiutiit Katimajiit Inc. Université Laval. CIÉRA.

————. 1994. "The Inuit Encyclopedia of *Mitiarjuk*." Collected, transliterated from Inuktitut, and translated by B. Saladin d'Anglure. *Tumivut* 5: 73–80.

————. 2014. *Sanaaq: An Inuit Novel*. Translated from French into English by Peter Frost. Winnipeg: University of Manitoba Press. Transliterated from Inuktitut into Latin script and then translated into French and edited by Bernard Saladin d'Anglure. Originally published in French in 2002 as *Sanaaq, roman*. Montreal: Éditions Alain Stanké.

Morgan, Lewis H. 1871. *Systems of Consanguinity and Affinity of the Human Family*. Washington, DC: Smithsonian Contributions to Knowledge.

Morin, Françoise. 2004. "La protection des noms de lieux et des sites sacrés telle que préconisée par diverses instances internationales." *Études/Inuit/Studies* 28 (2): 203–9.

Morin, Françoise, and Bernard Saladin d'Anglure. 2006. "Sexualité et Religion: le mariage mystique des chamanes." *Bastidiana* 53–54: 79–93.

————. 2007. "Excision féminine/incision masculine, ou la construction sociale de la personne chez les Shipibo-Conibo d'Amazonie péruvienne." In *La personne et le genre en sociétés matrilinéaires et uxorilocales*, edited by N.-C. Mathieu, 120–45. Paris: Éditions de l'École des Hautes Études en Sciences Sociales.

Murdock, George P. 1949. *Social Structure*. New York: MacMillan.

Murphy, Jane. 1974. "Psychotherapeutic aspects of shamanism on St. Lawrence Island, Alaska." In *Magic, Faith and Healing: Studies in Primitive Psychiatry Today*, edited by Ari Kiev, 61–69. New York: MacMillan/Free Press.

Nungak, Zebedee, and Eugene Arima, eds. 1969. *Unikkaatuat: Eskimo Stories from Povungnituk, Quebec*. Bulletin 235. Ottawa: National Museums of Canada.

Oosten, Jarich G. 1976. "The Theoretical Structure of the Religion of the Netsilik and Iglulik." Ph.D. diss., University of Groningen. Krips Repro-Meppel.

————. 1983. "The Incest of Sun and Moon: An Examination of the Symbolism of Time and Space in Two Iglulik Myths." *Études/Inuit/Studies* 7 (1): 143–51.

————. 1989. "Theoretical Problems in the Study of Inuit Shamanism." In *Shamanism: Past and Present*, 2 vols., edited by M. Hoppál and O.J. von Sadovski, 331–42. Budapest: ISTOR Books.

————. 2002. "Kiviuq: An Epic in the Making?" *Anthropologie et Sociétés*, 26 (2–3): 71–90.

Oosten, Jarich, and Frédéric Laugrand, eds. 1999. *The Transition to Christianity*. Vol. 1, *Inuit Perspectives on the 20th Century*. Iqaluit, NU: Nunavut Arctic College.

————. 2002a. "Canicide and Healing: The Position of the Dog in the Inuit Cultures of the Canadian Arctic." *Anthropos* 97: 89–105.

———. 2002b. *Inuit Qaujimajatuqangit: Shamanism and Reintegrating Wrongdoers into the Community*. Vol. 4, Inuit Perspectives on the 20th Century. Iqaluit, NU: Nunavut Arctic College.

———. 2007. "Bears and Dogs in Canadian Inuit Cosmology." In *La nature des esprits dans les cosmologies autochtones/Nature of Spirits in Aboriginal Cosmologies*, edited by Frédéric B. Laugrand and Jarich G. Oosten, 353–86. Quebec City: Presses de l'Université Laval, Collection Mondes Autochtones.

Oosten, Jarich, Frédéric Laugrand, and Wim Rasing (eds). 1999. *Perspectives on Traditional Law*. Interviewing Inuit Elders, Vol. 2. Iqaluit: Arctic College/Nortext.

Oswalt, Wendell H. 1979. *Eskimos and Explorers*. San Francisco: Chandler and Sharp.

Paniaq, Hervé. 1997. A variant of the epic of *Atanaarjuat*, recounted to Igloolik Isuma Productions.

Parry, Sir William E. 1824. *Journal of a Second Voyage for the Discovery of a North-west Passage from the Atlantic to the Pacific: Performed in the Years 1821–22–23, in His Majesty's Ships Fury and Hecla*. London: John Murray.

Piaget, Jean. 1971. *The Psychology of Intelligence*. London: Routledge. Originally published in 1947 as *La psychologie de l'intelligence*, Paris: Armand Colin.

Piugaattuq, Nua. 1990. Interviews recorded in Inuktitut by B. Saladin d'Anglure in Igloolik. Fonds BSA, Université Laval, Quebec City.

Poole, Fitz J.P. 1981. "Transforming 'Natural' Woman: Female Ritual Leaders and Gender Ideology among Bimin-Kiskusmin." In *Sexual Meanings: The Cultural Construction of Gender and Sexuality*, edited by S.B. Ortner and H. Whitehead, 116–65. Cambridge: Cambridge University Press.

Pouillon, Jean, and Pierre Maranda, eds. 1970. Échanges et communications: *Mélanges offerts à C. Lévi-Strauss à l'occasion de son 60e anniversaire*. 2 vols. Paris: Mouton.

Quassa, François. 1998. A variant of the epic of *Atanaarjuat*, recounted to Igloolik Isuma Productions.

Rabelais, François. 1684. *The Fourth Book of Pantagruel*. Translated by Thomas Urquhart and Peter Antonny Motteux. Originally published in 1552 as *LE* — *QVART LIVRE des Faicts et dits Héroiques du bon Pantagruel*. A Paris, de l'imprimerie de Michel Fezandat, au mont S. Hilaire, à l'hostel d'Albret.

Radcliffe-Brown, A. 1940. "On Joking Relationships." *Africa* 13 (3): 195–210.

Randa, Vladimir. 1986a. *L'ours polaire et les Inuit*. Paris: SELAF.

———. 1986b. "Au croisement des espaces et des destins: Nanuq 'marginal exemplaire': un cas de médiation animale dans l'arctique central canadien." Special anniversary issue, "On the Borders of Gender," *Études/Inuit/Studies* 10 (1–2): 159–69.

———. 1994. "Inuillu uumajuillu: les animaux dans les savoirs, les représentations et la langue des Iglulingmiut (Arctique oriental canadien)." Ph.D. diss., Paris: École des Hautes Études en Sciences Sociales.

Rasmussen, Knud. 1929. "Intellectual Culture of the Iglulik Eskimos." *Report of the Fifth Thule Expedition, 1921–1924*, 7 (1). Copenhagen.

———. 1930a. "Observations on the Intellectual Culture of the Caribou Eskimos." *Report of the Fifth Thule Expedition, 1921–1924*, 7 (2). Copenhagen.

———. 1930b. "Iglulik and Caribou Eskimo Texts." *Report of the Fifth Thule Expedition 1921–1924*, 7 (3). Copenhagen.

———. 1931. "The Netsilik Eskimos: Social Life and Spiritual Culture." *Report of the Fifth Thule Expedition, 1921–1924*, 8 (1). Copenhagen.

———. 1932. "Intellectual Culture of the Copper Eskimos." *Report of the Fifth Thule Expedition, 1921–1924*, 9. Copenhagen.

———. 1998. (based on the author's manuscripts) *Contes inuit du Groenland*. Translated from Danish by Jacques Privat. Paris: Hachette Littératures.

Robbe, Pierre. 1994. *Les Inuit d'Ammassalik, chasseurs de l'Arctique*. Mémoires du Muséum d'Histoire naturelle159, Ethnologie. Paris: Éditions de Muséum.

Sahlins, Marshall. 1968. "Notes on the Original Affluent Society." In *Man the Hunter*, edited by R. Lee and I. De Vore, 85–89. Chicago: Aldine.

———. 1976. *Stone Age Economics*. Chicago and New York: Aldine.

Saladin d'Anglure, Bernard. 1977a. "*Iqallijuq* ou les réminiscences d'une âme-nom inuit." *Études/Inuit/Studies* 1 (1): 33–63.

———. 1977b. "Mythe de la femme et pouvoir de l'homme chez les Inuit de l'Arctique central." *Anthropologie et Sociétés* 1 (3): 79–98.

———. 1978a. "L'homme (angut), le fils (irniq), et la lumière (qau), ou le cercle du pouvoir masculin chez les Inuit de l'arctique central canadien." *Anthropologica*, new series, 20 (1–2): 101–44.

———. 1978b. "Entre cri et chant: Les Katajjait un genre musical féminin." *Études/Inuit/Studies* 2 (1): 85–94.

———. 1978c. *La parole changée en pierre. Vie et œuvre de Daividialuk Alasuaq, artiste inuit du Québec arctique*. Prepared in conjunction with Richard Baillargeon, Jimmy Innaarulik Mark, and Louis-Jacques Dorais. Les Cahiers du Patrimoine 11. Quebec City: Ministère des affaires culturelles.

———. 1980a. "'Petit-ventre,' l'enfant-géant du cosmos inuit (Ethnographie de l'enfant et enfance de l'ethnographie dans l'Arctique central inuit)." *L'Homme* 20 (1): 7–46.

———. 1980b. "Violences et enfantements, ou les nœuds de la vie dans le fil du temps." Special issue, "L'usage social des enfants," *Anthropologie et sociétés* 4 (2): 65–99.

———. 1981. "Le syndrome chinois de l'Europe nordique entre le temps de l'astrolabe et l'espace du chronomètre." Special issue, "Voyage au pays de l'altérité," *L'Ethnographie* 76 (81–82): 175–221.

———. 1983. "*Ijiqqat*: voyage au pays de l'invisible inuit." *Études/Inuit/Studies* 7 (1): 67–84.

———. 1984a. "L'idéologie de Malthus et la démographie mythique des Inuit d'Igloolik." *Malthus hier et aujourd'hui. Congrès International de démographie historique*, edited by A. Fauve-Chamoux, 167–73. Paris: Éditions du CNRS.

———. 1984b. "The Route to China Northern Europe's Arctic Delusions." *ARCTIC* 37 (4): 446–52.

———. 1985. "Du projet PARADI (parenté, adoption, identité) au sexe des Anges, notes et débats autour d'un troisième sexe." Special issue, "Parentés au Québec," *Anthropologie et Sociétés* 9 (3): 139–76.

———. 1986. "Du fœtus au chamane, la construction d'un troisième sexe inuit." *Études/Inuit/Studies* 10 (1–2): 25–113. [See 1994b for a shorter version translated into English.]

———. 1988a. "Penser le féminin chamanique, ou le tiers-sexe des chamanes inuit. Special issue, "Chamanisme dans les Amériques," *Recherches amérindiennes au Québec* 18 (2–3): 19–50.

———. 1988b. "Kunut et les angakkut iglulik (des chamanes, des mythes et des tabous, ou les premiers défis de Rasmussen en terre inuit canadienne)." Special issue on Knud Rasmussen, *Études/Inuit/ Studies* 12 (1–2): 57–80.

———. 1988c. "Enfants nomades au pays des Inuit Iglulik." *Anthropologie et Sociétés* 12 (2): 125–66.

———. 1990a. "Nanook, Super-Male: The Polar Bear in the Imaginary Space and Social Time of the Inuit of the Canadian Arctic. In *Signifying Animals: Human Meaning in the Natural World*, edited by R. Willis, 169–85. London: Routledge. Originally published in 1980 as "L'ours blanc dans l'espace imaginaire et le temps social des Inuit de l'Arctique central canadien." Special issue, "L'Ours, l'autre de l'homme," *Études mongoles et sibériennes* 11: 63–94.

———. 1991. "Le chamanisme inuit, comme ancienne technologie de la reproduction." In *Se reproduire, est-ce bien naturel?* Cahiers du GRIEF 5: 57–77. Groupe de Recherche Interdisciplinaire d'Études des Femmes, Presses de l'Université Toulouse-le-Mirail.

———. 1992. "Au clair de la lune circumpolaire, la cosmologie des Inuit." *Interface* 13 (6): 14–28.

———. 1993a. "Brother Moon, Sister Sun, and the Direction of the World: From Arctic Cosmography to Inuit Cosmology." In *Religion and Ecology in Northern Eurasia and North America*, edited by T. Irimoto, 187–212. Tokyo: University of Tokyo Press. Originally published in French in a more extended version in 1990 as "Frère-Lune (Taqqiq), sœur-Soleil (Siqiniq) et l'intelligence du monde (Sila)." *Études/Inuit/Studies* 14 (1–2): 75–119.

———. 1993b. "The Shaman's Share, or Inuit Sexual Communism in the Canadian Central Arctic." *Anthropologica* 35: 59–103. Translated by Jane Philibert from the original 1989 French version, "La part du chamane ou le communisme sexuel inuit dans l'Arctique central canadien." *Journal de la Société des Américanistes* 75: 132–71.

———. 1993c. "Sila, the Ordering Principle of the Inuit Cosmology." In *Shamans and Cultures: The Regional Aspects of Shamanism*, edited by M. Hoppál and K. Howard, 210–25. Budapest: Akadémaia Kéido; Los Angeles: International Society for Trans-Oceanic Research.

———. 1994a. "The Mythology of the Inuit of the Central Arctic." In *American, African and Old European Mythologies*, edited by Y. Bonnefoy, 25–32. Translated by W. Doniger. Chicago: The University of Chicago Press. Originally published in 1981 as "Esquimaux: La mythologie des Inuit de l'Arctique central nord-américain." In *Dictionnaire des mythologies*, edited by Yves Bonnefoy, 379–86. Paris: Armand Colins.

———. 1994b. "From Fetus to Shaman, the Construction of an Inuit Third Sex." In *Amerindian Rebirth*, edited by A. Mill and R. Slobodin, 82–106. Toronto: University of Toronto Press. Originally published in 1986 in a longer French version as "Du fœtus au chamane, la construction d'un troisième sexe inuit." *Études/Inuit/Studies* 10 (1–2): 25–113.

———. 1996. "Shamanism." In *Encyclopedia of Social and Cultural Anthropology*, edited by Alan Barnard and Jonathan Spencer, 504–8. London and New York: Routledge.

———. 1998. "Entre forces létales et forces vitales, les tribulations du fœtus et de l'enfant inuit." In *Le fœtus, le nourrisson et la mort fœtus et de l'enfant inuit*, edited by F. Zonabend and C. Le Grand Sébille, 55–76. Paris: L'Harmattan.

———, ed. 2001a. *Cosmology and Shamanism*. Interviewing Inuit Elders 4: Mariano and Tulimaaq Aupilaarjuk, Lucassie Nutaraaluk, Rose *Iqallijuq*, Johanasi *Ujarak*, Isidore *Ijituuq*, and Michel *Kupaaq*. Iqaluit, NU: Nunavut Arctic College.

———. 2001b. "*Pijariurniq*: Performances and Inuit Rites of the First Time." In *Inuit Identities in the Third Millenium*, edited by Louis-Jacques Dorais, 34–59. Quebec City: Association Inuksiutiit

Katimajiit. Originally published in 2000 as *"Pijariurniq*. Performances et rituels inuit de la première fois." *Études/Inuit/Studies* 24 (2): 89–113.

———. 2002. "Rethinking Inuit Shamanism through the Concept of 'Third Gender.'" In *Shamanism: A Reader*, edited by Graham Harvey, 235–41. London and New York: Routledge. Originally published in 1992 in *Northern Religions and Shamanism*, edited by M. Hoppál and J. Pentikaïnen. Ethnologica Uralica 3. Helsinki: Finnish Literature Society; Budapest: Akadémaia Kéido.

———. 2003a. "String Games of the Kangirsujuaq Inuit (with comparative notes by Guy Mary-Rousselière)." Translation and appendix by J. D'Antoni and M. Sherman. *Bulletin of the International String Figure Association* 10: 78–199.

———. 2003b. "Ethnographic commentary." In *Atanarjuat, The Fast Runner*. Collective book in English and Inuktitut, written in collaboration with P.A. Angilirq, Z. Kunuk, H. *Paniaq*, P. Qulitalik, and N. Cohn. Toronto: Coach House Books and Isuma Publishing. [My comments are translated from extracts of the original 2002 book published as *Au pays des Inuit, un film, un peuple, une légende: Atanarjuat, la légende de l'homme rapide*, produced in conjunction with Igloolik Isuma Productions. Montpellier: Indigène Éditions.]

———. 2004. "La toponymie religieuse et l'appropriation symbolique du territoire par les Inuit du Nunavik et du Nunavut." *Études/Inuit/Studies* 28 (2): 107–31.

———. 2005. "The 'Third Gender' of the Inuit." Special issue, "Myths and Gender," *Diogenes* 52 (4): 134–44. London: Sage Publications. Translated from the original 2004 French version, "Le troisième sexe social des Inuit." Special issue, "Mythes et genres," *Diogènes* 208. Paris: Presses universitaires de France.

———. 2006a. "The Construction of Shamanic Identity among the Inuit of Nunavut and Nunavik." In *Aboriginality and Governance: A Multidisciplinary Perspective from Quebec*, edited by G. Christie, 141–65. Penticton, BC: Theytus Books. Translated from the original 2001 French, "La construction de l'identité chamanique, chez les Inuit du Nunavik et du Nunavut." *Études/Inuit/ Studies* 25 (1–2): 191–215.

———. 2006b. *Être et renaître Inuit, homme, femme ou chamane*. Preface by Claude Lévi-Strauss. Paris: Gallimard.

———. 2006c. "The Whale Hunting among the Inuit of the Canadian Arctic." In *Aboriginal Society and Aboriginal Rights: A Multidisciplinary Perspective from Quebec*, edited by Gordon Christie, 179–201. Penticton, BC: Theytus Books. Translated from the original 1999 French version, "La chasse à la baleine chez les Inuit de l'Arctique central canadien." In *La Baleine, un enjeu écologique*, edited by S. Bobé, 88–128. Paris: Les éditions Autrement.

———. 2006d. "The Inuit 'Third Gender.'" In *Aboriginal Society and Aboriginal Rights: A Multidisciplinary Perspective from Quebec*, edited by Gordon Christie, 167–78. Penticton, BC: Theytus Books. Translated from the original 1992 French version, "Le troisième sexe." *La Recherche* 245 (July–August): 836–44.

———. 2013. *Bowhead Whale Hunting among the Inuit of Canada's Arctic: Thirty Years of Challenges (1978–2008)*. Translated, reworked, and expanded from the 1999 original version in *Arvik! In Pursuit of the Bowhead Whale*, edited by Robert Fréchette, 59–81. Westmount, QC: Avataq Cultural Institute, Nunavik Publications.

———. 2015a. "Métamorphoses dans les relations inuit avec les animaux et les esprits." *Religiologiques* 32: 29–63.

———. 2015b. "Du *Sila* inuit au Qi chinois. Par les chemins de traverse du chamanisme et de la christianisation." In *Rencontres et médiations entre la Chine, l'Occident et les Amériques*.

Missionnaires, chamanes et intermédiaires culturels, edited by S. Li, F. Laugrand, and N. Peng, 113–34. Quebec City: Presses de l'Université Laval.

Saladin d'Anglure, Bernard, and Igloolik Isuma Productions. 2002. *Au pays des Inuit, un film, un peuple, une légende: Atanarjuat, la légende de l'homme rapide.* Montpellier: Indigènes Éditions.

Saladin d'Anglure, Bernard, and Françoise Morin. 1998. "Mariages mystiques et pouvoir chamanique chez les Shipibo-Conibo d'Amazonie péruvienne et les Inuit du Nunavut canadien." *Anthropologie et Sociétés* 22 (2): 49–74.

Saladin d'Anglure, Bernard, and Michel Treguer. 1997. *Igloolik Nunavut.* Colour documentary, Warchoaz Productions, FR3. http://www.isuma.tv/bernardsaladindanglure/igloolik-nunavut-part-1. http://www.isuma.tv/bernardsaladindanglure/igloolik-nunavut-part-2.

Saladin d'Anglure, Bernard, and Monique Vezinet. 1977. "Chasses collectives au caribou dans le Québec arctique. Commentaires des dessins de Nua Kilupaq et Juu Talirurnilik." *Études/Inuit/ Studies* 1 (2): 97–112.

Savard, Rémi. 1966. *Mythologie esquimaude: analyse de textes nord-groenlandais.* Travaux divers 14. Quebec: Université Laval, Centre d'Études Nordiques.

———. 1970. "La déesse sous-marine des Eskimos." In *Échanges et communications: Mélanges offerts à Claude Lévi-Strauss, à l'occasion de son 60e anniversaire*, 2 vols., edited by by J. Pouillon and P. Maranda, 1331–55. Paris: Mouton.

Serres, Michel. 1997. *The Troubadour of Knowledge.* University of Michigan Press. Translated by Sheila Faria Glaser and William Paulson. Originally published in 1989 as *Le Tiers-Instruit.* Paris: Éditions François Bourin.

Shao, Liang. 2012. *Logiques du tiers-exclus et du tiers-inclus, en sciences naturelles et dans les langues.* Accessed 27 April 2017, https://www.researchgate.net/publications/257738946.

Slwooko, G. 1979. *Sivuqam ungipaghaatangi II: Saint-Lawrence Island Legends.* From stories written by G. Slwooko, illustrated by J.L. Boffa. Anchorage: National Bilingual Materials Development Center, Rural Education Affairs, University of Alaska.

Sonne, Birgitte. 1990. *The Acculturative Role of the Sea Woman: Early Contact Relations between Inuit and Whites as Revealed in the Origin Myth of the Sea Woman.* Meddelelser om Grnland (Monographs on Greenland), Man and Society 13. Copenhagen: Museum Tusculanum Press.

Spalding, Alex, with the cooperation and help of Thomas Kusugaq. 1998. *Inuktitut Dictionary: A Multi-Dialectal Outline (with an Aivilingmiutaq Base).* Iqaluit, NU: Nunavut Arctic College, Nunatta Campus.

Spencer, Robert F. 1959. *The North Alaskan Eskimo: A Study in Ecology and Society.* Bureau of American Ethnology Bulletin 171. Washington, DC: Smithsonian Institution.

Spier, Leslie. 1925. *The Distribution of Kinship Systems in North America.* Publications in Anthropology 1. Seattle: University of Washington Press.

Sternberg, Leo. 1925. "Divine Election in Primitive Religion." In *Proceedings of the 21st International Congress of Americanists*, 2: 472–512. Göteborg: Göteborg Museum.

Taylor, Garth. 1993. "Canicide in Labrador: Function and Meaning of an Inuit Killing Ritual." *Études/ Inuit/Studies* 10 (1–2): 233–44.

Tcherkézoff, Serge. 1987. *Dual Classification Reconsidered: Nyamwezi Sacred Kingship and Other Examples.* Cambridge: Cambridge University Press. Originally published in 1983 as *Le Roi Nyamwezi, la droite et la gauche, Révision comparatiste des classifications dualistes.* Cambridge: Cambridge University Press; Paris: Éditions de la Maison des sciences de l'Homme.

Thérien, François. 1978. "Entrevues sur le chamanisme conduites à Igloolik et traduites en anglais." Manuscript. Team research project on the transmission of Inuit knowledge, directed by B. Saladin d'Anglure, and funded by the FCAC program (Formation de Chercheurs et Actions Concertées), du Québec. Fonds BSA, Université Laval, Quebec City, and Institut Culturel Avataq Montreal.

Therrien, Michèle. 1987. *Le corps inuit (Québec arctique)*. Collection "Arctique" 1, edited by V. Randa. Paris: Société d'Etudes Linguistiques et Anthropologiques de France (SELAF) and Presses Universitaires de Bordeaux.

Trebilcot, Joyce. 1982. "Two Forms of Androgynism." In *"Femininity" "Masculinity" and "Androgyny": A Modern Philosophical Discussion*, edited by Mary Vetterling Braggin, 161–69. Totowa, NJ: Rowman and Littlefield.

Trott, Christopher. 2006. "The Gender of the Bear." *Études/Inuit/Studies* 30 (1): 89–109.

Turner, Lucien. 1894. *Ethnology of the Ungava District, Hudson Bay Territory*. Extract from the Eleventh Report of the Bureau of Ethnology 1889–1890, 165–350. Washington, DC: Smithsonian Institution.

Ujarak, Juanasi. 1971. Interview conducted by B. Saladin d'Anglure. Unpublished.

Ujarak, Juanasi, *Iqallijuq*, and Isidore *Ijituuq*. 1971. Interviews conducted by B. Saladin d'Anglure with Igloolik elders. Unpublished.

Weyer, Edward M., Jr. 1932. *The Eskimos: Their Environment and Folkways*. New Haven, CT: Yale University Press.

———. 1956. "Daylight and Darkness in High Latitudes." Washington, DC: United States Navy (Op-03A3).

Williams, Walter L. 1986. The *Spirit and the Flesh: Sexual Diversity in American Indian Culture*. Boston: Beacon Press.

Willmott, William E. 1960. "The Flexibility of Eskimo Social Organization." *Anthropologica* 2 (1): 48–59.

Photo Credits

1, 2, 3. Photos by Therkel Mathiassen, Knud Rasmussen Collection, Courtesy of National Museum of Denmark; 4, 5. Knud Rasmussen Collection, Courtesy of National Museum of Denmark; 6. Courtesy of The Royal Danish Library, Photo Collection, KE011361, Photo by Peter Effelt; Copenhagen; 7, 8, 11, 12, 13, 14, 16, 17. Courtesy of Bernard Saladin d'Anglure; 9. Courtesy of Bernard Saladin d'Anglure, 1972; 10. Courtesy of Bernard Saladin d' Anglure, 1976; 15. Courtesy of Bernard Saladin d'Anglure, Igloolik, 1983; 18. Courtesy of Bernard Saladin d'Anglure, Iqaluit, 2006; 19, 20. Photo by Knud Rasmussen, 1922, Courtesy of National Museum of Denmark, Copenhagen.

Index

A

Aakulujjuusi, 41, 42, 55, 286, 321n2

Aamarjuaq, 185, 235–40, 243, 245

adoption, 43–48, 212, 215

ageing, 287

Agiaq, 42, 55, 321n2

Akpalialuk, 269

Aksarjuk, 260

Amarualik, 2, 248, 249, 266–67

amulets, 23, 53, 194–95, 211, 212–13, 243

Angiliq, 248, 270

animal adoption, 45–48

Annanack, George, 11, 273

Annanak, 273

anuses: and ermines, 194; and Itirjuaq, 211, 217; people without, 86–88, 89, 90; and sea urchins, 211, 213; soul escaping through, 67

Apitak, 261

Arctic char, 138–39

Arctic fox, 52–53, 126–33, 204, 322n15, 331n12

Arctic ground squirrel, 60

Arnainnuk, 4, 5, 6

Arnartaaq, 18, 25

Artcirq, 7

Atagudlik, 269

Ataguttaaluk, Cannibal Forebear story, 4, 247–72

Ataguttaaluk, Élise, 6

Atanaarjuat, 52, 232–46, 333n2

Atanarjuat: The Fast Runner (film), xv, 183, 328n11

Atlantic salmon, 138–39

Atuat: and Ataguttaaluk story, 247, 248; her version of Ataguttaaluk's story, 249–59; repeats what Ataguttaaluk told her about surviving, 259–68

Atungaq, 74, 325n15

Ava, 53–54

B

battered wife asks Moon Man for help story, 197–209

battered wife story, 152–76

Bazin, Étienne, xvii, 4

bearded seals, 237
bears, 46–47, 93–94. *See also* polar bears
Belmont, Nicole, 284
beluga whales, 82–85
bird skin, 23, 51–52
black bears, 136–37
blindness, 75–79
Boas, Franz: and adoption story, 43; and
    battered wife asks Moon Man for help
    story, 197, 206, 207; and battered wife
    story, 153, 168; and dog-penis metaphor,
    20; and girls playing at marriage story,
    142; interest in studying Inuit, xv, xvii;
    and Inuit cosmology, 39; and Itirjuaq
    story, 215, 216, 217, 332n2; mistreated
    orphan story, 177; moral of girls playing
    at marriage story, 144; on origin of
    death, 54; recipient of shaman's coat,
    3; and story of mistreated orphan, 177;
    and woman who refused to marry story,
    104, 107
bowhead whales, 134, 151, 237, 329n3
breath, magic power of, 194, 213–14
burial, 73

C

cannibalism: from Ataguttaaluk's point of
    view, 261–65; and Ataguttaaluk's story,
    254–59; commemoration and myth,
    272–73; and debts of blood, 269–70; at
    George River, 272–73; likened to incest,
    91, 95; treatment of person guilty of,
    265–69
caribou: battered wife becomes, 161–67;
    caught by eagle husband, 147; fat of, 86,
    88; and Ijirait, 110–11; Inuit hunting
    of, 162–67, 238; metamorphosed into
    human, 111, 113; seen as giant lice,
    264; as Sila's children, 68–69; in wife
    devoured by maggots story, 121; wolves
    hunting of, 157–61
caterpillars, 45–46
cat's cradle, 99–100, 117
ceremonial clothing, 191–92, 243
child betrothal, 103, 104, 223, 270
childbirth, 22–23, 71–73, 89, 174–75, 277–
    79, 324n11. *See also* pregnancy
childlessness, 121–26, 152, 172, 198, 212, 286

Christianization, 245, 279
clairvoyance, 212, 252, 281
cloud of childbirth, 22, 175
colour symbolism, 104
Comer, George: and Atanaarjuat, 233, 235,
    239–40, 241; and battered wife story,
    168, 169; contact with Inuit, xv, xvii, 3;
    and stone husband story, 143
confession to misdeeds, 82
confinement, 24, 90, 175
constellations, 93–96
cord-like objects, 16
cosmogony, 70–71
cosmology, 39–40, 58–59
cross-dressing, 3, 221, 222, 223, 228
cultural mother, 279

D

Damas, David, xix
daylight, origin of, 51–54
death, 54–56, 287
delousing, 263–65
disembowelment, 201–5
divination, 22–23, 163
dogs: battered wife turns into, 153–57;
    connection to bears, 78, 171, 199; and
    origin of constellations, 93–94; and
    penis, 19–20, 325n5; and puppy meat,
    324n8; in Uinigumasuittuq story,
    104–9; what Uinigumasuittuq's story
    tells us about, 119
Dorset people, 7
double-soul, 15, 17, 56
dreams, 15
dwarfs, 59–62, 323n4

E

eagle husband story, 146–50
Eber, Dorothy, 11–12
elders, 153
end of the world, 97
ermines, 125, 192–95
Ettuk, Jimmy, 233, 243
excrement, 88, 105, 127–29, 190, 191, 193

F

farting, 63, 67, 68, 132–33, 213–14, 328n11, 332n5
feminism, 211
fetuses, 12, 17, 18, 21, 173–74, 222, 276–79. *See also* childbirth; pregnancy
First Nations, 109–11
fog, 71, 108, 175
Fournier, Louis, 320n9
fox woman story, 126–33
Freuchen, Peter, 270
Frobisher, Martin, 324n8
fulmar, 113–16, 326n12
funerals, 73

G

games: of girls who played at marriage, 141, 151; and human finger bones, 117; imitating a wolf, 207; laughing, 203; and seasons, 99–100; to welcome a visitor, 190, 191
giants, 59–62
girls playing at marriage story, 141–51
goose woman story, 133–40
Guillaume (author's son), 6, 7

H

Hall, Charles Francis, xv
hollow man, 138–39
homosexuality, 221, 333n5
hood-covered head, 199
Hooper, Lieutenant, 73
Hudson's Bay Company, 110
human origins, 18–19
human races, origin of, 108–11
human society: five paradoxes of, 286–87; major rules of, 93, 118–19, 151, 175–76, 196, 209, 245, 288
human-animal relations, 151–76, 286–87, 322n12
humour, 61, 62, 64
hunter-game animal relationship, 286–87

I

Igalaaq, 186–87, 190–96
Igjugaarjuk, 67
Igloolik Island, xiii, xvii–xviii, 7–8
Igloolik Isuma Productions, 6, 7
Igloolik people, xiii–xv, xv–xvii, xviii, 6–7, 40, 41
Igloolik region, 102
Igloolik village, 1
Ijiqqat, 69, 110–11
Ijirait, 110–11, 112, 119, 246
Iktuksarjuat, 4, 6, 258, 267, 268–70
Imaruittuq, Bernadette, xix
imitating baby ritual, 50–51
imitating wolf game, 207
incest, 90–91, 118, 221
Innaarulik, Jimmy, 2
Inugagulligaarjuk, 59–61, 323n4
Inukpasujjuk, 41, 46, 59–62, 206, 233
Inullariit Society, 7
Inummariit Cultural Association, 7
invisible spirit world, 142
Iqallijuq: and Ataguttaaluk story, 247, 248, 259, 263, 268, 272; and caribou, 69; confused sexual identity as child, 26–27; and games, 100; and Guillaume, 6; and Itirjuaq story, 210; meets author, xix–xx; memories of being born, 12–22, 321n2, 326n5; on Naarjuk, 63; as newborn, 22–26; on origin of death, 55; and pregnancy, 67; on rejuvenating youth, 49; and rituals of childbirth, 72; seasonal rituals, 71; and Sila, 65; as source for author, 2–4; tells story of birth to Kublu, 28–38; tie to Qisaruatsiaq, 281–82
Iqallijuq (creator of salmon and char), 138–39
Iqipiriaq, 268, 269, 270
Irqaviaq, 11
Itiqanngittut, 86–88
Itirjuaq, 210–19, 231, 332n2, 332n7
Ittukusuk, 258, 261, 263, 264–65, 268
Ittuliaq, 17, 18, 21, 25, 26
Ivaluarjuk: and animal adoption story, 46; and battered wife asks Moon Man for help story, 197, 198, 199, 200–201, 207, 208; and eagle husband story, 147,

149; and girls playing at marriage story, 142; and lost on ice story, 187, 189, 192, 195; mistreated orphan story, 179, 181–82, 186; and narwhal story, 324n5; and origin of daylight, 52; and sculpin husband story, 151; and wife devoured by maggots story, 124

K

Kallu, 269, 270
Kannaaluuk, 117–18, 119, 327n21
Kaujjajjuk, 177–86, 186–96, 327n21, 330n10
kayak, 164, 329n4
Kinaalik, 120
Kiviuq, 66, 74, 131, 323n9, 325n15
Koonooka, Chris Petuwak, 332n3
Kuatsuk, 261, 264, 266, 268
Kublu, 26, 28–38, 65, 74, 82, 324n3
Kunnuk, 261, 262, 263
Kunuk, Zacharias, xv
Kupaaq: and Atanaarjuat, 233; as author's source, 4, 5–6; and Brother Moon and Sister Sun, 74; and girls playing at marriage story, 141; and Itirjuaq story, 210, 212, 217; on Kiviuq, 66; mistreated orphan story, 177; on Naarjuk, 63; and orphaned boy story, 95–96; and stories of unhappy man in loveless marriage, 121; and story of battered wife, 152; story of mistreated orphan, 177; story of woman who refused to marry, 103–19

L

laughing, 201–5, 331n7
lemmings, 125–26, 131–32
Lévi-Strauss, Claude, 283, 284
loons, 78–81, 164
lunar eclipses, 99
lynching, 192
Lyon, Captain, xiii–xv, 97, 101–3, 117, 333n2

M

maggots, 123–25
Malaurie, Jean, xix, 333n5
marine mammals, 116–17

Mark, Jimmy Innaarulik, xviii–xix
marked animals, 227, 231
marriage, 103–19, 121–51
Mary-Rousselière, Guy, 247, 248
menopause, 83
menstruation: and blood, 182; communication of, 22; of Iqallijuq, 27; keeping secrets about, 63; and looking at game animals, 22, 125; rituals of, 227–28; and women's separation, 83, 92
midwives, 21–22, 23, 278
miscarriage, 153, 172
mistreated orphan story, 177–86
moon, 92–93, 97, 99
Moon Brother, 75–93, 96–97, 107–8, 118
Moon Man, 171, 180–83, 198–209, 331n13
mosquitos, 131
Mutch, Captain J., xvii, 43, 44

N

Naarjuk, 57, 59, 62–63, 70, 192, 231
Nalikateq, 202, 206
name-soul, 17, 25, 156, 172–73
narwhal, 85
Nasuk, Noah, xix, 3
newborns: ability to change sex, 21–22, 174; care for, 24; and death seeking forces, 24–25; and dogs, 78; inability to connect to living world, 22–23; Iqallijuq's experience at being, 22–26; Qisaruatsiaq's experience at being, 279–80; words of advice for mother's of, 281
Niviarsiaraannuk, 269
Niviarsiat, 270
nuliksariit, 270
Nuvalingaq, Moses, 50, 51
Nuvvijaq, 13–22, 26–27

O

oil lamps, 92, 135–36
old woman character, 192–93, 240
omens, 252
opposites, 96, 99–100, 134
oral literature, 40
origins of world, 40–45

orphans, 95–96, 177–96, 210, 322n17

P

Padluq, 249–59, 266
Panniaq, Hervé, 200, 203, 233, 235
Parry, Captain, xiii, xv, 52
Peck, Reverend, xvii
penises, 19–20, 89–90, 122–24, 138
Pitsiulaaq, Piita, 11–12
Piugaattuq, 248, 260–61, 264, 268, 269, 270
polar bears: impersonating, 204, 205–6; killed
    by Moon Brother, 75–79; as mediator
    for battered wife, 170–71; as Moon
    Man's sled dogs, 171, 199; similarity
    to ermines, 194–95; and Walrus-Skin's
    revenge, 183–86
polygyny, 214–15, 236, 245
post-partum bleeding, 22, 24, 83, 90, 175, 182
post-partum taboos, 167
pregnancy, 18, 21, 67, 88–89, 139, 140. *See
    also* childbirth
puritanism, 211

Q

Qikirtaarjuk, 6, 105, 106, 108, 232, 233, 266,
    268
Qingailisaq, 3, 319n4
Qisaruatsiaq, 275–82
Qittuarjuit, 85–86, 87
qiturngaqatigiit, 270
Qitusuk, Aani, 11, 274, 275
Quassa, Francois, 233, 239, 241
Qumangaapik, 247, 252, 260–63, 269

R

Rasmussen, Knud: and animal adoption story,
    46; and Ataguttaaluk story, 247, 253,
    256; and Atanaarjuat, 233; and baby
    imitation ritual, 50–51; and battered
    wife gets help from Moon Man story,
    206; and battered wife story, 153, 175;
    and girls playing at marriage story, 142;
    and Inuit cosmology, 39; and Inuit oral
    literature, 40; and Itirjuaq story, 210–11;
    on Kinaalik's belt, 120; on magic power

of breath and farts, 213–14; mistreated
    orphan story, 177; on Naarjuk, 63; and
    origin of daylight, 51; on origin of death,
    54; and shamanism, 67; on Sila, 58; and
    story of mistreated orphan, 177; study of
    Iglulik Inuit, xvii; and Uinigumasuittuq
    story, 101; and whale husband story,
    146; and wife devoured by maggots
    story, 122
ravens, 52–53, 127, 169–70, 322n17
reincarnation, 12–22, 13, 17, 24
rejuvenation of youth, 49
reversibility of perspective, 45, 152–76, 284
ringed seals, 170–73, 186–87
rock ptarmigan, 252

S

Saittiuq, 3, 9–11, 320n1
Sanikiluaq, 11, 50, 246, 274
Sarpinaq, 248, 260, 261
Savviurtalik, 12–22, 25–27, 156
sculpin husband story, 151
sculpin's wife, 142
sea urchins, 212–13
seals, 24, 237. *See also* ringed seals
sex: after childbirth, 321n4; among
        Itiqanngittut, 88; and cannibalism, 266;
        and dietary code, 126; differentiation,
        70–71; and division of labour, xii, 173,
        215, 218, 220–31, 322n10; fashioning
        penises and vaginas from objects,
        89–90; fetuses ability to choose, 21,
        222; and goose woman story, 137; and
        humour, 61, 62, 64; newborns ability
        to choose, 21–22, 174; overlap with
        food in Inuit, 91, 124; phallic symbols,
        107, 113; punishment for sexual
        offenses, 118; symbolism of, 172, 180;
        in Uinigumasuittuq story, 104–5; and
        weather rituals, 71; in whale husband
        story, 145; and wife devoured by
        maggots story, 122–24; between woman
        and Moon Man, 206
shamans/shamanism: ability to inhabit
        different worlds, 228; access to
        invisible world of spirits, 153, 155;
        and Atanaarjuat, 245, 246; authorizing
        gender change, 222, 223; belts, 119–20;

and calling to name-soul, 25; and caribou divination, 163; cross-dressing of, 228; and delousing, 263–64; female, 210–19, 332n1; initiation for, 67, 138; and Kannaaluk, 119; learning to be, 199; and the left arm, 66; and loons, 81; and origins of the world, 41; and punishment for sexual offenses, 118; ritual of harpooning Sedna, 117; and solar eclipses, 97; and solving problems of human life, 288–89; as source of modern learning, 8; and spirits, 181–82, 330n4; transcending different scales of size, 151; transgender, 8, 221; trying to get people to laugh, 203; in Walrus-Skin story, 189–96; and weather, 63

shooting stars, 207

sickness, 210–11

Sigluk, 248, 261, 263, 268, 269, 270

Sila, 58–59, 65–66, 67, 69–71

sinew weaving, 147–49, 189

sipiniit, 21–22, 25

Slwooko, Grace, 220, 332n3

smell, sense of, 276

smiling with half face, 100

snow blindness, 75, 324n7

snowy owl, 88

solar eclipses, 97, 99

songs, 9–11, 135–38

souls, 12, 13, 15, 55–56, 59, 67–68. *See* double–soul; name–soul

speed, love of, 246

spiders, 131

spirits: ability to see earth, 206–7; access to invisible world of, 153, 155; and girls who play at marriage, 141–51; and humans entering spirit world, 198–201, 229; and Kaujjajjuk, 181–82; learning from, 8; source of, 40; taboos of humans mixing with, 207–9

spouse exchange, 72, 91, 122, 123, 127–28, 134, 286

St. Lawrence Island, 220

stars, 201, 207

stone blocks, 137–38

stone husband story, 143–44

strange man and his whale story, 220–31

suicide, 6–7, 153, 192

sun, 71–73, 92–93, 97, 99, 100

Sun Sister, 75–93, 96–97

Sun Woman, 200, 331n6

sweat, 230–31

symbiotic oneness, 276

T

Tagurnaaq, 50–51, 247, 248, 249–59, 260, 264

Taqqiapik, Dalasi, 73

tattoos, 205, 251, 325n21, 331n10

thirst, 13, 15, 155–56

Thule people, 7, 40, 144

Tivajuut festival, 2, 72, 98, 203, 321n5

transgender people, 8, 220–31, 288

Tuniit, 7, 110, 111, 326n8

turd woman, 127–29

Tutukatuk, 331n13

two-spirits, 221

U

Uinigumasuittuq, 6, 102, 103–19, 145, 326n5, 327n18

Ujarak, xix–xx, 2–4, 50, 53, 68–69, 248, 259

ukkusiq, 136

Ulluriaq, 321n2

Ululijarnaat, 201–6, 208

umbilical cord, 23

umiat, 108, 147

Uppik, Hannah, 278

Uqaittuq, Suapik, 279

urine/urination, 16, 145, 190, 191, 193

Urulu, xix, 101, 248, 258, 327n17, 327n18

Uumarnituq, 41, 42, 43–45, 55, 286, 287, 321n2

W

walking backwards, 198

walruses, 167–69

Walrus-Skin, 177–96

war, 56, 287

weather, 63, 65–66, 69–71

weaved caribou sinews, 147–49, 189

whales, 144–46, 225–31, 228. *See also* beluga
    whales; bowhead whales
white people, 109, 110
wife devoured by maggots story, 121–26
wolverines, 127–29, 131, 328n9
wolves, 131, 157–61
woman who refused to marry myth, 103–19
womb memories, 11–22, 45, 274, 275–79, 282
womb-igloo metaphor, 3–4, 16, 18
words, power of, 52

Y
youth renewal, 49

Z
zoophilia, 221